CRITICAL CRIMINOLOGY

9507D

COLL

6

CRITICAL CRIMINOLOGY

Visions from Europe

René van Swaaningen

SAGE Publications
London • Thousand Oaks • New Delhi

SAGE Publications Ltd
6 Bonhill Street
London EC2A 4PU

SAGE Publications Inc
2455 Teller Road
Thousand Oaks, California 91320

SAGE Publications India Pvt Ltd
32, M-Block Market
Greater Kailash – I
New Delhi 110 048

British Library Cataloguing in Publication data
A catalogue record for this book is
available from the British Library

ISBN 0 7619 5144 X
ISBN 0 7619 5145 8 (pbk)

Library of Congress catalog record available

Typeset by M Rules
Printed in Great Britain by Biddles Ltd, Guildford, Surrey

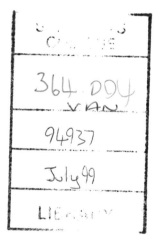

Contents

Foreword
Jock Young

Although criminology as a discipline emerged in Europe, both its comparative history and contemporary development have, until recently, remained largely uncharted. Now, the blanks on the map are beginning to be filled in with Paul Rock's *History of Criminology* (1994) and by the remarkable exegesis of the origins of European criminology in Piers Beirne's *Inventing Criminology* (1993). But neither book has the comprehensive intent of René van Swaaningen's text. For this book surveys and contrasts the different and uneven development of criminology across Europe both in terms of the orthodoxy of positivism and neo-classicism and, more recently, administrative criminology and its critical counter-balance. But, more centrally, it distils from countless conferences, common study sessions, interviews and debates, the contours and purpose of European critical criminology from its flourishing in the 1960s to its present crisis phase of the 1990s. Here is a hidden discourse, largely unknown to the textbooks of Anglo-American criminology. It is my task in this foreword briefly to underscore the importance of European critical criminology for the vitality of the discipline.

The two currents that have largely shaped contemporary criminology are, first, analytical individualism, whose impact has been paramount throughout the century, and, secondly, since the Second World War, the criminological thinking that has emerged in the United States. By analytical individualism, I mean criminology that focuses on the characteristics of the individual rather than on the properties of society as a whole. The two major staples of criminological thinking – neo-classicism and positivism – belong firmly in this camp: the first views crime as the moral lapses of the freely willed individual; the second, as a pathological determinism of individuals caused by genetic, family or social defects. Both of these prevalent and popular notions are given short shrift in many of the leading academic texts yet they recur, without fail, in every generation. They are often presented as contending theories, yet they coexist in practice; indeed, much crime-control practice involves a demarcation dispute as to which side of the line the offender belongs. They recur because a vast amount of criminological thinking is concerned with the practicalities of control: the needs of the prison governor to classify prisoners in terms of risk, the needs of the Minister of Justice to make pronouncements on the crime rate, or the judge to allocate the degree of culpability in the flux of mitigating circumstances. Such individualism is concerned with the administration of crime; it tends to involve minimalist theory, to be technicist and to require 'hard' facts to feed the demands of agencies and government. Above all, it is rarely critical of the core constitution of society: its focus is on lapses or defects in the individual. It is a cosmetic criminology that views crime as a blemish that suitable treatment can remove from a body which is, itself, otherwise healthy and in little need of reconstruction. Such a criminology *distances* from the core institutions and proffers technical, piecemeal solutions. It, thus, reverses causality: crime causes problems for society rather than society causes the problem of crime. Critical criminology challenges all these assumptions. From the point of view of the establishment, the offender lacks core values and is so inadequately embedded in the institutions of civil society that the criminal justice system is necessary to hold him or her in check.

But, from the perspective of critical criminology, within the problem of crime and its control lies a double irony. First, criminal behaviour is seen to involve the acting out of the core values of society – individualism and possessiveness – and to be spurred on by the key institutions – work and education – which impede success in society through the arbitrary denial of opportunities because of class and race. Secondly, the criminal justice system, by labelling and reinforcing stereotypes, makes criminals of people. The secondary harm of criminalisation is often more of a problem than the primary harm of crime itself.

As van Swaaningen demonstrates, a central attribute of critical criminology is its utopianism. From this perspective, there is a utopian ideal outside the system which allows a critical purchase on existing practices and values. From the point of view of administrative criminology, the ideal already exists in the steady job and the leafy suburbs; it is the behaviour of the offender that disturbs this ideal. Lastly, whereas criminological orthodoxy is aware of the inadequacies of the statistics, it sees such flaws as technical problems that can be scientifically overcome. For critical criminology, on the other hand, the statistics are not, nor could ever be, 'hard' data: they are a fabrication of power, a construction of stereotype and preconception. Thus, criminalisation is, by its very nature, a political process: the idea of a value-free and politically neutral criminology is an illusion which, as Thomas Mathiesen and Nils Christie argue, is functional to the existing system. Indeed, other critical criminologists of the abolitionist school would go further and suggest, with Louk Hulsman, that crime itself has 'no ontological reality'. It is a group of behaviours arbitrarily selected by those in power within the criminal justice system: hardly a secure basis for claiming a so-called science called 'criminology'. The debate about such matters is endless but what is important is to note that, without the critical tradition, criminology quite naturally remains at a one-dimensional level. It is the language of crime that emerges from the agencies of crime control and the academic research funded by central and local government to evaluate its performance. It is scarcely likely to evolve by itself self-critical debates that would question not only the core institutions of society but the very subject itself. For this reason alone, van Swaaningen's book is to be welcomed, but let us turn to his second focus: European criminology.

Criminology in the latter part of the twentieth century is dominated by the literature emanating from the United States. In no other country is there such a prolific academy, in no other advanced industrial country (with perhaps the salutary exception of Russia) is there a crime-control industry of such enormous proportion. Yet it is almost entirely self-referring; European work, where mentioned, tends to be that of the dead European precursors of present-day American theorists. The cast-iron test of this is the contrast with Canada; here, despite bordering on the United States, the literature referred to is much more wide in its orbit (see Young, 1992). It includes US sources to be sure, but it also takes cognisance of what is happening in Australasia and in Britain, as it does of the francophone debates of France and Belgium.

One reason for the insularity of US criminology and its dominance over the world literature has been, without doubt, the extraordinary creativity of American criminologists in the post-war period. It is difficult to imagine a literature without Howard S. Becker, James Q. Wilson and David Matza. Yet such creativity is a creature of exceptional circumstances: the crime rate of the United States is considerably greater than that of any of the stable Western democracies. To give an example: a young American male (of whatever race) is 52 times more likely to be murdered than his English counterpart, 22 times that of a Swede and 28 times that of a young Frenchman (Currie, 1996).

Let us note that disparities of such an order are remarkable. Critics, for example, frequently point to the sizeable gender differences in the incidence of offending and note, quite rightly, that such disparities must, of necessity, be of great significance to the criminologist. US–European differences in rates of violence are of a similar or, indeed, greater order, and must surely be held at centre stage when we consider any cross-cultural generalisations. Similarly, the rate of imprisonment in the United States is of a qualitatively greater level than in other Western democracies. It is over five and a half times that of the figure for England and Wales, which has one of the highest imprisonment rates in Europe, while the proportion of Americans either in prison or on probation or parole is ten times that of English people. Indeed, an extraordinary 1 in 37 of the US adult population was under some form of correctional supervision in 1994.

Such exceptional crime and imprisonment rates, while ensuring the ample funding of American criminology, should make us wary of simply transplanting US theory or corrective practices. It is as if biologists were to focus most of their research effort in the desert regions of the world, yet seek to generalise their findings about plant and animal behaviour to the temperate zones. It is obvious that to generalise, say, about the effect of deterrent sanctions from a country where criminal justice system interventions are a commonplace of life (indeed, one in four young black Americans is under supervision) to one where sanctions are a comparative rarity is fraught with difficulty. Similarly, it is obvious that the fear of crime debate must be distinctly different in a country where homicide is a major cause of death among young men, while arguments about gun control, neighbourhood watch, 'hotspots' and so on must be viewed in a very particular context rather than easily generalised from the United States to elsewhere. Indeed, Elliott Currie, of the University of California at Berkeley, has repeatedly warned (1996) of the frequent fallacy of importing willy-nilly American solutions to the crime problem into Europe. A clear paradox here is that, particularly in terms of the use of penal sanctions, this involves taking lessons from a country that has clearly failed in the 'war' against crime. It is an index of American cultural hegemony that such incongruous policy transplants are frequently discussed and implemented.

But this is not to suggest that there is nothing to learn from the United States. As Currie indicates, analysis can show what happens when certain variables are taken to their limits: when free-market policies dominate social relations and where control is attempted through the coercion of the criminal justice system rather than the pursuit of social justice. In this way it can give us a warning about paths that engender crime which it would be better to avoid rather than venture down. But, more than this, it can provide a wealth of experiment and improvisation in crime control which, if *carefully* transferred into another cultural context, may well have much to contribute. What is important here is that we learn to *transpose rather than transplant*; that we must take cognisance of the specific social, political and cultural context in which generalisations about crime are evaluated and the qualitative differences between societies. Jayne Mooney (1996) has shown, for example, how the British Home Office crime-prevention strategies seem to be based on an understanding of the patterns of violence that are characteristic of the United States rather than Britain (for example, a stress on greater danger in public places against men rather than violence that is as likely in private as public and more equally likely against women and men). And, elsewhere, it has been shown how the notion of neighbourhood watch, when transplanted from Detroit to London, ignored differences in the level of crime, the nature of community support, the degree of multi-culturalism, the system of control of the police and the general political climate (see Kinsey et al., 1986). Thus, just because we use the same phrase 'neighbourhood watch' in Detroit and London does not mean we are talking about the 'same' institution, and studies which blithely correlate the effectiveness of 'neighbourhood watch' around the world do so at their peril. The problem of specificity, of taking careful cognisance of the specific cultural setting of an institution, is, therefore, of great importance.

My intent in indicating the heterogeneity of the US and Europe is not to suggest the homogeneity of the latter. Indeed, the similarities between Western European nations are perhaps only evident in terms of their contrast with America. Of course, wide differences in crime and the institutions that control it occur across Europe. Paradoxically, the importance of a European criminology is not in the unity but in the diversity of social, political and cultural situations that occur. For nowhere in the First World does such a diversity occur in such a small geographical area. A multiplicity of nations with differing political systems, legal cultures and social structures exist next to each other.

Some have long histories, stretching back for centuries, others have arisen out of intense conflict and fragmentation: nowhere is the student's sense of diversity among advanced industrial societies so sustained and tested. There is no comparable situation in the United States. Sometimes it is suggested that the wide variety of immigrants in the United States has given rise to an exceedingly diverse society. But such immigration occurs anyway in Europe and such diversity consists of immigrants often from the actual extant, distinct and contiguous countries of Europe: which *are* the separate constituents *before* the melting pot.

It is in making comparisons within Europe that questions of specificity very forcibly become evident to the researcher. Thus, John Pitts (1994: 48) notes at the beginning of his project on juvenile justice:

> The first stage was a search for equivalence in which we attempted to find practices and system-components which did the same job in a different, but hopefully better, way than their home-grown counterparts. The implicit objective of the search for equivalence is piracy, wherein researchers comb the continent returning with new and exotic foreign solutions to old and intractable British problems. What we discovered, however, was that many of the practices we observed, while ostensibly similar, had no home-grown equivalents because the systems we encountered, while ostensibly similar, were designed to do different things and they did so in a different way.

Thus the French *juge des enfants* and the British magistrate in a juvenile court are similar in name only; seen in context they have totally different roles. And what is anti-racist good practice in one country is seen as racism and exclusion in another (see also Cooper et al., 1995). Thus, in two countries only 21 miles apart, the same terms are redolent with different and even opposing meanings. Furthermore, the process of comparative research, Pitts argues, makes us inevitably, if we are scrupulous in our investigation, excavate the bedrock cultural assumptions behind the institutions of a given country and, finally, to turn back reflexively to our own culture: '[the] answer to the question "what can we learn in Europe" is that by a willingness to immerse ourselves in the ideas, beliefs and assumptions which drive another national system we can gain a view not only of their final vocabulary but, crucially, of our own as well' (Pitts, 1994: 48).

And it is here that the present book takes on special significance. For van Swaaningen shows quite clearly the reflexive nature of European comparisons: that we learn a great deal about our own culture from the investigation of the context of others. As he freely acknowledges, the European Common Study Programme on Criminal Justice and Critical Criminology with which so many of us have worked since its inception in 1988 has opened the eyes of many of our students and been an education to all of us. Based at Barcelona, Bologna, Ghent, Komotini, Middlesex, Rotterdam and Saarbrücken, this ERASMUS programme has repeatedly demonstrated the need to understand cultural specificity while presenting the unsettling fact that only a few miles away in another First World country things are done differently. It has taught us also, as van Swaaningen shows, that the development of criminological theory is closely linked to the politics and culture of a particular country and that any simple linear progression, as beloved by the Anglo-Saxon textbooks, is erroneous.

René van Swaaningen talks of a crisis in critical criminology. In this he is undoubtedly right, although the crisis in the critical sphere is, so to speak, on the back of the seemingly perpetual crisis in establishment criminology over the past 20 years. For the rise in crime in the latter part of the twentieth century has called forth a plethora of theories, many of them recycled, and a host of piecemeal solutions, each introduced with a seemingly inexhaustible sense of self-congratulation only to be dumped unceremoniously and unnoted a few years later. The essential flaw of establishment criminology is, of course, to attempt to explain crime without touching upon reality, constantly to distance explanation from the basic social and economic problems of a divided society. But critical criminology, despite the many gains that I have listed, has all too frequently made almost mirror-image mistakes. For, as van Swaaningen notes, it has tended to play down the real problems of the ghetto and the inner city, it has focused lop-sidedly on the problems of criminalisation rather than the problems of crime, it has been 'impossibilist' about crime-control measures, it has detected 'net-widening' in every single attempt to ameliorate the crime problem and it has carried an all too 'sunny picture' of informal justice. As it is, as Elliott Currie (1992: 92) bitterly puts it:

> A world view that cannot even acknowledge the seriousness of a social problem is necessarily unable to come up with anything approaching a credible remedy for it; in the absence of any effort to provide a remedy, there are plenty of other takers . . . [this has] effectively ceded the political terrain on illicit drugs and violent crime to the political right.

Furthermore, the minimisation of crime leads to the neglect of aetiology. By ignoring, or indeed rejecting, the study of the aetiology of crime, critical criminologists have found themselves setting up their critical axis within the criminal justice system rather than in civil society. The alternative visions of reform revolve around the abolition of the criminal justice system and the development of alternative notions of social control rather than on the fundamental transformation of society. Not only is such a radicalism limited in its purchase, for it critiques the administration of society rather than society itself, but it also inevitably leads to the neglect of that part of the rich legacy of European criminology. This is particularly important in that the turn away from European criminology after the Second World War, traced by van Swaaningen, frequently involved a rewriting of the history of criminology allocating individualistic themes of crime to the European tradition and social explanations to the New World from the Chicago School onwards. Thus, Lilly et al. (1989: 47) write: 'Although exceptions exist, mostly early theories located the sources of crime *within* the individuals . . . As America turned into the twentieth century, however, a competing and powerful vision of crime emerged: a vision suggesting that crime, like other behaviour, was a social product.' And even where the European debate on the social causes of crime is acknowledged, it is regulated to a small mention, a relic of times gone by (see, for example, Vold and Bernard, 1986; Akers, 1997).

It is, of course, relevant to ask: what can be gained from re-examining the historical roots of criminology in Europe? The answer to this is negative only if one believes that criminology is a discipline that has progressed over the centuries from simple-minded theory to the more sophisticated. I doubt this; indeed, when one examines contemporary theory, one often gets more a sense of *déjà vu* than of change and, indeed, frequently precisely an opposite trend seems to be in operation. Of course, on the most elementary level, the study of the historical development of theory enables one to understand the process of concept formation. In particular, it quickly disallows us the conceit that concepts occur outside the political and social context of the time, what Ian Hacking (1981) calls the 'exterior' history of the discipline. But, more than this, there is a rich legacy in the actual content of past work. It is important to understand why, for example, the concept of relative deprivation occurred first of all to Adolphe Quetelet and did not occur to the later moral cartographers of the Chicago School. Or, with regard to the Classical School, the gradual chipping away at the thick patina of reinterpretation that has accumulated over the centuries begins to reveal its key thinkers, such as Cesare Beccaria, in a new light and provides dramatic contrasts with contemporary voluntaristic theories (see Beirne, 1993; Ahearne, 1994). The deep embeddedness of classicism in the problematic of social contract theory contrasts with the atomistic voluntarism conjured up by current rational choice theory. Beccaria's awareness of social causality, of the aetiology of crime in social inequality and exclusion, and, of course, the problematic nature of punishment, has much to teach the student. Finally, take the increasingly popular control theory of Travis Hirschi (see Gottfredson and Hirschi, 1990) with its supposed roots in the work of Hobbes and Durkheim. Of course, even the most perfunctory glance at *Leviathan* or *The Division of Labour* makes nonsense of this claim, but, more importantly, reading these classics immediately sensitises the student to the importance of human reflexivity and sense of justice in the adherence of the citizen to the laws and rules of the state – matters totally absent in control theory.

The European legacy is worth re-reading and re-evaluating, and van Swaaningen's contribution to this task must be seen in the light of what is discernible as a second wave of revisionism among radicals. The first, at the point of emergence of critical criminology in the 1970s, involved the re-appraisal of how traditional criminology had tackled the relationships of class and gender. *The New Criminology* (Taylor et al., 1973) and Carol Smart's *Women, Crime and Criminology* (1976) are important markers of this trend. The second, in this present period of critical criminology in crisis, involves, from varying perspectives, an appraisal of the historical development of the subject, and includes, for example, Piers Beirne's *Inventing Criminology* (1993) and Colin Sumner's *The Sociology of Deviance: an Obituary* (1994) (see also Garland, 1985; Roshier, 1989; Young, 1997).

The modernist gaze, which has dominated the standard textbooks in criminology, looks to the past for signs of origin and development which lead progressively to the theories of the present. Context is of less importance than tracing the line of progress. The gaze of late modernity differs fundamentally from this: it is interested in situating theory, context becomes all important, the line of history is seen as a social construction (indeed, constructions in the plural as there are several imputed lines), it discards progress and enters more readily into debates over time, it takes from the past in order to construct situated theories of the present.

Van Swaaningen's book must, therefore, be seen in this light. As he puts it, '[my] general thesis is that if criminology is to keep advancing as a discipline there is an urgent need for the resurgence of theoretical epistemological reflections on its foundations' (van Swaaningen, 1996b: 2). To go back to these foundations for him necessitates the revival of a concern with social justice, and with an alternative vision of social order. Thus he applies such a 'replacement discourse' to community safety and the position of the victim.

His strategy involves a side-step away from penal intervention to that which stresses a welfare, social justice approach. Thus, he counters the present pragmatic approach to community safety which is intent on limiting problems by increased use of formal social control and technical means. Instead, he argues for a welfare strategy that aims to provide community safety for all and attempts to bridge the social split in Western cities between 'urban third worlds', on the one hand, and super-protected residential areas, on the other. He thus moves safety politics into the framework of normal social politics and out of the domain of criminal justice. Likewise, he argues that the prime responses to the criminal act must be to assist the victim in a welfarist fashion and, *then*, to deal with the offender within the penal sphere. The real interests of the victim are not met by retribution but by material and social assistance outside the criminal justice system. This change in strategy involves a significant alteration in perspective within critical criminology. In the past 15 years, the two major tendencies have been abolitionism and realism. The abolitionist position, out of which van Swaaningen's own work emerged, has largely been based on a critique of the penal system. This has, as I have outlined above, a limited purchase: it is radical merely in its critique of punishment rather than in its call for a transformation of society. The realist perspective, in its initial formulations, tended to a similar error, albeit in the form of a mirror image of abolitionism: that is, it was intent on showing how democratic reform of the police and the establishment of truly popular institutions of justice would have great impact on the crime rate (see Lea and Young, 1984: Kinsey et al., 1986). It, too, tended to focus on the criminal justice system, albeit in a form that aimed to radicalise the system rather than abolish it. There is no doubt that such reforms are urgently needed but it would be wishful thinking to believe that such penal intervention would fundamentally alter the crime rate. The aetiology of crime lies in the unequal and competitive nature of the free-market society; such a criminogenic society can be exacerbated by a discriminatory penal system and it can be ameliorated by a criminal justice system that is fair and just. But to believe that the central plank of policy should lie in surveillance, policing and imprisonment, however minimalist, leads realism to a position that is either a left-wing version of the administrative criminology of the establishment or simply a radical version of neo-classicism. Therefore, realism needs also to stress that both short-term and long-term reform must focus upon the institutions of civil society rather than the penal instruments of the state. Such a convergence between the abolitionist and realist wings of critical criminology has arisen out of discussions at the meetings of the ERASMUS Programme on Criminal Justice and Critical Criminology. Differences, of course, remain and debate will, of necessity, continue. This book contributes greatly to the exchange of ideas, and reveals discourses often hidden from orthodox debates about crime but which offer to illuminate our understanding both of crime and the institutions we construct to attempt to control it.

Acknowledgements

This book has grown out of two concerns: apprehension about criminology's future as a scientific critique and the lack of teaching material on comparative criminology in Europe. In my attempt to indicate a possible future for critical criminology, I use specifically European debates and traditions of thought as 'new' points of reflection for a perspective that has largely been styled in an Anglo-Saxon fashion. This is how the two concerns come together.

Colleagues, students and staff members of our European Common Study Programme on Criminal Justice and Critical Criminology (CSP), and people I have met through the European Group for the Study of Deviance and Social Control have contributed a great deal to the actual formation of my argument. They have also been particularly helpful in gathering and checking information on their own countries. Many people provided me with useful insights, literature suggestions or data I would not have found as a foreigner to all but one debate. Others gave me linguistic assistance, supportive criticism or sharpened the analysis by giving my argument a sound slating. Some have, after careful reading of the manuscript, indicated lapses and flaws and made valuable suggestions to improve the book.

For all these very different reasons, I would like to thank Maria Archimandritou, Elke Bahl, Jolande uit Beijerse, Herman Bianchi, John Blad, Encarna Bodelón, Maria Teresa Brancaccio, Tineke Cleiren, David Downes, Hugo Durieux, Johannes Feest, Cyrille Fijnaut, René Foqué, Willem de Haan, Patrick Hebberecht, Constantijn Kelk, Nikos Koulouris, John Lea, Ronny Lippens, Ian Loader, Iñaki Rivera, Ben Rovers, Vincenzo Ruggiero, Andrew Rutherford, Mick Ryan, Karl Schumann, Gerlinda Smaus, Sonja Snacken, Tony Ward, Jock Young and Damián Zaitch. I would also like to express my gratitude to Anja van Aalst for her committed secretarial assistance at the Erasmus University's Department of Criminal Justice and Criminology, to Sue Ashton for the excellent job she did in 'brushing up' my English, and to Gillian Stern of Sage Publications for her gentle support and editorial advice.

1

Introduction

While criminology's epistemological and political foundations and presuppositions were questioned in the 1970s, the 1980s were characterised by a tendency to get 'back to normal': that is, back to positivism. At present, most European criminologists are engaged in research that is shaped by the logic, idiom and priorities of law enforcement, aimed at the practical utility of criminal justice policy, and often commissioned by the justice administration, local government, banks, insurance companies or other representatives of private enterprise. In this context, the poignant question is: is there still any need for a critical, theoretical perspective in criminology? Or can it suffice for criminologists to engage in so-called value-free research without challenging the ideology of crime control? The premiss of this book is that we cannot confine ourselves to such functionalist or positivist stances and that reflexivity and epistemological critique are indispensable for the scientific development of criminology as an academic discipline.

The retrieval of critical criminology is necessary to challenge criminology's restraining utilitarian ethos and thereby preserve its status as an independent academic field. However, since the heyday of critical criminology in the early 1970s, a great many things in society, politics and penal practice have changed so drastically that some of its positions have become untenable. The purpose of this book is to retrieve those elements of critical criminology that are worth saving and to revise those that can no longer be maintained. For this purpose, we first need to analyse critical criminology's historical roots. Under what conditions did it develop as a counter-paradigm and how did it lose this position? The analytical starting-point thus lies in the so-called crisis in critical criminology, situated on the 'cusp of change' from the post-war era, marked by 'inclusion, affluence and conformity', to the last quarter of the twentieth century, marked by 'individualism, diversity and a vast, widescale deconstruction of accepted values . . . where each of the certain keystones of society: the family, work, the nation and even affluence itself, became questioned and unobvious' (Walton and Young, 1997). An analysis will be made of the consequent changes in criminal justice politics in order to assess what critical criminology's most relevant contribution could be in the present era.

Instead of the negative critique of the state's politics of crime control, which came to dominate the critical project in the late 1970s, it seems more challenging now to present a contrasting, alternative vision of justice. The vision of a reassessed critical criminology, which unfolds in this book, entails a 'replacement discourse'; that is, a perspective that 'is not simply critical and oppositional, but provides both a critique and an alternative vision' (Henry and Milovanovic, 1996: 205). This replacement discourse starts from the normative, epistemological basis of critical criminology: a critique of criminal justice needs to include a critique of the sociopolitical context, and alternative visions of crime control need to be grounded in visions of a more just society with respect to the distribution of wealth and opportunities. Based on this premiss, three central themes in present-day criminal justice politics – crime prevention, the position of the victim and the value of legal safeguards – are subjected to the classical critical criminological touchstone: the demand for social justice. This implies a materially equal distribution of care for public safety and legal protection among all sections of society.

A nebulous concept like social justice can easily remain a mere 'feel good' slogan. By applying it to the three above-mentioned themes, I hope to avoid this danger. The main purpose of making the guiding principle of social justice explicit is, however, grounded in the acknowledgement that concrete ideas and measures in the sphere of criminal justice are always steered by a meta-discourse that happens to 'hang in the air' at a certain moment. One moment it is the common opinion among the professional élites that law enforcement first of all needs to be humanitarian; next, it is felt that the punitive side needs to be stressed. 'Justice' is an often contested concept, both in an analytical and a political sense, and yet we can hardly imagine doing without it if we speak about crime and crime control. The concept of 'social justice' is at least a bit more concrete because it stresses that only a material realisation can lend credibility to the abstract notion of justice. The same goes for human rights, which seem to be one of the few collectively shared anchors of morality in our era. The search for a normative foundation for critical criminology in the notion of social justice and human rights culture is based on an apprehension of criminogenic, 'a-social' tendencies in European societies and of the boundless, 'inhuman' political instrumentalism of crime-control ideology.

Going back to the specific European history of criminology, the search for alternative visions of justice is notably informed by legal-theoretical observations. A book that addresses European intellectual traditions, visions and debates in critical criminology does not as yet exist. By opening these themes up to an international audience, I hope to raise a more profound interest in the critical criminologies of the European continent. This book thus tells a previously untold story about European criminology and leads to a new critical perspective which looks quite different from the one that flowered in the 1960s and 1970s.

What is critical criminology?

As a distinct perspective, critical criminology is a product of 'the sixties', a decade which, as an epoch, actually ranges from 1963 to 1973, with the mythical year '1968' neatly in the middle. The social changes of that era had a particularly strong impact on criminology because this discipline occupies, more than any other social science,

> the crossroads of order and disorder, of law and morality. Indeed in many ways the sudden outburst of intellectual output occurring in the period 1968–1975 can be seen not so much as a series of academic 'break-throughs' occurring within the interior world of academic debate, but as strident signals of the change into late modernity occurring in the world surrounding the academy. For it is at times of change that fundamental revisions of academic orthodoxy occur. (Walton and Young, 1997)

A younger generation of criminologists argued that dominant traditions in the discipline reduced the crime problem to a problem of certain types of nasty individuals, and thereby implicitly defended the conventional social order. Mainstream criminology portrayed crime as an act which either derived from the offender's free will or was a product of pathological defects. Penal interventions aimed at retribution or at the correction of wrongdoers follow from such an individualising approach. Critics considered this a sociologically ill-informed vision. They argued that the bulk of the crime problem consisted of property offences, which have virtually nothing to do with any pathological defect and are only a product of rational choice in as much as they are latent forms of resistance to an unjust social order. They considered these relatively small offences primarily as a logical by-product of capitalism, which both produces consumer 'needs' and relative deprivation. By describing crime as 'deviancy', critical criminologists pointed to the political nature of the causes of crime, the concept of crime itself and crime-control politics. Rather than studying crime as a problem that particular individuals or groups represent to society, criminologists should study deviancy, normality and disorder as a problem of society in a more structural sense. An important objective in this respect would be to study the role of the media and criminal justice agencies as amplifiers of deviancy and to analyse which interests lead 'moral entrepreneurs' to define certain social problems as crime problems, while ignoring other dangers to society. In this latter sense, mainstream criminologists were criticised for their neglect of the crimes of the powerful. The impetus to include various white-collar and corporate crimes, sexual violence and human rights violations by the state among the common objectives of research lies with critical criminology.

The means to reduce the problem of crime need, according to critical criminologists, to be an implicit part of socioeconomic politics. The criminal justice system is said to do the opposite. It reproduces social inequality. The police seem mainly interested in the wrongdoings of the lower social class. These groups are also dramatically over-represented in the prison system. As a means of crime control, penal intervention is counter-productive because it brutalises and makes scapegoats of the most vulnerable groups in society. To counter the individualising aetiological discourse of mainstream criminologists, lawyers and psychiatrists, critical criminologists demonstrated the selectivity and ineffectiveness of the criminal justice system and revealed miscarriages of justice. In this way, the discourse about crime and crime control was lifted to a higher sociological level, which exceeded positivist aetiology.

Critical criminologists relate empirical analyses to social theory. The adjective 'critical' is indicative in this respect; it is derived from the *Frankfurter Schule's* critical theory. Though many implicit references to this famous school of German sociology have been made, few criminologists have explicitly worked within this style. The whole enterprise of critical criminology does, however, find its ultimate root in critical theory's central claim that scientific questions should always reflect social questions, and that science can be a means to change the status quo. A comparable implicit, but important, political theoretical inspiration is derived from French structuralism, notably from Louis Althusser's reflections on Marxism, and the Italian neo-Marxist intellectual tradition inspired by Antonio Gramsci. These orientations to social and political theory have led to macro-sociological reflections on earlier North American labelling and sub-cultural perspectives, in which questions of power are raised to a political level. Next to being a criminological perspective in the empirical sense of the word, critical criminology is an epistemological critique of positivism and functionalism. Such a competing paradigm on criminal justice as a servo-mechanism of hegemonic social relations and of crime as deviancy came to the surface in Western Europe in the early 1970s. In Chapter 5 a more detailed analysis of international disparities will be presented, but here we already need to indicate an important difference between Britain and the European continent.

David Garland (1994: 18) has divided the historical roots of British criminology into a Lombrosian project (which led to an individualising, aetiological and explanatory criminology) and a governmental project (leading to a criminology that seeks to enhance the efficient and equitable administration of justice). In this latter respect, British critical criminologists have notably argued against the hegemony of a Fabian administrative orientation to criminology. Continental European critical criminologists have, like their British counterparts, also argued against a Lombrosian project, but instead of the governmental project their particular critique is oriented towards jurisprudence rather than to an administrative criminology, which in many continental countries was marginal or non-existent before the end of the 1960s. Continental criminologists still orient themselves more towards the legal field than their British colleagues – and this is a tradition that we will focus on. On the European continent, the term 'critical criminology' is mainly used as an umbrella-concept for a criminology that includes a social critique, under which both materialist and interactionist criminologies find shelter. Literal distinctions between *radical* (referring to Marxist roots) or *new* (originating in the new left) are, in practice, less relevant. The adjective 'critical' has gradually become the demarcation line for scholars who oppose the utilitarian ethos that subordinates criminology to law-and-order interests. At the heart of critical criminology is to be found a combination of intellectual scepticism about the political determination of criminological subject matter and an explicit political commitment to social justice (Cohen, 1990).

Crises in critical criminology

After paving the way for alternative research and criminal political agendas, critical criminology reached a crisis with the changing spirit of the times – when idealism was replaced by scepticism, affluence by budget deficits, full employment by structurally high unemployment rates and the social politics of inclusion by one of exclusion. Thus, it cannot be sustained that symptoms of crisis are specific for critical criminology. The near demise of criminology was, moreover, announced from its very inception, now more than a century ago: either because its ultimate success would result in the abolition of its very object of study, or because it would fail to present adequate explanations of crime. Crisis is, furthermore, a necessary condition for development. Without crises we would be doomed to follow the same paths over and over again, unable to explore new ways. When pathologising stereotypes and theories about (the cause of) crime are disproved by empirical research, this implies a crisis in that particular theory.

None the less, critical criminology is a particularly paradoxical and thus crisis-prone project. A critical approach to deviance and social control would really exclude an un-critical adoption of normative legal concepts like 'crime' which is, after all, criminology's natural subject matter. The term 'deviancy' suggests that crime does not have any ontologically distinctive characteristics from other social problems. Thus, terms like emancipatory, reflexive or exposé sociologies of deviance and social control, deviologies, contrologies, empirical ethical studies or, indeed, micro-polemology (a term which suggests that crime is, like questions of war and peace, to be studied as a social conflict) have been proposed as alternative names for the new criminology. After intensive parochial debates, the term 'critical criminology' has been retained because, only if one stays within the realm of criminology, can an epistemological change, or a scientific revolution to speak in Thomas Kuhn's terms, be advanced.

Criminology's problematic academic status needs to be revealed. In name, it is taken to be a working field with an autonomously defined object of study; but, in practice, it has developed as an auxiliary discipline to law-and-order interests. Mainstream criminologists do not challenge the moral and political presuppositions in the legal definitions of its subject matter. Critical scholars compensate for this neglect; but, instead, critical criminology had become more a critique of criminology than a study of crime itself. Just like mainstream criminologists, critical scholars are also judged on the way they deal with the crime problem. The wider critique of how society deals with social problems is felt to suffer from moral relativism and scientific dilettantism. This conceptual and political problem is at the root of the crisis in critical criminology.

Analytical crises

An important internal reason for the crisis in critical criminology is that neither the empirical project nor the development of the alternative agenda has got off the ground. According to Italian critical criminologist Dario Melossi (1985), the impasse is fundamentally theoretical: critical criminology has never come to terms with its interactionist roots. Dutch critical criminologist Willem de Haan (1990: 13–14) also observes that critical criminology has never lived up to its initial promise to integrate materialist and interactionist perspectives. Instead of de-reifying the aetiological notion of crime or engaging in serious critical sociological research, critical criminologists have largely confined themselves to a display of moral indignation about social inequality and exploitation, and have largely reiterated their own ideology. Having become an actual paradigm, the critical perspective lost much of its initial competitive potential and began to look increasingly like an esoteric debating club on 'the real evils in the world', of which everyday crime is only a marginal part. Austrian critical criminologist Heinz Steinert (1978) posed the rhetorical question of whether socialism can be advanced by radical rhetoric and sloppy data. According to English critical criminologist Colin Sumner (1994), it is even now time to write the obituary of the sociology of deviance since too many of its readings are misleading or shallow.

Critical criminologists are also heavily criticised for neglecting the real social problems of inner cities, of which relatively small crimes are an important part because of their massive impact. Their critique of crime control is increasingly portrayed as playing down justified complaints about the disintegrating effects of such 'petty' crimes on the community and as creating an atmosphere in which virtually every police intervention is charged with being repressive, racist or biased against the lower classes. The 'just deserts' element of a wanton, unworldly 'left idealism' is stressed by critical scholars who, on this very premiss, build a so-called 'left realist' perspective. Having been a symbol of progressiveness for some years, critical criminology is now merely depicted as academic dilettantism, with fuzzy morals and flaky politics (de Haan, 1990: 17–35). Sectarianism, the delusions of theories of crime as a mere exponent of deviancy, an unwillingness to deal with positivist and statistical issues, and the message that as far as penal reform is concerned nothing works – these are the factors that mark an internal analytical crisis in critical criminology.

Ideological crises

These crises were embedded in a broader, cultural transformation. Belief in progress, social engineering, civilisation and emancipation was on the wane by the end of the 1970s. Illusions about the possibility of changing society had been shattered, and the belief in a possible just world was seen as a fundamental delusion. Critical criminology's socialist commitment had also become complicated. Following the Stalinist gulags and China's Cultural Revolution, Western sympathisers of Marxism-Leninism or Maoism had something to explain. In addition, the new hope derived from Latin American opposition forces against right-wing dictatorships, of which Che Guevara and Fidel Castro were the heroes of their time, disappeared as the Cuban model became established, despite an uneasy solidarity with this victim of the United States' isolationist politics. Marxist experiments in Africa were not very encouraging either; and, ultimately, the developments in state-socialist countries in Central and Eastern Europe, which finally collapsed in 1989, made it hard to embrace new socialist experiments whole-heartedly. As a social critique, historical materialism may still have important points to make in most parts of the world, but as a political strategy, or indeed as a model of society, it is widely regarded as something that has had its day.

At the same time, the image that progressive Europeans hold of the United States of America has also changed. Having been among Europe's liberators, just after the Second World War the US was widely seen as the country of freedom and progress, but a post-war generation now mainly associates it with anti-communist witch-hunts and its support for right-extremist forces in Latin America, other economically and ideologically biased demonstrations of 'world leadership', and an equally ruthless as mind-numbing 'commerciocracy'. To make the political anomie in Europe even greater: now that the traditional working class has become so prosperous that its interest rather lies in reducing taxes than in keeping up good public services, the very idea of the welfare state is declining. Since the Western European ideal of making a social-democratic society has been damaged, and not replaced by any other positive ideal, a suspicious or apathetic attitude towards any politics of change has taken the place of previous, more positive political commitments. Limiting risk and nuisance becomes the new, negative motive for state intervention. While a 'Fortress Europe' is built around the richest countries of the continent, nationalism grows both within and outside the European Union. In this context, the liberal-capitalist democracy, once a central object of critique for the left, is now widely perceived as the most reasonable political system – even when the heart is not in it.

The philosophical counterpart of this anomic complexity is generally referred to as the postmodern condition: an era in which leading modern ideologies and central beliefs that have guided and synchronised social questions become defunct. This vision is, in its most uncompromising form, elaborated by the French philosopher Jean François Lyotard. According to Lyotard (1986: 27, 38), 'modernity as a project aiming at the realisation of universalism' failed as a grand narrative when Auschwitz proved the 'tragically unfinished character of modernity'. This Nazi extermination camp has become the symbol of a turning-point in modernity. It marked the end of a philosophical period of confidence in the moral and reasonable autarchy of mankind. After Auschwitz, there was no choice but to abandon every claim for the absolute, the pure and the definitive. The disenchanted spirit of the 1980s was marked by a bitter, cynical or apathetic acceptance of the status quo, and a subsequent rejection of macro-sociological social critiques. This was not the most fertile political ground for critical criminology. While rejecting the often frivolous, Western ethnocentric and socially uncommitted visions of reality, we will follow the modest postmodern reconstruction of reality by smaller narratives.

Between critical theory and postmodernism lies, of course, the shattered dream of socialism. Yet the distinction between 'modern' and 'postmodern' should not be taken as absolute. On the one hand, many postmodern observations reflect on a society that is, in fact, hyper-modern in the sense that the modern process of industrialisation and rationalisation is driven to the extreme, rather than given up. On the other hand, many 'modern' philosophers of science had already radically questioned the methodological claim of rationality, as many interactionist sociologists long ago started to deconstruct reality. Social critics like Theodor Adorno, Jürgen Habermas and Herbert Marcuse warned against the same boundlessness of the human urge for power and possession as potential factors in the destruction of civilisation that postmodern scholars describe. Adorno (1950) keeps the closest to the metaphor of Auschwitz – after which writing (traditional) poetry would no longer be fitting – by pointing to the political-economic incentives to authoritarianism. Marcuse (1969) and Habermas (1973) spoke of the legitimation crisis of the welfare state and of the obscenity of our societies exactly because there is, as postmodern scholars would repeat some ten years later, ultimately no other binding ideology than the market and people's insatiable consumerism.

Why critical criminology is worth reassessing

There are good reasons to retrieve both the materialist and interactionist heritage of critical criminology. Criminologists tend to hop rather quickly from one academic fashion to the next. By simply discarding what has been done before, there is little accumulation of knowledge and scientific development hardly takes place. Currently, the 'real' criminologist deals with the police, crime prevention and with organised crime. But does this mean that studies of the penal system, moral panics or social deprivation have become less relevant? Does the fact that today's debates focus on control, opportunity and rational choice theory imply that interactionist and radical, Habermasian or Foucauldian perspectives have become outdated? Though actual conditions have changed, the old problems of unemployment, of class, race, age and gender discrimination, and of crimes of the powerful, are still there, and thus we still need criminological analyses addressing macro-sociological questions.

All European countries currently face grave crises in criminal justice. Given the failure of traditional penal approaches, there is a pressing need to elaborate precisely those criminological perspectives that deal in an alternative way with questions of crime and punishment. Once their central beliefs were criticised, however, critical criminologists either fell into analytical despair or adapted to the idea that they should primarily contribute to the penal fight against crime. The idea now dominant that the alternative approaches of the 1970s were either naïve or irresponsible has meant that old-fashioned 'tough' solutions (of which we know the social effects quite well already) are accepted with frightening ease by the general public and politicians as well as by many criminologists. In their rejection of 'the seventies', they fail to see, however, that many of today's criminal policies (for example, on community policing, crime prevention or non-custodial sanctions) are actually derived from critical criminological insights from this doomed era. Even when the original ideas have been implemented in ways quite different from what critics originally intended, there are intellectually more creative and politically more strategic responses to consider than the widely prevailing despair and resignation. According to Dutch legal theorist August 't Hart (1993), the Ministry of Justice currently monopolises the 'right' vision of reality and keeps people trapped in its stereotypes. A reorientation towards critical criminology is inevitable if we are to create an open space for alternative scenarios of criminal politics which compensate for the democratic deficit of a 'totalitarian' culture of an instrumentalist politics of law and order.

In the 1970s, 'grand theory' belonged to critical scholars. From the 1980s on, it became the domain of North American mainstream criminologists, who presented 'general theories' of crime (Gottfredson and Hirschi, 1990) and of 'expropriate crime' (Cohen and Machalek, 1988), or even related crime to 'human nature' (Wilson and Herrnstein, 1985). Critical scholars are currently rather silent about such big questions and have lowered their pretensions. Probably afraid of being chastised again for dilettantism, few even dare to address the poignant questions brought about by today's crucial political developments in the Western world, such as the criminogenic exclusion of lower-income groups from social life and the creation of new underclasses by the privatisation of public services (on which those people who can afford them the least are the most dependent), the replacement of real jobs by 'flexible' work on demand without realistic job prospects (so-called 'McJobs'), the automation and globalisation of labour, and ever more restrictive migration policies. The current picture of European criminology is, by and large, one of an increasingly dispersed, unreflexive and empiricist orientation towards actual questions of law enforcement (Robert and van Outrive, 1993). Though the increased number of empirical studies is a welcome development, criminologists risk the abolition of their discipline if too little attention is paid to its theoretical foundations. Criminology's value as an autonomous academic discipline next to 'normal' social sciences lies in its interdisciplinary character and its specific knowledge of the criminal justice system. This enables criminologists to show how various social phenomena relate to crime and criminalisation, how a legal construction and follow-up funnels this problem, and what the effects of specific penal and other social reactions are. As opposed to most other social scientists, (critical) criminologists (in particular) also take normative questions of law enforcement into consideration; the values of the rule of law under a constitutional state are part of the foundations of criminology. The big moral questions of Western law enforcement already outlined have to be related to this normative postulate of enlightened human values.

The study of social reactions to crime receded at precisely the time when a

large expansion and retrenchment of the penal system began, the competences of the police were widened, and pro-active interventions (that is, before
an actual suspect can be identified) and new criminalisations and sanction
modalities widened the penal net. There is a large tradition of empirical studies on law enforcement, labelling, stigmatisation, criminalisation, moral
panic, selectivity and so on, which can still make a relevant contribution to
these recent developments in criminal justice. They need sophistication –
analytical frameworks need to be adapted to present realities – but there is no
need to write off these critical orientations altogether. Critical criminologists have been among the first to point to the neglect of organised crime as
a crime of the powerful (for example, Alan Block and Bill Chambliss'
Organizing Crime of 1981). In The Netherlands, the whole field of organised
(drugs) crime has recently been subjected to thorough examination (van Traa,
1996). Far-reaching police methods (infiltration, setting up front-stores, 'controlled' supply of drugs, detailed observation, etc.) are applied to fight
organised crime. Now it is time for critical criminologists to bring this debate
back into the realm of crimes of the powerful, to engage in empirical studies
in this field, and to apply a social reactions approach to the effects of penal
intervention on the development of these crimes, on the social rule of law and
on civil liberties.

It is premature to write the obituary of critical criminology. If critical
criminology is to reconnect with the times, a central question is: which of its
concepts need revision, which ones are best forgotten altogether and which
ones have kept their validity?

Plan of the book

Chapter 2 examines some epistemological and methodological questions
brought forward by the adoption of critical theory, the interdisciplinary
approach of criminology and jurisprudence, and by the comparative nature
of the book.

The next two chapters consist of a search for critical impulses to criminology and penal reform from the 1880s on. The roots of European critical
criminology will be traced back to the European Modern School of integrated penal sciences, which gained momentum around the turn of last
century. Its pivotal questions will be outlined and explained in their particular sociopolitical settings. These chapters show how criminology has from the
outset been placed in a functionalist framework. Chapter 3 largely deals with
the situation in Italy, Germany, France, Belgium and The Netherlands, where
the Modern School was the most influential. Chapter 4 investigates how a
critical criminology *avant la lettre* developed in The Netherlands at the beginning of this century. Criminology as a distinct scientific area emerged on the
European continent in close correspondence with the legal discipline. In the
early phases, Anglo-Saxon scholars played a rather marginal role in its development. Anglo-Saxon criminology only really developed after the Second

World War in the realm of empirical sociology. The link with legal developments within the criminal justice sphere was less obvious. These different histories explain much about later differences between continental European and Anglo-Saxon criminology.

The next three chapters deal with the heyday of critical criminology and related penal reform movements till their virtual disappearance from the academic scene. First, a map of the state of the art in various European countries is drawn. Before the Second World War, the streams of inspiration largely flowed from the European continent to the 'New World', but from the 1950s onwards the direction turned around. Having contributed to politically vulnerable functionalist visions of criminal justice politics in the period prior to the Second World War, European criminology suffered from an unabsorbed past. Partly under the influence of Anglo-American schools of empirical sociology, continental criminologists also began to take a more independent line from legal scholars. Chapter 5 outlines how different critical criminologies emerged in Britain, Germany, Belgium, France, Italy and Spain. I will demonstrate how comparable criminological problems received different responses because scholars reflected upon different sociopolitical realities – from social-democratic welfare states, via more traditional class societies, to countries in transition from dictatorship to democracy. Chapter 6 indicates how Dutch critical criminology, unlike that of other countries, did not imply a rupture with the past, but was rather a radicalisation of earlier penal schools. A contextual analysis is given of the simultaneous development of a sociologised due process model of justice and an abolitionist perspective. In Chapter 7, related activities of radical European penal reform movements are evaluated. This chapter concludes with some theoretical lessons from these experiences with regard to the future of critical criminology.

The reshaping of critical criminology for the present era is elaborated in the remaining part of the book. The preceding academic and activist developments and the changing politics of law and order necessitate a reassessment of critical criminology, while its central epistemological critique and orientation towards social justice have kept their validity. Chapter 8 analyses the nature of the law-and-order campaigns of the 1980s and 1990s, which brought forward managerial visions of justice and moralising visions of crime. It investigates under which political, economic and macro-sociological circumstances a radical shift in penal and social values has taken place. This chapter marks a caesura in the analytical approach of the book in the sense that it bridges preceding analyses of what has been and the following thematic explorations into what might be. It both indicates the need for a reconceptualisation of critical criminology and shows why precisely now an orientation towards social justice is fundamental. Chapter 9 begins with an outline of general changes within the criminological discipline over the past 15 years and stresses the need to reaffirm a social reactions approach to law and order. It examines, furthermore, how more recent critical perspectives as left realism and neo-abolitionism have emerged, and how these perspectives can, in an integrated fashion, contribute to a replacement discourse on community safety. In

Chapter 10, legal guaranteeist and feminist perspectives are added, in order to construct an alternative vision of the political values of law. The normative theoretical exploration contrasts with the dominant instrumentalist discourse, which is directed at the criminal justice system's organisational 'efficiency'. The idea that justice is grounded in material provisions functions as a guiding principle in these last two chapters. It is elaborated in two distinct ways. In Chapter 9, we move towards a primary politics of social justice, aimed at a socioeconomically just policy of community safety. In Chapter 10, we move towards a secondary politics of social justice, focused on the role of the victim and the public need for an affirmation of norms. The need to set limits to penal intervention, the sociological role of legal principles and the function of law as moral-practical discourse will be oriented to the imperative human rights. Chapter 11 brings some final conclusions together. Following the developments analysed in earlier chapters, it reassesses some critical criminological hypotheses and analytical concepts. These form the incentive for both new visions of penal reform and of critical criminology's theoretical orientation. Warnings against wayward instrumentalism, a remoralisation of the social role of the state, and a reaffirmation of a normative orientation to social justice have been central in critical perspectives on criminal justice for over a century. Perhaps these values become most relevant when people seem to forget them.

2

The Value of Comparative Criminology

The claim to present a survey of critical criminology in Europe, and to reassess the critical project on this basis, encounters many structural limitations. First, the goal of outlining a future for critical criminology can easily conflict with the objective of offering a representative survey, which may distract from the main argument. With respect to the aim of giving as representative a picture as possible, a thematic survey may well result in an unintended ethnocentrism: themes are selected which are central in one's own national context, while issues pivotal in another country remain untouched. With the reservation of what will be argued in the next section, I have let developments in different countries tell their own story, without forcing them into one unifying theoretical framework. In exploring a future for critical criminology, a thematic approach can be adopted more safely and the focus on national disparities can be changed to one of similarities. This analytical transition becomes gradually visible during Chapters 7–9.

Secondly, because reassessing critical criminology's restructuring and constitutive role is the ultimate goal of this book, its related, earlier debates on penal reform are given more than representative attention. A focus on penal reform in the development of critical criminology has, however, major analytical advantages. At this point, critical criminology's original perspective of change and its political commitment become particularly apparent. It also offers a common focus, while national disparities in theoretical orientation and political situation can be respected. On the other hand, a survey of critical criminology can hardly do without an analysis of penal activism because this political pressure from 'below' forms an important empirical incentive for critical criminological studies into the objectives and effects of penal sanctions in all the countries described. Penal reform is (unlike many other themes) a common orientation in European critical criminologies, and is therefore very suited to comparative study. It is, furthermore, a subject with considerable historical continuity, and is a point where criminological and legal analyses meet. This is important with respect to the joint development of these two disciplines on the European continent. In most European languages, the term 'penal reform' exceeds questions of punishment alone, is not associated with reformism, and covers endeavours to reveal miscarriages of justice and to support alternative visions of crime control, by influencing public opinion, penal practitioners and politicians. It will be used in this broad sense of the word. Though certainly not all penal reformers have a political orientation related to that of critical criminology, I will, following the aim of this book, only deal with those who do.

Thirdly, the selection of what to stress and what to give less attention to is guided by the goal of presenting a survey of European critical criminology. Its most characteristic feature, which is also the most uncommon in the Anglo-Saxon world, is reflection upon the legal discipline. Themes which fall slightly outside this focus, but which have also played a role in European critical criminology, such as Marxist histories of crime and crime control, conflict theories on crime as resistance, methodological elaborations, empirical studies as such (in short, all those issues which we also find in Anglo-Saxon critical criminology) may remain under-exposed, as does the work of non-European precursors of critical criminology, such as North American labelling, sub-cultural or conflict theorists. It seemed, however, unnecessary to devote many pages to these already well-known traditions.

Fourthly, while speaking of 'Europe' in general terms, an actual survey can only be given of those European countries where an identifiable critical criminological strand can actually be distinguished. I have made a systematic inventory of the leading European critical journals, checked references, and asked key scholars in various countries for their vision of the state of the art in their country. None the less, I will surely have missed many relevant debates. Europe ranges from Russia to Portugal and from Turkey to Iceland, and it is simply impossible for one person to understand fully such a diversity of cultures, languages and political and academic traditions. Sometimes there is a significant critical school, as for example in Norway, which can only be dealt with superficially because I do not know the language sufficiently well to give a proper survey. In most cases I concluded, however, that we can hardly speak of a real critical criminological tradition. The political situation in the countries of Central and Eastern Europe, which have been under the sphere of influence of the former Soviet Union, makes a meaningful comparison difficult. If Marxism is the official state ideology, 'left idealist' observations from the West are not exactly popular among social critics in those countries (Falandysz, 1991: 16–17). Sometimes, the absence of a critical debate in a particular country has more to do with the lack of an empirical criminological tradition in general. In this respect I realise, however, that even when, for example, Irish (Tomlinson et al., 1988: 9) or Greek scholars (Bokos et al., 1992: 133) argue that there is hardly any empirical research on crime and law enforcement or any counter-movement in the penal sphere in their country, a Dutchman can well be criticised for a serious flaw if he just repeats this.

Finally, a book simply has a limited number of pages, and the survey must necessarily be incomplete if the book is to remain readable. I have therefore confined the survey to the main lines, and have not been able to go very deeply into each debate.

Writing a book such as this also involves other analytical problems which require some elaboration before the actual study can start. These are mainly epistemological questions about the status of knowledge in critical theory, the

different traditions of legal and criminological thought and the diverse international frames of reference that have to be taken into account while
comparing European criminologies. A central line in this respect is the question of what can be compared and what cannot; and, if things can be
compared, which conditions should be observed? These questions need to be
answered with regard to, respectively, the role of critique in the construction
of knowledge, the role of normative standards, and the role of culture.

The value of critical theory

'All human knowledge . . . is ultimately and irreversibly stained and impreg-
nated with human interests, goals, values and metaphysical assumptions. So,
of course, is criminology, though one can find a widespread reluctance in the
field to accept this epistemological position' (Sack, 1994: 3). This acknowledgement does not lead to a rejection of empirical positivism, as was the
original target of critical criminologists. It only stresses the necessity of prior
epistemological reflection. The positivist ideal of 'pure' science prevents us
from empirically ungrounded speculation. So-called 'hard data', acquired
through sound methodological analyses, are very well able to demonstrate
causal relations between different phenomena. They can also help to rule out
theoretical assumptions and can even say some useful things about the actual
effects which can be expected of certain politics. Positivism can, however, only
offer 'very partial, crude, and flawed explanation' because it focuses on 'short-
term, de-contextualised policies, that are intentionally disentangled from
integrated policy packages' (Braithwaite, 1993a: 388–93). 'Results of empirical studies largely say nothing about the possibilities of changing things.
Empirical social-scientific research can never offer us anything more than a
[series of] observation[s] which establish and interpret a specific situation'
(van der Vijver, 1993: 27). 'As a discipline criminology is shaped only to a
small extent by its own theoretical object and logic of enquiry. Its epistemological threshold is a low one, making it susceptible to pressures and interests
generated elsewhere' (Garland, 1994: 28). Raising epistemological questions
about the ideological foundations of criminology, as has been the objective of
critical scholars, can help to decrease this susceptibility. Critical studies are
extremely important in this respect since they 'keep us all on our toes with
regard to our own pre-suppositions' (Braithwaite, 1993a: 394–5).
    The problem for critical theory is of an epistemological nature. Positivists
accuse critical scholars of nothing less than giving up on science, by adopting
the position that 'everything goes' as regards the question of what makes a
claim to scientific knowledge. Though I agree that, without a certain reduction of complexity, hardly any rational discussion is possible, the real
question is how far such scientific reduction can go before a theory stops
making sense in a concrete social setting. For this purpose we need epistemological reflections. Here epistemology is not only understood as an
investigation into the question 'What can we know?', but also into 'What

determines what is to be considered as valid knowledge?' Michel Foucault answered the positivist critique with his famous counter-question 'Which knowledge do you want to exclude if you ask me "Is it science?"' Yet we need to accept that, in the 1990s, the onus of proof lies again on the side of scholars who do not follow all the mores of logical positivism. Though critical theory is only half a century old, the well-rehearsed argument against critical studies – the fact that they start from premises that do not follow from empirical testing – can be traced back to the old Kantian distinction between analytical pronouncements, based on the anatomy of a specific phenomenon, and synthetic judgements, in which different observations are, often *a priori*, combined. In 1781, Immanuel Kant argued that the foundations of all academic disciplines consist of synthetic judgements *a priori* which do not follow from any analytical pronouncements. These premises are taken as axioms that lie outside scientific observation. Kant's *Critique of Pure Reason* deals with the question of how such concepts are constituted. In this respect, Kant stresses the importance of critique as a critical judgement of the sources and limits of knowledge. Critical theory proposes to subject pre-scientific premisses to a critique of ideology and relate it to (economic) power relations in society.

A premiss of critical theory is that social scientists cannot confine themselves to acquiring knowledge about partial, precisely and empirically describable and operationalistic detail-phenomena which only confront the reader with scientific problems. They should also expose the problematic structures of society itself and confront the reader with social problems (Adorno, 1969: 142). Thus, theory should be grounded in society and contribute to changing reality instead of just describing it. With his famous consideration of knowledge-guiding interests, Jürgen Habermas (1968) made a distinction between power-knowledge (*Herrschaftswissen*) and emancipatory knowledge. Power-knowledge is knowledge that is affected by professional, commercial or hegemonic political interests. It does not question social relations as they are. Emancipatory knowledge challenges these interests by revealing the presuppositions on which certain analyses are based and aims to change the status quo. At this point, Habermas' insights match quite well with Foucault's argument that so-called disqualified, non-discursive knowledge should be revealed in order to get a more balanced picture of historical developments. The stipulations of both are ultimately based on the Marxist notion that professional knowledge belongs to the super-structure, and that we have to look for their material foundations.

The word 'discourse' refers to professional, coherently structured knowledge. Sources that can provide analytical insight into non-discursive knowledge about crime and punishment are scarce. They can to a certain extent be derived from judicial archives (as regards the offender's personal statements), and furthermore from pamphlets, manifestos, prisoners' autobiographies, contemporary novels, myths and the oral history of social movements – especially those of prisoners – which react to a certain (penal) reality from a position of 'subjection'. Social movements are understood as organised, but not yet fully institutionalised, groups, with a distinct identity based on a positive solidarity for a specific cause, an adversarial position towards the status quo on this issue, an action-orientation to change this situation and a tendency to link specific claims with broader social reform. This latter element, in particular, distinguishes social movements from other lobby and interest groups. Though empirical observations are largely derived from other criminological studies, the analyses of penal pressure groups in this book are also derived from unstructured interviews with penal activists in various European countries, as well as from personal involvement in some Dutch pressure groups: to call this 'participant observation' would, however, be to turn around the order of things. The use of activist knowledge and the analysis of academic debates in relation to their specific historical, cultural and socioeconomic grounding bring this study into the realm of critical theory. According to John Braithwaite (1993a: 394–5), criminologists need to 'nurture the contextual art of identifying similarities and differences from other contexts . . . nurture historical criminology, and nurture cross-cultural criminology'. That is the project I want to undertake.

The value of jurisprudence

The frames of reference of law and sociology are, at least in their ideal-typical positivist fashion, rather different. For a legal positivist, 'the truth' comes from above. The prevailing laws and the verdicts of the supreme court are the analytical limits lawyers set themselves. Beyond this exegesis of texts, legal observations soon get a hypothetical character. For a positivistic sociologist, 'the truth' comes from below, and can be constructed differently if empirical analyses require it. If the methodologically constructed data have spoken, 'the facts' are revealed. All knowledge beyond this scientific reconstruction is called speculation. Empirical testing can disprove a sociological theory but not a legal one. In jurisprudence, a theory is based on philosophical stipulation and serves as a normative standard, whereas sociological theories are grounded in empirical analyses and serve as an interpretative framework. These two distinct academic traditions have frequently clashed and been misinterpreted. In the history of European penal sciences, the idea that empirical criminological insights are useful in order to improve the effectiveness of law enforcement has been a *basso continuo*. Here, the perspective will be turned around: why would the study of law be useful for critical criminologists?

(1) The relation between criminology and jurisprudence is historically determined. Academic criminology, on the European continent, emerged and developed in close connection with the legal discipline. In most European countries, criminology is based in law schools. Criminology only gained an independent academic status as a social science in the mid-1960s: in Mediterranean countries it is still mainly carried out by lawyers. Though criminologists and legal scholars, partly under the influence of Anglo-American empirical sociology, drifted apart in the 1970s, European critical

criminology still cannot be understood without specifically dealing with its legal roots. Much of the theoretical work that in the English-speaking world is reckoned to the criminological field is done by legal theorists on the European continent.

(2) Empirical criminologists currently often demonstrate a limited awareness of debates and developments in jurisprudence. Criminology loses, however, its power-critical dimension if hegemonic legal concepts and structures are taken for granted, and its legitimacy as an independent academic discipline if specific knowledge of the criminal justice system is neglected. Criminology distinguishes itself from other social sciences precisely by its knowledge of the legal definition and administration of crime. Empirical analyses of crime and crime control can be interpreted in their proper context only by including this specific legal knowledge. Thus, knowledge of the nature of legal concepts and structures and their underlying political values is necessary if criminology is to keep its independent academic status.

(3) Considerations from both jurisprudence and criminology have often been used in an integrated way, notably in the development of criminal justice policy or, indeed, in penal reform. At these intersections, both criminologists and lawyers operate in an empirical as well as a normative style. The traditional positivistic distinction between law as a normative discipline and criminology as an empirical one is thus too simple. Over the past decades, new social movements affiliated to critical criminology have also held great expectations of law as an instrument of struggle. Many of the more critical European studies on criminal justice of the past decade have, furthermore, come from legal theorists rather than criminologists. The aim of this study is to prevent a further drifting apart of law and criminology. Mutual reflection seems the best way forward for both disciplines.

(4) The introduction of the legal rationale could demonstrate the value of normative thought, which is often avoided in the empirical sciences. While sociology observes and analyses an existing empirical reality, jurisprudence can also visualise strivings and open the door to what 'should be' and how it could be pursued. Normative considerations about legal principles can prevent criminologists from sliding down into uncritical empiricism. For this reason, critical criminologists have often connected empirical analyses with social or political theory. Legal theory has, however, been largely ignored. In view of their mutual history, a reflection upon the legal discipline is quite obvious in a study of European criminology.

(5) By following the axioms of orthodox Marxism, critical criminologists have argued in largely dismissive terms about law and the language of rights as ideological, anachronistic and illusory. By disregarding law as a product of the super-structure, they have, however, not taken the protective side of criminal justice seriously, and failed to see a shared normative, *a priori* and synthetic style of argumentation. The legal rationale has a 'counter-factual' character. This Habermasian concept refers to the continual dialectic relation between empirical reality and normative presuppositions. Jürgen Habermas (1981) has developed the concept of counter-factuality to

interpret the role of claims to validity for ideal communication. The counter-factual elements of law embody an institutionalisation of moral-practical rationality as a necessary impetus for social change. Legal principles thus play a mediating role in the interpretative practice of law enforcement. Legal guaranteeism is the clearest example of how a counter-factual vision is used in European critical criminology. The guaranteeist perspective, which will be introduced in Chapter 5 and elaborated in Chapter 10, is based on the classical legal aim to protect individual citizens from arbitrary state intervention by explicitly codifying when the state can intervene and when it cannot. Both the currently re-emerging dominance of sheer instrumentalist visions by new administrative criminologists, and a neglect of the protective value of criminal law by their critics, are reasons why I propose a renewed reflection on classical legal principles for criminologists, and, indeed, why a more profound knowledge of European traditions in criminology could be relevant to an Anglo-Saxon audience. In Romance languages, *'garantismo'* implies both an orientation to the substantial, political value of criminal law and the procedural value of legal safeguards. In Germanic languages, like Dutch, these two dimensions are covered by distinct concepts, referring respectively to the constitutional bedding (*rechtsstatelijk*) and the protective aim (*rechtsbescherming*). Though guaranteeism reflects an inquisitorial criminal justice system, a typical continental, normative accent on written law, and is, particularly in Southern Europe, embedded in critical criminology (Zaitch and Sagarduy, 1992), its basic political and epistemological contentions resemble Anglo-Saxon critical legal studies (Fitzpatrick and Hunt, 1987).

(6) Another branch of European critical criminology, abolitionism, which will be introduced in Chapter 6 and elaborated in Chapter 9, is also rooted in a counter-factual, legal way of thinking. Abolitionism is a normatively inspired replacement discourse in which an alternative vision of crime control is advocated that does not just follow from sociological analyses. A sociological input is reflected in the fact that abolitionist objections to criminal justice are largely motivated by empirical arguments about its ineffectiveness. Though a politics of abolition and a politics of rights may conflict on a practical level, both are critiques of the current legal practice, both argue along normative and functionalist lines and both include a perspective of penal reform. Moreover, abolitionists also propose to do away with the penal rationale and legal-political instrumentalism because these are seen to frustrate its protective functions.

(7) Technical legal knowledge had proved to be a suitable means for the realisation of the objectives of social movements. Thus, there is no reason to assume that law only benefits 'the powerful'. Legal activism can break the vicious circle of the impossible options trap that critical criminologists have fallen into. On the other hand, more concrete knowledge of the legal system can also lead to a more realistic understanding of the limitations of law enforcement in solving social problems.

From these seven points emerges a reflexive relation between criminal law and criminology at two levels: (a) a rather practical level (concerning a political translation of ideas), and (b) an epistemological level (where the very formulation of normative orientations and principles is concerned). These can be called respectively, a *functional* and a *normative* sociological reflection on criminal law. At a more technical level, both disciplines follow their own paths. Here, the criminological and legal disciplines have other standards of relevance, are ruled by another methodology, and serve other purposes (Moedikdo, 1974; Lüderssen and Sack, 1980). Thus, I do not propose an integrated approach to law and criminology *tout court*. Such an attempt will necessarily lead one of the disciplines into a position auxiliary to the other, but a reflexive confrontation can be very useful for the future of criminology.

The value of international comparisons

What use can be made of comparative criminology? Simply comparing rules and policies on a mere descriptive level – 'How is theft defined in country A?' or 'How are summons issued in country B?' – seems rather pointless, for it is questionable what one actually learns from such petty facts. The blunt argument that because this or that measure 'works' in country C it would be worthwhile to consider its introduction in country D makes just as little sense, since it misjudges the interaction of legal-political developments with specific cultural phenomena, economic conditions and political constellations. This section gives a global picture of these contextual factors that can serve as a general interpretative framework.

David Nelken (1994c: 221) gives a threefold assessment of the purpose of comparative criminology. This may first 'have as much to do with understanding one's own country better as it has with understanding anyone else's. Comparative enquiry has as one of its chief concerns the effort to identify the way a country's types of crime and of crime control resonate with other aspects of its culture.' Comparative criminology reveals the culture-bound quality of national criminology. A second goal is to overcome ethnocentrism: that is, the generally repressed, but none the less often implicitly felt notion that foreigners seldom have any particularly good ideas. And, thirdly, 'comparative work can also breathe new life into the sociology of deviance . . . because it poses the problem of how to understand the other without either resorting to stereotypes or denying difference' (Nelken, 1994c: 223).

Cultures of social control

For a correct understanding of critical thought in Europe, differences in cultures of social control have to be taken into account. A preliminary problem is the concept of social control itself. Stan Cohen (1985: 2) has described it as a 'Mickey Mouse concept' which covers 'all social processes to induce conformity ranging from infant socialisation through to public execution'. By using the concept of social control, many suggestions are raised but nothing is made clear. In critical criminology, social control has become 'a negative term to cover not just the obvious coercive apparatus of the state, but also the putative hidden element in all state-sponsored social policy, whether called health, education or welfare' (Cohen, 1985: 2). In this tradition, social control actually produces deviance. This perception of social control as an Orwellian conspiracy of the state and its accomplices is too negative to fit the proposed replacement discourse of this book and its state-centredness hardly reflects the current fragmented, largely privatised, forms of social control. Power now seems more dispersed among various institutions and informal, market-driven mechanisms whose mutual relations are quite opaque. We will adopt Cohen's (1985: 1) rather neutral definition instead: social control covers the 'organised ways in which society responds to behaviour and people it regards as deviant, problematic, worrying, threatening, troublesome or undesirable in some way or another'.

Modes of social control are rooted in specific cultural patterns. They reflect different histories, traditions, social codes and criminal justice systems. Dario Melossi (1991b) distinguishes between models of social control (in the critical, state-oriented interpretation) within the Western world of a 'Protestant' model that prevails in the North, and a 'Catholic' one in Mediterranean countries. In the first model, a dispersed and enterpreneurial state focuses on the self-control of the individual citizen; in the latter model, a more centralised and unresponsive state addresses people largely as representatives of a particular group, and control is basically external. The culture of social control is strongly determined by the level of public trust in the fairness and reasonableness of norms. David Nelken explains this element of social control by comparing Britain and Italy. Nelken (1994c: 230–1) operationalises trust in a twofold way: as a faith in institutions and persons; and as the predictability of social expectations. Despite the fact that the way in which trust functions in British and Italian social systems is very different, they should not be contrasted too much. Both are 'generalised means of exchange' which 'serve to eliminate uncertainty and allow a system to action'. Furthermore, the level of trust in interpersonal relations may turn out to be completely different from the trust one holds in institutions, and the trust in some specific institution may well coincide with a distrust of the system as a whole. Also, the trust between various systems can be quite different. In Britain, the judiciary and the political and administrative systems are considered as social systems that support each other. In Italy, there is a large distrust between the three. The same goes for the trust on which the internal relations of the system are built. The British criminal justice system is, at bottom, based on relations of trust between the various functionaries. In the British 'old boys' network', large policy discretions are allowed, whereas in the Italian context such a system seems too easy to excuse for corruption. Italian social systems are based on distrust. Italy is, however,

> characterised by both more and less trust; there is more inter-personal trust but less impersonal trust. As a generalisation we could assume that in Italy friends need to, and are willing to, do much more for you than could be expected in Britain. But the

very search for trust . . . only reinforces the sense of insecurity and lack of a larger
background on which to rely. (Nelken, 1994c: 236–7)

Britons would, in return, put more trust in 'their' institutions and less in
their friends.

The decision to trust, the manner of trusting and the level of trust in a particular society are again strongly rooted in its historical development. The
more social control mechanisms are oriented towards self-control, the greater
will be the trust in the accountability of functionaries. The level of trust in
social systems also increases with the level of establishment of a social-democratic welfare state. If institutions actually provide services for the citizens, the
more likely it is that people will identify with them. The more unresponsive
they are, the smaller public confidence will be. There is a larger degree of professionalisation and dependence on social systems in advanced welfare states
and a larger degree of clientelism and dependence on friends if the state primarily embodies power.

Visions of the 'state' mark a common misunderstanding among European
critical criminologists. For the sake of argument, these will be reduced here to
two cultural spheres: a Southern and Central European one, on the one hand,
and a North-Sea culture, on the other; The Netherlands belong, together
with the Scandinavian countries and the United Kingdom, to this latter tradition. Central and Southern Europeans have a pyramid-shaped image of the
state: a centrally organised body in which orders are hierarchically given
from top to bottom according to strict bureaucratic rules in order to establish
propter hoc democratic control. In North-Sea countries, the state functions
more as a management system, where comparable informally operating
authorities are *post hoc* subjected to democratic control. They carry out their
job according to rather general standards that can be applied with discretion.
Though over the past 15 years the tendency of governments in all Western
European countries to rely on (semi-)privatised agencies has led both to more
fragmentation and to more centralisation (this issue will be addressed in
Chapter 8), their different administrative traditions still play a significant
role. Because such notions are taken for granted and generally remain
implicit, discussions of 'the state' raise considerable unspoken misunderstanding; we often think we are speaking of the same body, but in reality we
are not.

Unlike many other nation-states, the formation of The Netherlands was
not the result of an aristocratic power accumulation, but originated in a
revolt against Spanish rule in 1579. Metaphysical considerations about the
state have not found much reflection in Dutch political practice nor in its state
philosophy. Rooted in a tradition in which the maintenance of the water balance was the first task of 'the authorities', the state basically represents a
public service. On the one hand, people have always expected something positive from their representatives and, on the other hand, these representatives
answer these expectations by inviting all kinds of opponents and dissident
forces to take part in discussions and negotiations. Perhaps even stronger

than in Britain, the organisational structure of Dutch institutions is rooted in relations of trust. Dutch organisational structures are ruled by the same culture of pragmatism as the British. Thomas Hardy's famous commonplace 'We Britons hate ideas!' applies just as much to the Dutch. According to Nelken (1994c: 228), from a continental viewpoint, it becomes 'pertinent to discuss the ingrained "pragmatism" (a term which is not intended as a compliment) of many British and American criminal justice procedures and practices'. The Dutch criminal justice system would be open to the same criticism. Nelken (1994c: 229) argues that it is tempting to 'assume that the countries or cultures concerned represent polar opposites . . . Often it is only after shifting to a perspective anchored in a third reality that the factors which the countries actually have in common emerge clearly.' When comparing Britain with the European continent, the Dutch situation is an excellent third reality. The Netherlands has continental (French) legal structures, but the working and rationale of various social systems is ruled by Anglo-Saxon pragmatism. This makes the Dutch situation an analytical 'bridge' between Britain and the continent.

Ideal-types of criminal justice in Europe

Because the history of European criminology is interwoven with jurisprudence, differences in legal culture may also be more determining factors for continental criminologists than for their Anglo-Saxon counterparts. An adequate description of various criminal justice systems cannot be given here. In order to sketch a global context of understanding, I will put forward some ideal-types of criminal justice. The two major traditions in European legal thinking do not follow a North–South line. In law, the distinction between Anglo-Saxon common-law systems (with an adversarial procedural structure) and continental legal systems based on the 'principle of legality' (with a more inquisitorial procedural order) is more fundamental. The trial is pivotal in common law, whereas investigative preliminary phases are more central in continental legal systems. In common law, a judge merely acts as a referee between two fighting lawyers who tactically cross-examine witnesses. A continental judge has an elaborate dossier knowledge of a case before the actual court session and he or she actively questions witnesses, whereas there is no real cross-examination by lawyers. The attribution of procedural responsibilities marks a related difference. In common law, the accused and defence play a rather active role (for example, with regard to finding counter-evidence to convince the judge and jury), whereas under a continental rule of law, non-cooperation of the accused has no formal consequences for his or her chances. In common law, the prosecutor is a member of the bar; in continental systems a member of the magistracy. In both systems, the prosecution has the task of giving a lawful and convincing evidence and the accused does not have to contribute to his or her own conviction.

In common law, the police operate in a rather autonomous fashion, whereas in continental legal systems they are (ideal-typically) embedded in a more hierarchical system of competences controlled by the public prosecutor's office and investigating magistrates. In respect of cultures of policing, Nelken (1994c: 221–2) gives a wonderful example of how these differences direct criminological knowledge.

> Much British writing on the police takes it for granted that nothing could be more ill advised than for the police to risk losing touch with the public by relying too much on military, technological or other impersonal methods of crime control . . . In Italy, however, two of the main police forces are still part of the military and in a recent opinion poll . . . one of these – the *carabinieri* – was voted the legal institution in which people had the most confidence.

The prominence of a more military style of policing is typical of Southern European countries. Both systems have their particular weaknesses. Forces oriented towards a military model have often been the docile instruments of an authoritarian *raison d'état* aimed at the repression of political activism and other deviant sub-cultures. On the other hand, examples such as the Guildford Four or the Birmingham Six in Britain show that a lack of control over the police can also have its particular democratic shortcomings. As an illustration of the fact that problems can equally be a result of too little trust as of too much trust, Nelken (1994c: 237) argues:

> In the United Kingdom the overwhelming majority of criminal cases are decided at first hearing; it is only as a result of a series of miscarriages of justice . . . that thought is now being given to automatic procedures for review. In Italy, on the other hand, many cases pass through two levels of appeal and almost all criminal cases have two trials on the 'facts'. But the benefits in trust and legitimacy that are gained from ensuring everyone 'a second bite at the cherry' are counter-balanced by the loss of trust in the system that comes from the delay which is its consequence.

Common law allows a more central place for unwritten law, whereas on the continent law enforcement is bound by the limits set by codification: the so-called 'principle of legality'. Nelken (1994c: 228) mentions this difference in legal culture as a major source of misunderstanding between Britain and the continent. 'It takes a Briton or American . . . to be puzzled by the continental "principle of legality" in prosecution decision making which in its extreme form – as in Italy – refuses to authorise any use of discretion in enforcement or prosecution by police or prosecutor.' The 'principle of legality' also implies a difference between the Anglo-Saxon idea of the rule of law and its continental equivalent of the *rechtsstaat*. The first concept refers to the guarantees a 'subject' holds against state intervention, whereas the second notion holds the principle that every state action that curtails the freedom of the citizen should be explicitly based on and legitimised by a specific written legal paragraph. When speaking of the continental situation, we will use the word *rechtsstaat* as an accurate English translation would be too long.

Common law allows for lay magistrates in criminal cases, whereas most continental systems use professional judges only. The jury system, felt to be a crucial element of criminal justice in common-law countries, is not by any means so obvious on the continent. Both the presence and absence of a jury system is motivated by arguments of democracy. In common-law countries, the jury system is felt to be the democratic element in criminal proceedings because it guarantees a public input into the legal system. The main democratic argument against a jury is the danger that justice will de-rail into populist lynching when lay sentiments prevail over more rational, professional legal principles. It is hard to draw any meaningful conclusions about the democratic calibre of a country by the presence or absence of a jury system. Germany and The Netherlands do not have a jury system in criminal cases; Belgium and France only use it in serious cases (*assize*), a system recently introduced in Italy and Spain. As far as democratic government is concerned, most European countries allow for a broader public input in politics by referendums, inquiry procedures and proportional representation than is the case in Britain, where even the feudal system is maintained in the right of hereditary peers to enter the 'senate' (House of Lords).

Among continental criminal justice systems there are also major differences. Two extremes, Spain and The Netherlands, are used as ideal-types of a doctrinal and a pragmatic system. In Spain, legal scholars largely deal with weighty philosophical questions called 'penal dogmatics'; whereas, in The Netherlands, lawyers tend to focus more on policy, case law and procedural aspects. In doctrinal systems, like the Spanish, law enforcement consists of logical system-internal deductions by which an autonomous reality is given to legal principles and dogmatic constructions which do not necessarily have any reflection in social practice. In The Netherlands, law enforcement is oriented towards achieving practical results. In this pragmatic approach, logical and dogmatic consistency often comes second place. In Spain, the principle of legality is strictly followed in every phase of the penal process. It forces all legal officials to act exactly as the law prescribes and to transfer a case to a next phase in the penal process. In The Netherlands, this same principle determines the maximum breadth and level of penal intervention, but not the minimum. Whether a case is, within this limit of legality, dealt with in a criminal lawsuit, diverted to less custodial means of social control or, indeed, dismissed, is left to the discretion of various officials. Nearly every single act of a Spanish judiciary needs to be explicitly regulated by law, whereas the Dutch system allows for wide discretion in this respect. The other side of the coin is that in Spain every single citizen (victims, grassroots groups) can personally initiate penal prosecution, whereas in The Netherlands it is the absolute monopoly of the public prosecutor to decide whether or not a case is prosecuted. As far as sanctions are concerned, Spanish law provides for a very strict framework of minimum and maximum sentences, along with mitigating and aggravating circumstances, which leaves the judge little room for interpretation, whereas the Dutch system has only maximum sentences and the art of balancing every individual case, according to person- and offence-specific circumstances, is seen to be the core of the judicial profession.

While the major distinctions between European criminal justice systems may not correspond with the dividing line between the two main modes of social control, the differences in legal orientation among continental law systems do. A strict interpretation of the principle of legality reflects a pyramid-shaped model in which the state symbolises the centre of power and law is mainly an imperative. An expediently applied system reflects a more managerial governmental structure in which law is a means rather than an end. In such a system, policy considerations, laid down in guidelines, White Papers, pseudo-law and municipal regulations, 'adapt' abstract legal ideals to reality. Dutch Minister of Justice Winnie Sorgdrager (1995: 9) has argued in this respect: if, in Northern Europe, the content of a specific norm is no longer considered to be just or practicable, this norm is changed. 'The danger of this adaptation of norms to practice is that norms will eventually lose their cogency in a more general sense. This danger is called the inclined plane.' In Southern legal cultures, 'norms are preferably left intact, no matter how unjust or impracticable, while violations of these norms are condoned in complete silence. This includes the danger of norm and practice drifting completely apart. This could be called hypocrisy.' This different culture of dealing with rules explains a lot about the continuous French scapegoating of the Dutch politics of tolerance with respect to the control of drugs. President Chirac's conservative administration holds the view that The Netherlands should repress not only the trade but also the consumption of drugs by penal means because the Dutch have signed various treaties in this respect, whereas the Dutch government claims that its harm-reduction approach is more suc- cessful in the prevention of street crime and health risks, and is thus in accordance with the spirit of these treaties. Both are right according to their national legal cultures.

Tolerance as social control: the Dutch case

In the international literature, the 'Dutch model' of social control is often put forward as an example of a tolerant and mild penal climate. In many of these analyses, the sociocultural context is either ignored or misinterpreted as a product of a country with a homogeneous population and low crime rates. Foreign observers who treat a proverbial Dutch tolerance as an example of ultimate humanism, as well as those who see it as an indifferent or even immoral attitude towards pernicious anomalies or who depict it as a border- less naïvity, are equally wrong in their observations. Possible contrasts in tolerance reflect above all socioeconomic, political and cultural contrasts. In his comparative study in *Contrasts in Tolerance* between Britain and The Netherlands, David Downes (1988a: 69–74) rejects the idea of a general, principled Dutch culture of tolerance. There are, however, tolerant outcomes of the Dutch politics of crime control. Norwegian criminologist Nils Christie (1993: 41–6) has described the Dutch mode of social control as 'tolerance from above,' from an intellectual rather than an economic élite. Erhard Blankenburg (1993: 363) therefore argues that Dutch social control has a democratic deficit, for it depends on the defining power of a changing group of dominant professionals. Because of an enlightened and somewhat imperi- ous style of government, and because of the many highly institutionalised and professionalised social movements, the actual management of social systems is kept out of the glare of too much public scrutiny. In this way, an authoritarian style of administration can be maintained, while at the same time politics can be more tolerant than the population.

Dutch tolerance should be seen as a means rather than an end. It is a consequence of both political pragmatism and an ideologically and historically produced reciprocal relation between state and citizens. Despite all normative arguments for tolerance in Dutch history (from Desiderius Erasmus and Baruch Spinoza to the Protestant plea for religious freedom during the Dutch revolt against the Spanish), it cannot currently be considered as a principle *per se*. It is rather a moral appeal for self-control and a pragmatic *modus vivendi* to keep things as quiet as possible by not provoking unnecessary unrest in society. It is a benign form of utilitarianism. Its rationale is that approaches to deviance of a predominantly moralistic nature tend to be counter-effective because they only alienate those people who have already strayed from the norm and do not address those still sharing the norm. Solely pragmatic responses, however, offer no normative standard for either expressing the value the law aims to protect or for assessing the ethical, human or political justness of certain reactions. It implicitly assumes that the middle way offers the maximum attainable in convincing people of the reasonability of a norm, and that, sometimes, with a slight variation on Edwin Schur, a relative non-intervention is socially less damaging or disruptive than repression.

Tolerant law enforcement?

Dutch legal culture is characterised by a strong policy orientation, a comparably less frequent use of the deprivation of liberty, a rather broad acknowledgement that easily accessible welfare provisions also function as a means of crime prevention and that health care (drugs), social work (juvenile delinquency) or administrative means (prostitution) play at least an equally important role in social control as criminal law. The existence of a large network of client-oriented welfare agencies, with some 8,000 professionally trained social workers employed in the (para-)legal field, is an important explanation for the traditional mildness of the Dutch criminal justice system. This 'mildness' is most strongly expressed in the least tangible phenomena: a wide trust in and respect for the various players in the judicial system and their colleagues in social services and public health institutions; a 'family-like' trial atmosphere; calm relations between guards and inmates in prison; and a relatively subdued reporting of crime in the media (Hulsman and Nijboer, 1993).

A clear legal translation of tolerance is the actual decriminalisation of certain victimless offences (like the possession of soft drugs for personal consumption) without actually taking these formally out of the criminal code. The idea behind a rather strict separation between law and morality is quite pragmatic. If a particular moral judgement is not forced upon people who do not share that morality, if treatment by police and judiciary is perceived as decent, the length of sanctions reasonable, and prison conditions acceptable, the risk of revolt or escalation of violence becomes less and the penal system remains manageable. This notion implies limited intervention in cases where no individual victim makes a claim for state intervention, such as drug-taking, abortion, euthanasia, pornography and prostitution. These morally loaded issues are the subject of endless public debate, and the policy of tolerance (*gedoogbeleid*) adopted in these areas is carried by a rather wide consensus – at least amongst the 'élites' who participate in the public debate. Such a policy of tolerance does not imply that the authorities think that all these practices are without problems, but rather shows a realist appraisal of the modest possibilities of social engineering by penal means, as well as an awareness of the counter-effects of penal intervention as regards effective control. A relatively tolerant penal approach is a product of pragmatic considerations combined with an ideology of benevolence and humanism, and coincides with other means of social control, including health care and social work.

Though the Dutch prosecution system is based on the principle of expediency, there is political control over the general policy of prosecution, and the general operation of discretionary powers is regulated by written and publicly available policy guidelines (*beleid*). These are a go-between between law and practice and have the status of pseudo-legislation. In *Dutch Legal Culture*, legal sociologists Erhard Blankenburg and Freek Bruinsma (1991: 39) call *beleid* 'a very Dutch legal term indeed'. In German or French, one would need a whole sentence to cover its full meaning, whereas the English equivalent 'policy' covers only part of its significance: 'as a legal term in the technical sense it is unique.' Blankenburg and Bruinsma argue that *beleid* has become an additional source of law, forming a bridge between informal or customary law, on the one hand, and formally codified law, on the other. Rotterdam legal philosopher René Foqué (1995: 62) sees the way in which law and practice can be attuned in this way as a major advantage of Dutch legal policy. Currently, however, it also carries the danger of being used as a political instrument ruled by administrative opportunism.

European intellectual traditions, as well as the legal rationale and cultures of social control, differ significantly from the Anglo-Saxon situation. In addition, the value people attribute to normative or pragmatic considerations and the trust they put in other persons or institutions are quite different in Britain and on the continent, but also in Northern and Southern Europe. In a book on comparative criminology, these contextual frameworks need to be enunciated. This chapter should make that clear. Because The Netherlands form in some respect a 'third reality' between Britain and the 'real' continental culture, and because an analysis of 'Dutch tolerance' as a model of social control touches upon important paradoxes of penal reform, specific attention is paid to the Dutch case. The dilemma of creating a practical and flexible legal system, while at the same time opening the door to an administrative, political instrumentalism of the rule of law, is a central problem for penal reformers. This dilemma has its roots in a central debate in European penal science of the second half of the nineteenth century. Let us therefore, in the next chapter, begin at the beginning.

3

The Early Criminological Critique of Penal Reform

On the European continent, critical criminology developed in a different context from Britain, reflecting both different traditions in criminology and different penal realities. In this chapter this historical context will be examined. Criminological insights have, from the 1880s onwards, mainly been applied to jurisprudence and penal reform. Most criminological textbooks start with Cesare Beccaria's classic *Dei delitti e delle pene* of 1764. Conventional histories generally echo a story of uneven progress, in which epistemological problems and questions of power receive only a marginal place – if any. Michel Foucault has played a crucial role in the establishment of an alternative vision of criminological history. He has provided the incentive for studies on the history of criminology as 'a study of disciplinary practices . . . in order to analyse the role of the human sciences in the operation of modern forms of power' (Garland, 1992: 412). Consequently, many critical histories now tend to interpret criminology as a legitimation discourse of law and order. According to Garland, such views should, however, not be viewed as *the* history of criminology, 'but instead as a genealogy of one of its elements', which needs to be accompanied by an intellectual, institutional, social and cultural history of the discipline. This is the aim of this chapter.

The Modern School of integrated penal sciences in Europe

It is not difficult to understand the debates on criminal justice of a century ago. The absence of technical facilities such as telecommunications or rapid means of transport affected the actual administration of justice, but at a somewhat higher level of abstraction the debates are quite comparable with those of today. In the 1880s, people feared that social turmoil, strikes and other forms of (socialist) 'rowdyism' would endanger the hegemonic social order. These fears were sublimated by defining such activities as crimes and by interpreting general public anxiety as a rational response to rising crime. Newspapers reported allegedly soft judicial reactions, and argued for an expansion and intensification of repressive penal control as the only just and warranted answer. Various European academics began to realise that classical criminal law was no longer a suitable means of social control because it did not touch upon the causes of crime. Progressive scholars among them proposed social measures to do something about the causes of crime. Both strictly instrumental and critical visions of criminology were in evidence from the beginning, and there was hardly any political consensus about the 'purpose' of this new discipline (Baratta, 1980 versus Fijnaut, 1984a). As a result of these paradoxical political aspirations, various parts of the criminal justice system, and most notably the police, were given tasks that were both repressive and of a social, caring nature to safeguard the legal order (Fijnaut, 1979). At the same time as more stiff penal repression was advocated, preventative social legislation was also introduced. This amalgam of progressive and conservative considerations resulted in a subtle concerted action between reward and control, by affiliating social policy to the fight against crime, which Garland (1985) has called the 'penal–welfare complex'.

On the European continent, this penal–welfare complex has been most notably advocated by the Modern School of penal science. The adjective 'modern' is used to contrast this new, empirical scientific approach to law with the Classical School in jurisprudence, of which Beccaria is the most well-known representative. The classical postulate of law is that of a pure legal system, free of political influence. The classical principles aim to offer the individual citizen a safeguard against arbitrary state interference. By the 1880s, the classical legal system was criticised for being blind to the social reality of crime. It would need to be fundamentally reformed. Therefore, so-called modern scholars proposed an integrated study of criminal law and criminology. Scientific insights should make law enforcement more effective and enable something to be done about the causes of crime. The Modern School emerged in the tumultuous time of the industrial revolution, the rise of socialism and the rapid progress of the natural and social sciences. It developed during a period of major political change: the *fin de siècle*, the *belle époque*, the First World War, the Bolshevik Revolution in Russia, the Weimar Republic in Germany, the radical left politics of the Second Spanish Republic and the following Civil War, the world economic crisis of the 1930s and the subsequent move towards extremist right-wing politics, such as Spanish Franquism, the Salazar regime in Portugal, Mussolini's fascism in Italy and Hitler's National Socialism in the German Reich, which was joined by Austria through the Anschluß, annexed western parts of present-day Poland and the Czech Republic, and was supported by pro-Nazi governments in Bulgaria, Croatia, Finland, Hungary, Romania, Slovakia and the Vichy regime in the south-eastern half of France. The fact that important centres of the Modern School of integrated penal sciences were established in Germany and Italy, while the school had largely political aspirations, explains how some modern scholars could follow the spirit of the times so alarmingly closely.

The criminological theories of the nineteenth century can hardly be imagined to have emerged in the 1880s without the prior development of the theories of Charles Darwin and Louis Pasteur. Darwin's findings in *On the Origin of Species* (1859) and *The Descent of Man* (1871) gave important impulses to the medical and natural sciences, from which so-called criminal anthropology emerged. In 1876, Italian prison doctor Cesare Lombroso published his famous book *Trattato antropologico sperimentale dell'uomo delinquente* (Criminal man). Lombroso argued that criminals and the feeble-minded were evolutionarily deprived people. Their physical characteristics resembled those of more primitive species. Because of this atavism, crimes committed by such people could not be considered to derive from free will: this belonged to a higher step in the development of mankind. Lombroso's book gave rise to the so-called *Scuola positiva*, the Italian Positivist School.

The most important opposition to the *Scuola positiva* initially came from the French Environmental School. The intellectual basis of their social-psychological approach to crime had been developed half a century earlier by statisticians. In 1833, the Frenchman André Guerry had shown in his statistics of morality what influence factors like age, gender, season, education and so on have upon criminality. Guerry contested the belief that crime was largely a product of poverty, but it was also the first empirically based breach in the dominant theory of crime in terms of morality. In 1835, Belgian mathematician Adolphe Quetelet implicitly undermined the ideology of free will, by indicating the statistically relatively constant level of crime, the great regularity in the frequency of certain offences regardless of variations in the social reactions to it, and the fact that every type of person (and not a specific category) can become involved in crime. Quetelet can also be seen as the intellectual father of the notion of relative deprivation because he pointed out that great inequality between wealth and poverty in the same place is a central incentive to crime, for it excites passions and provokes temptations of all kinds.

In opposition to Lombroso's biological determinism, and inspired by Pasteur's bacteriology and other recent discoveries in the natural sciences, medical doctor Alexandre Lacassagne argued, in 1885, that the criminal may be the bacterium of society, but that this bacterium cannot grow without the cultivating medium of his environment. This is also the context in which Lacassagne's famous line that every society gets the criminality it deserves should be read. Manouvrier showed an early reflexive insight into the fact that the label 'crime' can also be used morally to censure acts of the powerful when he described, in 1893, the slaughtering of the *communards* by the *Versaillais* forces (when the proletarian democratic Parisian commune of 1871 had already been crushed and its defenders disarmed and detained) as a criminal act.

The French Environmental School, of which, next to Lacassagne and Manouvrier, Gabriel Tarde is the most important representative, mainly gave rise to a more sociological study of crime. Tarde's *Laws of Imitation* of 1890, in which examples from the immediate surroundings are seen to be a major incentive to crime, was especially important in the development of a social-psychological criminology; for example, Edwin Sutherland's differential association theory of the 1930s can be traced back to Tarde's work. In 1895, the French sociologist Émile Durkheim argued that crime should be considered as a normal phenomenon, which is functional to society as the necessary negative to stabilise and integrate a collective conscience. Most penal scientists of his time, among them Gabriel Tarde, have forcefully rejected Durkheim's 'immoral' thesis. After its initiating role, the French school no longer took a leading role in the further development of the Modern School. Environmentalist ideas were most explicitly taken up by the Belgian penal scientist Adolphe Prins.

An initial confrontation between the Italian and French Schools was followed by a merging multi-causal theory, whose connecting element was determinism. As both theories presupposed in their own way an identifiable criminal class, which happens to be located in the socioeconomically most deprived groups in society, present-day critical scholars tend to speak about these criminological schools in large negative and rejective terms. Both schools imply an apartheid model of society (Bianchi, 1980: 47–75) and a bourgeois ideology of social defence which would give penal repression a new legitimation (Baratta 1982: 35–44). Though not representative of the French sub-cultural approach *avant la lettre* as a whole, this can hardly be argued about Manouvrier. Critics rightly argue that Lombroso's ideas, in particular, demonstrate an authoritarian, imperious and overtly racist political vision. In the original texts, the political consequences – for example, the necessity of capital punishment for the incorrigible – are made quite explicit – be it often in prefaces or afterwords. Dutch criminologist Willem Bonger (1905: 106) had already pointed to the socioeconomic biases of the Italian School. Lombroso's ideas were used politically as an ideological legitimation for the low standard of living in Southern Italy, which was now 'proved' to be due to the mental inferiority of people from the *mezzogiorno*.

On the epistemological field the story is more complex. Many critics glossed over the fact that an empirically grounded determinism also implied a radical critique of dominant classical legal concepts such as the guilt and accountability of the individual, which originated in the liberal, bourgeois enlightenment. Furthermore, it is not generally acknowledged that the initial hegemony of the anthropological approach was, in a relatively early phase, replaced by predominantly environmental orientations. Only few present-day critical criminologists pay attention to the fact that a large number of the representatives of the Modern School were critical of the hegemonic social order and that some of them were even committed socialists. Bonger (1932: 200) pointed out that the Modern School's ideology of social defence was not at all new. Though it ultimately came down to retribution, punishment had always served the protection of society as well. However, in the late nineteenth century these arguments were put forward in a more explicit way, and many legal scholars came to advocate social defence as an official legitimation of punishment over retribution – whereas previously it had been the other way around.

Franz von Liszt's Marburg programme

The person who most explicitly pointed to the consequences that multi-causal empirical deterministic findings should have for the classical rationale of criminal law was the German legal scholar Franz von Liszt. He proposed to implement positivist criminological insights into penal dogmatics. In his inaugural address, in 1882, to the University of Marburg on the *Zweckgedanke im Strafrecht* (Goal-orientation in criminal justice), von Liszt made a number of proposals to reform classical, Beccarian criminal law into a more efficient instrument in the fight against crime. This idea became known as the Marburg programme. It implied a fundamental critique of the classical dogmatic idea that criminal law should have a theoretical goal in itself. In von Liszt's perspective, law is to be treated as a means rather than an end. The ethical and metaphysical elements of penal dogmatics need to be replaced by more down-to-earth considerations about effective law enforcement. A doctrinal system-internal orientation should make way for empirical analyses of the functioning of law in empirical practice. The classical idea on punishment is, according to von Liszt (1905: 132), a 'blind, instinctive and impulsive reaction', a 'social zest of survival', which is 'not supported by one single functional consideration'. Von Liszt refers to the criminogenic effects of prison sentences on corrigible first offenders. An approach to criminal law which takes social scientific knowledge into account implies an important contribution to more effective crime control because it enables lawyers to make differentiations in reactions to different offences and different types of offenders.

Critics argued that von Liszt misjudged and underestimated the meaning of retribution. They doubted that much of the classical postulates of criminal law would remain if von Liszt's ideas were followed (von Birkmeyer, 1907). It should be mentioned that these advocates of the Classical School were to be found on the conservative side of the political spectrum and von Liszt and his followers represented the liberal left. Though he considered social policy to be more effective than penal measures, von Liszt did not pay much attention to the relation between the development of crime rates and economic conditions at a macro-social level, as was, for example, put forward in 1867 by the Bavarian statistician Georg von Mayr. Von Liszt remained too much the lawyer to go beyond the idea of individual deterrence. His reference to social policy, however, never led him to throw any of the classical legal principles overboard. Von Liszt described the principle of legality as the Magna Charta of the offender – and thus of every citizen and indeed of the *rechtsstaat*. Written law remains the threshold beyond which no penal intervention may ever go. Criminal law should, however, no longer be directed at the criminal act but at the actor, and needs to deter criminal behaviour by contributing to the improvement of criminals susceptible to it and to the incapacitation of those who are not. This latter contention represents the most dubious, and most often criticised, point. The Marburg programme contains no criteria according to which the level of corrigibility of an offender can be judged, and it is consequently unclear to whom social services are to be offered and to whom these should be denied. In practice, every offender who has relapsed twice is regarded as an incorrigible habitual offender. These represent some 35 per cent of all offenders (Naucke, 1982).

International support for the Marburg programme led to the foundation of a broad international association of penal scientists. The main points that these scholars agreed upon was the fact that criminal law had become alienated from social reality and had fizzled out into doctrinalism. In January 1889, the German Franz von Liszt, the Belgian Adolphe Prins and the Dutchman Gerard van Hamel established the International Union of Criminal Justice (*Internationale Kriminalistische Vereinigung – Union international de droit pénal,* henceforth IKV–UIDP). This Union did not aim at any theoretical elaboration of the French or Italian Schools, but at the application of positivist criminological insights to penal practice. The Union consisted, to a large part, of lawyers from all over Europe, for whom shared political aspirations on law enforcement were the major motives for co-operation. The statutes of the Union thus focused on this issue. In the second paragraph, the goal of the Union was summarised as

> (1) the fight against crime as a social phenomenon. Because crime is rooted in social conditions, (2) results of anthropological and sociological research need to be taken into account both in penal science and in criminal legislation. In this respect the Union supports (3) crime prevention; (4) a differentiated approach to occasional and habitual offenders; (5) the inclusion of penitentiary matters into the general discourse of law enforcement; (6) the improvement of prisons; and (7) the replacement of short custodial sanctions by alternative means. (8) The length of custodial sanctions should not only be determined in court, but it must be possible for prison authorities to accommodate it; and (9) incorrigible habitual criminals need to be incapacitated as long as possible. (Groenhuijsen and van der Landen, 1990: 35)

Under this eclectic and functionalist umbrella, both conservative and more progressive scholars and practitioners found shelter.

Initially, annual conferences were organised (starting in 1889 in Brussels), but from 1895 onwards the Union met less regularly and held its last conference in 1913 in Copenhagen. The First World War put an end to this form of broad international cooperation. The Union counted one thousand members, from nearly all parts of Europe. The majority came from Italy, Germany and north-western Europe, but it is interesting to note that many active participants also came from Eastern European countries, notably Serbia and Poland. Notably absent in the Union were England and Spain. The Modern School had a low impact in Spain because when it emerged, as a (partly) progressive initiative, Spain was ruled by right-wing dictators, the Kings Alfonso XII and XIII and General Primo de Rivera. When the Modern School's social defence ideology got an authoritarian character itself, the left was ruling in Spain's Second Republic. In those days, the director general of the prison department, Victoria Kent, proposed the introduction of preventive social measures, while at the same time strengthening the legal position of prisoners. The economic crisis and the Spanish Civil War put a premature end to these radical penal reforms (Rivera Beiras, 1995: 76–81).

British intellectuals and penal officials also played a marginal role in the early development of criminology (Garland, 1994: 42), but the reason for their absence was quite different. It is also remarkable, since the British penal–welfare complex was comparable with that of The Netherlands and Belgium. English supporters of the Union, such as Havelock Ellis and William Douglas Morrison, were largely greeted with scepticism by British scholars because their ideas did not fit the British scientific tradition – a tradition 'more modest, more acceptable to the institutional authorities and organised by engaged professionals rather than by maverick intellectuals'. Criminology had initially a very low impact in Britain (Garland, 1988: 4–6). Leon Radzinowicz (1966: 21) argues that the whole idea of 'schools' is alien to the British legal tradition. On the continent, schools could flourish partly because of the powerful positions held by academics in the administration of justice, which is not the case in Britain. The British penal climate is ruled rather by a pragmatic muddling through than by any all-embracing doctrine. David Garland also points to the fact that the Modern School's deterministic tendencies did not fit the voluntaristic British culture. The Gladstone Report of 1895, in which the possible policy input of criminology is examined, is quite explicit about this: it is considered to be a 'plain fact that most criminals, with important exceptions, are indeed reformable, no matter what these scientific theories might imply' (Garland, 1985: 174; 1988: 3). This is contrasted with the Modern School's idea that habitual offenders are incorrigible, or indeed with the positivistic idea that criminals have genetically determined deficiencies. This scepticism towards positivistic determinism culminates in Charles Goring's rejection of the very existence of a distinct anthropological criminal type on statistical grounds, although Goring does not deny possible genetic differences between criminals and non-criminals. Garland (1994: 42–3) points to the fact that many British psychiatrists, such as Henry Maudsley and J. Bruce Thomson, held very comparable 'Lombrosian' views on degeneration and the 'genuine criminal' in the 1860s. By 1913, when Goring's *The English Convict* was published, these assumptions had lost most of their credibility on the continent as well.

The English critique of the impracticability of anthropological ideas, and their ill-informed opinions of crime, is largely directed at the purist Italian pioneers of the Modern School. Particularly in the Low Countries, the eclectic and pragmatic ideas of the Modern School were also brought forward and implemented by practitioners, who, just like their British counterparts, linked a practical commitment to professional tasks. In many of their writings, Dutch representatives of the Modern School expressed a strong sympathy for the British respect for individual freedom and even argued for the adoption of the British adversarial legal system in The Netherlands – to replace the Napoleonic codes. The idea of maverick Europeans and British pragmatics is a mock-contrast that may just be a perfect illustration of the fact that the British have actually never seen themselves as Europeans. The public understanding of 'Europe' as something that mainly threatens virtuous and superior Albion with all kinds of moral and other dangers really ranges from the days of the British Empire to the present day in which Tory Eurosceptics want to 'protect' their 'ragged old lady' from 'Brussels bureaucrats'.

Differences in legal culture may also be a factor in the ambivalent British attitude towards the idea of integrated penal sciences. The Modern School's critique of legal doctrinalism simply does not find any reflection in common law. In Britain, both the process of legislation and the administration of justice have, moreover, to a greater degree than on the continent, been in the hands of the aristocracy. Their desire to keep social relations as they are is reflected in a simple hatred of disorder. As if they are governing a boarding school, they interpret disorder mainly as a lack of discipline which is to be countered by stiff punitive responses. Continental judges all receive an academic grounding, they are generally younger and from a more diverse class background than their British counterparts. Therefore, they may also be more inclined to take scientific research a bit more seriously. Apart from these speculations, the fact remains that British criminology and jurisprudence have developed independently from each other and that, until today, mutual reflections are scarce. On the European continent, this is still more common.

The political development of the Modern School

The ambiguity of the Italian Scuola positiva

The political development of the leading Italian positivists is most fascinating (Vervaele, 1990: 271–317). Cesare Lombroso initially fostered a deep distrust towards the working classes and saw anarchists especially as born criminals *par excellence*. Without really changing this opinion, Lombroso became a member of the Socialist Party in 1893. He played a leading role in this party after he dropped, in 1897, his atavism hypothesis under the influence of Enrico Ferri. Ferri is the most interesting representative of the Italian Positivist School. Praised as an excellent orator and debater, he argued predominantly against the classical school in criminal law. Not without irony, Willem Bonger (1932: 96) maintains that Ferri was not only clever enough to see that Lombroso's biological assumptions were scientifically untenable, but he was also able to convince Lombroso himself of this sad fact. Ferri's integrated bio-social concepts formed the paradigmatic basis of dominant models of thought on crime and punishment.

In 1883, Ferri wrote, in his book *Socialismo e criminalità* (Socialism and crime), that socialism is an abstract metaphysical theory that goes against human nature. Some eight years later, he made a sharp distinction between anarchism and socialism. The first is based in misery and crime, whereas the latter should be considered as a step forward in civilisation. Thus, there is no contradiction between socialism and social defence, and Ferri joined the International Union of Criminal Justice. From 1892, in his book *Sociologia criminale* (Criminal sociology), Ferri developed an eclectic aetiological penal theory of social defence, in which socioeconomic deprivation is included as a cause of crime.

In 1921, Ferri finished a draft for a new Italian criminal code in which the penal question is addressed in remarkably non-moralistic and non-retributionist terms. Ferri proposed a more professional approach to criminals.

Critics pointed out that it would be impossible to put Ferri's project into practice because judges were not educated in psychology and the state's financial means were insufficient to pay for all the social workers and civil servants who would have to be employed in Ferri's system. One year later, the fascist leader Benito Mussolini came to power. After the Italian parliament rejected his bill in 1924, Ferri resigned from the Socialist Party and began to show an increasing sympathy towards the fascist government. The fascists used Ferri's bill to undermine the classical legal principles of legality and guilt. At the same time, a greatly increased level of penalties was defended from a perspective of social defence, and capital punishment was reintroduced for attacks against the state, murder and so on. No changes were made in the education of judges, and social workers or civil servants were hardly employed. None the less, Ferri embraced the new criminal code of 1927, a fascist adaptation of his draft, which is still known as the *Codice Rocco*. All revolutions coincide with a natural reinforcement of authority against preceding anarchy, Ferri argued (Vervaele, 1990: 441). Having presented himself as a socialist for most of his active academic life, Ferri, in 1927, was, in a political sense, back to the point where he started in 1883. He had, however, always defended and refuted all his (irreconcilable) political ideas with the same originality and vigour.

After the First World War, Ferri tried to reunite modern scholars, but universal aspirations on criminal justice politics could no longer be held in the inter-war period. Unlike Ferri himself, other scholars from the International Union did not join the new *Association internationale de droit pénal* in 1924, which would, after the Second World War, develop into the *Défense sociale nouvelle*. In the middle of Ferri's career, Willem Bonger devoted 36 pages to his work. Particularly when he deals with Ferri's *Socialismo e criminalità*, Bonger (1905: 136) is clearly irritated by his ignorance of basic elements of historical materialist thinking and his decided tone against it at the same time. 'The author attacks the socialists as "excessively anti-scientific and sentimental", while he vaunts the "great scientific character of the sociologists". Yet these last, notwithstanding their great scientific character, combat a doctrine which they know only in part or not at all.'

Penal systems tend to recruit their clientele from the most powerless groups in society. In order to counter the tendency to criminalise socialists and anarchists, Italian scholars like Turati and the Sicilian physician Napoleone Colajanni established the so-called *Terza scuola* (Third School) which strongly argued against the idea of metaphysical natural law. Colajanni argued that law is a human construction and that the study of law is thus necessarily part of sociology. Lombroso's atavism hypothesis is countered by analyses of the way Southern Italians have been exploited as cheap labour in the Northern provinces. Colajanni wrote in his book *Sociologia criminale* of 1889 that, in order to minimise the level of crime in a particular society, there should be a certain level of security as regards the means of sustaining life, economic stability and an equal distribution of welfare. Since this is not the case in Italy, higher crime rates in the South should not come as a surprise. Positivistic theses about the criminogenic influence of socialism, as well as its contention by the *Terza scuola*, were copied in other European countries in a slightly more moderate way.

German gesamte Strafrechtswissenschaft

Franz von Liszt was born to a well-to-do Viennese family and raised in a pro-Prussian and pro-Bismarckian atmosphere. With such a family background, membership of the national conservative party was only natural. After the fall of Chancellor Otto von Bismarck, von Liszt joined, during the authoritarian reign of Emperor Wilhelm II, the progressive liberal party, for which he first became a member of the Prussian parliament and later of the *Reichstag*. Looking at von Liszt's sympathy for Bismarck's strategic politics, it is tempting to think of von Liszt's political development in comparable terms to Ferri's. There are, however, notable differences between the Italian and German situations. The anthropological determinism of the Positivist School was not adopted completely by von Liszt – and, later, he was rather a partisan of the Environmental than of the Biological School. In 1905, Bonger still dealt with von Liszt's thought in his chapter on the bio-sociologists, but in a footnote to the English edition of *Criminality and Economic Conditions* (1916: 189), he happily concluded that von Liszt had changed his opinion, and could, since his article of 1899 on the social factors of crime, in fact be ranked with the partisans of the Environmental School. German academics, especially lawyers, have traditionally been strongly influenced by Hegel and Kant's idealism, in which deterministic concepts like the 'born criminal' do not fit very well. In fact, von Liszt's instrumentalism marked a breach with the dominant tradition of rational metaphysics in German jurisprudence. Furthermore, German intellectuals did not have the same leading positions in the socialist movement as their Italian counterparts. Von Liszt's political position was also less explicitly visible in his work and, unlike Ferri, he never refuted the essentials of his initial ideas, though he adapted his criminological preferences to the spirit of the times. Von Liszt never abandoned the idea that the principle of legality should remain an absolute condition for any legitimate penal intervention. He always opposed the extra-legal security measures that both Bismarck and the Emperor introduced as political means of law enforcement. Von Liszt did not elaborate the theoretical integration of criminology and criminal law. His focus was on penal policy (Fijnaut, 1986a: 13). In Germany, a penal–welfare complex could be more easily established than in Italy, and von Liszt's idea of a *gesamte Strafrechtswissenschaft* – an integrated legal and criminological approach to the penal subject matter – fell on more fertile ground.

During von Liszt's life, Germany developed from a conservative 'night-watchman' state into a deeply interventionist state in which the civil service, the nobility (*Junker*) and the army played a central role. Elaborate legislation on social security, introduced within a militaristic and conservative political system, essentially served to stop the development of socialism. Critics have argued that the political aspirations and instrumentalist approach to law made von Liszt's ideas vulnerable to being used as a legitimation of conservative and paternalistic politics (Foqué and 't Hart, 1990: 246), or indeed that von Liszt's 'credulity of the modern state-idea' made him 'an active witness of Bismarck's anti-socialist laws' (Stangl, 1988: 88). During the first years of the socialist Weimar Republic of 1918 (when Emperor Wilhelm II received political asylum in The Netherlands), Minister of Justice and legal philosopher and pupil of von Liszt, Gustav Radbruch, actually introduced some of von Liszt's proposals. Von Liszt died in the same year that revolutionaries Karl Liebknecht and Rosa Luxemburg were murdered: 1919.

The authoritarian development of the Modern School itself only began after von Liszt's death, when the economic situation of the Weimar Republic headed for catastrophe and the political situation became increasingly vulnerable to totalitarian developments. In this context, the 'sociological school', as von Liszt's perspective was called, was criticised for being soft on crime, and thereby of undermining the credibility of the *rechtsstaat*. This opinion is reflected in the *Kriminalbiologische Gesellschaft*, in whose establishment in 1927 in Vienna IKV–UIDP member Franz Exner played a central role. This group from then on became a mere German and Austrian affair. In further defence of von Liszt, it should be mentioned that the first thing the Nazis did was to do away with the principle of legality, which von Liszt had always forcefully defended, and indeed to ignore any empirical findings on the social causes of crime. Under Nazi rule, law was interpreted as a means of regulating relations between members of the community and their alleged enemies, and was to be informed by sound popular feeling (*gesundes Volksempfinden*). When German lawyers *en masse* adhered to these views, and left the German Juridical Association several months after Hitler's inauguration in 1933 in order to join its Nazi equivalent, the legal system could be radically transformed without altering a single statute. Following the *Führer*-principle, commands from hierarchically higher-placed persons now received the status of law, and public education and social defence became central aims of law enforcement.

At the International Conference on Criminal Law and Penology in Berlin in 1935, the German Minister of Propaganda Joseph Goebbels stressed, in his opening address, the important role of criminal law in National Socialist doctrine. The conference's president, Minister of Justice Gürtner, announced the abolition of the principle of legality and the transformation of the principle of guilt into one of 'criminal will' (*Gesinnung*), by which the difference between preparatory acts, attempts or completed crimes is blurred, and offender typologies are used as 'guilt-supporting factors' (Gradisen, 1988). It is worth mentioning that the International Society of Criminology (ISC), which was established in 1938 in Rome under Mussolini's rule, emerged from Exner's *Kriminalbiologische Gesellschaft*. In his report of the ISC's first congress, Dutch penal scientist Willem Pompe (1940) praised the informative character of this first 'completely criminological' conference which had attracted 1,100 participants from 44 different, mainly European and Latin

American, countries. Pompe was, however, very reserved about the dominance of the biological school and the 'new fascist realism' which surrounded
the conference, as well as the prominence of 'military exercises' for offenders
as a means of a 'totalitarian re-education'. Nor did he appreciate the strongly
felt presence of Roland Freisler, the German State Secretary of Justice and
later president of the infamous People's Court (*Volksgerichtshof*), which dealt
with anti-Nazist activities (so-called 'crimes against the German people'), as
one of the general reporters at the conference. Together with the conference's
president di Tullio, Freisler proposed 'with martial vigour' the foundation of
an International Society of Criminology to explore the further development
of the 'technical auxiliary sciences to criminal justice'. With a certain relief,
Pompe remarked that 'fortunately the Jewish question has been ignored. In
this company and in this era an unbiased debate on this subject would not
have been possible' (1940: 156). In the conclusion to his report, Pompe (1940:
160) posed the question whether 'the successful – and in many ways important – first conference of criminology will due to this war also remain the
last?'

Belgian poenaal positivisme

Belgian founding father of the Modern School, Adolphe Prins, can initially
be considered as the school's left liberal. His political and scientific opinions
cannot be understood separately. He saw the adaptation of criminal law to
modern discoveries in natural sciences also as a sign of progress in the moral
and political sense (Tulkens, 1990). Prins' political position is, however, not
unambiguous. His career was based at the Free University Brussels, a stronghold of free-thinkers and social scientists. Prins was active in liberal political
circles, but also kept close relations with the ex-milieu of the first
Internationale. He considered the proletariat to be a latently criminal group
because of its inclination to vagrancy, but also pointed to the fact that only
industrial capitalists would gain profit from an unlimited freedom. He considered liberalism to be a too rationalistic ideology and claimed that socialism
went against egoistic human nature. Prins argued that a compromise between
liberalism and socialism would be the key to the solution of many social
problems.

Prins saw jurisprudence as part of the social sciences and penal policy as an
integral part of social policy. In this sense, Prins is much more of a criminologist than von Liszt, who did not go beyond the liberal individualistic
postulate of law. In opposition to the Italians, Prins did not consider classical criminal law as a superseded ideology, though he criticised its abstract
doctrinalism. With regard to the question of free will, Prins rejected complete
determinism and opted for a sociological position of relative free will within
the limits of given social conditions, an idea inspired by Tarde. According to
Prins, there is no necessary contradiction between criminal law as a means of
social defence and an insistence on the moral responsibility of the individual.
Prins was also the first to use the term 'social defence', by which name the

school would become best known. In 1910 he wrote a book entitled *La défense sociale et les transformations du droit pénal* (Social defence and the transformation of criminal law). For Prins, a criminal justice system as a goal-oriented mechanism of social defence should start with a social prevention politics. This should activate social mechanisms that can reduce socioeconomic misery and establish the positive social reintegration of offenders into society. Therefore, knowledge about the social circumstances under which a crime is committed needs to be included in penal policy. An economic stimulus in sanctioning needs to be introduced in order to enable the offender to earn money with prison work by which he can compensate the victim – especially if this would imply a longer sentence. Ferri proposed the establishment of a state fund for the compensation of victims.

Belgium was one of the first countries to introduce modern insights of criminal law into penal practice; as, for example, the introduction of conditional conviction and parole in 1888. Important reformers in this respect were the catholic Minister of Justice Jules Lejeune and, most notably, directly after the First World War, socialist Minister of Justice Émile Vandervelde. The Belgian law on social defence of 1930 is generally considered to be the most notable practical implementation of penal positivism – because it was not affected by fascism. This law (*Wet op het sociaal verweer*) includes a regulation of hospital orders, in which the social defence context is quite dominant, as is shown, for example, by notions of the 'abnormality' of habitual offenders and the general threat they represent to society. Initially, Prins focused on social prevention and on the positive reintegration of the offender into the community, but in his later works more paternalistic and repressive elements concerning the need for social defence against incorrigible offenders became increasingly dominant and eventually Prins even advocated penal intervention *ante delictum* (Vervaele, 1990: 378).

The Dutch nieuwe richting

Co-founder of the IKV–UIDP, Amsterdam criminal justice professor Gerard van Hamel, was the Modern School's major advocate in The Netherlands. Van Hamel was educated as a classical lawyer and worked as a public prosecutor. In his inaugural address to the University of Amsterdam, *De grenzen der heerschappij van het strafrecht* (The boundaries of criminal law's dominion), he wholeheartedly embraced the principles of classical legal theory and even warned against paternalist intentions with respect to criminal law enforcement: 'Criminal law should not seek for everything it can potentially punish, but should only punish what it legally has to' (van Hamel, 1880: 7). Van Hamel (1890: 534) mentions two major reasons for the emergence of the Modern School: the increase in crime and recidivism, which shocked many classical lawyers out of their a-social system-internal doctrinalism, and the attractiveness of natural scientific research methods tracing back causes of crime and the practical possibility of adapting law enforcement to these findings.

Van Hamel was a rather conservative liberal who accepted more of the Lombrosian aetiology than either von Liszt or Prins. He was, however, quite critical of the criminal justice system. While he praised the humanitarian, precise and well-educated qualities of lawyers, he also saw them moving the mill of the criminal justice system, which always turned round in the same dogmatic way, unaware of many developments in real life. At the same time, van Hamel never disputed any classical legal principle. It is thus quite unlikely that van Hamel would have said in 1905, as the Soviet lawyer Evgeni Pashukanis suggests, that the main obstacles to modern criminology were the three concepts of guilt, crime and punishment. Nor was van Hamel a representative of the sociological school, as Pashukanis seems to argue (Cohen, 1988: 28). Pashukanis may well have used van Hamel's liberal critique of the lawyer's blind spot for the limits of free will 'by the facts of real life' to support his argument for a materialist theory of penality. After the end of the class struggle, the state and classical legal principles would also, according to Pashukanis, gradually wither away and be replaced by an educational and exclusively protective legal system – a point of view for which Stalin had him executed as an enemy of the Soviet Union.

Nor is it justified to compare the dispute between van Hamel and Pashukanis with the present-day critical criminological debate between idealism and materialism, as Stan Cohen (1988: 28) does. It is, though, true that van Hamel, unlike his Belgian colleague Prins, did not link changes in the penal system with any structural changes in society, nor did his work witness any implications that could be read as critical of the hegemonic social order. Nor did he mingle in controversies within criminology – in fact, he knew very little about it. Van Hamel was even afraid of the absorption of criminal law by criminology. In particular, the firm statements of criminal-anthropologists about supposedly outdated legal beliefs made him critical of integrated penal science:

> the more strongly we embrace the new anthropological-sociological direction . . .
> the stronger our respect should be for the gains of the Classical School in jurisprudence. It remains the champion of individual freedom against misuse of state power, even when it is called justice. What Lombroso means for scientific development . . . has meant Beccaria for our sense of justice. (Fijnaut, 1984b: 18)

Dutch penal scientists, as well as Dutch penal practice, have to a great extent been influenced by the Modern School. No attempt, however, was made to draw up new legislation based on modern principles: if it could be done by accommodation, why create a revolution? According to Fijnaut (1986c), the modern project had been a competing paradigm within jurisprudence until 1920. It encountered a mixed reception between 1920 and 1930, and received a virtually unanimous acceptance after 1930. The Modern School's determinism does not fit with the Dutch Calvinist *habitus*, which is based on the principle of free will. Thus we find the most fierce opponents of the Modern School among doctrinaire Calvinists. Voluntarism is, however, so deeply rooted in Dutch society that determinism has not been embraced even by the school's adherents. Socialist support for the modern project is seen to be only logical.

> In the same way as our catholic social theory relates to that of social democracy, our catholic penal theory relates to that of the Modern School . . . The purely atheist–materialist character of modern penal theory makes it completely understandable that this theory receives such a sympathetic and benevolent reception among socialists. The mutual affinity is very strong indeed. (van Wijnbergen, 1910: 74–5)

The Dutch orientation towards compromise has led to an eclectic legislation based on classical principles refined with modern elements. The idea of minimal penalties was, for example, already excluded in the bill for the new criminal code of 1886 – when modern thoughts on penality were still hardly enunciated. Many Dutch legal scholars, among whom was the new criminal code's principal author, Minister of Justice Modderman, argued that it would be undesirable to criminalise vagrancy. Under pressure from the senate, vagrancy was none the less introduced as a summary offence. Modderman argued that the remedy of penal intervention should never be worse than the disease of crime. It should, on the contrary, be of a higher moral level. Most of the more direct and practical measures in this respect were, however, introduced well after the new legislation of 1886 (such as juvenile criminal law in 1905), and most of them even after van Hamel had changed his professorial chair in 1909 for a parliamentary seat for the liberal party (such as conditional conviction in 1915, a law on fines in 1925, and a law on the criminally insane in 1928). The new Dutch criminal code formally included the possibility of conditional release or parole, but it was hardly ever applied. The new code of criminal procedure of 1926 showed the increased influence of the Modern School, but formed no general guiding principle for the new legislation. In many ways it was a pragmatic compromise between quite opposite views of common-law-inspired adversarial components and inquisitorial elements from continental law.

The modern idea of a criminal justice system oriented towards the person of the offender had already begun with the establishment of the forerunner of the probation service, The Netherlands Society for the Moral Improvement of Prisoners, in 1823 (Janse de Jonge, 1991: 16). The Modern School gave this shift from an orientation towards the criminal act to a focus on the actor an enormous impulse. Probation was seen as a practical instrument to do something about the causes of crime and to give shape to the rather abstract concept of rehabilitation. Modern moves on probation, like keeping 'non-dangerous criminals' out of prison and the creation of relief work for ex-prisoners had been introduced in the 1890s. Both the repression and the care of criminals, as well as the orientation to law and order and social defence, can be distinguished. Though social care for the masses was largely provided from a perspective of policing, this does not take away the fact that the modern insights had a largely softening effect on sanctions and also contributed to a certain extent to undermining the central position of the prison sentence as a mechanism of social control. Welfare provisions, social and labour legislation, health care and education also fulfilled useful functions in the control of the masses and the prevention of crime (de Swaan, 1989).

The success of the Modern School was to a large extent determined by the facility with which its messages could be translated into actual policy. The liaison between social care and repression appeared to be particularly politically attractive. It enabled the various agents of social control to be severe and benign at the same time. Criminal law was no longer the only instrument of control; various educational and medical programmes was also at one's disposal. The euphoria about this duality was most aptly described by a follower of van Hamel, the statistician de Roos (1902: 336–7):

> The new approach aims at nothing but the very best. It wants to banish penal slavery; it no longer accepts that a human being, who has by a mental disposition or environmental circumstances fallen into crime, will be completely degraded and brutalised by imprisonment, so that his aversion to society, in which he found no place, swells to an intense hatred, because the expelled is worked to the bone instead of being offered a helping hand. Through the new ideas goes a breath of compassion with the fallen human being; a compassion which does however not step back from severe measures with regard to the defence of society against dangerous individuals . . . Through the new ideas goes a breath of pureness and cleanness. Hygenics, extermination of the unhealthy and decadent, that will be the character of the future of criminal law.

In the latter part of this quotation, the potential danger of the modern approach comes clearly to the surface: its ultimate consequence is a boundless criminal justice system. Despite a moderate and pragmatic implementation of modern thought in penal practice, many progressive academics have drawn attention to its possible dangers. In the 1930s, the idea that law enforcement had become too soft was also widely shared in The Netherlands, but the new German measures to counter this tendency were generally rejected as a destruction of the *rechtsstaat*. We will return to this ambiguous position in Chapter 4.

It would be too simple to argue that the authoritarian development of the social defence movement could have been prevented if warnings against the boundlessness of a fully modern penal legislation had been taken more seriously, when we look at the dramatic economic context in which this development took place. But it can be, and indeed often has been, defended that the lack of a normative-ethical component, which Pompe (1940) also implicitly indicated, and the failure to implement a discussion of the basic values which would need to underlie such a new criminal law, facilitated its a-moral development. Due to the fascist infection, the idea of social defence lost its credibility after the Second World War.

Post-war attempts at integration

Later European scientific criminological developments cannot be understood without realising the tremendous influence of the Second World War. It both produced deep disillusionment about the idea of technically facilitated progress in civilisation and created deep distrust between various European states. It was soon followed by an era of economic reconstruction, by attempts at European integration aimed at the prevention of further wars on the continent, by a wide process of de-colonisation, but also by the Cold War, beginning with the *putsch* in Prague and siege of Berlin in 1948, which generated anxiety about a new world war.

In this context, humanism and individualisation became new keywords in the penal field. This should have given the idea of 'social defence' new credibility. In the Dutch situation, the Modern School's humanising and progressive influence on the sanction system have been stressed (van Ruller, 1988: 102; van Kalmthout, 1990). This view of the modern heritage is similar to what Leon Radzinowicz (1966: 123) has said:

> The rigidity of the classical school on the continent of Europe made it almost impossible to develop constructive and imaginative penal measures. Had our system of dealing with crime been confined within the pattern laid down in *Dei delitte e delle pene* virtually all reforms of which we are most proud would have been excluded, because they would have conflicted with the principle that punishment must be closely defined in advance and strictly proportionate to the offence. There would have been no discharge, no adjustment of fines to the means of the offender, no suspended sentences, no probation, no parole, no special measures for young offenders or mentally abnormal.

Though mistakenly suggesting that continental criminal justice systems would have remained untouched by the Modern School's influence, the dilemma Radzinowicz suggests, between an impractical system with many procedural guarantees and a more practical and less protective one, is a problem penal reformers continue to face.

Défense sociale nouvelle: *a humanist impulse*

In 1949, the Italian lawyer Filippo Gramatica re-established an international movement oriented to social defence, the *Société internationale de défense sociale*, at a conference in the Belgian city of Liège. Gramatica cannot really be called a humanist. He had been a high-ranking civil servant under Mussolini, and still argued in a Machiavellian style that every human being was a potential natural dictator. Because everybody has a natural will to power, there needs to be rigid social discipline. The classical concept of guilt is of little sociopolitical relevance, according to Gramatica, and the concept of *antisocialità* (anti-social behaviour) should function as an alternative principle. The state has the duty to reintegrate 'anti-social abberations' into society. With regard to 'normal' criminals, Gramatica proposes *provvedimenti pedagogico emendative* (pedagogical provisions) and for those who cannot be held responsible *misure curative* (therapeutic measures). According to Gramatica, such transformations from the legal to the pedagogical and therapeutic fields should, however, be preceded by socioeconomic change. In his book *Principi di difesa sociale* (Principles of social defence) of 1961, Gramatica's utilitarian position is so dominant that questions of an axiological nature, notably the question of the legitimacy of state intervention, are ignored.

Gramatica may have been 'a colourful person in the dun post-war social defence movement' (Machielse, 1979: 72–3), but because of his dubious political history, his rejection of the classical principle of guilt and his insistence that penal scientists should only study human behaviour with the methods of the natural sciences, Gramatica was not acceptable as a leading spokesman of the new group. The more moderate Frenchman Marc Ancel, who became his successor, rejected, at a conference of the social defence movement in 1954 in Antwerp, Gramatica's goal of adapting the individual to society. Political objectives remained viable for a new social defence movement, but in the post-war era the effectiveness of sanctions should be primarily oriented towards humanisation and individualisation (Ancel, 1954: 272). The questionable pretension that natural sciences can determine what is an anti-social act was a scientific weakness of Gramatica's position. Ancel devoted considerable energy to trying to convince people who associated the new social defence movement with authoritarian tendencies that they were wrong. Such 'intolerance' would retard the implementation of a humane policy of penal sanctioning (Ancel, 1964). In his humanist political agenda, Ancel based himself on Prins' pedagogics of responsibility. For Ancel, this process of humanisation had already started with the Classical School, from which he adopted the principles of equality before the law and of legality, in order to stress the need (a) to underline an individual's personal responsibility; (b) for procedural guarantees against the state; and (c) for specifically defined penal sanctions that are to prevent over-reactions and cruel and undue punishment.

From the Modern School, Ancel adopted the general critique that classical abstractions do not correspond with penal practice and thus retard effective law enforcement. His main disagreement with modern scholars is that the new social defence movement should be more strongly oriented towards the protection of the individual. Ancel (1967: 7) wanted to break with the Modern School's 'biological or sociological fatalism'. The question of determinism or free will is, according to Ancel, a question for philosophers and people interested in metaphysics, but not for lawyers. They need to start, for practical reasons of law enforcement and for the sheer logic of criminal responsibility, from the assertion of a relative free will. In Ancel's writings, the Modern School's focus on the perceived dangerousness of the offender makes way for a vision of the offender as a person who primarily needs care and compassion. In this way, he gives an impulse to the idea of a re-socialisation by means of probation. For Ancel, attempts at rehabilitation should always respect the dignity and integrity of the individual. This is to be procedurally guaranteed. Rehabilitation is also presented as a rational strategy of crime prevention.

Ancel (1954) proposes a critical study of the criminal justice system and its underlying values, and the development of a multi-disciplinary approach to crime, in which all human sciences play a role. Respect for human rights and the dignity of mankind are the limits beyond which no penal intervention should go. The approach of the new social defence movement also implies, however, a rather paternalistic procedural order in which the conflict character of a criminal process is ignored (Machielse, 1979: 77). In Belgium, Léon Cornil can be considered as a follower of the new social defence movement. In the post-war period, Cornil played an important role in the development of the probation order in his country, and at the penitentiary congress of 1950 in The Hague he advocated the abolition of the prison sentence because imprisonment is an important obstacle in a prisoner's rehabilitation (Franke, 1990: 663).

German-language critics of the penal rationale

In a social history of penal reform in post-war Austria, Wolfgang Stangl (1985) concludes that criminological insights have hardly played any role in political debates and that most of the earlier reforms of the penal system were initiated and implemented by legal practitioners alone. In Germany, the situation was not very different. The world of dogmatically oriented penal scientists was closed again and was barely influenced by any criminological insight. It was now felt to be crucial first to restore the perverted classical *rechtsstaat* and to reaffirm the doctrinal study of legal principles – at least, this was the vision in the West German Federal Republic. The development of a socialist legality in the German Democratic Republic was notably different, but falls outside the scope of this book. Whereas a sociologically oriented criminology in England received an important impulse in the 1940s, notably from German immigrants with a legal background such as Hermann Mannheim or Max Grünhut, a comparable empirical criminology would emerge in Germany itself only in the late 1960s. Georg Rusche's theory of 1933, about the relationship between developments in the labour market and those in the penal sphere, which had in 1939, in cooperation with Otto Kirchheimer, led to the penological classic *Punishment and Social Structure*, received much more attention in the United States than in Germany, where it was only rediscovered in the 1980s.

　Gustav Radbruch, who was dismissed from all his positions by the Nazis and died four years after the war, argued that the protection of legal values (*Rechtsgüter*) should be the sole legitimation of penal intervention. Legal contemplations on morality and conviction (*Gesinnung*) as constituting elements of an offence (*Tatbestände*) were best forgotten. According to Radbruch, the positivist fallacy of blind obedience to law, even when it is based on immoral foundations, should be overcome by taking respect for human rights as the touchstone of the legitimacy of law. The ultimate goal of penal reform is consequently a criminal code without penal sanctions, and the replacement of criminal law by something better. An abolitionist perspective, in which the offender is not medicalised and crime is seen in relation to its social context, was developed by the Austrian Julius Vargha at the beginning of the twentieth century. Vargha advocated, in his book on the abolition of penal subjugation (*Die Abschaffung der Strafknechtschaft*), a so-called social custody (*Bevormundung*), which comes close to a present-day community sanction (Stangl, 1984).

The most radical post-war penal critique in the German-speaking world had its roots in psychoanalysis. The work of the progressive psychiatrist Otto Gross and, indeed, of Sigmund Freud heralded a long tradition of radical critiques of the punitive rationale. This began in the 1920s with Theodor Reik's plea to replace punishment by confession and absolution (*Geständniszwang und Strafbedürfnis*) and Franz Alexander and Hugo Staub's incisive critique of criminal justice by examining the dominantly irrational relation between the offender and his judges (*Der Verbrecher und seine Richter*). It was followed in the 1940s, in Erich Fromm's *Escape from Freedom*, by Freudo-Marxist observations of conformism, authoritarianism and destructivism as reactions to mankind's inability to be free. This tradition culminated in Arno Plack's (1974) bulky plea for the abolition of criminal law (*Plädoyer für die Abschaffung des Strafrechts*). In a way, Plack was a forerunner of anti-oedipal and Lacan-inspired postmodern scholars.

These studies imply a fundamental, albeit sometimes rather crude, critique of aggression and destructivist urges as the main source of crime. The book *Die Gesellschaft und ihre Verbrecher* (Society and its offenders) by the Swiss legal theorist Paul Reiwald, turns the traditional focus of Freudian criminology around by examining the psychoanalysis of those who see the need to punish. In connection with the Modern School's argument, Reiwald (1947: 310) argues that 'the effect of criminal law must indeed be better examined, albeit not the effects on those who have to endure it, but on those who impose it.' The foundations of the social reaction approach were laid. As a true postwar scholar, Reiwald begins his analysis by problematising the concept of hostility to society (*Gesellschaftsfeindlichkeit*) which had dominated the idea of social defence in the preceding decade. According to Reiwald, the criminal justice system has been vulnerable to be infected by such concepts because the very penal rationale is, like fascism, based on irrational affects. Punishment is no more than an irrational response to an irrational act; it answers an affect with an affect, despite all pretensions to judge the motives of a criminal act as if it were a normal part of the legal discipline. According to Reiwald (1947: 221–3), it is high time to disprove such delusions, which do not become rational just because they are held by scientists. The criminal judge does not differ fundamentally from a Catholic inquisitor. He would do better to model himself on King Solomon, the Shakespearean character of Portia, or, indeed, on Miguel de Cervantes' *Don Quixote's* helper Sancho Panza.

According to Reiwald (1947: 288), not only crime but also criminal justice finds its roots in aggressive and destructive urges. It has developed into a 'just, formalised and partly sublimated form of aggression against the unjust, formless and primitive aggression of the a-social'. This rationalisation of irrationality has little to do with justice, argues Reiwald. Doing justice implies a reaction that mirrors the act, aims at redress and is led by the principles of non-violence and human dignity. The 'ancient tactics' of opposing change and improvement with the argument that one should strive for the impossible is rejected by Reiwald (1947: 304). Such an argument is 'particularly easy for criminal lawyers'; they have 'thousands of years of experience' and 'the power of affect' on their side. Reiwald's visions of sanctioning are the contrary of the penal (ir-)rationale, which really fosters the authoritarian personality and is therefore the enemy of democracy. Therefore, Reiwald (1947: 311) concludes, using the words of the Swiss humanist Auguste Forel, 'the future of criminal law lies in my view in its abolition; that is, in its drifting away from any right to punish.'

It is interesting to return for a while to Arno Plack, who used, like Reiwald, largely psychoanalytical lines of thought and had clear criminal political objectives as well. Plack explicitly advocated therapy instead of punishment, and proposed replacing the common interpretation of retribution by an orientation towards redress. Seen from a present-day perspective, it is particularly interesting that Plack (1974: 6–7) motivates the need for penal abolition by the fact that it is not enough to liberalise and humanise the penal system because it is unconvincing continuously to minimise the consequences of penal intervention if one holds the ideology as such to be incorrect. This will not be understood by the people and will eventually alienate them against reform. According to Plack, the fact that retributionist legitimations of the penal system would recede more into the background proves that, since this is, in the final analysis, the core of criminal law, the system as such would be in its last days.

European criminology developed in a functionalist legal context. In Britain, criminology hardly had an effect on jurisprudence and developed more in the realm of psychiatry. The European Modern School of integrated penal sciences was motivated by progressive and conservative political considerations alike. This ambiguous political basis resulted in a predominant authoritarian politics in the 1930s and a humanitarian tendency after the Second World War. Now we will take one step closer towards critical criminology by explicitly focusing on the ideas of critics of authoritarianism. Since early Dutch criminology offers a rich palette of such critiques, we will focus on this specific context in the next chapter.

4

Precursors of Critical Criminology

Socialists and criminal justice

In 1889, Ferdinand Domela Nieuwenhuis, the first socialist member of the Dutch parliament, attacked Minister of Justice Ruijs de Beerenbrouck on the 'fundamentally wrong foundations of the current penal system', which did not incarcerate the guilty, he argued, but rather the victims of society. Marxist analyses of the penal system were supported by the criminological findings of Ferri, Lombroso and Garofalo (who had disproved the voluntarist hypotheses of classical criminal law), and by the over-representation of the working class in prison. The low wages prisoners received for prison labour were a more fundamental form of theft, he maintained, than those acts criminalised as such. Domela considered the cell system an equally pointless as well as refined form of cruelty. It 'idiotises' inmates and turns them into 'mean hypocrites, unsuitable for social co-existence'. Scientific socialism had shown on historical grounds that all so-called legal questions were no more than power questions (Franke, 1990: 487–8). In 1897, the socialist journal *de Jonge Gids* initiated a survey among prisoners in order to reveal the appalling treatment of political prisoners. The many reactions of respected jurists meant that the inquiry could not be discredited as socialist propaganda.

> The fact that they could accuse precisely those gentlemen, who are so convinced of their own decency, of such pointless and barbarian cruelties, must have given them great satisfaction. The gentlemen could hardly defend themselves against these accusations without providing new ammunition for the attacks on their sentiments. This has made the socialists' role particularly influential. (Franke, 1990: 492)

In this context, a socialist strand also emerged within criminology.

Willem Bonger: socialist and sociologist

Amsterdam criminologist Willem Bonger has been put forward as a predecessor of critical criminology (Turk, 1969; Taylor et al., 1973). He was among the first criminologists to make thorough, quantitative analyses of the relations between economic conditions and crime. Bonger was an active member of the Dutch Labour Party. To call him a 'self-proclaimed Marxist', as Taylor et al. (1973: 222) do, is incorrect. Bonger was a confirmed social democrat, a revisionist who had an aversion to both Marxism's autocratic tendencies and to revolutionary idealism. Bonger was a 'socialist at the University', but also remained a 'professor in the Labour Party' (van Heerikhuizen, 1987: 168–74). Bonger derived his inspiration from Marx's scientific work rather than from actual Marxist politics. In a footnote, which first appears in the English edition of *Criminality and Economic Conditions*[1] of 1916, Bonger (p. 246) argues:

> To require that a book like mine should once more set forth and defend the theory of Marx *in extenso*, is as impossible as to require that a modern biologist, who proceeds on Darwinian theory, should prove over and over that his basis is sound. That there may be more or less error in detail in the theory of Marx, as in that of Darwin, is possible, but in general they have resisted, like a wall of bronze, all attacks in the most pitiless of contests, that of opinions.

This is Bonger's most explicit identification with Marxism. As such, his work is, however, an example of economic sociology rather than of historical materialism, and his vision of social development is evolutionary rather than dialectical.

Bonger put much effort into countering the thesis that socialism is conducive to crime. He advocated the improvement of socioeconomic conditions as the best way to prevent so-called 'crimes of misery' – crimes committed because of insufficient means of existence. Bonger called himself a convinced determinist, but only for socioeconomic reasons. He considered the Modern School to be an impossible compromise between determinism and voluntarism. This is a contention that cannot have pleased the supervisor of his dissertation: Gerard van Hamel (van Heerikhuizen, 1987: 69). Bonger praised the French School for its initiating role in suggesting the relation between economic conditions and crime. Despite his criticism of Tarde's theory on imitation as the main causal explanation of crime, Bonger (1905: 161) judged positively about Tarde's scientific contribution: from his work it was possible to gain more in-depth comprehension, even when it did not bring solutions to the problem any closer. For Bonger, Manouvrier's studies on the origins of crime were 'the best'. Bonger (1905: 175) praised him for 'saying in fifty pages more than many in a bulky volume' and translated various of his works into Dutch. Bonger adopted many ideas of the Environmental School, but he also wanted to take a step further by indicating some possible solutions to the problems they had signalled. Bonger refuted Lombroso's atavism theory as a fable about the continuing progress of civilisation. He criticised Lombroso for not paying attention to the question of who determines which activities are called 'crime', and argued that it is simply untrue that moral opinions are universal in time and place. Lombroso is seen as a relic from an era in which people still believed in natural law. If there are physical differences between 'criminals' and 'non-criminals', it is mainly because misery also causes physical degeneration (Bonger, 1909). In his inaugural address to the University of Amsterdam, Bonger (1922) begins his analysis of the evolution of morality by outlining how 'primitive' people deal with deviance and social control. They are often able to handle their social problems more peacefully than we in our capitalist societies. This also disproves Lombroso's atavism theory.

With the emergence of capitalism, a social climate was created which incites egoism and increases the opportunities to commit crime. According to Bonger (1922), this has demoralised the working class. Lowered moral standards become particularly conducive to crime under deprived socioeconomic circumstances. The reports of the probation service clearly prove this. By social politics and education, the morality of the working class can be uplifted and the volume of crime can be limited. For this reason, Bonger argues that the probation service deserves more support from the workers' movement. In order to realise a more just economic order, the means of production have to be socialised gradually, while the previous private owners should be compensated in order to prevent disorder. With his 'progress-optimism', Bonger is a clear representative of the utilitarian socialism which in Britain is known as 'Fabianism'; it is also the kind of socialism against which critical criminologists would direct their fire in the 1970s. For Bonger, crime is only a negative social phenomenon. He does not share Durkheim's thesis on the positive social function of crime in the ascertainment of 'good' and 'evil'.

With his social-psychological egoism thesis, Bonger remained quite close to the French School. In contrast to what has been argued by Taylor et al. (1973: 223), it is not at all 'strange' that Bonger began his thesis on crime and economic conditions with an exposé of psychological theories. Not only do they play an important role in his own work, but these theories were dominant when he wrote the book. Bonger (1905: 98) directs his criticism at the implicit thesis that economic conditions are of little influence on the level of crime. The *Scuola positiva* is mainly criticised because it is ill informed about the nature of crime, as well as about the nature of the capitalist production process. Bonger is equally elaborate about the observations of other precursors of criminology (statisticians, environmentalists, spiritualists and socialists) in this respect. Bonger (1911) feels ideologically closest to the socialist Italian *Terza scuola*, but distances himself from Colajanni and Turati's rhetorical, crude and emotional observations which are not supported by empirical data and are insufficiently aware of scientific socialism.

Statistics (in those days court statistics rather than police figures or, indeed, victim surveys) play an important role in Bonger's work. He counters the thesis that socialism is conducive to crime by statistically comparing (both in time and place) the development of criminality and the number of socialist voters in the same area. Bonger found no generalisable relation between the two: both the 'most socialist' province (Groningen) and the 'least socialist' provinces (Drenthe and Brabant) had a rather high number of convictions for criminal offences. The highest conviction rates were found in the (non-socialist) Catholic province of Limburg, and the lowest rate in the relatively secular and socialist province of North-Holland. From a comparison of socioeconomic conditions in these provinces, Bonger concludes that the relation between crime and the exploitation of the working classes is more significant than any religious denomination. Bonger did not problematise the way judicial statistics are constructed. He presupposes that the percentage of crimes that are reported, cleared up and dismissed remains unchanged. He pays no attention to a possible class-biased selectivity in the criminal justice system, nor to the fact that tolerance towards crime is also determined by socioeconomic conditions (Fiselier, 1976: 168–9).

Critics often maintain that Bonger suggests that all crime would diminish if socioeconomic circumstances were improved. Bonger's position is, however, more subtle. He argues that 'crimes of misery' can decrease under better socioeconomic conditions for the working class. This would, however, have much less effect on crimes of a different nature – caused by sexual demoralisation, alcoholism, war and so on. So-called 'crimes of greed' would probably even increase. 'Statistics show that simple theft is very sensitive to economic trends, whereas this is much less clear for embezzlement and fraud. These crimes increase when economic misery decreases. Apparently, a higher level of welfare generates greed and thereby increases the level of crimes related to these urges' (Bonger, 1932: 115). Bonger also deals with professional crimes committed by entrepreneurs, bankers and stockbrokers and tradesmen. We can find most of the basic themes of Edwin Sutherland's theory of white-collar crime of 1949 in Bonger's (1905: 599–607) thesis. Most of his analyses, however, like those of the French School, deal with the common crimes of the working class.

Bonger pointed to the moral and bourgeois premises on which the concept of crime is based. By giving the example of how strikes are criminalised, Bonger (1905: 379) argues that 'power is the necessary condition for those who wish to class a certain act as a crime.' While rejecting essentialist definitions, the question of what crime is, according to Bonger, is not simply determined by class interests. Bonger barely elaborates the notion that criminal law is also used as an instrument of the ruling class, and, in his later work, this element becomes even less prominent (Fiselier, 1976: 160–1). Even though the same behaviour is not criminalised in all times and places, the concept of crime consists of some common elements. 'It is warranted to say that in modern countries nearly all criminalised acts are also considered to be immoral by nearly all citizens – albeit to a different extent. Even the professional thief will say that theft really is an immoral act' (Bonger, 1932: 2). Bonger interprets crime as a sub-set of the category 'immoral behaviour', namely that kind of immoral behaviour that is anti-social. The immoral part is presented as the subjective element of crime and the anti-social part the objective. Bonger's biographer, Bart van Heerikhuizen (1987: 198) calls Bonger's definition of crime 'sociologically relativistic' because, for him, the 'objective' element of crime relates to the social reactions it provokes. By calling the anti-social element of crime 'objective', Bonger, is, however, inconsistent with his earlier rejection of essentialism and his observations of the broad disparities in culture and time with regard to the kind of acts that are criminalised. Bonger fought the same struggle about the definition of crime that many criminologists would do after him, and failed to find an acceptable position between relativism and essentialism.

Clara Wichmann's radical critique of penality

Clara Wichmann is an internationally less well-known precursor of critical criminology than Willem Bonger. Bonger was active in the Labour Party; Wichmann was a representative of the libertarian left. Bonger was born in 1876 as the youngest son of a large middle-class family; Wichmann was born in 1885 to a small family of German immigrants who belonged to the well-to-do bourgeoisie and was, although at a distance, politically associated with the workers' movement. Bonger worked till his professorship in 1922 as a clerk in his father's company; Wichmann worked as a defence lawyer before she became bankrupt in 1914, and later at the Central Bureau of Statistics before her early death in childbirth in 1922. During her law studies in Utrecht, Clara Wichmann attended intensive classes of the Amsterdam professor of philosophy Bolland, who had, around the turn of the century, begun a left-wing Hegel revival in The Netherlands. Here, she also came in to contact with libertarian socialists, who would become very important in her later life. As a woman, a socialist and a lawyer, Clara Wichmann felt an obligation to engage in the Union for Suffrage. By this involvement, she came into contact with and wrote about ethical feminism. At the same time, in 1908, she became, under the influence of Bertha von Süttner, active in the peace movement. In 1915 she coordinated a manifesto against compulsory military service. She entered into a 'free marriage' with conscientious objector Jonas Beniamin Meijer. Inspired by the Russian Revolution, she participated in the Union of Revolutionary Socialist Intellectuals in 1917 (Pit, 1984).

In 1919, Clara Wichmann linked her political ideas with her professional working area, criminal law. Together with kindred souls from the anarcho-socialist movement, she established the *Comité van actie tegen de bestaande opvattingen omtrent misdaad en straf* (Action Committee against the Prevailing Opinions on Crime and Punishment, henceforth CMS).[2] In its manifesto of association, the necessary interrelation of science and politics is taken for granted. As general secretary of the CMS, Wichmann pointed out that structural penal reform will not be achieved by theory alone, nor just by socioeconomic changes. The potential for structural reform lies precisely in their indirect connection. Theory and practice should always be reciprocal, and the incentive for innovation is formed by social movements. Reactions to the CMS manifesto from the scientific community varied from mild to very enthusiastic.

The CMS was a political platform which found its basis in various revolutionary groups, and strove for penal abolition. Opposition to the state's right to punish is as old as the state itself. Late nineteenth-century philosophers and writers, such as the German Friedrich Nietzsche, the Frenchman Jean Marie Guyau, or the Russians Leo Tolstoy and Peter Kropotkin, all put forward abolitionist arguments with regard to the *ius puniendi*, the state's right to punish. Nietzsche's abolitionism follows from his *Umwertung aller Werte*, the revaluation of all values. His idea of the moral autonomy of the enlightened 'over-man' (*Übermensch*) makes the state's 'lies in the name of

the people' illegitimate. It currently retards innovation by 'calling oppositional forces criminal'. In Guyau's thought, the abolition of criminal law
follows from the libertarian ethics of a *morale sans obligation ni sanction*.
Tolstoy's radical pacifism has been an important source of inspiration for the
rejection of criminal law as an expression of violence. And Kropotkin is of all
anarchists the most explicit about the idea that criminal law is one of the
most repressive instruments of the state, which should disappear with the
abolition of the state itself. The CMS did not use the word 'abolitionism',
which stemmed from the early nineteenth-century anti-slavery movement. In
the penal field, fighters against capital punishment and torture were, slightly
later, also referred to as 'abolitionists'. In relation to the penal system, the
term 'abolitionism' is only used from the late 1970s onwards, but as such the
idea certainly 'hangs in the air' in the *belle époque*.

Next to libertarian socialism, the ethical pacifist ideas of Tolstoy and
Gandhi were central incentives for the CMS. For some other members, the
political commitment to penal abolition was directly inspired by personal
prison experience. In 1916, later CMS co-founders Bart de Ligt and Lode
van Mierop had been imprisoned as fine defaulters – they were fined for
drawing up a manifesto against the imprisonment of conscientious objec-
tors. Their support for these political prisoners' hunger strike was
criminalised as 'agitation'. The CMS saw a direct link between the penal
and the military systems, and regarded both as man-created institutions of
pointless and repressive cruelty. By retaliating against the evil of crime with
the evil of punishment, the threshold of answering violence with violence is
continually lowered. Punishment is a form of unresponsive violence, and
the CMS rejected, following Tolstoy, its legitimacy – both as retribution and
as rehabilitation. The socioeconomic conditions under which crime
emerges, as well as the treatment of delinquents, need a better solution
than repression (Wichmann, 1924: 92–8; 1930: 81–95). Clara Wichmann
relates the *ius puniendi* to historical materialism, social ethics and other
cultural developments.

> All is in all, Multatuli [a critical, nineteenth-century Dutch novelist] said. Whether
> one just wants to repeal abuses within the boundaries of the prevailing penal
> system, or one holds the opinion that the penal system as a whole is wrong . . . can
> hardly be a question of judicial conviction only. Questions of crime and punish-
> ment are no isolated areas; they are linked with other social issues and indeed with
> questions about the philosophy of life. (Wichmann, 1924: 103)

The materialistic foundation of modern penality

In 1912, in her dissertation *Beschouwingen over de historische grondslagen der
tegenwoordige omvorming van het strafbegrip* (Reflections on the historical
foundations of the present-day transformation of penality), Clara
Wichmann advocates the idea that current manifestations of crime are inherent in the capitalist structure of society. She wrote her thesis under the
supervision of a Utrecht representative of the Modern School, David

Simons. In the preface, Wichmann thanks both Simons and the Amsterdam neo-Hegelian Bolland. She expresses the hope that they will accept her gratitude for everything she has learned from them, despite the fact that she has chosen a way other than both men might have hoped. Though approvingly using many of the Modern School's ideas, Wichmann seeks debate with its followers. She advocates the addition of an ethical dimension to the instrumental pragmatism of the Modern School. In this respect she takes up the discussion on the foundations of modern criminal law, notably lacking in the work of many modern scholars.

Clara Wichmann concentrates her critique of the penal system on the area of sanctioning. She argues for penal reform with an educational orientation. As opposed to the Amsterdam Lombrosian penal abolitionist *avant la lettre* Arnold Aletrino, she does not believe that the biological determination of the criminal makes imprisonment an indefensible option, but stresses socio-economic factors that limit freedom of action. Contrary to the 'Fabian' Bonger, Wichmann rejects probation as a form of bourgeois charity that frustrates the political struggle of proletarian outcasts. In her thesis, she treats both the French and the Italian Schools with respect, but stresses, at the same time, that even 'born criminals' would probably not commit crimes if their social circumstances were better. On this issue, she is just as critical of the French 'bourgeois environmentalists' as of the Italian positivists because neither devotes much attention to the responsibility of the state to improve living conditions for the proletariat.

The way in which Clara Wichmann defends the Modern against the Classical School is worth mentioning. Classical critics of the Modern School point to the ultimate consequence of a boundless criminal justice system. In reality, she argues, hardly anybody has ever defended this position. Referring to ultimate consequences is the best strategy to retard innovation, since the ultimate conclusion of *any* idea will be totalitarian. The point is, therefore, not to focus on ultimate solutions at all, but rather on finding a workable practice. Theoretical insights are to be used as guidelines, a direction in which concrete measures should be sought, namely doing social justice in individual cases (Wichmann, 1912: 153). Modern scholars provided a useful impulse by judging the criminal justice system on its social functions instead of on its dogmatic purity, but Wichmann criticises their neglect of the criminogenic nature of capitalist social structure. While carefully avoiding mention of the modern penal reform movement as one unanimous school, Wichmann outlines the general innovative value of those aspects in which it differs from the Classical School. These elements can be summarised as: the attention given to the personal circumstances of the accused, especially with regard to the necessity of separate reception and criminal procedures for juveniles; the focus on so-called social precaution, prevention and effective crime control; the relation between punishment and the dangerousness of the accused; and the introduction of a concept of guilt as 'imputability', which is based on empirical psychology instead of metaphysical armchair considerations (Wichmann, 1912: 130–1; 1923: 261–5).

Wichmann considers these criteria, however, insufficient for a fundamentally different vision of criminal law. In the prevailing economic order, punishment is still an egoistic self-defence of the ruling classes. She rejects the modern tendency to individualise social problems; in this respect, modern scholars have learned just as little from social sciences as classical lawyers. In her important essay on the right to punish, *Het recht tot straffen* of 1919, she calls Cesare Beccaria the original 'triumpher of abstract individualism' and the 'Adam Smith of criminal law' (Wichmann, 1923: 248). Any really modern idea should go beyond this liberal rationalism. Because the modern critique of classical, bourgeois legal principles incoherently adopts a liberal, individualistic view of mankind itself, it is suitable to be used for bourgeois purposes of social defence (Wichmann, 1924: 257). Wichmann sees the fact that the Modern School did not touch upon crucial socioeconomic notions as its 'ethical shortcoming'. She considers it 'a tragic development' that modern scholars have not seen how the consequences of their own research should lead to a radical attack on the capitalist system, which brings forward so many of the social evils the school describes itself as the causes of crime. Thus a theory of penality needs to be grounded in historical-materialist principles.

The strong emphasis that Clara Wichmann puts on the relation between crime and socioeconomic conditions is reminiscent of Bonger. Bonger, however, never referred to Clara Wichmann. Wichmann depicts Bonger's theory as a social-democratic variety of the French School's bourgeois environmentalism because Bonger also localises most crimes within the working class. She also points to the fact that Bonger does not address the selectivity of criminalisation in the legislative process and has hardly ever argued against apparent cases of class justice (Wichmann, 1912: 121–2). Clara Wichmann was the first Dutch penal scholar to write about the class interests that guide the process of criminalisation. Wichmann shares Bonger's rejection of punishment as a general deterrent. In 1917, she referred to a particularly severe sanction for wood theft, which was motivated by the argument that an example needed to be set in order to deter people from stealing fuel in the coming winter. A true commitment to general prevention would, according to Wichmann, have led this particular judge to signal the problems the poor would probably have to cope with in the coming winter in war time. The verdict should have urged social measures to prevent this misery. Instead, the judge did not exact retribution for the offender's guilt, but merely used him as an example to others (Wichmann, 1930: 69–81). Wichmann considers the concepts of crime and punishment, which modern scholars have uncritically adopted from the Classical School, as far too limited. With the unfounded suggestion of a direct causal relation between crime and punishment, the political character of criminality is obscured; poverty and repression do not receive the label 'crime', but the consequences of poverty and repression. In line with both the traditions of the Modern School and of Bonger, she classifies various forms of offence on the basis of their cause: crime from material necessity; crime as resistance to socioeconomic disparities; and crime as anti-social behaviour. Wichmann believed that the revolution, which was thought to come at any moment, would bring an end to the first cause of crime and to a certain extent also to the second, whereas other reactions, with a clear educational goal, should be developed for the third category.

Clara Wichmann's utopian socialism is not simply naïve. She rejected the idea that, after the revolution, all crime would disappear. Crime has always been and will always remain. Its massive character is, however, not self-evident and can be limited by social measures. The realisation of socialism will first of all change the nature of crime, and perhaps also diminish the level of crime as a whole. In this sense, Wichmann's analysis is not fundamentally different from Bonger's. Wichmann ascertains, in the line of Maria Montessori, that truly educational reactions cannot be of a punitive nature, but should indeed offer positive stimuli to the individual's personal development. The attempt to teach somebody social skills will, however, only be effective if they appeal to a personal motivation (Wichmann, 1930: 103). A truly critical – what Wichmann (1930: 181) calls 'dialectic-ethnological penal' – theory needs to imply another conception of the historical development of criminal law, of the definition of crime, of human responsibility, justice, and of people's education. Wichmann herself did not have the opportunity to elaborate these themes further herself, but in the establishment of a 'new criminology' in the early 1970s we will touch upon comparable themes.

The humanitarian and authoritarian face of social defence

Clara Wichmann was by no means the only person to point to the dangers of social defence. Head of the judicial statistics department, de Roos (1911) concludes, after comparing developments in criminology with those in penal practice, that the implementation of modern criminological ideas in penal policy would be likely to have a hardening rather than a mitigating effect. Even allegedly benign representatives of the Environmental School, like Lacassagne and Tarde, advocated a rigorous application of capital punishment because soft remedies would lead to an increase in crime. David Simons (1911: 35) indicates the dangers the Modern School implies for the legal safeguards the offender holds against the state when the predominant interest of a stable social order is put forward. Wichmann (1923: 260) writes that 'the idea that this theory will lead to sentimentality . . . is completely amiss, because the Italian School knows, next to a humanitarian side, there is also a less scrupulous counterpart. Garofalo in particular has preached the elimination of the criminal from society by means of capital punishment or banishment. This same hard line can be observed in van Hamel's opinions on the incapacitation and medicalisation of 'the degenerated', and in his defence of emergency legislation against anarchists and of sanctions of indeterminate length (Franke, 1990: 464; Vervaele, 1990: 382).

These ideas were not unanimously shared by all modern scholars. David

Simons, an advocate of a humanistically inspired socialisation of punishment based on modern ideas, always forcefully rejected the idea of indeterminate sentences (Janse de Jonge, 1985: 306). As a former defence lawyer, Simons discards the idea that tougher penal sanctions are an adequate means in the fight against crime. 'One wants to maintain a system by continually increasing sentences. That has never succeeded and will not succeed today. Continual appeals to the sharp sword of criminal justice are indeed the sharpest condemnation of the very system itself. In the end, liberty will gain the victory over punishment. *Victa vincit libertas*' (Simons, 1918: 4). In his valedictory address in 1928, Simons argued that the criminal justice system needed to be humane or not exist at all. Simons' successor in the Utrecht chair of criminal law, Willem Pompe (1928: 10), argued in his inaugural address of the same year that: 'the French School has already shown that the criminal is, at least potentially, and perhaps also actually, equal to other human beings. In this way, it has remained loyal to the French tradition of the *citoyen* and has saved criminal law at the same time from the Italian abyss.'

Bonger's warnings against authoritarianism

Willem Bonger's contribution to the debate on criminal justice politics became explicit in the 1930s, when authoritarian tendencies began to prevail. When Taylor et al. (1973: 235) suggest that Bonger might have had some sympathy for a war on crime, or indeed for a kind of socialism of the Soviet type, they do him great injustice. Bonger's biographer, Bart van Heerikhuizen (1987: 259), raises fundamental objections against such anachronistic, unfair, crude and incorrect observations: 'Anyone who is able to write such a sentence disqualifies himself as a serious observer of Bonger's work.' Bonger's book *Problemen der democratie* (Problems of democracy) of 1934 is a fundamental defence of democratic principles and a warning against autocratic tendencies leading to totalitarianism. Despite the fact that 'Europe has for the greater part become undemocratic – of its roughly five hundred million inhabitants, more than three hundred million live under autocratic regimes' – Bonger insists that democracy will eventually defeat autocracy. His argument is predominantly pragmatic. Modern capitalist, industrial societies have a vulnerable production process. As they are over-sensitive to social unrest and violence, they can only survive in a democratic system. This is the only way in which important shifts in power balances can be managed in a non-violent way. This makes democracy the system that fits best with modern social economic relations.

Though he rejects their voluntarism and celebration of capitalism, Bonger always felt a strong sympathy for the down-to-earth and pragmatic approach of the English. His aversion to philosophy, to abstract speculations not grounded in empirical reality, is also a reason why Bonger was so strongly anti-German. He always saw the specific combination of German absolutism about 'big ideas' and the 'expansionist and aggressive Prussian spirit' as a danger to democracy (Valkhoff, 1946). When theories of the superiority of the Nordic race and of criminogenic factors inherent in 'inferior races' began to dominate criminological discourse and the political reality in Europe, Bonger wrote, in 1939, a book on race and crime, in which he shows that there is no significant empirical relation between the two. In the same way as in his earlier analyses of crime and religion, he explains racial disparities in crime rates by differences in socioeconomic position.

Bonger is very explicit about the idea that an individual may never be sacrificed to the communal interest of social defence. In an unprecedentedly outraged article, Bonger warns against the rather supportive and docile Dutch observations of the new German visions of criminal justice. Bonger (1935) argues that those who do not see the relation between this modern criminal law and dictatorship are simply blind. He points to the *Kriminalbiologische Gesellschaft* which has applied a Nazist ideology to the penal area. He severely criticises Nico Muller, a progressive judge and leading force in the Dutch probation service who travelled through 'new Germany' to study the new penal system in that country, with the words: 'what should we think of someone who has a look at prisons, but forgets to tell us about the existence of concentration camps?' The tone of Bonger's article was so furious that the journal's editor 'had to' delete too personalistic attacks (as stated in an editorial note to the article). Bonger did, however, not stand alone in his opinion. Such highly acclaimed lawyers as van Oven and Langemeijer argued with respect to the Dutch participation in the penal congress in Berlin in 1935, that they found it 'inexplicable if representatives of a civilised nation are going to talk about criminal justice and the penal system in the country of concentration camps and Gestapo' (Gradisen, 1988: 365). Groningen professor of criminal law, Simon van der Aa, was a mouthpiece for the majority when he responded that staying away would probably be interpreted as a diplomatic offence to the German government. Despite van Oven and Langemeijer's appeal that in such questions of principle more guts than diplomatic courtesy was required, many Dutch penal scientists went to Berlin, and discussed the new order of German law enforcement, albeit in a mainly rejective way (Gradisen, 1988).

How deeply Bonger's rejection of any (both left and right) authoritarian tendencies and his commitment to democratic principles went is best illustrated by his personal life story. In the run-up to the war, he not only opposed the new German penal order and its racist bias, but also advocated the decriminalisation of abortion and the liberalisation of divorce law, and took up a position against the increasing social exclusion and stigmatisation of homosexuals (Valkhoff, 1946). He was an important member of the *Comité van waakzaamheid* (Committee of vigilance) against Nazism. When, on 10 May 1940, the Germans actually invaded The Netherlands, Bonger knew he would be on the list of people to be arrested first. He considered it a spineless act to flee to the savage capitalist (Britain or the United States) or Stalinist countries (Soviet Union) he had always criticised. At the same time, at 64 years old, he was pessimistic about his personal role in the resistance. On the evening of the Dutch capitulation, 14 May 1940, he met novelist Etty

Hillesum at the Amsterdam Museumplein. During their conversation, which has become famous through Hillesum's diaries, she asked him whether he still thought democracy would overcome. Bonger answered: 'It will certainly overcome, but it will cost more than one generation.' These would be his last words. That night, Bonger took his own life. In a letter to his son, he wrote: 'I cannot see any future for myself and I cannot bend to the scum who are going to rule now' (van Heerikhuizen, 1987: 157).

It is interesting to see how his colleagues reacted to Bonger's self-chosen death. Fear of the German oppressor surely contributed to the fact that not a single word was devoted to it, but the reactions of various academic journals are none the less revealing. Bonger's (1939) last book, *Ras en misdaad* (Race and crime), was reviewed in an awkward way by criminal lawyer Taverne (1941). A substantial part of this review article is devoted to the problem of so-called Jewish crime, which Bonger mainly explains as a consequence of an anti-semitic exclusion from society. This opinion is rejected by Taverne, who, by way of conclusion, 'just wants to indicate briefly that the author rejects the superiority of the Nordic race' (1941: 39). The only remark Taverne makes about Bonger's death is that this event prevented him from bringing forward some of his earlier criticisms of this study. It should be noted that there was no German censorship over academic journals. In another review, criminal lawyer Röling argues that Bonger has disproved various widespread but incorrect common beliefs about race and crime, and hopes that younger criminologists will, after Bonger's death, remember his 'tempestuous enthusiasm and the honesty of his convictions' (1940: 457). After this review, the tone of Röling's memorial article of 1942 is quite striking. Given the widespread practice of self-censorship in those days, one can still understand why this late obituary does not refer to the motives of Bonger's suicide. Röling wants, however, 'to highlight the flaws and inconsistencies' in Bonger's work. He calls him 'prejudiced, one-sided, here and there uncritical, and blind to certain areas of life'. Bonger mainly 'tried to illustrate his hatred against capitalism with figures that present it as the root of all evil'. Bonger, in his outraged article about Nico Muller's support of the 'new' German visions of penality, only rejected these ideas because they no longer fitted his era (Röling, 1942: 110).

The development of Muller's ideas is one of the most illustrative examples of how the consequent implementation of modern thought followed the spirit of the times. Initially, Muller focused on the individual education of offenders. He rejected the idea of the unreformable offender. Muller's dissertation of 1908, in which he developed a psychologically oriented classification of property offenders which was aimed at non-custodial measures, was highly praised by Bonger (1932: 23). Despite his academic activities, Muller was predominantly a practitioner. He was known as a sincere and benign man, who, for two decades, was the embodiment of care for the offender. In the second half of the 1930s, the dominant idea was that the massive burden of crime during the economic crisis had outgrown an individual approach and that a general education of the masses was needed to

counter the 'wrongly oriented philanthropy of the past'. In this sociopolitical context, Muller accommodated his initial ideas on individual education to
the notion of general prevention and social defence (Janse de Jonge, 1991:
15–61). In defence of Muller it should be noted, as Bonger (1935) also explicitly mentions, that his celebration of Germany's new penal order was written
in 1931 – two years before Hitler came to power. Bonger's objections were,
however, more fundamental: he considered the whole idea of general prevention incompatible with any sense of justice because it sacrificed the
individual to a state display of power. The whole notion of *Gemeinschaft*
(community) was dangerous and suspect, argued Bonger.

Post-war developments in criminology

After the liberation of 1945, the Holocaust was the central problem to be
coped with. In Dutch criminology, Ger Kempe's (1947) essays on 'crime and
inhuman behaviour' formed a clear reflection of the widely felt anxiety, aston-
ishment and dismay at the dehumanisation that had taken place under Nazi
rule. Willem Nagel's (1953) *Volg het spoor terug* (Follow the traces back) is its
more essayistic counterpart, written under his literary pseudonym J.B.
Charles, which stems from his time in the Resistance. The Dutch authorities
were immediately confronted with the difficult question of how to deal with
all those political delinquents (Nazis and their collaborators) who were over-
populating Dutch prisons – and the concentration camps still in existence.
Under emergency legislation and military criminal law, 152 people were sentenced to death and 40 of them were actually executed. Three months after
liberation, a national action committee against capital punishment for war
criminals (it had already been abolished from common criminal law in 1870)
was founded by philologist Piet Meertens and criminal lawyer Jacob van
Bemmelen.[3] Though reaction to Nazi arbitrary rule primarily resulted in a
strong reaffirmation of the democratic *rechtsstaat*, more radical penal
reforms were also advocated. A national association of ex-political prisoners
under the Nazi regime was founded by the end of 1945. It aimed at a general,
humanitarian penal reform. While recognising that their situation had been
quite specific, these ex-political prisoners emphasised the brutalising conditions of Dutch prisons. Their action found broad support among the
previous Resistance, as well as among the probation service, penal scholars
and the judiciary. In 1946, the utopian socialist Bellamy Party defended, in
line with the radical Freudian traditions in criminology, the abolition of prisons and their replacement by psychiatric means. Others advocated an
orientation towards redress because nobody gains from incarceration
(Franke, 1990: 633, 662–3).

On 28 May 1949, Meertens established, together with radical psychiatrist
Musaph and medical doctor Storm, the *Vereniging tot vernieuwing van de
opvattingen omtrent misdaad en straf* (Association for the Renewal of
Opinions on Crime and Punishment, henceforth VOMS). They knew each

other from the circle around the utopian socialist weekly *de Vlam*, which had emerged from the resistance. VOMS, presenting itself as the successor to Clara Wichmann's CMS, wanted to keep a radical critique of the penal system alive. Their radical critique of penality was rooted in discomfiture about the fact that only now that people from the higher social classes had been imprisoned was it possible to reform the penal system. In line with the spirit of the times, VOMS oriented itself towards rehabilitation. Retribution was rejected as a legitimation of punishment. VOMS organised public hearings and symposia in which liberation from the Nazis was interpreted as a liberation from coercion in a broader, psychological sense. As the initial revival of utopian socialism soon faded, and the more concrete proposals for penal reform were soon adopted, both VOMS and *de Vlam* ceased to exist in 1952.[4]

After the war, the Dutch economy lay flat, the city of Rotterdam had become a ruin after the German bombardment of 14 May 1940 (and by a mistaken Allied bombardment in 1942), Amsterdam had lost its characteristic Jewish heart and in many Dutch cities the traces of destruction were still visible. The sphere of economic reconstruction and the Dutch government's problems with Sukarno's independence movement in the Dutch East Indies, were not a good starting-point for any cultural reconstruction. After the evident powerlessness of the country against the Germans and its impotence to defend the colonies in the Far East against the Japanese, both the economic position and the national pride of the Dutch were severely damaged. The colonial war the Dutch fought (from 1947 to 1949) in the now independent republic of Indonesia was a painful last convulsion of a political dwarf who thought he owned an empire. With the beginning of the Cold War, all initial euphoria evaporated and The Netherlands fell back on pre-war imperial structures.

In the penal field, things changed importantly in the 1950s. It is hard to single out one cause of change. The 'official', yet not uncontested, scenario is the following: under normal conditions penal policy-makers do not experience prison life. During the war, many of them were, however, imprisoned by the Nazis. After this experience, the improvement of prison conditions, and of the chances people have before they commit a crime and after they are released, became a matter of much stronger, personal consideration. In this context, the latent progressive influence of modern scholars of various penal schools could become manifest. The government appointed a committee (Fick) to study the restructuring of the penal system. This committee's policy recommendations of 1947 were followed in 1951 by new legislation on penal principles and prison conditions. The Utrecht School, in particular, is seen to have had an important influence both on the committee and on the judiciary in this political climate in which the need for a more humanitarian prison system was forced upon many notable people. Ger Kempe argued that the war tore The Netherlands away from its fatal indolence in penal matters. It forced upon people the conclusion that 'the delinquent is one of us.' Kempe's idea that the treatment of prisoners mirrors the level of civilisation of a society was widely shared among the general public. People apparently learned from the experience of an authoritarian regime that social danger-ousness is a tricky legitimation of penal intervention because it has no intrinsic limits. Nico Muller made his excuses about his political naïvety of the early 1930s and invested all his energy in the humanisation of the prison system (Franke, 1990: 632).

The Utrecht School found a ready reception among legal authorities for the idea that offenders first and foremost have to be understood and 'encoun-tered' as fellow human beings and not as a deviant species. Law enforcement became the politics of bad conscience (de Haan, 1990: 64–82). The fact that the School had educated many judges and high civil servants at the Ministry of Justice is said to have contributed to the codification of the preparation of offenders for their return to society as the main purpose of imprisonment. The School also contributed concrete proposals for the humanisation of detention as a means of bringing the principle of rehabilitation into practice. These included: the introduction of a more 'communal' prison regime with one prisoner to a cell and communal activities outside the cell; the organisa-tion of various educational courses; social-work activities and psychological assistance; and the formulation of basic rights for detainees. The Fick Committee also recommended the replacement of the informal grievance boards by a more sound legal system of supervisory committees, which would provide prisoners with a legal right to appeal against the decisions of the prison governor. These moves to establish a system of prisoners' litigation were stopped by the director general of the prison department Lamers, and its introduction was delayed until 1977. Gradually, the opinion came to pre-vail that the best way to prepare a prisoner for his return to society is to curtail his liberties and rights no more than is strictly necessary for the exe-cution of the prison sentence. The judiciary also came to share the idea that imprisonment, because of its damaging and stigmatising effects, fails to pro-tect the society to which the prisoner returns. Thus, rehabilitation is not just based on humanitarianism, but can also be understood in terms of self-inter-est; prisoners should not be sent back to the streets embittered or rancorous. This heralded a period of reduction in incarceration from 1950 to 1975.

Criminology and the realm of criminal law

Before the Second World War, Dutch criminology was dominated by Willem Bonger. His views may not have been widely shared, but they were broadly respected, and partly accepted, even outside social-democratic circles (van Weringh, 1986: 147). And as Bonger's introduction to criminology for a long time remained the only Dutch-language handbook, virtually every student derived his or her criminological knowledge from Bonger. Bonger's own theory was, however, just like Clara Wichmann's, by and large forgotten, only to be rediscovered in the 1970s. In the 1930s, various initiatives were taken to establish independent institutes of criminology. In 1934, Willem Pompe opened the first institute of criminology in Utrecht, and in 1938 Jacob van

Bemmelen founded the first professional body for criminologists as a section of The Netherlands Society for Mental Health. The 'criminology section' mainly consisted of criminal lawyers and psychiatrists, but there were also psychologists, sociologists and probation officers. With Willem Bonger and Nico Muller among the board members, and a younger generation, such as Jacob van Bemmelen as president and Willem Pompe and the Groningen advocate of integrated penal science Maarten Vrij among the keynote speakers, the first national criminological conference of 1938 marked the transition towards the development of criminology as an autonomous academic discipline. After the war, separate chairs in criminology were established at various universities, and by the end of the 1950s the Dutch journal of criminology (*Tijdschrift voor Criminologie*) was founded on the initiative of Herman Bianchi, to be followed slightly later by an independent criminological association (SICCO).

Utrecht criminologist Ger Kempe explains the rapid development of criminology in the post-war era by the fact that many progressive lawyers had become sadder and wiser men after the war, and their belief in the *rechtsstaat*, as a cognisable moral order, had been shattered by the fact that it had not afforded much protection against totalitarian abuses. From now on, it was acknowledged that the *rechtsstaat* was also a human construct, and that the 'bloodless picking of doctrinal jurists' is a socially rather useless activity. Psychology and the social sciences could offer more impetus for penal reform. Criminology and criminal law were seen as distinct disciplines which can, however, not be separated (Kempe, 1968b). The ethical critique of the Modern School now became particularly apparent. According to Kempe (1967: 299), the Modern School had considerable 'ethical disqualifications' because of its rigorous instrumentalism, as well its introduction of the positivist objectification of the delinquent human being as a species from a stigmatising offender-typology, and particularly because it wrote off a group of people as 'incorrigible'. These criminologists from shortly after the Second World War also showed their irritation with the petty-bourgeois worldview embedded in von Liszt's ideas. Ger Kempe (1968a) cynically describes the groups of parasites von Liszt proposes to incapacitate as *Untermenschen* (sub-human beings) who obviously need to be excluded from society. Leiden criminologist Willem Nagel (1981: 213) argues that 'one unfortunately has to say that the extraordinary authoritarian penal science, which became dominant in Germany approximately one decade after von Liszt's death, should be attributed to his school.' With the ultimate consequence of the lack of normative principles in the project of the Modern School, we touch upon the limits of instrumentalism.

Integrated penal sciences in Leiden

At the Leiden Institute of Criminology Jacob van Bemmelen, and later Willem Nagel, took modern ideas about criminal justice a step further. Willem Nagel suggested the need to study crime in its empirical social context. Reciprocity between the development of criminality and penal policy formed the central pragmatic focus of these Leiden scholars. Van Bemmelen (1935: 2) drew attention to the catastrophic consequences of long-term unemployment on the level of crime: 'will we ever be able to see that every crisis will result in rising crime and that it is pointless to respond in a solely punitive way?' After the war, van Bemmelen held, contrary to many of his contemporaries, no high expectations of penal reform. His vision was to do less harm, rather than more good. Since punishment, in whatever shape, is after all an evil, we should economise in the use of this necessary evil.

Van Bemmelen was an important advocate of integrated penal science, and his studies covered both the legal and criminological fields. Besides some essayistic attempts, and an observation of the consequences of psychological research on the legal concept of guilt (1955), van Bemmelen separated the two disciplines. According to van Bemmelen, the relation between criminal law and criminology resembled the average marriage: based more on good intentions than on passionate love. Van Bemmelen argued that criminologists should not try to question the legitimacy of criminal law (by proposing to replace it with therapeutic models) and, conversely, that criminal lawyers should take the empirical nature of crime into consideration, even when this leads to incongruences in their theories.

Van Bemmelen also wrote a second Dutch-language introduction to criminology, which appeared in the war-year of 1942. The preface to the second edition of 1948 starts with a description of the lessons which have to be learned from the experience of the Holocaust and the Occupation, in which van Bemmelen notably leans on Paul Reiwald and on the value of classical legal principles. But, even in this post-war edition, all criminological theories are just summed up without any commentary: even those on supposedly typically 'Jewish' crimes such as fraud, and explicit Nazi ideologies such as Stumpfl's offender typology or Exner's criminal biology. His assistant of those days, Willem Nagel, argues that van Bemmelen had never defended any of these (before the war widely acclaimed) German theories and later explicitly contested them. Yet it remains a bit strange that van Bemmelen

> regularly quoted German scholars as if it was business as usual – which it probably was according to him. What would suddenly be so wrong about Franz Exner and all those others who one knew from writings and conferences of the times before Hitler, and who one had known as respectable and scholarly scientists? That is indeed the question! (van Weringh, 1986: 152–3)

Jacquelien de Savornin Lohman (1975) attributes the post-war penal humanisations in The Netherlands also to Marc Ancel. We saw in Chapter 3 that Ancel added a practical-ethical dimension to the idea of social defence which was lacking in its pre-war variety. The direct influence of his *Défense sociale nouvelle* on Dutch post-war penal scholars is, however, equivocal. On the one hand, many penal scientists were attracted by its humanist elaborations to the Modern School, but, on the other hand, only two Dutch scholars, Jacob van Bemmelen and Willem Nagel, actually joined the *Société Internationale*. The prominence of 'confused writings of certain dubious

Italians' (Gramatica) aroused suspicion about the ethical standard of this new movement and led many others to stick to, sometimes religious-inspired, more deterministic visions of crime causation. Since Ancel's writings have been characterised as 'one of the few clear' ones, which 'deserve our greatest interest', it is not surprising that the ideas of the *Défense sociale nouvelle* received a more prominent place on the agenda once Ancel became their spokesman (Nagel, 1956: 27).

The Utrecht School

For the Utrecht School, closely connected with the names of jurist Willem Pompe, psychiatrist Pieter Baan and criminologist Ger Kempe, the creation of a meaningful encounter with offenders is the central purpose of the penal process. With an ethical humanism, the Utrecht School tried to understand the deviant other, and his or her motives, as a fellow human being. The Utrecht 'encounter model' required a more fundamental dialogue between offender and magistrate than was possible within the prevailing penal process. Psychiatry and criminology, in particular, were thought to provide the necessary individual and social knowledge. As the lawyer of the school, Willem Pompe (1957) stressed that legal concepts such as accountability and responsibility were the limits that no penal intervention should exceed. According to Pompe, the general level of trust in fellow human beings and in society at large is in inverse relationship to the depth of penal intervention – low trust leads to a highly punitive society and vice versa. The humanisation of criminal law is needed for the restoration of its lawful character. This element, which was perverted by the Nazis, consists primarily of the re-establishment of trust (Pompe, 1963).

The Utrecht School argued strongly against any idea of general prevention and social defence. This implies an instrumentalist vision that does not take the person of the offender into consideration, and thus violates human dignity. For this reason, Utrecht scholars also had their reservations about the new social defence movement. Particularly for Pompe, the retribution of guilt is both the core and the limit of punishment. Retribution is in this view established when the judge metes out the penalty. Its theoretical conceptualisation is placed in the context of existentialist visions of guilt. Morally loaded concepts such as exoneration of blame, forgiveness or penitence are adopted to stress the fact that rehabilitation is the necessary counterpart of retribution after the offender has been sentenced. The need for retribution is over as soon as someone has dealt with his guilt. Punishment serves to bring someone back to himself, and thereby to the community (Pompe, 1954).

The Utrecht School should not be understood as a school in a theoretical sense. It is better described as a working group of lawyers, psychiatrists and criminologists, originating in a personal friendship between Willem Pompe and Pieter Baan. It emerged in 1948, had its heyday around 1958 and ended around 1963. This working group was labelled a school by the Frenchman Jacques Léauté (1959), for whom the group embodied a new modern anthropological perspective. Perhaps Ger Kempe comes closest to such a portrayal, but, as such, the idea of one uniting theory is too large a claim. The Utrecht School placed a practical, critical accent on the administration of justice and, over the years, became strongly penologically oriented.

The optimistic Utrecht philosophy of freedom and responsibility, with its deep respect for human dignity, can only be understood as a reaction to the experience of war and the preceding period of crisis. With the prospect of renewal, mankind could be liberated from its galling bonds in order to be able to create its own design of life (van Weringh, 1986: 165). The offender-centred approach of the school was inspired by phenomenology, but notably also by existentialists such as Simone de Beauvoir and Jean-Paul Sartre, as well as by actual penal developments before, during and after the war. The philosophical sources of inspiration of the Utrecht School were most explicitly expressed in Ger Kempe's inaugural address of 1950 and in an influential article on an existential examination of criminology.

> In the classical vision the offender is no concrete reality; for Lombroso he is only a criminal species; in sociological approaches he is only a member of the community; and seen in the light of the newest developments, the offender is an existential reality in his being human. His act is a specific way of giving shape to this humanity. (Kempe, 1952: 178)

Kempe does not only discard Lombroso's ideas as sub-human, but accuses the Modern School in general of a lack of vision of mankind and of society.

Another scholar of the Utrecht School, Rijk Rijksen, was an important advocate of sociological criminology. In his inaugural address of 1955, Rijksen spoke of an 'impasse' in this respect. This should also be seen in the context of the dominant effect psychiatric and psychological studies had on Dutch criminology. In 1958, Rijksen published a book of interviews with prisoners that were so critical of the role of the police, judiciary and the prison system that the Ministry of Justice, which had commissioned the inquiry, prevented its general publication. It was first 'confidentially circulated' among people for whom it held a 'professional interest'. In an accompanying letter of January 1959, Kempe and Rijksen agreed with the Minister that an initial 'professional judging' of the book was desirable in order to prepare for eventual necessary changes in penal policy. When the book was made public, it was chastised in the media for 'unscientifically rousing public sentiment'. Only Herman Bianchi's review (in *Trouw*, 7 November 1959) was whole-heartedly in agreement with the book, though Bianchi raised no objections to its initial banishment from the public domain and praised the Ministry of Justice for its open-mindedness in the face of criticism by initiating the project of Rijksen. David Downes (1988a: 84–5) also signals the strong influence of this book, generally referred to as 'the green book' (after the colour of its cover) on the judiciary. He quotes a Dutch judge who said in the 1980s:

> One of the books that made a great impression on me was the 'green book' of professor Rijksen . . . For most people, the only time that really counts are the first weeks, the first months in prison, and the first time they are in prison, and every

other time does not make any difference. So why should we do it when it costs so much to put them in prison?

In an (undated) letter accompanying the public edition of the green book, Rijksen argued that 'at present, the Minister of Justice is of the opinion that it is meaningful to enrich the public debate on penal problems with a voice that has not been heard yet: that of prisoners.' Fijnaut (1986a: 30, 55) argues that the initial censorship of the green book may have been at the root of the disturbed relations between the universities and the Ministry which would become manifest in the 1970s.

Towards critical criminology

Ger Kempe

Ger Kempe has always stressed that he is not a lawyer – a demarcation line within the Utrecht School as well as a means of opposing the general idea of 1950s Dutch academia that criminologists were actually 'dressed up' lawyers. Though his major empirical work, his dissertation on the relation between crime and religion in a Weberian sociological tradition, dates back to 1937, Kempe's career really gained momentum after the Second World War. His work was also strongly marked by this war: Kempe had been active in the Resistance until his imprisonment by the Nazis in 1944. In his inaugural address, *Schuldig zijn* (Being guilty) of 1950, in which nearly everything that has driven him in his later social and academic work can be found, he expressed his gratitude to the governor of the prison in which he had been incarcerated during the German occupation for his personal mitigating influence on the regime and the conditions under Nazi rule. In the 1950s, Kempe engaged in probation work and became a member of the Fick Committee (Janse de Jonge, 1991: 91–6).

Taking his war experiences explicitly on board, Kempe (1947: 23) outlines the criminologist's dilemma in respect of the most adequate definition of crime.

> The criminologist is forced to put some limits to the subject matter of criminology. If he wants to include all social interaction and inhuman behaviour in his study, he inevitably loses contact with reality and he will not be able to move beyond general abstractions about 'the anti-social' which are of no use to anybody. On the other hand, there are criminologists who think they can pass by notions of public morality and only act as an accountant, and nothing more.

From 1951, Kempe re-edited Bonger's introduction to criminology, aiming to keep the book as much as possible in line with Bonger's thought, and confining himself to updating it. Kempe indicated where research has really disproved Bonger's deterministic theory and where Bonger would have been likely to have insisted on his determinism. In his own work, Kempe argued against determinism because, in practice, deterministic ideas have led to the exclusion of quite specific groups from society and will inevitably continue to do so. For comparable reasons, Kempe (1952) also argued against the growing influence of the Chicago School. In 1967, Kempe stated that his thought had developed too far in a different direction from Bonger's and he published an introductory textbook of his own.

In his later writings, Kempe increasingly doubts to what extent the criminal justice system can really be influenced by social sciences – and by probation. He becomes quite critical of those psychiatrists (implicitly referring to his colleague Pieter Baan) who think in their ecstatic paternalism that they should actively take part in legal considerations from a place behind the table of the judiciary. This desire is at odds with the ethics of the medical profession (Kempe, 1963). The Utrecht School has done its job, but should not be continued. Criticising its paternalistic and inquisitorial character, Kempe now declares the penal process beyond reform because it is 'structurally determined by a discriminatory character'. Under the influence of the media, stereotypes about the criminal as a sub-human being are continually reproduced. These stereotypes reinforce the selectivity of the criminal justice system and structurally drive deprived groups in society into the arms of the law. In 1975, Kempe praised, for the first time, Clara Wichmann for her pioneering role in the study of class justice as well as for her radical rejection of punitive responses. According to Kempe (1975: 19), dispute settlement should be the touchstone of justice. In 1976, he proposed abandoning the idea of a policy-oriented penal science. In an analysis of the moral entrepreneurs behind the Dutch vice laws of 1911, he concludes that the major task of the criminologist lies in challenging the political and professional power relations which label social problems (or non-problems) as penal problems. Willem Nagel (1981: 215) argues: 'In 1957, his [Kempe's] articles were entitled "probation in a changing society", at the end [mid-1970s] we should better characterise them as "changing visions of society".' From an optimist, Kempe became a cultural pessimist.

Kempe did not elaborate his later ideas, but his torch was to some extent carried on by Herman Bianchi. Bianchi (1974b) always argued that the Utrecht School gave an important impetus to the politics of decarceration. However, from the way in which the Utrecht scholars dealt with the initial censorship of the green book, and the absence of a clear vision of society, Bianchi also concludes, that the Utrecht School was too law-abiding and did not have any affinity with the politics of radical criminology. Willem Nagel (1981: 225) has made a similar observation. The school's rather uncritical attitude towards the democratic *rechtsstaat* is generally explained by the post-war context in which the Utrecht School emerged. Bianchi is accused of unfair moralism and anachronistic argumentation because he judges ideas which emerged just after liberation from completely arbitrary Nazi rule by the standards of the 1970s (Hoefnagels, 1975; Moedikdo, 1976).

Willem Nagel

For Willem Nagel, the key problem of the rule of law is embedded in the dialectics of freedom: how much freedom are we willing to give up in order to empower the state and enable it to protect us against encroachments on civil liberties by crime? The level of the state's tolerance should equal that of the citizens. In order to establish this balance, judges should actually personally experience what deprivation of liberty really means, and offenders must get a fair chance to reintegrate into society (Nagel, 1975). Nagel also warns against the tendency for criminal law, despite its rhetorical foundation in the interests of the citizens, to develop in a high-handed and authoritarian fashion.

Nagel differentiates between legal and sociological definitions of crime and suggests the relativity and the selectivity of the penal rationale. For Nagel, the fact that critical criminologists also use the pejorative adjective 'criminal' as a label for awful human behaviour that is not listed in the criminal code is not a problem, but rather a fact that lawyers should take into consideration. The criminal justice system does not apparently deal with, or even refuses to act against, social wrongs that are really serious 'crimes' in the sociological sense – such as crimes committed by the military in totalitarian regimes (Nagel, 1976). Nagel adopts, like Kempe, a normative concept of crime beyond the definitions of criminal law. The ontological kernel of crime is embodied in the tendency to overcome weaker subjects. Nagel argues that evil is inside all of us: 'in every person lives a squirt, an old Adam, a little bastard. That is the fascist in the bud' (Nagel, 1962: 300). At this point, Nagel's concept of crime comes close to what Johan Galtung (1977) calls 'structural violence'. With this term, Galtung refers to socially accepted, or even applauded, behaviour that in a subtle way puts other people down or harms them. According to Nagel (1975: 176), law enforcement under a democratic rule of law can be directed to the reintegration of the offender into the community, but in military regimes or police states this ideal cannot be pursued. Here one can only hope for revolution. Nagel (1975: 176) argues that 'the specific sociopolitical conditions of a country are the major factors which determine what kind of criminology is the most significant.' Under a totalitarian regime there is hardly any meaningful criminology possible and, in such situations, a criminologist has really only two options: leave the profession or leave the country.

According to Antonie Peters (1983b), Nagel should also be considered as a critical criminologist *avant la lettre* because he was one of the first to apply sociological insights not only to crime, but indeed to law enforcement itself. Cyrille Fijnaut (1986b: 81) argues that Nagel, in his dissertation of 1949 on the development of crime in the town of Oss, in which he combines person-oriented aetiological material with social-ethnographical analyses and a sociological study of the selectivity of law enforcement, comes close to an empirical elaboration of Clara Wichmann's socialist visions of penality. In 1956, Nagel characterised Clara Wichmann as 'the champion of the Modern School', but also put a question mark over the notion that radical ideas like hers, which seem so humane, will actually have a humanising effect once they are implemented. Wichmann's subjectivist position may challenge hegemonic morality, and consequently criminal law, but Nagel doubts whether it is in a more general sense wise to distance oneself from the existence of a sharp line between good and evil. In this respect, Nagel points to 'those too subjectivist extremists in the Modern School', who have led this generally 'promising orientation into a dehumanising direction'. With their determinism, these modern scholars have 'created a completely unfree, morally unaccountable offender, which is no longer human. Taking responsibility for one's acts is a key characteristic of being human. A human being without guilt is indeed sub-human' (Nagel, 1956: 24–5).

Nagel was an important advocate of empirical sociological criminology. Once this became established, and its studies more or less implemented in penal policy, Nagel was also the first to argue that sociological input should not degenerate into a careful counting of facts like the number of children in criminal families, the number of months the father has been unemployed and so on. Nagel (1965: 230) rejected a 'scientistic A causes B criminology' in which insights and methods from the natural sciences are applied to social questions. At the same time, Nagel argued, however, that 'it is certainly possible to be impressed by frequently coinciding social factors and developments in crime, or to take apparently fatal environmental conditions into account, without adopting a classical scientistic criminology.' On various occasions Nagel expressed his irritation with the fact that post-war criminological conferences by and large dealt with the same, rather trivial, issues as before the war, and by the fact that the same people dominated the scene, including, among them, the Germans – as if nothing had happened in the meantime which should have led criminologists to change the whole scope of their discipline. For Nagel (1974), the conflict character of criminal law had become the central theme.

Like Kempe, Nagel too began to doubt the policy input that criminology could actually have, and his personal development also came close to cultural pessimism. Nagel gradually abandoned the idea of integrated penal science because the criminological and legal perspectives are fundamentally different. He urged criminologists to free themselves from the law schools because criminology needs a closer connection with sociology and social psychology if it is to make any methodological progress. 'There are many juridical disputes which do not really impress the criminologist at all, whereas there are areas in sociology and psychology where the lawyer . . . cannot remain an outsider . . . the criminologist's vision of penalised deviance should be a completely different one from that of lawyers' (Nagel 1976: 8–9). With an approach to crime as structural violence and law enforcement as social conflict, Nagel (1976: 8–9) re-names criminology 'micro-polemology'. By pointing to the political dimensions of crime, contesting the idea that criminology should confine itself to the study of acts that are made punishable by law, and his resistance to a 'scientistic' aetiological criminology, Nagel made the patchwork of critical criminology visible.

This chapter is based on the question of why critical criminology in The Netherlands developed in such a different way from the way it did in Britain. With a less sharply polarised political climate, which is more susceptible to social change, Dutch critical criminologists could continue on a path already marked out by Bonger, Wichmann, Kempe and Nagel. We will see, in the next chapter, how British, German, Italian and other critics had to 'fight their way in' to a predominantly administrative criminological or legal establishment.

Notes

1 The original French book *Criminalité et conditions économique* was published in 1905. It originated in a contest initiated by the University of Amsterdam in 1900: present a systematic and critical analysis of the literature on the relationship between crime and economic conditions. The contest was not won by Bonger's work, but by Joseph van Kan's book *Les causes économiques de la criminalité*, published in 1903.

2 Co-founders were Kees Boeke, J. Brommert, Bart de Ligt, H.E. Kaspers, J.W. Kruyt, Jo Meijer, Lode van Mierop and Felix Ortt. Amsterdam professor of criminal anthropology and novelist Arnold Aletrino (1858–1916), who was also active in libertarian left circles, and who was both a Lombrosian and a penal abolitionist, died too soon to participate in this movement. It would have been interesting to see whether people with comparable political ideas but contrasting scientific visions could have cooperated constructively.

3 After 1870, capital punishment remained constitutionally possible under extraordinary and military legislation. When Meertens and Van Bemmelen's action committee was finally granted an audience by Queen Wilhelmina to plead for a more sensitive application of the Royal pardon, she listened but did not say a word and insisted on countersigning executions. The executions came to an end in 1948 when Wilhelmina's daughter Juliana came to the throne. It was in 1984 only that the death penalty became constitutionally impossible under all circumstances (art.114 Grw).

4 There are only few accounts of VOMS' further meetings (manifesto in *Tijdschrift voor Strafrecht*, vol. 58 (1949), p. 324; Bianchi, 1951; Rogier, 1979; Franke, 1990: 633). Further information is derived from personal communications with Herman Bianchi, who was a close friend of Meertens.

5

The Patchwork of European Critical Criminology

'The sixties', the mythical era of social protest in which critical criminology has its roots, heralded 'the dawning of the Age of Aquarius', a positive spirit of love and peace, flower power, teach-ins and sit-ins. 'Paris 68', the ideal-type of European student revolts, announced the more militant era of the 1970s, characterised by a politics of opposition, with students' and other left-wing movements who wanted to enforce a new democratic appeal in society. Alvin Gouldner (1970) saw student activism and the new social movements as having a great potential for both a fundamental change in the nature of sociology and, indeed, as a spearhead of 'the revolution'. A more law-abiding part of society feared that their countries would become ungovernable and, indeed, face a possible revolution. Both left and the right seemed to agree on one thing: 'the times they are a'changing.'

By the end of the 1960s, platforms of critical criminology had emerged in some European countries, but in others empirical criminology as such was still in its infancy. The extent to which social critique in academia emerges has to do with the level of welfare and the actual political constellation in a particular country. The dictatorships of Salazar and Caetano in Portugal or of the Greek colonels simply did not offer much common ground for any 'Aquarius' spirit. Consequently, the phase of a 'euphoric left' did not affect these countries. The following 'angry left' implied both a liberation from and a reaction to dictatorship. In Portugal, the transition to democracy began after the Carnation Revolution of 1974, which was initiated by the movement of the armed forces of the conservative general de Spinola. From that time on, left-wing forces could operate in public. After some right-wing counter-pressure from de Spinola's side, which could not accept that the days of the colonial Portugese empire were over, this has resulted in a series of left-wing governments. In Greece, the bloody crushing of student demonstrations in Athens in 1973 (and the international outrage against this massacre with which the junta showed its true face) announced the final collapse of the military regime one year later.

In Portugal, critical 'criminological' studies, most obviously of state violence, emerged by the end of the 1970s. The first critical scholar was Boaventura de Sousa Santos, whose studies on popular justice as an embodiment of a duality of state power have become well known internationally. Slightly later, studies on democracy, socialism and law enforcement were undertaken by Manuel da Costa Andrade, Teresa Pizarro Beleza and Jorge Figueredo Dias (Beleza, 1987). Though criminological research oriented towards empirical sociology is hardly carried out at Portugese universities, all the typical critical issues, like the repressive sides of law and order, crimes of the powerful, class, and, more recently, gender and migration politics, are discussed in relation to criminal law. This critical strand in law schools is typical of countries where criminology has not really developed as a social science.

In Greece, a critical movement among criminologists only emerged in 1990. The start was given by the joint text of Maria Archimandritou, Charalambos Dimopoulos, Nikos Koulouris, Ioannis Panousis, Ioannis Tzortzis, Sophie Vidali and others in the newspaper *Epochè* of 23 December 1990 against the brutal conditions in Greek prisons after a series of serious disorders in that year. They advocated social interventions based on criminological research (Bokos et al., 1992). Leaving aside some articles or essays (some of them in English) on radical criminology, Maria Archimandritou's books on alternatives to prison of 1994, and on the evolution of the labelling approach in critical criminology, system theory and abolitionism of 1996, are pioneering studies in the Greek language.

These two examples prove how important it is to include some basic historical facts if we are to say something sensible about academic developments. It is simply not the same to be radical in stable social democracies like Scandinavia or The Netherlands, in more polarised welfare states like Britain or Germany, or indeed under military regimes in Portugal or Greece. The personal consequences are also fundamentally different.

The British Empire of critical criminology

Without doubt, the British debates represent the richest tradition in European critical criminology. Since these have already been covered in many excellent surveys, it will be hard to say anything new about them. This section therefore serves to indicate some main lines of development and to see how the British case relates to the European context. For this reason, some specific factors as to why critical criminology was actually born in Britain have to be mentioned first.

First, David Downes (1988b: 45) points to the overall rapidly growing number of criminologists in Britain. Before 1968, criminology was a term associated with orthodoxy in which only a few dozen people were interested. When criminology became intellectually more challenging, when it was liberated from its utilitarian, crime-fighting ethos and broadened to a study of deviance and disorder in social terms, a wider group of sociologists began to show interest. Secondly, there was by that time also an empirical crisis in British mainstream criminology, located in 'the amateur, muddling-along ethos of British life combined with the Fabian type of pragmatism' (Cohen, 1981: 70). In most continental European countries there was no such thing as administrative criminology. Thirdly, material resources for radical social critics to actually establish a competing paradigm were to some degree available in British social science departments. This was not the case in many universities on the European continent, where criminology was based in law schools, which certainly in those days were ruled more by orthodoxy than were faculties of social sciences. Fourthly, the British Labour Party to some extent adopted the new left, whereas in most continental countries the orthodox left prevailed. In global terms, the new left took a more libertarian stance towards organisational structures and action programmes than the orthodox left, and expected greater impulses for change from various new social movements than from traditional political parties and labour organisations. Finally, the British culture of pragmatism also facilitated a criminology in which political commitment to social practice could be integrated. On the continent such orientations were, under the classical positivist sway, widely discarded as 'unscientific'. The polarised political situation of Labour and Tory was, in addition, a more constitutive element for a conflict model in criminology than the political constellation of many continental European countries, marked by coalition politics with an omnipotent Christian Democrat party nearly always in the middle.

While critical criminology may have been established in the aftermath of the 1960s, some of its intellectual and conceptual roots stem from times well before that era. These are first of all the European social theories of Louis Althusser, Antonio Gramsci, Jürgen Habermas and Karl Marx. The labelling approach of North American scholars such as Howard Becker (whose classic essay on *Becoming a Marijuana User* dates back to 1953), Ed Lemert and Erving Goffman also had a tremendous influence on critical criminology. The labelling perspective turned around the very scope of criminology from a focus on the offender and the offence to one on the controllers and the social reactions to crime. It also problematised the legal definition of crime by revealing the interests that direct the labelling process.

Various notions from David Matza's sub-cultural approach, and Richard Cloward and Lloyd Ohlin's 'strain theory', have also had a significant effect on critical criminology. Because these theories were, however, generally associated with North American functionalism they did not fit very well to a reflexive European perspective. Therefore, British scholars read them in the context of conflict theory, as developed in the late 1950s in Europe by Ralf Dahrendorf and in the early 1970s in the United States by Richard Quinney and Bill Chambliss. Steven Box proposes, in *Deviance, Reality and Society* of 1971, to start from a conflict perspective and to elaborate this with empirical data. The leading doctrine in sociology that one should work the other way around (from the empirical reality to theory) is, according to Box (1971), in reality not upheld or one never actually reaches theory formation. Implicit visions of society are obscured. When these sub-cultural and strain perspectives were combined with neo-Marxist, conflict and structuralist theories, in particular, they played an important role in British critical criminology. In this tradition, Stuart Hall and Tony Jefferson's *Resistance through Rituals* from 1975, and notably their (and others') *Policing the Crisis* (1978), form the intellectual *tour de force* which exemplifies 'all the strengths and weaknesses of Marxist sociology' (Downes and Rock, 1988: 263). It offers 'a fascinating spectacle' of the 'epistemological dilution of structuralist Marxism through its confrontation with the nasty business of empirical reality' (Sumner, 1981: 277–8). Hall analyses how moral panics are constructed, how they are used to exclude certain groups from society and to translate problems resulting from economic crises into penal problems, and how groups resist their subordinated position.

Deviancy theory primarily emerged from a critique of the labelling approach. Labelling scholars were accused of a liberal attitude which lacked an understanding of power structures and of the most important actor in the process of definition: the state. On this critique, known as the Becker–Gouldner controversy, Taylor et al. (1973: 139–71) base their 'fully social theory of deviance'. Labelling scholars are said to overemphasise social reactions to deviance and to neglect causes and motivations. Furthermore, it is seen to be morally relativistic and liberal in its social commitments. This is a really classic refrain in criminology: Tarde accused Durkheim of moral relativism, German classical lawyers did the same with von Liszt, and in the 1980s 'realists' used the same label for so-called 'left idealist' criminologists. Labelling theory's founding father Howard Becker (1967) is, however, quite explicit about his commitments when he argues that sociology should be an academic support for the underdog, who he defines as the victim of power. With hindsight, it is hard to understand why deviancy theorists polarised so strongly with labelling scholars. Stan Cohen (1988: 242) has rightly described critical criminology as the 'tougher successor of labelling theory'.

Though it still seems a justified criticism that the labelling approach explains very little about the causes, or indeed the creation, of primary deviance, the accusation that labelling scholars ignored 'the power question' now looks a bit far fetched. In an interactionist perspective, social dynamics are analysed at a meso- and micro-social level, whereas the analytical value of Marxist and structuralist theory lies more at a macro-sociological level. They offer different tools meant for different analyses of the empirical reality, which can well be attuned at a meta-level. Defining 'crime' as behaviour that is labelled as such does not mean one would not take crime seriously as a social problem. Crime is a legal definition of certain acts. Some of these are dangerous or annoying and some not really; and, vice versa, not all harmful events are criminalised, especially not those of more powerful groups in society. For some critical criminologists, such crimes of the powerful do not only include forms of white-collar crime, but also military interventions, the creation of unsafe working conditions or the exploitation of people in order to maximise profits. In this respect, a logical step to match the transition from the labelling approach to deviancy theory is a shift in research attention from stigmatisation to criminalisation. The question now becomes why certain behaviours are criminalised and others are not.

Stan Cohen's *Folk Devils and Moral Panics* (1972) marks a transition from the labelling approach towards deviancy theory, by demonstrating how the

media create 'moral panics' and how certain juvenile sub-cultures are labelled
as enemies of public morality. Jock Young's study, *The Drugtakers* (1970),
which also has the amplification of deviance through the media, and by the
police, as its central theme, is rooted in a tradition which marks the start of
the National Deviancy Conference in the late 1960s. Young criminologists
engaged in research which had the specific combination of class and youth as
a key focus. Ian Taylor wrote in 1968 from a specific class position on football
hooliganism, Stuart Hall in 1970 on hippies, Phil Cohen and Geoff Pearson
on youth cultures in general, Paul Walton in 1971 on the student movement
and Paul Willes in 1972 on motorbike sub-cultures (Taylor, 1973).

'The birth of radical criminology in this country in an organisational form
was the National Deviancy Conference (NDC), formed in July 1968 as a
breakaway from the Third National Conference of Teaching and Research on
Criminology at the University of Cambridge', and, indeed, from 'the intellectual ghetto of positivism' (Young, 1988: 161). 'Official criminology was
regarded with attitudes ranging from ideological condemnation to a certain
measure of boredom'; in order to get away from this kind of criminology
'some sort of separate subculture had to be carved out within the sociological world. So, ostensibly for these reasons . . . seven of us met in 1968,
fittingly enough in Cambridge, in the middle of an Institute of Criminology
conference opened by the Home Secretary' (Cohen, 1981: 80). These seven
'rebels with a cause' were Kit Carson, Stan Cohen, David Downes, Mary
McIntosh, Paul Rock, Ian Taylor and Laurie Taylor. The latter organised the
first meeting of these seven people, and some friends, in November 1968 in
York. From this 'York group' emerged the NDC. Its political basis lay in the
new left's critique of the extension of the state by welfarist interventions in
society. Together with anti-psychiatric movements such as Red Rat, People
not Psychiatry and Humpty Dumpty, penal pressure group Radical
Alternatives to Prison, prisoners' movement PROP, the squatters, the London
Street Commune, and the militant social work organisation Case Con, radical criminologists became part of the British new left.

Laurie Taylor and Stan Cohen were the group's anchormen during the
first years, whose institutional centres were the universities of York and
Sheffield. The first NDC attracted 20 people, but by 1973 the NDC counted
400 members (Taylor, 1973: 210). Though the NDC existed from 1969 to
1979, the first three years were the most productive. During this period, ten
conferences were held, of which the collected papers were published in 1971
as *Images of Deviance* (edited by Stan Cohen) and in 1972 as *Politics and
Deviance* (edited by Ian Taylor and Laurie Taylor) and in 1973 as
Contemporary Social Problems in Britain (edited by Roy Bailey and Jock
Young).

Despite its prominent place on the new criminology's research agenda
(Taylor et al., 1973: 274), actual research attention for a political economy of
social reactions became increasingly marginal, and the link with interactionism became gradually more tenuous. During the 1970s, British critical
criminology was mainly an epistemological critique and a critique of the

state's law-and-order politics. Opposition to the positivist ideal of value-free science, where it concerns a politically determined subject such as deviance and social control, takes a central role in this respect. Critical scholars refused to practice criminology as an auxiliary discipline to criminal law enforcement, and saw it as their task to examine the functioning of the criminal justice system as an instrument of the state to keep power relations as they are. The prison system, in particular, was studied with regard to its role in perpetuating, if not reproducing, class relations and brutalising people. For these reasons, it is counter-effective in the fight against crime. Stan Cohen and Laurie Taylor's *Psychological Survival* of 1972 is a pivotal study in this respect, for it is the first critical empirical account of long-term imprisonment in Britain.

By the mid-1970s, a growing disparity can be observed within the NDC. Conferences were held less frequently, while individual scholars elaborated their own particular theory. A neo-Marxist criminology was established in the footprints of Taylor et al.'s (1975) compilation *Critical Criminology*. Laurie Taylor, Stan Cohen, David Downes and Paul Rock reassessed an inter-actionist approach to social control because, as the first two authors argued, there was no esoteric group left to study (Cohen and Taylor, 1975: 22). Stuart Hall's Birmingham Centre for Contemporary Cultural Studies focused on sub-cultures of imagination and resistance, in which the idea of 'giving meaning to life' no longer depends on work.

This split was deepened when a second generation of radical criminologists aligned themselves more explicitly with Gramscian observations on hegemonic structures and with neo-Marxist conflict theory. They discarded the intellectual challenge of deviancy theory as 'intellectualism' and the NDC's organisational structure as 'patriarchal'. Paul Hirst and Colin Sumner, respectively, rejected and advocated a Marxist theory of deviance. According to Hirst (1975), there is no place for such unspecified, super-structure concepts as deviancy in orthodox Marxism, whereas Sumner (1976) argues that the concept of deviancy needs to be re-worked in Marxism's basic categories. When the new right began to dominate the British political landscape, with Margaret Thatcher's electoral victory of 1979, any optimistic tone about a possible post-capitalist society was definitely gone. A grim dismay about an emerging authoritarian state, which privatised one social service after another and pushed whole categories of people (miners, working-class youth, blacks, single mothers) over the edge of the poverty line, took its place. There was a huge disparity between neo-liberal rhetoric on democracy and the materially undemocratic content of Thatcher's politics. The image one holds of state intervention in one's private life reflects a person's political role:

> the perception of the state as a benevolent provider may well be changed by the experience of intrusive investigation into the life of a social security claimant. For some the state may appear as the defender of civil liberties but such a perception may well depend on whether you are a trade unionist on a picket line, the owner of the factory being picketed, or a riot policeman responsible for 'defending public order'. (Hillyard and Percy-Smith, 1988: 14)

Many of the critical studies on criminal justice agencies of the 1980s reflect the image of a democracy in decline and state interventions of an increasingly coercive character. The police were studied as an institution which has repressed (black) counter-movements fighting against Thatcherism – in Brixton, Liverpool and elsewhere – by Paul Gilroy, Paul Gordon and Stuart Hall. Expansionist sentencing policies, an increase in long-term imprisonment, and overcrowding and inhumane prison conditions which have ultimately lead to deaths and revolts in various prisons were analysed by Joe Sim, Mike Fitzgerald, Mick Ryan and Tony Ward, and Phil Scraton and Kathryn Chadwick. These analyses were all the more poignant in the case of Northern Ireland, where a series of studies on the criminalisation and media representation of so-called 'political crime' and 'subversive activity', and on human rights violations by the so-called 'special powers' and the prison system were undertaken by Paddy Hillyard, Dermot Walsh, Bill Rolston, Mike Tomlinson and others.

Analyses of discipline and state power now dominated British critical criminology, and the 'liberal' perspective of interactionism hardly received any attention. Particularly in the hostile political climate, the second generation of British radical criminologists felt that political commitment needed to be confronted with social action. To some extent, a 'criminology from below' against the 'authoritarian state' (Scraton, 1987), which already existed about the prison system (to be elaborated in Chapter 7), was now extended to the police, the conflict in Northern Ireland and racism and sexism. Penal reform was now also analysed in terms of fighting back: reform does not only not work, it also strengthens the hegemonic structures of Thatcher's authoritarian state. The penal system was seen to be 'working for the clampdown' (Sim, 1986). While 'solidarity' with subjected groups became something of a populist mission, a heavy load of theorical reflections on Gramsci, but also on Althusser, Foucault and Habermas, often gave empirical studies a theoretical burden they could not bear. 'You could not go anymore without a dictionary', Ian Taylor would argue with respect to later NDC conferences (van den Boogaart and Seus, 1991: 66).

The second generation of British radical criminologists brings us far beyond the traditional criminological subject matter of crime and punishment. By pushing critical criminology's initial epistemological incentive to the extreme, they brought about the important analytical problem that little expertise is produced that can be grounded in concrete empirical research. Deviance had become an ideology, argues Colin Sumner (1994). The aim to reveal 'the real' problems of society and 'the real motives of the state' gained a pretentious, if not dilettante tone. It suggested a kind of conspiracy theory, in which evil men, fanned by one very evil woman, designed shrewd and cynical policies. This really gave too much credit to the new right, which seemed to be mainly led by managerial considerations such as efficiency. Stuart Hall (1988) shifted the focus from an authoritarian politics of law and order to the 'authoritarian populism' in society that this politics appeals to. This analysis, which seems more challenging than a focus on the state as such, will be elaborated in Chapter 8, when the development of law-and-order politics during the 1980s and 1990s will be examined at a European level.

With a conference with the revealing title Permissiveness and Control: the Fate of the Sixties Legislation in 1977, the NDC announced its obituary. Its actual swan-song followed in 1979 when the NDC organised, together with the Conference of Socialist Economists, a conference on Capitalism and the Rule of Law. By the 1980s, when critical criminologists were taking largely defensive positions, the project's restructuring nucleus had actually been emptied of its meaning. A consensus on the negative could well have facilitated neo-conservative sentiments because it lacked an *élan* about what 'should be'. This 'ideological negativism' seems a specifically British element in the crisis of critical criminology.

Downes and Rock's compilation, *Deviant Interpretations* (1979) can be seen as an interactionist answer to this increasingly straightforward neo-Marxist critical criminology. Italian critical criminologist Dario Melossi (1985: 197) argued that interactionism's micro-sociological and Marxism's macro-sociological approach were still in need of conjunction if the crisis in critical criminology was to be overcome: 'it is . . . around this issue that we can try to understand whether critical criminology has actually been able to go beyond labelling theory.' In Britain, this split cannot be mended any more, but on the European continent various attempts to do so have been made.

Ian Taylor and Jock Young's perspectives gradually changed from working-class criminology to left realism. Jock Young (1975, 1979), in particular, subsequently forcefully rejected the 'relativistic romanticism' of the NDC and its 'crass inversion' of utilitarianism in which crime was treated as if it were an alternative way of spending one's leisure time. The term 'deviancy' was dropped, and the leading idea now is that all crime has to be 'taken seriously', as it tends to hit the most vulnerable parts of society. In Young's (1988: 174) realist version of the crisis of critical criminology, the radical position has become untenable because of its underplaying of the problem of crime and its creation of taboos about police intervention, as well as its unwillingness to deal with positivism, aetiology, statistics and reform. As left realism heralds a reassessment of critical criminology it will be dealt with in more detail in Chapter 9.

British critical criminology received an important new impulse in 1976 when Carol Smart's *Women, Crime and Criminology* appeared. Next to Smart, Frances Heidensohn, who began her work on gender and deviance back in 1968 and has worked on these themes ever since, and Mary McIntosh, who addressed the issue of women and the state within the NDC, have been trendsetters of a feminist critique of criminology. Feminism played a key role in critical criminology in the 1980s. The number of feminist studies which then appeared in British critical criminology is really too vast to deal with here. We can only mention some key themes: Jill Box-Grainger published widely on rapists; Maureen Cain on epistemology; Pat Carlen on female offenders and prisoners; Sue Edwards on women on trial; Loraine

Gelsthorpe on sexism; Sandra Harding on feminist theory; Jeanne Gregory
on gender and class; Sue Lees on rape trials; Jayne Mooney on domestic violence; Alison Morris on women and criminal justice; Kate Painter on feelings
of unsafety; Marcia Rice on black women; and Sandra Walklate on victimology. Since feminism played its innovative role in respect of both the
theoretical basis of critical criminology (on the conceptualisation of power
and domination) and its empirical elaboration (victimology), it will be taken
up again in Chapter 10. Following Carol Smart (1990), we will deal in particular with its visions of law.

The European Group for the Study of Deviance and Social Control

In 1973 the European Group for the Study of Deviance and Social Control
broadened the scope and audience of the NDC to the European continent.
The group wished to be an impetus to overcome the inertia produced by sub-
group, class, ethnic, sexual and national boundaries. The European Group
contributed to the fact that themes like feminism, crimes of the powerful, the
conflict character of criminal law, the role of prisoners' and patients' movements in penal and forensic psychiatric reform, and violence were introduced
into European criminology. Conversely, many developments in continental
critical criminology were made known to an international audience through
the European Group. Stan Cohen (1981: 87) characterised the group as 'the
most notable institutional achievement' of critical criminology and 'an influential force in bringing together like-minded sociologists and activists in
Western Europe'. The European Group was a pioneer in the internationalisation of critical criminology.

In 1970, Stan Cohen, the Italian Mario Simondi and the German Karl
Schumann shared an office in the renowned critical school of criminology in
Berkeley, California. They did not know each other previously. In their home
countries, all three had their own experiences with the establishment of an
alternative criminology. Though the objects against which it needed to be pos-
tulated were different, a dissatisfaction with the dominant law-and-order
interests which tend to determine the criminological agenda and a positive
commitment to social justice were common factors. It is paradoxical that
Europeans had to go to the United States to get together, but Europe's specific history and its large cultural and linguistic diversity prevented such a
concerted action growing on the continent itself.

Back in Europe, the three men met in Florence, and wrote, together with
Laurie Taylor and the Italian Margherita Ciacci, a preliminary draft of a
manifesto to be circulated among critically minded colleagues all over
Europe. The purpose was to organise a first Europe-wide conference on critical criminology. Among the invited speakers were the Dutchman Herman
Bianchi, the Norwegians Thomas Mathiesen and Tove Stang Dahl, representatives of various patients' and prisoners' movements, radical and social
lawyers, and, above all, the German and English young interactionist and

neo-Marxist criminologists and their Italian counterparts, as well as the important anti-psychiatric group around Franco Basaglia. In 1973, a conference was organised in the Italian town of Impruneta (close to Florence) under the theme of 'Deviance and Control in Europe: Scope and Prospects for a Radical Criminology'. The establishment of the European Group became a fact. Herman Bianchi (1974c; 1980: 302–7) characterised this new criminology as a 'blue jeans criminology' which had been transferred 'from York to Florence'. Bianchi gives accounts of 'sleeping-bag and sit-in conferences', which were a 'true relief' in comparison with the conferences of the International Society of Criminology, with their frumpy ladies' programmes and posh conference suites, where criminologists discussed, in Mussolini's Italy, problems of the level of bicycle theft, and later, in Franco's Spain, in close harmony with Latin American participants in fine military uniforms, virtually the same things. The aim of the European Group was to free criminology from this suspect ideology and to reform it into a critical discourse on state-organised social control.

The group's commitment became particularly manifest when, just prior to the first conference, Pinochet's military coup against the democratic socialist Chilean government of Salvador Allende took place. The conference participants joined the demonstration in Florence against this act of terror and expressed their solidarity with the Chilean workers' resistance. The spontaneous decision of the participants was more than a joint action; it embodied an outspoken unanimity about the necessity of political commitment on the criminological subject matter (Humphries, 1974; Bianchi et al., 1975; European Group, 1975). The European Group wished to be a forum for progressive academics and activists alike, in order to get those themes addressed which were so notably lacking from mainstream criminological conferences. The group also wanted to show its solidarity with new social movements and its commitment to social justice. In this respect, it was felt to be an important issue to match the theme, the conference venue and commitment to local political action.

The development of the European Group followed, by and large, the same line we observed in Britain. It can be divided into four periods: before 1977; from 1977 to 1981; from 1982 to 1989; and after 1990. The first period, after a merely tentative direction had been mapped out in Florence, was characterised by filling in the radical agenda with more concrete themes: prisoners' actions and penal reform (University of Essex 1974), white-collar crime (Free University of Amsterdam 1975) and economy and crime (Vienna 1976) (Ciacci and Simondi, 1977). In the second period, the role of the state and the terrorism debate became central topics. In this way, the tradition of linking the conference theme to issues central to the national setting of the host country, expressed in resolutions adopted by the conference, also started. It can therefore hardly come as a surprise that in Catalonia, which had just entered a period of transition after the Franquist dictatorship, discussions were about state security (Barcelona 1977); in Germany, in the heyday of militant political activism, on terrorism and political violence (Bremen 1978);

and in Ulster on the combination of both these themes in the specific Northern Irish situation, where, during the conference, a hunger strike of prisoners from the Irish Republican Army (IRA) took place (Derry 1981). The explicit request for solidarity with these prisoners caused a serious split within the British contingent, which made emotions run so high that it presented a threat to the further existence of the European Group as such.

The third period was clearly marked by the crisis in critical criminology. It seems as if the conflicts within the NDC were, after its demise in Britain, continued in the European Group. Accounts of Thatcherism were, however, less relevant to an international audience, as they often presupposed a too-detailed knowledge of actual British politics. From this time on, the debates taking place within the European Group were not representative of the whole picture of European critical criminologies. Debates on interactionism and abolitionism in Northern Europe or on left realism in Britain were, for example, far more central than one would expect if one visited a European Group conference. The strongly activist alignment with the political issues of the day also left little room for the more legal-theoretical, reflexive academic tradition of Central and Southern Europe. Furthermore, what could be called a 'third generation' of critical criminologists, who were just children in 1968 and had grown up under the neo-conservative reaction to this era, had little affinity with the second generation's big words and revolutionary slogans.

The group's secretary, Swedish criminologist Karen Leander, and editors and distributors of its working papers, Anglo-Irish sociologists Paddy Hillyard, Bill Rolston and Mile Tomlinson, pulled the European Group through this difficult time. In the fourth period, various attempts at a re-adjustment of critical criminology towards the political reality of the 1990s were made, by dealing with such pressing themes as the internationalisation of policing, migration politics and the emergence of Fortress Europe, or the new meaning of citizenship in a European legal order. In this period, the group's activities also expanded to previously unrepresented countries in Central and South-Eastern Europe. At the same time, the European Group faced a new problem. Before the mid-1980s, the group was a unique international critical forum but, since then, many new European common study and research programmes, with more or less critical foci, have emerged. Because these international initiatives often cover rather specific issues of criminal justice politics and because 'social struggle' in the 1990s has a different character from that of the 1970s, it may be wise for the European Group to take a more general programmatic position and focus on the necessary theoretical and political reassessment of critical criminology and its central objects as such.

German critical criminology

The development of German critical criminology was quite different from the British. In Germany, there was hardly any sociological criminology before the 1960s. Criminology suffered from a politically heavy-burdened bio-psychological heritage. Within law schools, criminology had to fight for its survival. The main orientation within penal sciences was on doctrinal legal issues, which were thought to offer the best protection against a renewed political usage of criminal justice. Most criminal law professors included some criminology in their courses, but they took rather traditional positions: an offender-oriented aetiology aimed at law enforcement (Schumann, 1975a: 59). Criminologists were seen as conspirators against the purity of law. They were suspected of trying to substitute the dogmatic juridical deductive approach by empirical findings. Fritz Sack (1969) calls this period one of an unabsorbed past and uncertain future (*Unbewältigte Vergangenheit und ungewisse Zukunft*).

The emergence of German critical criminology cannot be seen as a reaction against administrative criminology, as in the British case, but rather against penal dogmatics, and against an offender-oriented aetiology. The birth of critical criminology in Germany was marked by the establishment of the *Arbeitskreis Junger Kriminologen* (Working Group of Young Criminologists, henceforth AJK) in 1969. The AJK fulfilled a comparable forum function to the British NDC. Today, the AJK still exists and edits the *Kriminologisches Journal*. Having started in 1969 as a bulletin of the working group, it has developed into Germany's first journal of critical criminology (Sack, 1969: 405; Schumann, 1975a: 60).[1] It is not completely clear who established the AJK; its structure may even be too loose to speak in these terms. It all started with some incidental meetings of isolated younger critical scholars who discussed, in Bielefeld, theoretical issues and research findings. When these meetings gained the character of a permanent working group, the AJK was born. Key figures in the AJK's early years were Manfred Brusten, Marlis Dürkop, Johannes Feest, Hans Haferkamp, Hans-Jürgen Kerner, Rüdiger Lautmann, Dorothee Peters, Helge Peters, Liselotte Pongratz, Stephan Quensel, Fritz Sack and Karl Schumann. The latter describes the AJK as a forum which was set up to develop a counter-discourse to the dominant criminology of criminalistics and psychiatric diagnostics, grounded in empirical study. In this way, a common ground was created for a long, necessary series of studies on selectivity in social control by schools, companies, police, the judiciary, social work and prison, as well as on related social problems such as stigmatisation and destigmatisation of minorities, and action research on penal reform (Schumann, 1973: 81–2).

A more detailed research agenda in 1973 formulated as central aims for the AJK: breaking the dominance of an offender-orientation in criminology by studies on institutional social control and on crimes which are not reported to the police; expanding the reach of criminological study beyond the traditional crimes dealt with by the criminal justice system; questioning the social consensus on norms and values; and indicating the historical and political context of criminalisation. An interesting point was made about the practical commitment, or 'solidarity', of critical criminologists. Such a commitment was taken for granted, but it was also stressed that the AJK employed a concept of 'praxis' which should be distinguished from the merely pragmatic and equally limited judicial or micro-social idea of practice oriented towards the status quo. Only by understanding the individual act in the context of its historical social structure, could the AJK facilitate a change of hegemonic practices. Such an understanding of social practice made a more profound sociological focus indispensable. It was, however, not self-evident which interpretative framework would be the best way to advance the desired social changes: action theory, sociolinguistic analyses, conflict theory and Marxist social theory were all proposed. Although this theoretical controversy was not resolved, it has not prevented an extensive number of empirical studies on the social practice of various institutions of the criminal justice system (AJK, 1974b; Kerner and Schumann, 1974: 15).

The theoretical ground for German critical criminology was prepared in the early 1960s, when a Durkheimian sociologist, René König, inspired quite a number of young sociologists, among whom was the founding father of German critical criminology, Fritz Sack. Sack (1972) criticises the selective and distorted perception of the labelling approach as a liberal *cri de coeur*. He argues that it should be understood in relation to Marxist theory in order to reveal how crime is defined. An orientation towards social reactions is needed in order to compensate for the suspect ideology (*Ideologieverdacht*) of dominant pathologising, offender-oriented criminology, which is subordinated to law-and-order interests. This orientation has led to a focus on classical individual crimes such as murder, offences against public morality and, primarily, property offences, whereas crimes against the environment, economic crime and war crimes remain out of focus. Marxist social theory can serve as an explanatory model of why this selectivity takes place, and as an explanation of the a-historical and a-political taken-for-granted notions of traditional criminology (Kerner and Schumann, 1974: 7).

Sack argues that because criminal lawyers largely deal with sociological issues and concepts, such as norms, deviance, sanction and social structure – and thus not so much with biological or psychiatric themes – a sociological criminology is the most appropriate. Particularly in Max Weber's analyses of the rationalisation and professionalisation of social systems, and Émile Durkheim's on the production of common beliefs and values as well as his interpretation of crime as a socially useful phenomenon for the maintenance of social order, Sack sees a rich sociological criminological tradition. This should be elaborated in a 'norm-centred' criminology, of which Taylor et al.'s *The New Criminology* is a key example (Sack, 1969: 312–14).[2] The study of social control should be connected more closely to both normative theoretical and interpretative paradigms in sociology.

Looking at the kind of studies published in *Kriminologisches Journal*, this tentative direction has been followed very closely. Hans-Jürgen Kerner and Karl Schumann, editors of the 1974 compilation *Kritische Kriminologie*, speak of a paradigm change from positivism to an orientation towards both social theory and labelling. Though the explanatory power of the labelling approach was questioned quite soon after its introduction, the intense controversy within Anglo-Saxon critical criminology between neo-Marxists and allegedly liberal labelling scholars was not so strong that it caused a division within the AJK. This is probably due to the fact that the two paradigms emerged largely simultaneously in Germany. The key advocate of the labelling approach, Fritz Sack, always stressed the importance of studying labelling processes in connection with materialist social theory. This made possible a common research focus on social inequality and crime (Kerner and Schumann, 1974: 8).

Sack's (1972) pivotal article on Marxist-interactionist criminology was followed by a critique by Karl-Dieter Opp (1972), who rejected the polarisation between 'new' and 'old' criminology. He argued that questions of an aetiological nature cannot be answered by an orientation confined to social reactions. Many (mainstream and critical) criminologists added their contribution to this debate on the usefulness of aetiology and the rejection of 'old' criminology. Sack argued against the criticism that a social reactions approach lacks an aetiological component, that including it would imply that the relevance of the labelling approach is still interpreted from a positivist rationale and is not judged on its own merits. This discussion may well have been the impetus for the rather large number of interesting theoretical attempts to integrate, or at least attune, the interactionist approach with subcultural, conflict and Marxist perspectives. This prevented German critical criminology from getting as much out of touch with its interactionist roots as its British counterpart. Though also in Germany the labelling approach was seen to have become too much part of mainstream criminology, the level of self-reflection within the critical paradigm was larger than in Britain. The main criticism applied to all German critical criminologists is that they had expanded the object of criminology to an unacceptable degree, by making it implicit in a general social critique (Kaiser, 1976).

The strong external opposition to critical criminology as a whole prevented large ideological controversies within the AJK. A neo-Marxist critique by Werkentin et al. (1972) caused some debate. Their position that criminology is subordinated to police interests, was, however, rather flatly formulated and was not supported by empirical findings. Their plea for a Marxist sociology of deviance rather prevented than advanced its development within the AJK, whose adherents keep moving between progressive liberalism and conflict theory. Fritz Sack remained loyal to his initial Marxist-interactionist orientation, which, some ten years later, was theoretically elaborated by Gerlinda Smaus (1986b).

Gradually, German critical criminology developed in a more epistemological direction, in which the labelling approach was brought back to the explicit political dimension of the process of definition, reification and discipline (Hess and Steinert, 1986). Looking at the content of *Kriminologisches Journal* over the years, there are initially quite a number of participant observation and other qualitative studies on groups of juvenile delinquents, and on drug policy, the police and other institutions of the criminal justice system, within a labelling framework. Important scholars are, respectively, Stephan Quensel, Erhard Blankenburg and Johannes Feest and Manfred Brusten.

There is also a respectable number of studies, inspired by conflict theory, on the disciplinary role of the prison system, on crimes of the powerful and on petty crimes as a form of latent resistance to unequal social relations, most notably by Heinz Steinert, Hans Haferkamp, Rüdiger Lautmann and Karl Schumann. An orientation that is fairly marginal in the Anglo-Saxon world, and which over the years has become more important in Germany, is the ideology critique of critical theory and an epistemological study of the leading interests behind criminalisation.

A possible explanation for the increasingly theoretical orientation of German critical criminology is the fact that relative unity in practical political commitment became by and large impossible when, in the second half of the 1970s, the 'terrorism discussion' divided minds. After the death in custody of militant activist Ulrike Meinhof in 1977, the idealist students' movement from which she came (which had already become more militant after the murder of student leader Rudi Dutschke by self-defined anti-communists in 1969, when 'commando actions' were carried out by the *Baader-Meinhof Gruppe*) gained a grim and violent character in the *Rote Armee Fraktion, Bewegung 2. Juni* and *Revolutionäre Zellen*. Some critical criminologists wanted to use the treatment of these 'political activists' by the police and penal system as an example of how criminal law is used as a state instrument to repress political enemies. Others argued that the excessive violence that these radical groups themselves apply invited repressive state reaction. Of course, the example of terrorism is particularly interesting for critical criminologists because it demonstrates perfectly how a very coercive and interventionist state of social control is employed and how this leads to serious miscarriages of justice. It shows, furthermore, how moral entrepreneurs play a role in the criminalisation process; how news is manufactured in such a way that the Red Army Faction's political critique remains out of focus; how emergency legislation is introduced which perverts basic legal principles; and how, in fact, the whole left is criminalised by a politics of so-called *Berufsverbote*, regulations that make it very hard for people on the left to find work, particularly in the public sector. When it comes, however, to the Beckerian question of whose side we are on, it all becomes much more problematic. On this latter point exactly, conflicts took a serious and personalised character, which made the idea of one critical criminological project impossible. The intellectual rock bottom was reached when explicit accusations of 'collaboration with the state' were made to critical criminologists who engaged in a research project on terrorism funded by the German Home Office and Bureau of Criminal Investigations (*Bundeskriminalamt*) (Behr et al., 1981 versus Hess et al., 1988).

Academic discussions about the disciplinary functions of criminal law continued, and even increased, but the battleground shifted from actual political problems, such as militant activism, to historical and theoretical studies in a Marxist or Foucauldian fashion. In this context, new analyses of the famous thesis of Georg Rusche and Otto Kirchheimer of the 1930s, on production relations and modes of punishment, were also initiated (Schumann, 1981).

Historical studies on penology also led to abolitionist conclusions. Henner Hess and Johannes Stehr investigated under what historical conditions the notion of 'crime' came to emerge as a public law concept. Stephan Quensel related this to the emerging 'hypostatised' state: that is, a state that is treated as an autonomous actor. Wolfgang Stangl (1988) pointed in the same direction when he analysed how the state gained dominium over more and more conflicts. Stangl interprets the Modern School's functionalist orientation as a reflection of the modern state, whose power should be based on rational principles rather than on the premodern 'God-given commandments of natural law'. By replacing metaphysical speculations about punishment with an empirical testing of the effect of sanctions, von Liszt has, according to Stangl (1988: 88), laid the basis for the 'myth of exactness and rationality' of criminal law. The modern linkage of criminal law's legitimacy to its ability to defend society against crime would be a 'marvelous bluff' because this social defence thesis cannot be proved empirically. Next to this point, Stangl's (1988: 94) abolitionist position is also based on the shift of visions of crime from the private to the public sphere and the subsequent transformation of the aggrieved into a passive and dependent victim.

With a growing theoretical and historical orientation towards social history, from which a social theory of discipline and of the genesis of norms emerged, attention to concrete penal politics decreased. This created a vacuum in political commitment. Other reasons for a specific German crisis in critical criminology were the absorption of interactionist studies in epistemological dimensions (which made the possibilities of empirical studies more difficult) and the fact that interactionism as such both practically and theoretically lost its innovative impulse. The argument that the stigma caused by penal intervention would exclude people from society was felt to have become less powerful; with steeply rising unemployment, non-penalised people are also excluded from society (Hess and Steinert, 1986). In British critical criminology, the balance between interactionism and Marxism tipped in favour of the latter, but on the German scales more weight has always been put on the first. Thus, the crisis in critical criminology also took a different shape.

Feminist studies had emerged in German criminology by 1978, though Dietlinde Gipser had already begun her studies on (why there are so few) female offenders in 1969. Other pioneers of German feminist criminology were Marlis Dürkop, who published on female 'terrorists', women in prison and wrote a feminist critique of the labelling approach; Gerlinda Smaus, who published on women's visions of justice, the paradoxical relation between abolitionism and feminism and on feminist epistemology; and Sabine Klein-Schonnefeld who wrote on state control and on terrorism. In general, the German women's movement and academic criminology have remained more separate fields than in Britain. In the 1980s, the feminist debate was, however, lifted to a parliamentary level by the Green Party (*Grünen*). Though German feminist criminology is not as elaborate as in Britain, there were, by the end of the 1980s, a growing number of feminist studies, of which I will mention just a few. Martina Althoff wrote on concepts of femininity and investigated how feminism relates to Foucault's theories; Helga Cremer-Schäfer added a feminist dimension to her work on media representation; Sabine Platt wrote on feminist legal theory; and Lydia Seus on gender biases in social control (Althoff, 1995). Studies on racism, or indeed on ethnicity and crime in more general terms, were rare before the 1990s, when some studies on right-wing groups such as skinheads came out.

German scholars have been able to carry various debates of the 1970s through in an adapted fashion, rather than completely rejecting a certain debate and confronting it rapidly with a new, obviously better, truth. Discussions on labelling and critical theory led, by 1983, to an interesting debate on abolitionism. The attempt to develop a theoretical foundation in the realm of critical criminology is an important German contribution to abolitionism. In Chapter 9 we will expand on this debate. Empirical studies inspired by abolitionism have been undertaken on crime prevention (by Gerhard Hanak, Wolfgang Stangl, Johannes Stehr and Heinz Steinert) and mediation (by Hubert Beste, Christa Pelikan and Arno Pilgram).

German critical criminologists, aware of their roots in law schools, also took a step that their British counterparts never took. They have reflected upon legal issues and investigated the possibilities of a renewed integrated penal science on the basis of an equality between criminal law and sociological criminology. In this debate, the first attempts were again made by Fritz Sack (1975), now together with lawyer Klaus Lüderssen. After three bulky volumes of German and Anglo-Saxon sociological studies on the genesis of social norms and of social reactions to crime, a fourth volume in this series *Abweichendes Verhalten* (Deviant behaviour) contained the *deus ex machina* of how these empirical insights are to be applied to criminal justice politics and jurisprudence. Another series of two volumes followed in 1980, in which a lawyer and a social scientist took turns to comment on a comparable theme from penal dogmatics or on the same legal paragraph. These two volumes were called *Vom Nutzen und Nachteil der Sozialwissenschaften für das Strafrecht* (On the benefit and disadvantage of social sciences for criminal law). This enterprise has been of significant academic value: the intersection of two different disciplines has been examined very thoroughly. The different positions on the relation between criminal law and criminology move between a complete rejection of integrated penal science by Alessandro Baratta and Wolfgang Naucke, because 'integration' will in practice always lead to a subordination of criminology to law-and-order interests, and a 'demagogic', indeed instrumentalist, use of empirical research to increase the efficiency of law enforcement by Richard Lange. A 'well-intended reception', aimed at the socialisation of criminal law, by Claus Roxin and Winfried Hassemer, covers the middle ground (Blankenburg et al., 1980).

The cooperation on equal terms, which Sack aimed at in 1974, did not get off the ground. The professional culture and frame of reference of lawyers and social scientists turned out to be too different. Lawyers seemed not really interested in solving social problems and insisted on observations directed to the question of which reactions are most consistent with legal doctrine. They held a juri-centric worldview which under-rated non-legal, social factors and skills, and would, furthermore, be unable to distinguish between empirical observations and normative judgements. Lawyers appeared not to be impressed by what they saw as the fragmented explanations and frivolous theories of social scientists, from whom they experienced a lack of understanding of the task lawyers actually have to perform: come to a concrete decision under pressure of time (Lüderssen, 1980). The fact remains that important sociological themes were translated into legal structures of relevance and indicated the disparities between actual law enforcement and judicial decision-making, on the one hand, and the correct doctrinal application of law, on the other. These studies also drew attention to social factors lawyers tend to overlook: namely, those which precede the moment when a problem becomes juridically relevant (hidden crime statistics studies, selective criminalisation, selective police perception and registration, and so on) and those that play a role after penal intervention (stigmatisation, the limited role of criminal law in respect of crime prevention and so on).

Sack is quite pessimistic about the legal adventure when he distinguishes the following phases. First, criminologists accept the definitions and objectives of the criminal justice system. In this way, criminology is reduced to a sociology of criminal law. In a second phase, the rationale of criminal law is still accepted, but the agenda is expanded to other relevant subjects. Criminology has become a sociology of penal control. In a third phase, both the agenda and the rationale of criminal justice are rejected, and criminology becomes a sociology of formal and informal control of social problems. This separation is caused by the acknowledgement that criminal law will, because of its very nature, never concern itself with social problems which exceed the individual level and incite important political changes (Sack, 1988: 23–8). This disappointment in the possibility of changing the criminal justice agenda is yet another incentive for abolitionism. It is, however, worthwhile to give the reflections of law another chance. The abolitionist incentive to reconceptualise law may offer new perspectives for this project. This theme will be elaborated in Chapter 10.

The Belgian connection to Latin Europe

South European countries do not generally have a strong sociological tradition in criminology. Here, critical theory has not been able actually to change the dominant statistical and aetiological positivist orientation in criminology, whereas this has often succeeded in disciplines like sociology, philosophy and, indeed, law. In Southern Europe, critical 'criminology' is generally a theoretical and epistemological critique of criminal law.

Belgium marks an interesting intersection of northern and southern traditions. Criminology is a strongly developed, independent branch of study at Belgian universities. Traditionally, the study of criminology is firmly focused on the police – vocational training in criminalistics is, for example, part of the study of criminology – but, as far as research is concerned, an independent sociological tradition prevails. With regard to cultures in government, policing and social control, Belgium is more a South than a North European country. This is, for example, shown in its formal, hierarchical social relations and impenetrable institutions, and an interpersonal culture of trust, a low identification with the authorities and a subsequent clientelism which forms a constituting factor in government. It is also shown in the long military tradition of the Belgian *rijkswacht (gendarmerie)*. In the 1960s, the Belgian radical left mainly involved itself in student groups which defended the interests of the proletariat in a Maoist or Trotskyist way, rather than in new social movements. The orthodox left also oriented themselves towards the penal field. In the 1970s, initiatives like *Passe Muraille* or *Doorheen Tralies* (meaning respectively 'through the wall' and 'through the bars' in French and Dutch) tried to make the prisoners' case part of the class struggle. They remained, however, marginal groups with no notable links with critical criminology. A Brussels-based group of lawyers around the journal *Pro Justitia* had more impact on the Marxist debate on criminal justice, as had the political scientist and Trotskyist activist Nathan Weinstock and the sociologist Severin-Carlos Versele. On the whole, however, criminology remains strongly geared towards police interests, and the social changes of the 1960s are hardly reflected.

From the 1960s onwards, Steven de Batselier set a tradition in studies of deviance and discipline within the psychiatric sphere. At the end of the 1970s, Lode van Outrive (1978) analysed the Belgian prison system from a Foucauldian focus on the disciplinary role of rehabilitation and correction. His work originated in the 1976 disturbances in the central prison of Louvain. In the same context, Chris Eliaerts completed a thesis on prisoners' rights. Under van Outrive's supervision, Paul Ponsaers made, in 1983, a structuralist analysis of workplace inspection as a social control institution which touches upon the heart of the capitalist economy, and a study of terrorism inspired by conflict theory. It was also around van Outrive that a group of students, with Luc Vanheerentals as initiator, united in the early 1980s as *Radicale criminologen*. This group wrote a brochure in 1982 on alternatives to criminal law, and commented on the 'political' use of remand. However, it never really got off the ground as a critical criminological platform. In 1977, penal reform became a target for the Flemish League of Human Rights (*Liga voor Mensenrechten*), in whose establishment John de Wit and Lode van Outrive (1986) played a central role. Through its critical journal on law enforcement and probation, *Fatik*, the Human Rights League entered the public debate on penality. Gradually, the penal reform movement engaged in the debate on abolitionism, which it only adopted in a modest, reductionist way.[3]

An important root of critical criminology in Belgium lies in a critique of the paternalistic protection ideology in juvenile law in the second half of the 1970s, in which Eugeen Verhellen and Lode Walgrave played a central role. Walgrave's work was followed in the 1980s by an impressive series of studies on social vulnerability in various settings, the problems young people encounter in the labour market by Jaak van Kerckvoorde and Nicole Vettenburg, and, in the 1990s, by explorative studies into restorative justice. Patrick Hebberecht (1984) completed a thesis on primary criminalisation which is notably inspired by conflict theory. A study on depenalisation, and of 12 alternative, less stigmatising and less offender-oriented, systems of social control was undertaken by Michel van de Kerchove (1987). Relations between sociopolitical developments and criminal law were also studied at the French-language universities, of which Christian Debuyst's studies on the definition of 'dangerousness' deserve special mention.

In recent years, many critical empirical studies on the prison system (by Kristel Beyens and Sonja Snacken), feelings of insecurity and crime prevention policy (by Peter Colle and Hans Hofman), the way the police deal with drug use, with racial conflicts and people's fear of crime (by Jan Capelle, Dan Kaminski and Georges Kellens) have appeared. Recent theoretical critical criminological studies in Belgium are Yves Cartuyvels' analyses of new forms of social control in a risk society; Mathieu Deflem's work on the abolitionist 'misuse' of Habermas' thesis on the colonisation of the lifeworld; and Ronny Lippens' study of the influence of the 'globalisation' of the economy and the 'fragmentation' of the normative debate on national criminal justice politics.

Belgium has a strong tradition in sociological criminology – it virtually missed the 'euphoric' or 'left idealist' phase of the early 1970s and critical criminology did not actually represent an influential enough branch to be discarded in the 1980s. Furthermore, over the past decade public confidence in the police and judicial authorities has sunk below zero, due both to the structural mis-management and in-fighting between the different police forces (*guerre des flics*) and a series of scandals and unsolved murders, from the failure in policing the European football cup final between Liverpool and Juventus on 29 May 1985 in Brussels' Heizel stadium which cost 39 Italian supporters their lives, the unsolved case of the Nijvel gang who killed about 30 people during the 1980s, the CCC-terrorism, the many corruption and other scandals involving highly placed politicians (particularly the suspicion of involvement in the unsolved murder of Walloon politician André Cools in 1991), up to the total loss of public faith in the police and the judiciary sparked off by the apparent failure in 1996 of the investigation into a series of child abduction cases where it turned out that the children were sexually abused and murdered (particularly the Dutroux case). This deep sense of crisis in criminal justice also contributes to the fact that Belgian criminology is, at present, more critical and reflexive than, for example, the Dutch, in which a basic belief in law and order is hardly questioned at all.

France: positivist criminology and critical theory

In contrast to Belgium, and despite the pioneering and internationally renowned work of André Guerry, Gabriel Tarde, Émile Durkheim, Marc

Ancel and Jean Pinatel, criminology has never really become 'emancipated' into an independent academic discipline at French universities. Criminological studies are mainly carried out by institutions affiliated to the national research council, CNRS. The greatest number of empirical studies comes from the *Centre de recherches sociologiques sur le droit et les institutions pénales* (henceforth CESDIP), based at the Ministry of Justice, but too independent to be called a stronghold of administrative criminology (Robert and van Outrive, 1993: 115–67).

The social developments of the 1960s found notable reflection in French academia, but not in criminology, which is concentrated outside the universities. Philippe Robert (1973) included a comparable critique about labelling theory's neglect of primary deviance, but the critical paradigm was not adopted. Typical subjects of critical enquiry, such as drug culture and policy, white-collar crime and gender studies, have hardly been subjected to criminological analyses. On the other hand, traditional – medical and psychological – clinical studies continued to play a central role in French criminology till 1990. Another striking difference with other countries is that even politically committed scholars have kept up a rather positivist profile. Debates on the limits of quantitative studies, or indeed on the possible value of qualitative research methods, are hardly in evidence. Claude Faugeron (1981) argues that a mainly statistical tradition is to be upheld in order not to get bogged down in theological speculation. In the light of the crisis in critical criminology, this latter danger is not inconceivable. According to Faugeron, there is no contradiction between applied, quantitative and so-called fundamental research with respect to the level of political commitment. She illustrates this thesis by pointing to a large number of critical, quantitative studies on marginality and on the relation between socioeconomic developments and levels of crime. There is also a large number of studies on various legal institutions: notably the prosecution service and the advocacy (the latter is particularly exceptional in other European countries) and on the so-called 'language of law'. Claude Faugeron, Philippe Robert and other collaborators of the CESDIP established a series of representation and attitude studies on criminal justice, deviance and social control. It seems, however, as if in France empirical analyses and theoretical explorations belong to two different worlds. Quantitative studies are seldom used in theory formation, and theory or macro-political or cultural analyses hardly incite new fields of research, with the aforementioned blind spots as a consequence.

Though the journal *Déviance et société* is not specifically a critical criminological journal, it warrants some explicit attention because it was, according to the first editorial in 1977, established to fill a gap in French-language criminology with respect to the study of social theories of deviance, social mechanisms which create deviance and social control. Belgian scholars, of whom the Fleming Lode van Outrive and the Walloon Christian Debuyst deserve special mention, played an important role in supporting the critical debate in this journal.[4] Quite a number of articles in earlier volumes of *Déviance et société* deal with class analyses of social marginality (Gérard

Manger) and of the biases of law enforcement (Thierry Godefroy and Bernard Lafargue), white-collar crime and legal activism (Pierre Lascoumes), penal reform (Monique Seyler) and, indeed, with the definition process of criminalisable violence and the social construction of dangerousness. These critical studies remain, however, a minority. Most studies, particularly those on youth, have a strongly liberal, 'do-gooder' orientation.

By the 1980s, *Déviance et société* had a less critical profile, marked by a tendency to forget Foucault and Marx and to reinforce the positivist orientation. At the beginning of the 1990s, a more critical orientation can be observed. Claude Faugeron took up the crisis in criminal justice, mainly in the prison system. Clinical studies and 'do-gooder' work on youth protection have largely disappeared, and 'realist' approaches become quite prominent. Left realism may not have been taken up as a theoretical perspective or a political critique in France, but its critique of the ignorance of the problems crime causes in respect of the quality of urban life and its plea to take up questions of social aetiology again were notably echoed. Renée Zauberman, who had carried out research on victimisation and the fear of crime from the early 1980s, was the first scholar to be mentioned in this respect. In her earlier studies, people's answers to interview questions were barely embedded in a theoretical framework. Her later work, in which she relates the hegemonic political discourse on unsafety with people's own definition of the problem, has a stronger explanatory power (Lagrange and Zauberman, 1991: 234–41). In 1984, Hugues Lagrange suggested that people's feelings of unsafety were as much grounded in loneliness and social vulnerability as in an actual fear of (street) violence. In 1987, René Levy and Frédéric Ocqueteau related people's anxiety to the fact that decreasing police concern for minor property offences particularly hit the most vulnerable groups in society, which are, at the same time, also the main victims of a new glorification of property as the main symbol of social status. In 1989, Pierre Boitte related crime-prevention politics to the debate on poverty. After an investigation into structural explanations of crime, Boitte argued that crime-prevention politics should incite social rather than penal intervention.

Also, in the present situation, where the extreme right *Front National* is able to put a particularly strong mark on President Jacques Chirac's law-and-order politics, studies on racism, multi-culturalism or race and crime are hardly in evidence in *Déviance et société*, with Frédéric Ocqueteau's work of 1983 on the xenophobic attitude of the French police as an exception. The same goes, too, for the drugs topic: despite the moral panic France's government creates around a certain 'narco state' within the European Union (The Netherlands), the debate on drugs still seems to be left mainly to the medical discipline.

Déviance et société is an academic journal; *Actes* can be considered as its more activist counterpart. *Actes*, in which the sociologist Pierre Lascoumes played a central role, was established in 1974. *Actes* aims to give room to the more militant debate on criminal justice. The activities of the small Bakounin-oriented abolitionist movement, the radical prisoners' movements and other social movements have all been covered in *Actes*. In this way, it has, as the editors argue, 'introduced the dimension of social struggle and critical reflections of the state into the legal and judicial practice'. Prison is a frequent topic, but also themes like law and literature, political refugees, family law, labour and health politics, and indeed the position of the left, are covered in a collection of many, mostly short, articles by academics and activists alike.

On the whole, criminology's subject matter is, in France, interpreted in a rather restricted way, oriented to criminal justice. There is, however, a critical tradition in disciplines like sociology, social psychology, social and political theory and, indeed, in jurisprudence, history and philosophy that also touches upon criminological themes. The lack of a common platform makes French critical criminology hard to trace, but it cannot be sustained that French influence on critical criminology is thus negligible. We only need to think of the French debates on Maoist-inspired existentialism, Marxist psychoanalyses or structuralism and deconstructivism, which have all left clear traces in criminology. All the way through from Jean-Paul Sartre and Jacques Lacan, to Louis Althusser, Jacques Donzelot, Claude Levi-Strauss, Michel Foucault and Gilles Deleuze, to the feminists Lucy Irigaray and Julia Kristeva, to postmodern and other philosophers like Jean-François Lyotard, Jean Baudrillard, Pierre Bourdieu, Alain Touraine and Jacques Derrida, French theorists are widely read and included in Anglo-Saxon critical criminological studies. This shows something of the complexity we face if we want to analyse the development of critical criminology in France. As an epistemological critique it is implicit in general social and political theory, and it can hardly be distinguished in an empirical fashion.

Michel Foucault, who always refused to be associated with all the above-mentioned labels and thus probably also with that of critical criminology, made a particularly important contribution to its development – also in France, where criminology consists of a 'garrulous discourse' with 'endless repetitions'. With these observations, Foucault (1975b: 47) comes close to deviancy theory's critique of administrative criminology:

> Have you ever read any criminological texts? They are staggering. And I say this out of astonishment, not aggressiveness, because I fail to comprehend how the discourse of criminology has been able to go on at this level. One has the impression that it is of such utility, is needed so urgently and rendered so vital for the working of the system, that it does not even need to seek a theoretical justification for itself, or even simply a coherent framework. It is entirely utilitarian.

Foucault gave a particularly strong impulse to historical studies of the prison system – and to a lesser degree of psychiatry – which represent a critical tradition in French criminology. In opposition to the dominant discourse of a continuing humanisation, Foucault demonstrates in *Surveiller et punir* (Discipline and punish) how the purpose of punishment as such has changed. The prison is subsequently transformed from a mere symbol of the power to punish into a machine designed for the production of docile bodies, which serves to discipline men inside and outside the institution. At an epistemological level, he demonstrates that the production of valid knowledge takes place under the influence of power relations. Therefore, Foucault proposes to rewrite the history of the psychiatric and medical professions, of the penal system, and of sexuality. For this purpose, he uses disqualified knowledge – the knowledge of the lunatic and the patient, the criminal and the pervert.

Foucault's argument that humanitarianism is an insufficient motivation for radical penal reform had a significant effect on all European critical criminologies. Many critical criminologists derived an ethic of non-participation from Foucault's work. Despite his highly abstract analyses, his auto-separation from Marxists, Maoists and structuralists, and all his pessimistic observations about penal reform, we cannot consider Foucault as an a-political meta-theorist. It was only after his participation in the French prisoners' movement that he came to his penological analyses. Foucault's idea of the disqualified knowledge of prisoners, which guides a penal reform politics from below, will be examined in Chapter 7. While analysing his activist path, we will touch upon Foucault's ideas on political strategy, in which power is perceived as a relational rather than a one-dimensional concept. This notion will be used in the replacement discourse that will be elaborated in the last chapters of this book.

Italian deviancy theory

Italy may not have a large empirical tradition in criminology, but to conclude that Italian critical criminology is thus meaningless, would, according to Teresa Lapis (1981: 155) be an expression of the Anglo-Saxon 'cultural imperialism which reigns over the discipline'. Italy has a forum for critical criminology around the journal *La questione criminale*, which was founded in 1975 and changed its name in 1983 to *Dei delitti e delle pene*.[5] In the absence of an administrative tradition, critical criminology in Italy also developed in a different context.

In view of the specific history of the anthropological *Scuola positiva* and the authoritarian social defence movement, critical reaction to this particular heritage might be expected. Tamar Pitch (1990: 47), indeed, observes that Italian critical criminology 'comes up against two well-established traditions: jurisprudence and clinical criminology. If the object of the former is more the system of criminal law and procedure than of the criminal justice system, the object of the latter is the criminal.' Italian critical criminology's political origins lie in Franco Basaglia's anti- or democratic psychiatric movement and in the students' and workers' social movements of the 1960s. It reflects a process of democratisation of the control of deviance and crime.

Franca Faccioli (1984) distinguishes three roots of critical criminology in Italian sociology of the 1950s. First, there are the many sociological studies on marginalisation, sub-cultures and poverty. A second tradition was formed by studies on social reactions to deviance, which find their roots in interactionist (legal) sociology. Considerable research was done on selectivity in the administration of justice, and of the social construction of juvenile delinquency.

Basaglia's anti-psychiatric experiments provoked a large number of studies on total institutions – which are called institutions of structural violence. A third root of Italian critical criminology is to be found in the intellectual tradition which followed in the footsteps of Antonio Gramsci, the political theorist who was one of the Italian Communist Party's (PCI) founders in 1921. A central concept in Gramsci's thought is 'hegemony'. Though hegemonic structures shape reality, they do not represent a permanent state of domination. Because they are continually challenged by class contradictions, they are always rendered unstable. Gramsci's thought forms a *basso continuo* among the Italian left.

Italian critical criminology began with macro-sociological, neo-Marxist, structuralist and Gramscian reflections on the dominant traditions of the discipline. It consisted of three major orientations (Iani, 1994). First, analyses were made of the neglect of crimes of the powerful, (women's) socialisation in traditional family models, and, most notably, the functions of imprisonment in relation to the labour market. Of the large number of penological studies, Dario Melossi and Massimo Pavarini's *Carcere e fabbrica* (Prison and factory) of 1977 has become the best known. Secondly, Gaetano de Leo and Allessandro Salvini (1978) contributed to the emergence of a sociopsychologically oriented deviancy theory, of which their book *Normalità e devianze* (Normality and deviancy) is a key example. A third category of critical studies was rooted in legal philosophy. From a strongly anti-instrumentalist tradition in the Italian legal discipline, Alessandro Baratta built a bridge to critical criminology. He developed principles for a democratic rule of law and theories on the interventionist state, which ultimately resulted in his (1982) book, *Criminologia critica e critica del diritto penale* (Critical criminology and the critique of criminal law).

The Italian state system of social control is quite specific. Discussion of social control has always been of an authoritarian kind. Italian penal legislation still bears the traces of a fascist heritage. It is supposed to function along strict hierarchical lines, but in practice it remains largely symbolic. Massimo Pavarini (1994: 50) argues that 'the adoption of a particularly severe criminal policy at the level of primary criminalisation has always been contradicted . . . by particularly lenient, if not openly indulgent, judicial and administrative strategies.' Italian state expenditure largely goes on the creation of, sometimes completely useless, jobs and labour projects, particularly in Southern Italy. Modes of social control in the rich North vary notably from those in the 'under-developed' South. An orientation to the labour market is, in the Italian context of interpersonal clientelism, more logical than in the comparably well-functioning and more autonomous North European administrative systems. According to Pavarini (1994: 52), the great influence of Antonio Gramsci and the PCI (in size and ideology rather to be compared with the Labour Party in Britain than with other European communist parties) has, partly because the Christian and Social Democratic nomenclature has successfully kept the PCI out of government till 1996, forwarded a popular culture in which 'a conflictual political paradigm persists which construes problems of social order in terms of domination, hege-mony – in one word, power'.

A central debate in the 1970s was the relation between Marxist social and political theory and criminology. The most influential of these theorists were Pietro Barcellona and Norberto Bobbio. Massimo Pavarini elaborated a political economy of punishment in the realm of criminology. Dario Melossi took up the Marxist classics and investigated the significance of the penal question for criminological study. Contrary to the British Marxist theorist Paul Hirst (1975), Melossi concluded that Marxist scholars should take up criminological studies because otherwise the left's position on crime and pun-ishment would continue to consist of liberal eclecticism. Alessandro Baratta pointed to a bourgeois tendency in the social defence movement and to the reproduction of social marginality by the penal system. Filippo Sgubbi (1975) contributed to theories on criminalisation by indicating the diffuse interests underlying a discourse of rights limited to the classical crimes. Sgubbi pro-posed, in a way comparable to Schwendinger and Schwendinger (1975), a redefinition of interests to be protected by criminal law. Sgubbi was thinking in this respect of health, safety in the workplace, and the environment.

Studies of deviance are of a slightly later date. They herald a second phase in Italian critical criminology. Originating in social psychology, the critique of deviancy was aimed at its instrumental use as a pathological concept to mar-ginalise 'difficult' people. In *Normalità e devianza*, de Leo and Salvini (1978) listed criminals, juveniles, psychiatric patients, drug addicts and sexual deviants as categories of people who are excluded from society, either by repressive or by pathologising means of correction. Tamar Pitch (1975) expanded the concept of deviancy to the sphere of penal control. Vittorio Cotesta examined the cultural determination of the concept of normality, and Giuseppe Mosconi analysed the significance of sociopsychological stud-ies to carry the critical criminological debate of deviancy further. At the beginning of the 1980s, these debates were connected with more structuralist analyses of dispersed institutional social control by Gianvittorio Pisapia (1978). Tamar Pitch (1983) criticised deviancy theory's global focus on mar-ginalisation. Also, the feminist critique of criminology, which became a rather important orientation by the early 1980s (Pitch et al., 1983), mainly developed in the realm of this critique. Franca Faccioli analysed the way in which female delinquency is first of all interpreted as a deviation from the social role of women, and Tamar Pitch argued against a 'soft', welfarist social control over women, and stressed the need for women's rights to counter these paternalist approaches.

Interest in legal issues always mounts when important legal changes are introduced, such as the new penal laws of 1975 and 1981. An orientation towards penal politics and towards depenalisation marks a third phase in Italian critical criminology. This kind of study really gained momentum between 1979 and 1981, when authoritarian elements of the emergency laws against the extra-parliamentary militant action of the *Brigate rosse* (Red Brigades) penetrated common criminal law, and when the 50-year anniversary of the fascist criminal code, the *Codice Rocco*, was critically commemorated. This critical legal orientation marked a fundamental difference from British critical criminology. *La questione criminale* covered the 1981 round-table discussion on the fascist heritage embedded in the criminal code (*Il Codice Rocco cinquant'anni dopo*). It was followed by 20 commentaries from critical scholars, in which central themes were the excessive use of remand and the rigorously retributive nature of penal laws.

In 1980, Franco Bricola analysed a number of trials and showed how fundamental aspects of due process had been violated, and how the frequent use of ideological justifications for exemplary penalties and longer periods of remand, such as rehabilitation or the prevention of social anxiety, can obscure the political use of criminal law. Eligio Resta analysed the dubious democratic quality of Italian judicial practice, which was increasingly ruled by decrees, emergency laws and secret trials. A larger report on political detention in Italy (detention based on emergency laws or decrees and an expansion of the legal concept of guilt to collective responsibility) was presented by Lucio Castellano. In this context, Alessandro Baratta drew up a series of principles for minimal penal law. Luigi Ferrajoli criticised the extremely inquisitorial nature of the Italian penal process, with a detailed description of the trial on 7 April 1979 of a lecturer from the University of Padua, Antonio Negri, who stood accused of being the secret head of Italian terrorism and of instigating the murder of the Christian Democrat politician Aldo Moro. Negri was acquitted of all charges, but was none the less kept in custody, on the substitute charge of collaboration with a forbidden organisation and some other minor charges. The entire first issue of *La questione criminale* (1979) was devoted to terrorism, including a contribution by Negri himself. Ferrajoli (1983) argued that the whole idea of emergency legislation embodies a metaphor of war, and that the process of regarding this as something normal should therefore be forcefully rejected under a democratic rule of law.

By the mid-1970s, Vittorio Cotesta was analysing the Italian penal reality from a Foucauldian perspective, while concrete parliamentary debates on new penal legislation were critically examined by Franco Bricola (1975) and Guido Neppi Modona (1976). A new bill was meant to improve prisoners' rights and to create more open prison regimes. Many critics feared, however, that the proposed expansion of discretionary powers for various authorities would increase the arbitrary nature of law enforcement. In a series of commentaries, Bricola criticised the particular way in which probation was employed in Italy, namely as a pre-trial favour of the judiciary to avoid remand, which is, according to Bricola, of little help in preparing the offender for reintegration into society.

The wide rejection of rehabilitation in the 1980s, most notably by Gaetano de Leo and Massimo Pavarini, is to be understood in this context. These developments, and the particular Italian legal context of a both paternalist and instrumentalist orientation towards social defence, were also significant for the largely negative reception of abolitionism. Pavarini (1985) maintained that its powerful arguments against the penal system were quite useful for critical criminologists, but that its alternative political agenda was better forgotten because its pre-trial focus on diversion and its 'social' responses (which were interpreted as if they were something similar to Gramatica's ideas of the 1950s) would reinforce a further instrumentalist orientation. Ferrajoli (1989: 234) also pointed to abolitionism's theoretical inconsistency. Abolitionists made the normative mistake of trying to disprove the principles of punishment by using functionalist arguments. Italian critical scholars opted for a strictly formalistic perspective in which the legal definition of crime was adopted, for flexible sociological or anthropological conceptualisations do not set any limits on the extent of state intervention. Classical legal principles were thought to offer the best protection against the danger of sliding back into the law of the jungle.

This orientation developed into the perspective of penal guaranteeism – which marks a fourth phase in Italian critical criminology. Guaranteeists start from a conflict view of society. They do not, unlike Anglo-Saxon conflict sociologists, put deviance forward as a latent form of resistance to a class society. Because society is conflictive at a structural level, organised resistance is the only politically relevant struggle (Ferrajoli and Zolo, 1977). Later, this Marxist vision was toned down, and Beccarian and Benthamite visions of enlightened utilitarianism and classical criminal law became more prominent (Ferrajoli, 1989). The dialectical relation between hegemonic legal definitions of crime and the interests of the working class (Ferrajoli and Zolo, 1977) or, as it was later called, the vulnerable groups in society, still has to be equated. Law (which belongs to the Kantian category of the *Sein* – being) and morality (belonging to the *Sollen* – ought to be) are treated as separate fields which can only be questioned from a position that is, respectively, internal and external to the legal rationale. Moral and political positions only play a role in a stage before values are translated into legal terms: as such, Filippo Sgubbi's (1975) reformulation of legal values (*Rechtsgüter*) fits the guaranteeist perspective. Only acts that cause actual social damage should be criminalised. In this way, guaranteeists wished to exclude the use of criminal law as a means of stigmatising personal moral choices. The guaranteeist perspective became a central debate after the publication of Luigi Ferrajoli's (1989) bulky volume *Diritto e ragione* (Law and reason).

The role that progressive judges, united in a professional forum called *Magistratura democratica*, play in Italian penal debates should not be underestimated. Despite high rates of serious crime and an old positivist penal code of fascist origin, judges managed to realise a practice of decarceration by making ample use of their power of discretion. This led to the virtual abolition of juvenile prisons by the 1980s, and decreasing incarceration rates between 1984 and 1990. Massimo Pavarini (1994: 49) reveals the a-typical cultural and political context in which this (short-lived) 'Italian penitentiary paradise' emerged. Next to an influential critical tradition among lawyers, Pavarini explains the Italian practice of decarceration by the indulgence of the administration, and the broad public perception of crime as a political problem. The Italian left has never been 'soft on crime', but has claimed instead that the wrong people, the powerless, are imprisoned. The crime problem is also perceived as part of the Southern question: the over-population of people from the *mezzogiorno* in Italian prisons resembles the situation of blacks in the United States. In line with the above-mentioned discussions of the dubious politics of emergency laws and legislation by decree, Pavarini (1994: 52–3) argues, furthermore, that the 'red terrorism', which 'in Italy was construed as an all too understandable phenomenon in its politico-cultural roots', was beneficial for strengthening a diffident culture 'prone to suspicion', and which 'has been more concerned about the perils of repressive agencies than the perils of criminality'.

Crisis, what crisis?

The crisis in Italian critical criminology is not so evident as elsewhere. First, the moral credibility of Italian critical criminology is not questioned so much: it is not accused of relativistic positions on crime. Secondly, critical criminology is simply not such an identifiable group as in Britain. Thirdly, the initial idealism and euphoria of Anglo-Saxon critical criminology was less evident. Because material and political relations are still sharply contrasted, the position of the left in general is also more obvious than it is in the declining welfare states of Northern Europe (Baratta, 1990). This argument, however, mainly addresses the external crisis we distinguished in the introduction, and leaves most of the internal, theoretical crisis untouched. Melossi's (1985) argument that the impasse in critical criminology is fundamentally theoretical (and not political) also becomes more understandable in this context. In the British and German cases, the terrorism debate has been an important element in the crisis of critical criminology. In Italy, it mainly facilitated a critical attitude towards law and order. It also caused, however, an important political controversy within the left. The attitude towards the Red Brigades must be distinguished from the opposition to emergency legislation on terrorism. Whereas the latter issue strengthened the left, the first rather divided minds between those who did not want to be associated with violence, and thereby enstranged themselves from their potential social basis, and movements of political prisoners who feel betrayed by the 'bourgeois left'.

Franca Faccioli (1984: 637) argues that critical criminology lost much of its relevance because it was unable to formulate convincing responses to two of the major problems that had come to dominate the public debate: terrorism and organised crime. Guaranteeism also suffered from this problem. It emerged, in the aftermath of the mass trials on terrorism, as a reaction to a growing tendency to derail the democratic *rechtsstaat* by *ad hoc* emergency legislation and government by decree. Strict and detailed codification, in which legal guarantees for the accused are laid down, should curtail this tendency to arbitrary state intervention. The violation of the principle of legality through the back door, by emergency legislation, is therefore answered by a demand for a very strict upholding of the legality principle in all stages of the process, which allows the police and judiciary as few discretionary powers as necessary. There are, however, considerable complications with the guaranteeist postulate in the current Italian political situation. It seems unclear why more trust should be put in the legislator to make good laws than in the judiciary to interpret them. There is a general crisis in the Western world in the parliamentary political system, but the Italian case – of structural political clientelism and rendered services – is exemplary in this respect. When the traditional political nomenclature collapsed in the early 1990s, it was not the Italian parliament but the judicial power that initiated the operation *mani pulite* (clean hands). There is quite a perverse element to guaranteeism as well: it came about in reaction to the instrumental use of criminal justice against the left, but is now mainly employed by mafiosi and other (political) fraudsters who are best able to mobilise the law and exploit legal guarantees.

A second element in the crisis of critical criminology, observed by Faccioli (1984: 637), is that its social basis in the democratisation movement fell away when many reforms in the field of deviance were, to a certain extent, realised. Tamar Pitch's (1983: 6) argument that deviancy theory mobilised an important language of resistance points in the same direction. This language has now become largely obsolete because of its imprecise and deterministic focus on marginalisation. 'The social and political events of the past ten years contributed to undermine that ideological and reductive reading of reality. The old dichotomies revealed themselves to be false and it was suddenly discovered that the social dynamic could not be read through the assumption of the centrality of the working class.'

The Italian crisis in critical criminology of the early 1980s also challenged its initial economic determinism. Subsequently, studies on forms of social control which cannot be reduced to economic relations, as for example those of Gaetano de Leo or Tamar Pitch, received more attention. This development accompanied the second phase in Italian critical criminology. After a third period of critiques of legal practice, penal politics and depenalisation, a fourth phase followed, in which earlier negative critiques were bent in a more positive, constructive direction by, for example, Alessandro Baratta or Luigi Ferrajoli. Their studies of a minimal penal law and guaranteeism reflected upon the question of how a socially just legal system should look. This counter-factual perspective will be elaborated in Chapter 10.

Spanish critical scholars as guardians of state power

Spain is a very specific case because, until the death of dictator *Generalísimo* Francisco Franco in 1975, and really not until after the period of transition towards democracy in 1978, the country remained, by and large, untouched by foreign influence. Under Franquism, critical voices were not appreciated. Social sciences could not emerge and, even today, have a marginal position in Spanish academia. At some universities there are departments, mainly staffed by psychiatrists and lawyers, called 'institutes of criminology', but hardly any empirical research is done here. Mainstream sociological criminology, by and large, does not exist in Spain. With disorder and state control as its central themes, critical criminology provoked a lot of interest in post-Franquist Spain, but it has hardly been able to gain a stable position, as universities are still bastions of orthodoxy. Critical 'criminology' mainly consists of a critique of criminal justice in the realm of legal sociology or philosophy. Next to juri-centrism, the Spanish political and academic culture is characterised by parochialism and distrust. The dominant, suspicious concern about the democratic deficit of various institutions becomes particularly understandable if we see that, even today, basic democratic control mechanisms are lacking at various organisational and political levels, and that blatant abuses of power are still, in the 1990s, systematically covered up by the authorities. Social protest should be seen in this context.

The heritage of the past 40 years of dictatorship, which both forced the left to operate underground and always remained visible in the higher echelons of the judiciary and the police (*guardia civil*), explains why a defensive orientation towards legal safeguards against the state, which is by and large still seen as the (potential) enemy, remains the dominant focus. Many social movements, and participants in the critical debate on penal reform, have their roots in the resistance to Franquism: practising lawyers, as well as active members of the anarcho-syndicalist trade union CNT, urban guerrilla GRAPO, or Catalan and Basque separatist movements such as *Terra Lliure* and *Herri Batasuna* (meaning 'free land' in, respectively, Catalan and Basque).

The first critical 'criminological' studies appeared at the end of the 1970s. They were directed at topical issues in the democratisation process, such as state security, abuses of the state, police action against terrorism and the abolition of the death penalty, and, indeed, the establishment of women's rights (for example, abortion) and penal law (Miralles and Muñagorri, 1982). A crucial step in respect of the democratisation of the judiciary was taken by a judge, Perfecto Andrés Ibáñez (1978), who translated and commented upon the work of Italian guaranteeists. He also established, after the Italian example of *Magistratura democratica,* a platform for progressive judges in Spain: *Jueces para la democracia.*

The ground for critical studies of the penal system was also prepared by the Basque professor of criminal law Antonio Beristain, whose focus on the treatment of offenders was, during Franquism, strongly interwoven with politically more acceptable ideas on Christian charity and compassion. Beristain also supervised critical Basque scholars, such as José Luis de la Cuesta and Ignacio Muñagorri, who published widely on 'terrorism', drug control and citizenship. The introduction of specific critical criminological debate in Spain has, however, come from Latin America – where Anglo-Saxon critical criminological studies have been published in Spanish. Paradoxically, these ideas have come to Spain through people who had to flee from dictatorial regimes in their own countries. For a country trying to establish a democratic system, Latin American analyses of lost democracies, and the Italian reckoning with its fascist past of some decades earlier, are seen to be the most relevant reflections. In this context, Argentine Roberto Bergalli and Chilean Juan Bustos arrived at Barcelona's two major universities.

In one of the first critical criminological collections in Spain, the transition towards democracy was explicitly put forward as an argument for introducing a critical perspective on criminal justice to Spanish academia. Though it would facilitate the internationalisation of Spanish academia in general, a concrete Spanish critical criminology should, for reasons of comparability, be based in a Latin cultural context (UAB, 1980). Bergalli (1980) combines the materialist critique of the labelling approach from the Anglo-Saxon literature with the German and Italian reflections on these debates. According to Bergalli, it is worthwhile to take the labelling approach seriously in the Spanish context because it has given an important impetus to questioning the behaviour of the authorities. One needs, however, to include the missing questions of why people are stigmatised and why secondary deviance plays such a dominant role. Bergalli adds that deviancy theory can explain something about the material social relations in which primary deviance arises. In this same volume, Àngel de Sola Dueñas (1980) argues that the transition towards democracy needs to be accompanied by adequate social policies and by a differentiation in sanctioning possibilities. Under a socialist criminal justice politics, penal law can finally become the *ultimum remedium* it is meant to be in the dogmatic postulate of the *estado de derecho* (rule of law). In the Italian tradition of Bricola and Sgubbi, de Sola (1980) stresses that this can only take place within the limits of carefully codified legal safeguards. The paradoxical relation between these two strategies means that, in the Spanish context, the latter, guaranteeist considerations have prevented the development of the former, social politics. Together with Juan Bustos and Teresa Miralles, Bergalli (1983) edited an influential collection of international criminological studies called *El pensamiento criminológico* (Criminological thought). This joint enterprise continued in 1986 with the establishment of the critical criminological journal *Poder y control* (Power and control), which unfortunately was not published for very long.[6]

Gradually, European critical studies on alternatives to custody and crime prevention were translated and discussed at regularly organised conferences. In Bustos' department, Elena Larrauri played an important role in support of critical criminology in Spain by writing, in the 1980s, various surveys of decarceration and abolitionism, her book *La herencia de la criminología crítica* (The heritage of critical criminology) in 1991, and by editing a book on feminist criminology (Larrauri i Pijoan, 1994). At the beginning of the 1990s, other young Catalan scholars of Bergalli's have engaged in critical studies on the classical theme in mainstream criminology: the police (Amadeu Recasens); a central theme since the period of the transition, the prison system (Iñaki Rivera); and an orientation that has just appeared in Spanish academia, feminism (Encarna Bodelón). A connecting factor between these studies is their focus on legal-philosophical considerations of *raison d'état* and on critical notions of citizenship.

The study centre of the Catalan department of justice, the *Centre d'Estudis Jurídics i Formació Especialitzada*, plays, in comparison with the universities, a central role in empirical research on criminological themes which are not confined to the criminal justice system, such as juvenile delinquency, public opinion and feelings of unsafety, as shown by Esther Giménez-Salinas and Jaume Funes in their survey of Spanish criminology in the 1980s (in Robert and van Outrive, 1993: 81–114). In addition to these three locations in Barcelona, young criminologists at various Basque universities currently undertake critical studies on the prison system (César Manzanos) and on (the normalisation of) drugs (Xabier Arana). The Basque government, and the establishment of the International Institute for the Sociology of Law at Oñati, play an important role in the stimulation of the critical debate.

Looking at the overall picture, legal and psychiatric orthodoxy still dominates criminological discussion in Spain and little empirical research is carried out. Critical scholars largely focus on foreign debates and on studies of legal and political theory. One area that has, indeed, been the object of many studies is the prison system, whose historical development as a disciplinary institution, the rejection of rehabilitation ideology along Italian lines of thought, and the functioning of prisoners' rights have been the most common themes. The role of platforms of welfare agencies in the judicial field (*Coordinación de servicios sociales*) and progressive syndicates of jurists, such as *Jueces para la democracia*, is quite significant and bar organisations (*Colegios de abogados*), in particular, regularly write statements on miscarriages of justice or reports on penal reform. The pressure from this side can be explained by the fact that in Spain (young) social critics cannot really earn a living with their, often marginal, positions at the university. Consequently, many of them also work as practising lawyers. These associations also played an important role in the later development of Spanish penal pressure groups, whose origins lie directly in the struggle for democracy in the late 1970s.

This chapter has demonstrated how the Anglo-Saxon sociological tradition led to important innovations in continental European criminology. Not all of these analyses of social control, however, fitted well to the political reality of European coalition politics (rather than the British Labour–Tory duality) and different cultures of social control on the continent, which largely lacked a tradition of administrative criminology. The activist commitment that marked British critical criminology in the late 1970s was generally less 'radical' on the continent, in the sense that a more reflexive attitude towards crime as a social problem was maintained. European critical criminologists also stayed closer to their interactionist roots than their British counterparts. Whereas, in Britain, law has often been treated as a mere instrument of the state, many European social critics have been educated in law and take a more nuanced position in this respect. They have always stressed the protective side of law (which British scholars tend to ignore) and thereby a central normative epistemological threshold for criminology. These three elements, which also explain why the crisis in critical criminology was less profound than it was in Britain, will be elaborated in the reassessment of critical criminology.

Notes

1 Another important journal on critical criminology was the Austrian *Kriminalsoziologische Bibliographie* (merged in 1992 with the journal *Neue Kriminalpolitik*), while the *Monatschrift für Kriminologie und Strafrechtsreform* also increasingly publishes critical criminological work.

2 This book has not been translated into German. The critical publishing house Juventa argued in a review that the innovative value of *The New Criminology* was mainly embodied in the last chapter, which was, by and large, published in German in 1974. The rest of the book contains a critical survey of criminology of a kind which was also available in German. It has, furthermore, a strongly British touch to it, which was felt not to be the most suited to the German educational system (van der Boogaart and Seus, 1991: 56–7).

3 One of the few inventories of the Belgian penal lobby, which also includes some probation-oriented initiatives, but does not mention the proletarian groups, is to be found in the Flemish journal of integrated penal sciences, *Panopticon* (1983: 289–96). The Belgian case will not be taken up in Chapter 7, on the penal lobby, because these initiatives have not really found any reflection in academia.

4 Most of what follows is based on a survey I made on the occasion of *Déviance et société*'s 20-year anniversary, celebrated in May 1996 in Liège (van Swaaningen, 1997). References to the studies mentioned in this section can be found in this article.

5 *La questione criminale*, meaning 'The penal question', is called a journal of research and debates on deviance and social control (*rivista di ricerca e dibatti su devianza e controllo sociale*). Its successor *Dei delitti e delle pene* ('On crime and punishment', after Beccaria's famous book) is called a journal of social-scientific, historical and juridical studies on the penal question (*rivista di studi sociali, storici e giuridici sulla questione criminale*), which sub-title is more in accordance with its actual content.

6 The journal was presented as a Spanish-language equivalent of the Italian *Dei delitti e delle pene* and of the German journal of critical legal studies *Kritische Justiz* – and thus not of the critical criminological journal *Kriminologisches Journal*. Despite the sociopolitical focus on (mainly state-organised) social control, the majority of contributions were of a legal nature and not of an empirical sociological kind, and they were oriented to the criminal justice system and not to any other system of social control. Personal conflict amongst the editors was a key reason why the journal came to an end.

6

Criminal Justice as a Social Problem

The critical tradition in Dutch criminology and penal reform of the 1950s, together with the spirit of the sixties, and the subsequent boom in social sciences, paved the way for a broad reception for critical criminology in The Netherlands. In the 1960s, the Dutch grew out of the traditional Calvinist straightjacket and the country experienced a wide process of secularisation, a sexual revolution, a political shift to the left and a wide variety of alternative lifestyles oriented to post-material values. The major action group of the early 1960s, Provo, had a nimble, anarchist character. It was closely related to student, anti- (US intervention in) Vietnam and ban-the-bomb movements, and directed its playful actions mainly against the police and the local authorities, who generally reacted with repression. In 1967, Provo transformed into the political (ecological) party Kabouter.[1] This party had some influence on Amsterdam's city council, but Provo's imaginative revolutionary élan is gradually waning. The radical women's movement, Dolle Mina, arose in 1968. It initially focused on the issues of women's choice in respect of contraception and abortion, and slightly later on pornography and sexual violence. After a phase of street protest, the women's movement focused on the legislative level in order to get its demands acknowledged.

The 1970s both demonstrated a different kind of social protest and heralded a turning-point in policing protest. Various small, militant movements of the orthodox (Marxist-Leninist, Maoist, Trotskyist) left emerged, but the larger social movements of the 1970s, such as the women's movement and the peace movement, arose as exponents of the new left. These groups largely refrained from subversive activities or radical rhetoric in case it endangered the fairly wide basis of social support they enjoyed. More militant social movements also emerged, such as the anti-militarist group *Onkruit* (a pun, meaning both 'weed' and 'anti-gunpowder'), who publicised, stole and destroyed military dossiers or equipment, or the squatters' movement. In the late 1970s, all social movements discovered legal activism to support their struggle, particularly squatters, who showed considerable success in this respect.

In the early 1970s, the new left exerted a strong influence on the Dutch Labour Party (*Partij van de Arbeid*), while the Radical, Pacifist Socialist and Communist parties also had large electoral successes. These developments made the authorities receptive to social change. The police began to respond to social action with a more pragmatic approach, aimed at negotiation. Only when compromises were rejected was violence used (Moerings, 1983). The inclusion of a period of negotiation, in which the authorities were willing to compromise and invite opposition groups to give their opinion, are, according to Moerings (1989), together with the representation of the radical left in parliament, and a traditional disinclination to violence among the Dutch left, important reasons why terrorist activities have been rare in The Netherlands.[2] The terrorism issue, which complicated the development of critical criminology in Germany, Italy and Britain, is thus largely absent from The Netherlands.

In the legal field, many things have changed. Critical academics have established free legal-aid shops (*rechtswinkels*) attached to the universities, and a critical 'young bar' (*jonge balie*) aims to fill the class gap in litigation. Such a critical commentator as Hans Tulkens has been appointed director of the prison department. And the president of a governmental advisory committee on the purposes and functions of remand, van Hattum (1975: 33), has written about the need to abolish the 'obsolete' prison sentence: 'This has been said before. Yet I would argue that it is thus high time that the government does its utmost to make this penalty disappear from our criminal justice system.' In 1975, redundant prisons were closed and the imprisonment rate fell to the historically lowest point of 17 detainees per 100,000 inhabitants. Abolitionism is thus not just a weird, maverick idea: there was a social basis for prison abolition in The Netherlands, and, indeed, it looked rather close for some time, even though the abolitionist Herman Bianchi criticised (in *de Groene Amsterdammer*, 12 October 1977) the van Hattum Committee for ignoring recent criminological research on the net-widening effects of the advocated 'alternatives' of community sanctions and compensation orders.

The emancipation of criminology

Jacquelien de Savornin Lohman (1975: 101) argues that, during the 1960s, a 'sociologisation' of progressive Dutch lawyers took place. Lawyers looked for new relevances for the criminal justice system, which was widely seen as an embodiment of imperious and outdated visions of society. In the 1950s, the scope of criminal justice shifted from a focus on the act to a focus on the actor. During the 1960s, this actor perspective changed to a systems approach, in which criminal law was mainly seen as a public service.

Over this period of time, criminology became 'emancipated' from the legal discipline. Before the second half of the 1960s, criminology was largely a subject for individual professors with one or two assistants, but, with the growth of university education in the 1970s, full-blossomed departments of criminology were established. Like other social sciences, criminology was a prominent growth area in Dutch academia. Among newly appointed criminologists, scholars with a legal background became the exception rather than the rule – the majority were sociologists or social psychologists. From the second half of the 1960s on, younger staff members of the seven Dutch criminological institutes – 'the young criminologists' – gathered on a regular basis to discuss each other's research findings and the development of criminology in a more general sense. In 1974, this group established a new professional platform, which they named The Netherlands Society of Criminology (NVK). The NVK cannot be compared with the NDC or AJK, for it set itself the task of supporting the further development of criminology in a general sense. The previous professional body, SICCO, was abolished, and most of its members joined the NVK. The NVK never got involved in the debate between what Bianchi (1974a) called governmental and non-governmental criminology.[3] The debate on the criminological relevance of Althusser, Foucault, Gramsci and Habermas did not take place in the journal of criminology (*Tijdschrift voor Criminologie*), but in those of critical legal studies, *Recht en kritiek*, and of social theory, *Te Elfder Ure*. The Dutch case is, in fact, rather odd. There was a large 'native' tradition of critical criminology from the beginning of the century, and the 'new' themes of the 1960s were all addressed at a fairly early stage and empirically elaborated slightly later. Yet, political and epistemological critique remained limited to incidental shots, while in actual research a traditional, positivistic approach was maintained.

The perspectives of labelling and stigmatisation were introduced by Herman Bianchi in 1968, and elaborated by his Rotterdam colleague, Peter Hoefnagels, in books such as *The Other Side of Criminology* (1969) or *Rituelen ter terechtzitting* (Court rituals, 1977). Willem Bonger's social democratic and quantitative criminology found followers in Groningen, where a tradition in studies on the relation between youth and class was set by Fokke Dijksterhuis, Siep Miedema and Jan Nijboer. These studies began, however, from a focus on traditional juvenile delinquency. Studies on counter-cultures in the NDC-style were hardly done. Whereas the squatters' movement of the 1980s figured in many novels, Dutch criminology continued to circle around the traditional themes of criminal justice, leaving the study of counter-cultures to general sociology. The very name of the new social movement Provo was coined by the criminologist Wouter Buikhuisen (1965), in his thesis on so-called 'nozems' – a rather a-political youth culture of the late 1950s, early 1960s. The more encompassing political counter-culture of the 1960s adopted the term as an honorary nickname. Criminologists also commented on these provos (Frenkel, 1966), and included conflict analyses of the phenomenon, but actual empirical research did not follow. After his participation in NDC conferences, Bianchi introduced deviancy theory into Dutch criminology in 1973. At his institute at Amsterdam's Free University, he appointed critical scholars Koos Dalstra and Willem de Haan, and a working group within the students' union, Crime Does Pay, was established which applied Anglo-Saxon neo-Marxist analyses of criminalisation and of the criminal justice system to the Dutch context, although an actual neo-Marxist criminology never emerged in Dutch academia. Whereas many academic criminologists individually incorporated the critical body of thought, virtually no one associated him- or herself explicitly with radical criminology.

The development of feminist criminology echoed the same story. There were various academic precursors (notably Clara Wichmann, but also

Cornelis Loosjes in the early twentieth century or Johanna Hudig of the Utrecht School), and a strong women's movement in the 1960s and 1970s, whose topics were widely subjected to empirical research, but an actual feminist branch of criminology never really got off the ground. The second feminist wave reached Dutch criminology by 1978, when Yvonne Quispel, Noor van Liebergen, Joke de Vries and others established the working group Feminist Radicals in Criminology (FRIC) at Amsterdam's Free University, together with women of the Oslo Institute of Criminology. For some three years, FRIC played an important role in Dutch criminology, with publications on the image of women in criminology, girls' crimes, pornography, feelings of unsafety, and the psychiatricisation of female delinquency. The group gradually fizzled out, however, mainly because these students did not gain positions at the university. Other pioneers in feminist criminology were the Nijmegen academic Ronnie Dessaur, who wrote feminist critiques of criminology, and publicist Jeanne Doomen, who had, by the mid-1970s, actually made rape into a key issue in criminal justice politics. From the 1980s on, considerable research was done on issues raised by the women's movement, but a feminist perspective was less evident. This was notably demonstrated in 1987 when The Netherlands Society of Criminology organised a conference on women and crime, with a rather tedious, mainstream agenda. There were a few studies on female offenders, the vast majority on women as victims, and no presentations on feminist epistemology or critiques of criminology. For one reason or another, the critical tradition was hardly represented in the volume of conference proceedings (Bruinsma et al., 1987). This latter tradition can be divided into three categories: (a) problem-oriented research; (b) epistemological critiques; and (c), the largest group, studies of law enforcement. Some examples of the first category are Margo Andriesen's publications on the clients of prostitutes; Nel Draijer's work on the sexual abuse of girls; Joyce Outshoorn's analysis of abortion legislation; Sari van der Poel on boys' prostitution; and Renée Römkens on domestic violence (see van Swaaningen et al., 1992: 31–6). In the second category are a considerable number of feminist critiques of social sciences or of philology which touch upon criminological themes; various feminist reflections on abolitionism (see Rolston and Tomlinson, 1990: 211–84); Heikelien Verrijn Stuart's criticism of the identification of women with the role of victim and her advocacy of empowerment; and the work of Loes Brünott, Jenny Goldschmidt, Marjet Gunning, Riki Holtmaat, Dorien Pessers, Ria Wolleswinkel and others on feminist jurisprudence. Within the third category, many studies either criticise a lack of serious police or court attention or argue, in an abolitionist fashion, for an alternative approach because they see the criminal justice system as structurally unhelpful. In this tradition, Roelof Haveman writes on 'queer-bashing' (homo studies are generally categorised under gender studies); Joyce Hes on restraining orders by civil law injunctions; Renée Kool on the courts dealing with child sexual abuse; Jacquelien de Savornin Lohman on victimology and on sentencing rapists; and Marianne Wöstmann on the police attitude to wife beating, particularly in Turkish and Moroccan families.

Critical criminology has, in The Netherlands, not arisen in contrast to the dominance of administrative criminology. If it emerged in contrast to anything at all, it was the legal and psychiatric hegemony of the 1950s. The emergence of administrative criminology, with the establishment of the Ministry of Justice's research department WODC, by Wouter Buikhuisen in 1974, may, on the contrary, be better described as a reaction to the growth of a too critical academic criminology, which was said to refuse policy-relevant research. Critics and administrative criminologists in The Netherlands share a dominant focus on penal practice, and theoretical elaborations have been scarce (by contrast, see van Dijk, 1981). Such a practice-oriented and critical approach to the police, judiciary, prison and probation follows from a strong culture of trust (both in institutions and individuals), a relatively non-polarised political climate with relatively small social contrasts and a social practice which was, in the 1970s, fairly susceptible to progressive suggestions for change. With the exception perhaps of the mid-1980s, when academic institutes of criminology were closed and the WODC continued to expand (van Swaaningen et al., 1992: 10–13), the controversy between critical and administrative criminology has never been so sharp in The Netherlands as in Britain. In fact, both move, by and large, between the limits of liberal and social-democratic pragmatism. From the mid-1980s on, academic criminology became – under financial pressure – more policy-oriented.

Whatever issue in current Dutch criminology is taken, one will generally find a rather critical tone on law and order, a rather restricted, mainstream vision on criminological themes, few references to social and political theory, and a disciplined methodological (quantitative and qualitative) attitude in which 'speculative' innovations are shunned. On the typical topics of critical criminological enquiry, next to studies on class and gender, media representation (Chrisje Brants, Herman Franke), white-collar and corporate crime (Frank Bovenkerk, Chrisje Brants, Henk van de Bunt, Petrus van Duyne, Grat van den Heuvel), drugs (Peter Cohen, Otto Jansen, Dirk Korf, Marcel de Kort), and later topics such as multi-culturalism (Frank Bovenkerk, Willem de Haan, Marta Komter, Yusel Yeşilgöz) or the private security industry (Bob Hoogenboom), empirical analyses are shaped less by the logic and scope of the criminal justice system, and relations with the sociopolitical context are more notably drawn. Let us now examine four centres where a critical tradition in criminology was established around 1970.

Class analyses of the Groningen School

From 1966 on, Groningen scholars Wouter Buikhuisen and Koos van Weringh were involved in experimental field research on crime prevention and in effect studies. But with Riekent Jongman's inaugural address of 1972, on unequal chances in the penal process, the Groningen research agenda for the next 20 years was set. No criminological school in The Netherlands has carried out a research programme with so much consistency. By the second half of the 1970s, the Groningen perspective was widely shared. In 1978, the NVK conference dealt with selectivity in the criminal justice system, and the published congress proceedings open, rather obviously, with an article by Riekent Jongman (Gunther Moor and Leuw, 1978). Jongman and his staff produced an impressive number of empirical studies of class justice, or 'justice by prognosis' as they called it. Various pioneering studies on the ideological and disciplinary functions of the prison system (Buitelaar and Sierksma, 1972), victimisation risk and related problems (Smale, 1977), relations between crime and unemployment (Jongman, 1978), and on the lifestyles of heroin users (Janssen and Swierstra, 1980) are landmarks of the Groningen School.

In their book on power relations and the prison system, Wout Buitelaar and Rypke Sierksma (1972) question the idea of resocialisation. They argue that the very nature of imprisonment, with its inherent exclusion of people from society, makes resocialisation impossible. This implies that penal reform directed at resocialisation, which leaves the incapacitating core of imprisonment untouched, will have no effect or will even be counter-productive. This notion, which Buitelaar and Sierksma (1972: 106) consider the backbone of their study, shows that 'there are contradictions in prison organisation, which can only be removed by the actual disappearance of the prison.' Such abolitionist arguments were, however, a-typical of the Groningen School. Jongman argued that criminological research results can be used to draw attention to the social consequences of economic inequalities and as a force to change these. This premiss is, however, not reflected in their research methods or theoretical perspectives. The Groningen scholars themselves prefer to speak of a research model rather than a theory.

Jongman stresses in nearly every publication that social inequality cannot be (politically) justified, and that feelings of relative deprivation induce a tendency to commit criminalised acts. He also explicitly argues that scientific results can be used to advance social change. None the less, Groningen criminologists see methodological advantages to a positivistic approach. Though some of them have also used qualitative methods and have carried out action research, a quantitative approach is felt to produce more hard evidence, and is thus seen to be a more suitable means of supporting policy recommendations. Various critics, most notably the previous head of department, Wouter Buikhuisen, who established the ministerial research department WODC in 1974, opposed the Groningen conclusions about existing class effects in law enforcement. His WODC reprocessed the data with different techniques (covariance instead of data-splitting analyses) and came to different conclusions. Nearly the whole 1977 volume of the Dutch journal of criminology is dedicated to the critique and defence of the Groningen studies on class justice. As the authors indicated in one of their responses, when political interests and interpretations clash, the debate is often transformed into a struggle over techniques and ends up in methodological hair-splitting (Jongman et al., 1977).

In the 1980s, Groningen scholars focused on socioeconomic crises and recessions as incentives to the breakdown of people's bonds with society, which may previously have prevented them from breaking rules. Other typical research topics of the Groningen School, in which strain theory and control perspectives were integrated, are the relation between youth unemployment and juvenile delinquency, social position and ethnicity of suspects, and sanctions on tax fraud. Observations of crime as an expression of resistance against an unequal society are based on empirical studies, and suffused with a mild social-democratic sauce (Jongman and Timmerman, 1985). The major problem of the Groningen approach is its lack of explanatory power. Positivism falls short if such a complex subject as social inequality has to be operationalised in quantitative terms, and, without a clear theory, the studies reveal a lot but explain little. Peter van Koppen (1994: 270), in a review article of a collection of Groningen studies, called the 'Groningen swan song',[4] writes that it 'clearly explains *how* the relations between social position, criminality and penal reactions lie, but after reading it, I still do not know *why* these relations are as they are; which factors explain which other factors?'

Neo-Utrecht legal guaranteeism

In Utrecht, the traditional link between criminology and criminal law is maintained. Martin Moerings (1977) empirically elaborates Rijksen's work by analysing the actual effect of imprisonment on external social contacts in interactionist and social-reaction perspectives oriented towards the ideas of Howard Becker and Erving Goffman. This finds a legal counterpart in Constantijn Kelk's study of prisoners' rights. Kelk (1978) sees an independent system of litigation for prisoners both as a means of diminishing the negative effects of imprisonment and as a necessary element of a democratic *rechtsstaat*. Kelk was also a member of the van Hattum Committee, set up after prison revolts in Groningen in 1971, which studied the remand system. Moerings and Kelk revised later editions of Rijksen's introduction to penology and made sure that the Utrecht School maintained a strong focus on penal law and penology.

The so-called 'neo-Utrecht School', established by Antonie Peters, is marked by a perspective of legal guaranteeism. This is based on the classical idea of criminal law as a means of protection against arbitrary state intervention. It reacts against the dominance of the *Défense sociale nouvelle* movement's rational functionalism. As one of the few Dutch scholars of the 1970s, Peters opposes this position and opts for a conflict model. Peters blames the social defence movement for a wayward instrumentalism and for blocking an intellectually sound legal discourse. If criminal law is primarily seen as an instrument of social defence, it loses its function of providing the socially weak with legal guarantees to fight discrimination against them (Peters, 1986). According to Willem Nagel (1981: 214), the difference between Kempe's first and Peters' second Utrecht School is that the first had been critical towards any instrumental use of criminal law, whereas the neo-Utrecht

School does not oppose instrumentalism *per se*, but only the use of criminal law as an instrument of the state. It chooses the side of the powerless. This can be the victim of theft as well as the thief. The neo-Utrecht School actually hardly deals with victims or with the social consequences of crime. It remains a defensive approach, which is, moreover, largely confined to procedural issues.

In 1974, Paul Moedikdo examined the relevance of sociology for the guaranteeist perspective at a more theoretical level. Functionalist sociology could provide more rational guidelines for state intervention. This perspective is most appropriate for refining the line of thought set out by Marc Ancel. Secondly, legal principles can, in the realm of normative social theory, be interpreted as a specification for political principles. With this normative and empirical acknowledgement, the legal guaranteeist perspective gets a stronger epistemological basis. In this way, the content of classical legal principles can be reaffirmed, without falling back on the legal doctrinal games of German *Begriffsjurisprudenz*, by which an autonomous reality is created for concepts and fictions that are really derived from system-internal deductions and constructions which do not have any necessary reflection in social practice. With a socially grounded legal guaranteeism, more justice is done to the power-critical function of law, Moedikdo (1974) argues.

Peters initially held a combined chair in criminal law and the sociology of law. His earlier work is of a largely penal dogmatic nature, but, after his return from Berkeley, where he worked with Philip Selznick, his writings became increasingly interwoven with sociological notions, while his teaching activities were concentrated on the sociology of law. In Peters' perspective, 'law and other social institutions should offer people the space and opportunity to encounter each other, but also to avoid each other if this is necessary. Too many bonds are bad for people, but too few as well. The voice of Durkheim continuously reverberates [in Peters' work], as do those of Weber and Marx . . . Only the intensity varies' (Gunning et al., 1993: 7). In his inaugural address, Peters (1972) argues that the essence of criminal law is embodied in its classical function to protect people against undue and arbitrary state intervention. With the acknowledgement that no legal provision alone will be able to provide adequate protection to the underprivileged, Peters (1979) insists that structural material conditions need to be changed as well. In order to optimise people's legal position, protective rules should be seen from the client's perspective and should include both legal procedures and socioeconomic factors. In this way, Peters combines classical legal guarantees with notions from conflict sociology. Courts are interpreted as forums for a fight over social conflicts. Criminal procedures are the rules of the game, regulating dialogue and debate. The level of criminal procedure's actual contribution to the emancipation of citizens (notably in the delicate position of the accused) is the measure of the democratic quality of the *rechtsstaat*.

Though lawyers held a dominant place in the neo-Utrecht School throughout the 1980s, criminologists could maintain a rather autonomous position. Chrisje Brants should be explicitly mentioned as a criminologist who has, with her studies on white-collar crime and moral panics, maintained a critical social-scientific tradition in Utrecht during the 1980s. By the end of that decade, when the anthropologist Frank Bovenkerk was appointed professor of criminology, empirical research, notably on crime in a multi-cultural society, received new impetus. Sociological insights certainly played an important role in setting out the legal guaranteeist research agenda, but actual studies carried out in this tradition were of a more juridical, notably procedural, kind. This guaranteeist perspective has been applied to the legal position of target groups as different as the military, political activists, psychiatric patients, juveniles, and, most notably, prisoners. It has contributed significantly to the commitment of many lawyers to social justice. It remains, however, a defensive position, which can also retard other, possibly more effective and more humane, approaches to social problems culminating in crime. This latent conservatism may be due to the fact that the sociological imagination has played only a marginal role. In Chapter 10 the guaranteeist perspective will be challenged with new sociological reflections.

The abolitionist perspective

The word 'abolitionism' has already been used many times. It has, in fact, become the best-known Dutch contribution to critical criminology. To deal with this perspective in a more detailed way, some analytical distinctions need to be made. In general terms, 'abolitionism' stands for a perspective directed towards the abolition of punitive responses to criminalised problems and their replacement by dispute settlement, redress and social justice. In this sense, we have encountered abolitionist scholars *avant la lettre* since the turn of the century. As actual founding fathers of an abolitionist perspective in European criminology in the 1970s, the Norwegians Nils Christie and Thomas Mathiesen and Dutchmen Herman Bianchi and Louk Hulsman should be mentioned. In the 1980s, this first generation's visions of alternative criminal justice politics were linked with insights from critical criminology, first with interactionism and (de-)constructionism and later also with more radical social theories, notably by German and Dutch criminologists. This second-generation abolitionism, which will be dealt with in Chapter 9, has actually become a continental branch of critical criminology.

The word 'abolitionism' was adopted from the North American anti-prison movement. In this, Canadian Quakers, in particular, take up their historical mission from the anti-slavery movement. They see prison as an institution that fulfils the same social functions today as slavery did in the last century. They established the international penal abolitionist movement, ICOPA, by organising its first conference in 1983 in Toronto (van Swaaningen et al., 1989). Though European academics use the word 'abolitionism' after this North American example, their perspective has a different origin and orientation. In comparison with the Western European situation, North American abolitionism is grounded rather in religious inspiration than in considerations of the counter-effectiveness of criminal justice; situated rather among the grassroots than among academics; and focused rather on prison reform than on punitive modes of social control in a more general sense. In Europe, abolitionist social movements were, in the early 1970s, formed by prisoners' unions and radical penal reform movements. These will be dealt with in Chapter 7.

Although the literal meaning of the verb 'to abolish' suggests otherwise, European abolitionism cannot be conceived in absolute terms. Abolitionists do not argue that the police or courts should be abolished. The point is that crime is not to be set apart from other, non-criminalised social problems and that the social exclusion of 'culprits' seldom solves problems. Instead, crime problems should be treated in the specific context in which they emerge, and reactions should be aimed towards inclusion in society. Abolitionists do not argue against social control in general terms. It is, indeed, hard to imagine social coexistence without some form of social control. The problem is the top-down, repressive, punitive and inflexible character of penal control. For this reason, abolitionism includes most of the arguments about informal, reflexive and participatory justice. Abolitionists both question the ethical calibre of a state that intentionally and systematically inflicts pain upon other people, and point out that, because generally accepted goals of general and special prevention cannot be supported with empirical data, the credibility of the penal rationale is at stake. Thus the criminal justice system is both problematic in a moral sense and dysfunctional according to its own ends.

Abolitionism has both a negative and a positive moment. It implies a negative critique of the fundamental shortcomings of criminal law to realise social justice, and aims to make a positive contribution to the prevention and control of criminalised problems by social means. In the negative aspect, depenalisation (reducing the punitive character of reactions) and decriminalisation (against the labelling of social problems as crimes) are the central topics. Stan Cohen (1986a: 127–8) characterised abolitionism's 'destructuring moves' as: decarceration, diversion (away from the institution), decategorisation, delegalisation (away from the state) and deprofessionalisation (away from the expert). In the positive aspect, a distinction is made between abolitionism as a way of thinking (an alternative way of understanding crime and punishment), and as a way of acting (a radical approach to penal reform). In the first sense, abolitionism is an example of a replacement discourse. In the second sense, linking abolitionism with Anglo-Saxon debates, it moves between Hal Pepinsky and Richard Quinney's vision of 'criminology as peacemaking' and John Braithwaite's theory of 'reintegrative shaming'. It is more modest than the former, for it is aimed at mechanisms of social control rather than rebuilding community spirit, but is embedded in a more radical position on penality than the latter.

In their attempts at depenalisation, abolitionists first directed their fire at the prison system. By 1980, the attention shifted to (the pros and cons of) non-custodial alternatives. Warnings against the net-widening effects of such sanctions were contrasted with their potential value in the reduction of the penal system. The recognition that sanctioning modalities at the end of the penal chain do not change its punitive, excluding character, meant that the focus was directed at the diversion of cases in preliminary phases. The aim of this was the prevention of the stigmatising effects of both trial and punishment. This focus was followed by an orientation to an alternative procedural rationale, which should lead to non-punitive responses to social problems, and indeed to the decriminalisation of certain behaviour, which means taking it out of the realm of criminal law.

Despite the central position Dutch scholars have taken in the abolitionist debate, the position of abolitionism within Dutch criminology is rather marginal. Though, around the early 1970s, abolitionist ideas may have been more widely shared, as a school it only represents a very small branch, which is considered to be a serious debating partner by only peripheral groups – and perhaps as the indispensable radical frills of national folklore by the rest. It is a remarkable achievement, indeed, that a small group has been capable to convince many foreign readers, and even some Dutch (van Dijk, 1989). Rather than emerging as a counter-paradigm, abolitionism gradually followed on from existing critical traditions in Dutch criminology.

Herman Bianchi's ethical appeal at depenalisation

The phenomenological line of Ger Kempe's first Utrecht School was, to a certain extent, continued by Herman Bianchi. In his inaugural address to the Free University Amsterdam, Bianchi (1958: 18) indicated the support he experienced from the Utrecht School. Bianchi follows Kempe in his opposition to a reductionist empirical criminology and in his argument for the development of an independent criminology. In his dissertation *Position and Subject-matter of Criminology*, Bianchi (1956) advocates the 'liberation of criminology from the lap of criminal law' because most attempts to integrate both penal sciences have always resulted in the reduction of criminology to an auxiliary science of criminal law. According to Bianchi, criminologists need to determine their own object of study. The formal legal concept of crime as a punishable act (*strafbaar feit*) is, unlike the more normative description as wrong doing (*misdaad*), an unsuitable starting-point for the criminologist. This theoretical contention does not, however, imply that the study of criminology and criminal law should be separated in their more practical orientations as well. Bianchi (1958: 16) is as optimistic about the blessings penal intervention can bring in respect of rehabilitation as the Utrecht scholars. The criminologist's task is to indicate factors that prevent the offender's reintegration into society. In the 1950s Bianchi was, like Kempe, engaged in probation work.

Criminology is an inadequate name for a 'huge and hybrid science' which aims to address the problem of crime in its full complexity, Bianchi (1956: 208) argues. For less-reductionist analyses, the criminologist needs to be equipped with knowledge from many scientific fields. 'The risk which is brought by this essential demand is rather obvious: the criminologist must be aware of degenerating into a Jack of all trades.' Therefore, the criminologist should focus on a metaphilosophical level. He should focus on the relations between different disciplines relevant to criminological themes, rather than really plunging into all of them. Sociology or psychology would result in partial and one-dimensional visions of crime. Bianchi expects more of social and cultural anthropology, phenomenological and moral philosophy and, indeed, of theology. Because the very concept of justice is a normative one, questions about the judgement of problematic acts should be answered in a normative style as well. Problems of guilt and accountabilty require a phenomenological approach (Bianchi, 1956: 71). Here, Bianchi adopts Kempe's (1950, 1952) position. Bianchi argues that Bonger's definition of crime as an anti-social act is 'one-sided' (1956: 104), and criticises Bonger's lack of philosophical interest (p. 123). In later writings, Bianchi (1975a, 1976) largely praises Bonger's contribution to the establishment of a critical perspective in criminology.

Following the penal system in an empiricist way, without seriously reflecting upon the philosophical foundations of the discipline, would, according to Bianchi (1956: 4), imply the euthanasia of criminology as an independent discipline. A dominant orientation towards a descriptive level does not problematise the timely and culturally determined definitions of crime, and thereby retards innovation. In the 1950s, Bianchi was one of the few scholars who did not hold the vision that criminology could actually contribute to a reduction of crime. He warned against prediction studies. These are not only merely metaphysical speculation, they are also ethically untenable because they reduce human dignity to scientific categories (Bianchi, 1960). Consequently, Bianchi (1961) rejected the ideologies of general prevention and social defence. These are not only unproved and unlikely assumptions, they are also dangerous objectives because they open the door to the political usage of criminal law. According to Bianchi, penal intervention cannot be legitimised by any functionalist consideration, but solely by its contribution to doing justice in the classical legal sense. In a polemic style reminiscent of Willem Nagel, Bianchi points to the crimes committed by authoritarian regimes which have often been supported by ideas of social defence.

Bianchi drew the ultimate, abolitionist conclusion from the 1950s Utrecht encounter model. In his 1964 book, *Ethiek van het straffen* (Ethics of punishing), Bianchi criticises the moral foundations of the penal system and proposes a model of reconciliatory justice instead, including the ethical Utrecht considerations of forgiving guilt and of repentance as a means of clearing blame. Though the French Revolution expelled the worst excrescences, the rationale of continental criminal law is rooted in the Inquisition. The Old Testament's touchstone of equalising justice, *tsedeka*, should replace these inquisitory structures, and the *anomie* caused by penal repression should be replaced by a *eunomie*, socially integrative and normative orientations, which can be forwarded by interventions aimed at redress (Bianchi, 1964). Civil law is a more suitable means of achieving such a eunomie than criminal law. Bianchi reconceptualises the notion of 'guilt' as an indication of to what degree an offender is able to carry and accept his punishment.

Willem Pompe (1965) wrote a mildly positive review of Bianchi's book; albeit because he felt attracted to its reconciliatory and empathic message. Kempe (1964), however, was straightforwardly negative. He warned against the injustice that can follow from Bianchi's opaque notion of guilt. Though Bianchi aimed at a reduction of the penal system, his approach could well lead to interventions far beyond the limits of legality. Also interesting is Louk Hulsman's review. Hulsman (1965b) shares Bianchi's criticism of the penal practice, but defends the statute of classical criminal law, as Bianchi had also done four years earlier. Bianchi directs his fire at the wrong target, Hulsman argues, because, instead of concluding for a necessary separation of law and morality, he introduces a new speculative and metaphysical vision of justice as reconciliation. This idea hardly fits in our highly urbanised society and the rationale of its criminal justice system. At core, Hulsman's rejection of moral judgements and allegedly speculative alternatives remains a main point of difference between these two founding fathers of Dutch abolitionism.

The reactions to *Ethiek van het straffen* recall the paradox of social defence: how far can humanitarian intentions be transferred to penal practice, without resulting in counter-effects in respect of legal guarantees? Despite the many positive reviews Bianchi also received, he felt the rejection of his work by those whom he saw as his most important examples (Pompe and Kempe) as a great disappointment. Despite the fact that he later presented himself as a follower of Clara Wichmann rather than of the Utrecht School, Bianchi's ideas on restorative justice are really an updated elaboration of the Utrecht encounter model. Bianchi (1974b) argues that the mere phenomenological encounter that the Utrecht School wanted to realise cannot be sincere if power differences are not, first, acknowledged and, secondly, neutralised as much as possible. This has been an important omission of the Utrecht School. We have seen before how Bianchi's critique was rejected as anachronistic (Hoefnagels, 1975; Moedikdo, 1976).

In the 1970s, Bianchi concluded that anomie is partly caused by criminal law's false claim to reflect consensual opinions on norms and values, and by the fact that decisions are forced upon people without paying attention to the question of whether or not these actually correspond with their own particular vision of the problem. In order to overcome such a hegemonic definition of the problem, Bianchi proposed in 1979 an 'assensus' model: a conference-like session where the conflicting parties themselves define the nature of the problem during the procedure, rather than starting from the penal categories and principle of 'objective' truth-finding. As this aim cannot be achieved, it should not be the object of a trial – a word that also reflects the rationale of the Inquisition. Finding a solution upon which all parties can agree is a more realistic and a more fruitful aim of a court session. Assensus is a way between the 'consensus' model of criminal law and the 'dissensus' embedded in conflict models. These two perspectives imply a fight over the representation of the facts instead of a focus on the follow-up. With these contentions, Bianchi rejects both functionalist and conflict sociology. Instead, he adopts a normative position oriented at informal justice and argues, along the same line as Nils Christie (1981), for a model of participatory justice. Bianchi proposes to change the role of the public prosecutor into that of the *praetor* from antique Roman law: a person who brings the parties to justice and acts as a referee who takes care that power differences are equalised. In order to create an open space for dispute settlement, Bianchi proposes the (re-)establishment of sanctuaries (*vrijplaatsen*) which cannot be reached by the arm of the law. Such sanctuaries would have a legal basis in the right of asylum held by churches and embassies. If the parties in a conflict find a satisfactory solution, the prosecutor should lose the right to proceed (Bianchi, 1985, 1994). Bianchi's ideas on sanctuary did not remain theory alone. A practical experiment was carried out in 1974. This initiative found support among various academics, lawyers, public prosecutors and judges, as well as among rabbis and vicars, who were attracted by the Old Testament notion of *tsedeka* justice and the right of the synagogue and church to offer asylum. Public sympathy for these ideas ceased when they become more radical in a practical political sense. In the public press, the idea of sanctuary is now portrayed as an ideological support of squatters' strongholds and of claims of 'illegal' immigrants who sought asylum in an Amsterdam church to prevent extradiction (Steenstra, 1988: 86–9). When his attempts to realise an alternative to criminal justice through the right of asylum failed, Bianchi adopted Thomas Mathiesen's distinction between positive and negative reform.

Bianchi's work forms one big philippic against prisons – starting in the 1950s with piecemeal reform within the probation service and ending in a non-reformist abolitionism oriented at alternative procedural structures. Next to this criminal political *leitmotiv*, Bianchi also continued to work on the more theoretical criminological issues set out in his dissertation of 1956, yet in an explicit radical style. These studies began in 1967, with an essayistic book on the relation between authority, law and order, and the blind adoration of this 'Lord of the Flies'. Yet, without many theoretical references, and clearly inspired by the social turmoil in Amsterdam of those days, Bianchi points to the insatiable nature of the penal system in its tendency to exclude various deviant groups from society. In this way, he introduces the concept of deviancy without reference to any Anglo-Saxon scholar. Bianchi (1971) elaborates these ideas theoretically in a book on stigmatisation, in which he combines Ed Lemert's notion of secondary deviance and Harold Garfinkel's analyses of degradation ceremonies with examples derived from the work of the French writer, Jean Genet, and the Dutch anti-psychiatrists, Jan Foudraine and Kees Trimbos.

From this time on, Bianchi engaged mostly in international debates and increasingly estranged himself from Dutch penal practice. In various publications between 1976 and 1978 he followed the radical academic fashions very

closely. He argued against the word 'terrorism' as a product of power knowledge and plunged into the French debates on structuralism. But
phenomenology remained the theoretical thread which connected all
Bianchi's observations. His critique of the Utrecht School comes down to the
idea that it remained too confined to 1950s micro-phenomenology. In the
1960s, a meso-phenomenology became visible in symbolic interactionism and
the labelling perspective. In the 1970s, structuralist analyses made a macro-
phenomenology of deviancy possible (Bianchi, 1975b, 1979). These
fashionable flings were not really thought through. Whereas structuralists
reduced the influence of the individual in the transformations of society to an
absolute minimum, phenomenological orientations, and certainly those of the
Utrecht School, focused on the individual. Bianchi never dealt with this
apparent philosophical contradiction. In his imaginative alternative introduction to criminology *Basismodellen*, Bianchi (1980) applies Foucault's
analyses of power-knowledge to the history of the criminological discipline,
adopts Mathiesen's analyses of penal reform, and comes, following the
French philosophers Gilles Deleuze and Félix Guattari, to an anti-oedipal
criminology in which such writers as the Marquis de Sade, Jean Genet,
painter Hieronymus Bosch and actor Charlie Chaplin are portrayed as the
greatest criminologists. *Basismodellen* is one of Bianchi's most intriguing
works, but its political analyses do not really fit with his phenomenological
ideas. Not all his theoretical positions are equally convincing. His conspiracy
theories, included in his emancipatory strategy model, are, in particular, heavily criticised as 'boy-scout bungling'. Bianchi himself is called the Isaiah of
criminology (van Weringh, 1981).

Bianchi has been judged too much (and written off) by this particular
book, which, indeed, contains too many mistakes and loose ends. If only
because the gap between the general plan of *Basismodellen* (to relate criminological paradigms to sociohistorical developments and visions of society)
and its slapdash elaboration has never been filled by any other criminological
handbook, I have come to a carefully appreciative judgement of this expressionistic work. Perhaps purely intuitively, Bianchi foresaw certain developments rather aptly. More positively put than van Weringh's portrayal, but
probably pointing to the same kind of animation, Willem de Haan (1988)
called Bianchi, following the idea of liberation theology, a 'liberation criminologist', and compares him therefore with Richard Quinney. Bianchi's
suspicion of rulers and their repressive strategies towards deviants includes a
form of self-liberation, which gives his criminology a para-religious component (Kelk, 1988: 34). When criticised for being a preacher rather than an
academic, Bianchi seemed not too insulted. He actually admits to feeling
closer to Augustine's *dubito ergo sum* than to Descartes' *cogito ergo sum*.

In 1958, Bianchi argued that mankind is unable to answer the fundamental questions of criminology, and over the years he has stayed remarkably
close to this non-rational premiss. He argues that it is quite healthy to keep
some religious doubts about scientifically proved truths. When people comment that his work is of a profoundly Protestant character, he replies that

progressive impulses have more often come from churchmen, and that, more-over, the prophet Isaiah is not the worst person to be compared with (van Swaaningen, 1988: 9–10).

Bianchi has probably taken the credo of the 1960s – that imagination should come to power – more seriously than any other Dutch academic; he is one of few persons to walk on the artistic edge in his approach to research. Before 1964, his work was of a balanced and relatively precise style, but then he began to adopt a far more expressionistic style. Apparently, Bianchi never felt even tempted to return to what he has termed 'naturalism' (the docu-mentary approach of traditional academic research), after having been marked out as a militant, an extremely controversial figure and an agitator. In the 1970s and 1980s, Bianchi was one of the few Dutch academics who took explicit political positions (some radical, but also some theological observa-tions which did not please his left-wing constituency) and actually investigated the relevance of new critical theories. His radical flings of the mid-1970s certainly provoked the emergence of the neo-Marxist and feminist working groups at his institute. His historical focus in the 1980s was an impulse for historical criminological research on the abolition of torture (Sjoerd Faber) and capital punishment (Sibo van Ruller), on sanctuaries (Marijke Gijswijt), dispute settlement by church councils (Herman Roodenburg) and the prosecution of homosexuals (Theo van der Meer). The odd thing is, however, that Bianchi had little affinity with neo-Marxist and feminist initiatives, while historical studies were hardly supportive of his ab-olitionist ideas.

The elaborated English edition of Bianchi's last book *Justice as Sanctuary* (1994) is again written in a more precise style. It contains a system of notes and references much appreciated in the academic world and other traces of 'naturalist' 'nitty gritty'. Bianchi's macro-theoretical and radical political reflections of the 1970s are not included in his ideas on assensus and sanctu-ary. They do not actually correspond with his rather individual-centred abolitionism. In a new chapter on strategies for change, structuralist and macro-political considerations about the feasibility of an alternative system of crime control are lacking. In this respect, this chapter is, for better or worse, about the opposite of his emancipatory strategy model of 1980. An interesting addition to this English edition is the inclusion of a paragraph on human duties accompanying human rights. Human rights require a precept to renounce certain action. Human duties, on the other hand, require active personal commitment. These elements of social justice are each other's necessary counterparts.

It remains Bianchi's main concern to reduce reliance on prison as much as possible, by replacing it with non-punitive alternatives. Bianchi represents an abolitionism oriented at depenalisation, and his critique is of a strongly ethical kind. In contrast to many other Dutch penal scientists, Bianchi's approach is remarkably non-functionalist. Bianchi does not reject the concept of crime as a moral condemnation – as sinful acts at the beginning of his career and malicious and egoistic acts at the end. He never pointed to any anti-social aspect of crime because this would be inconsistent with his principled rejection of social defence and general deterrence. Above all else, Bianchi opposed the repressive, punitively oriented way that these crimes are dealt with in the penal system.

Louk Hulsman's perspective of decriminalisation

Louk Hulsman does not owe his reputation so much to an impressive oeuvre as to his influence on the political debate on criminal justice. As a previous civil servant in the Dutch defence and justice administrations, he radically challenged the system's internal logic and the dominance of often purely bureaucratic considerations. This practical orientation led Hulsman to engage in many national and international committees on crime problems (Blad et al., 1987b). His critical, down-to-earth approach is also represented in his inaugural address to the Erasmus University Rotterdam in 1964, *Handhaving van recht* (Enforcing law) (Hulsman, 1965a). Criminal law is not the embodiment of a socio-ethical code, but a means of social control among many others – among which administrative and civil law are the most closely related. Crime only differs from other social problems in respect of its technical definition and follow-up. The study of criminal law enforcement should therefore also include the study of other instruments of social control, especially if these are likely to be more effective. According to Hulsman, the optimal sanction will mostly be a minimal one. Hulsman thus shows himself a true scholar of Jacob van Bemmelen and Willem Nagel, with whom he studied and worked. Hulsman took good notice of van Bemmelen's golden rule to economise on the use of criminal law. He radicalised this vision by linking the legitimacy of penal intervention to its contribution to public welfare and dispute settlement (Janse de Jonge, 1991: 149). Hulsman rejects metaphysical legitimations of punishment, such as retribution. Since human suffering cannot be measured, retribution cannot be equally enforced. Retribution can be a means, but no purpose in itself. The purpose of sanctions lies in the possibility of influencing undesirable behaviour. The limits of intervention are set by its ethical justification as well as by practical possibilities. This corrective function of sanctions is not the domain of the penal system alone; there is a wide spectrum of informal and more formal sanctions throughout society which all serve this same purpose (Hulsman, 1969). In his later work, Hulsman reserved the term 'punishment' for non-institutionalised forms of correction alone because anonymous penal reactions are not based on the affective relation that is needed actually to influence a person's behaviour through punishment.

Hulsman was strongly influenced by Marc Ancel, but also by his Rotterdam colleague Jack ter Heide, who developed a functionalist perspective in legal philosophy. According to ter Heide (1965), the protection of society and the liberty of the delinquent are two sides of the same coin: the most secure return of the delinquent into society is the central goal of sentencing. Hulsman's approach is more normative and politically committed than ter Heide's. His thought is ruled by the imperative to contribute to social welfare. The influence of the new social defence movement, in which Hulsman participated, can be clearly noted in his inaugural address, when he opts for a humanitarian and rational critique of the criminal justice system. Hulsman's focus on criminal justice politics finds its roots in this source of inspiration. In a *liber amicorum* for Marc Ancel, Hulsman (1975) argues that the next step on the path of social defence is to draw up criteria under which penal intervention is legitimate and in which cases the state should withdraw.

The development of criteria for legitimate penal intervention was a central part of Hulsman's work in the early 1970s. As absolute criteria against penalisation, Hulsman (1972) mentions the tendencies to (1) impose moral convictions and to (2) use criminal law as a stick behind the door for social work interventions. He also rejects penal intervention (3) when the frequency of the acts implies that it cannot be controlled because the system's capacity will be exceeded, or (4) when it does not contribute to any form of welfare, dispute settlement or redress. As a relative criterion, indicating that one should be extremely careful with penal intervention, Hulsman mentions, among other things, that law enforcement should not be focused on acts that are concentrated in socioeconomically deprived settings. Hulsman (1971) strongly argues against a 'professionalisation' of the probation service, by which it is actually transformed into an instrument of law enforcement rather than a welfare institution. Herewith, the probation service bargains with its own principles of rehabilitation, and increasingly 'fails' to point to the sometimes apparent dysfunctional role of criminal law as regards dispute settlement and social welfare. He calls this the 'betrayal of the pen-pushers'.

The function of criminal justice cannot be reduced to that of sanctions. Law enforcement should follow sociocultural developments by legislatory innovations; the legal concept of unlawfulness should correspond as much as possible with what society holds as undesirable. And, next to the sanctions which contribute to dispute settlement, social welfare can also be advanced by the prevention of dysfunctional conflicts. As far as law enforcement is concerned, this contention implies that the level of tolerance towards relatively innocent forms of deviance should be increased, that disputes over the actual content of norms and values should be possible, and that law should manage normative conflicts rather than declaring the one vision 'right' and the other 'wrong'. Furthermore, the social conflicts of the 1960s have shown that the application of means of coercion should be regulated in a more detailed way. Hulsman calls the fact that these things hardly take place 'frustrating', and argues that a stronger focus on policy, rather than legislation, would be a necessary step to overcome the fact that criminal law lags behind so many developments in society (Hulsman, 1967).

Seen in the context of the progressive political climate of the time, Hulsman's position is understandable, but it is equally understandable that, in the following era of restoration, many progressives wished that developments in criminal law would lag a bit more behind those in society. Paul Moedikdo (1974: 43, n. 54) contests Hulsman's political aspirations, by arguing that his 'policy-technical' vision of law 'tends to over-estimate the meaning of rationality and social techniques' as a means of advancing a humane coexistence. He adds that a more sound theoretical reflection might temper optimism about the possibilities of social engineering by law enforcement. Hulsman adds a normative element to his functionalist vision of law. He sees law as an instrument of social change, but explicitly argues that neither every goal nor all means are acceptable. Both should independently pass an ethical test before they are given an internal dynamics in legislation. After this is effected, the question of legitimation needs to be answered in terms of legality alone (Hulsman, 1968).

Like Bianchi, Hulsman also became more radical under 'the spirit of 68'. In his argument that instruments of social control should not create unnecessary and improper conflicts over norms and values, an implicit influence of the labelling approach can be identified. It should be noted that, despite the increasing criminological development of his thought, Hulsman also continued to do very typical juridical work during this time: writing commentaries to case law. In this era, he participated on various governmental committees: for example, on the decriminalisation of some offences against public morality, and on the establishment of a more liberal policy on the consumption of soft drugs. By the end of the 1960s, a new source of intellectual inspiration can be observed in Hulsman's work: symbolic interactionism. Hulsman's aforementioned colleague, Peter Hoefnagels' (1969) interactionist studies ultimately led Hulsman to a focus on what he would later call the 'life-world'. A first example of this micro-sociological approach is linked to the question of crimes which are never recorded in any statistics, because they are not registered by the police; the so-called 'dark figure'. The vast majority of crimes never reach the criminal justice system. Whereas this is a matter of concern for many lawyers, it makes Hulsman rather optimistic. Since society is still not in complete decay, the prevalence of a high 'dark figure' implies that most problems are dealt with quite effectively by informal, self-regulatory mechanisms of social control in the community. As far as crime control is concerned, criminal law thus turns out to be a relatively unimportant instrument. It furthermore proves that there are large disparities between the practice of criminal justice and its discursive representations. These disparities are not legitimised by any rational choice or analysis. If criminal law is to be judged on its actual effects, while empirical research shows that it does not play such a central role in social control, and often dysfunctions as regards its proclaimed goals, we are forced to reconsider the legitimacy of the system as such.

Hulsman's orientation towards decriminalisation is an intermediate step in the direction of abolitionism. The transition from Hulsman's earlier work, via his influence on the Council of Europe's *Report on Decriminalisation* of 1980, to his final abolitionist perspective does not imply a principally different position. Next to a full, *de iure* decriminalisation of certain offences, Hulsman also advocates a *de facto* decriminalisation. This means that certain acts will formally remain illegal, but will not be prosecuted. This focus is directed at

Hulsman's earlier arguments for an expansion of the policy discretions of the prosecution. In the Council of Europe's report three rationales behind decriminalisation are distinguished. In a 'type A decriminalisation' the behaviour referred to is no longer considered to imply something wrong. In 'type B', certain norms are not shared by a large part of the population, but it is not considered to be a task of the state to determine right and wrong in this respect. A 'type C decriminalisation' involves cases which are still considered to be wrong, undesirable or socially harmful, but there are other means of social control more effective and less stigmatising than criminal law. Many studies of the 'civilisation' of justice (transferring criminalised problems to a civil lawsuit), which have been carried out in particular by Hulsman's staff member Joyce Hes and practising lawyer Job Knap, follow from this aspect of Hulsman's abolitionism. In the realm of his strategy of decriminalisation, the 'normalisation' of drugs, studied by staff members Tom Blom, Hugo Durieux and Hans van Mastrigt, becomes a key topic.

According to Hulsman, we do not need to wait for radical political reform or structural analyses of criminalisation in order to begin decriminalisation: coercion needs legitimation, giving up on coercion does not. Through the ages, this practical anticipation of a formal abolition has been a typical Dutch strategy of reform. This pragmatic, political approach makes Hulsman's perspective an interesting challenge for those 'intellectual sceptics' who advocated radical penal reform but became paralysed by all the structural configurations it implies – which led them to the idea that nothing works. On the other hand, it makes the rationale of Hulsman's ideas very dependent on a cooperative political climate. Decriminalisation can also be used as an attractive label for the state to clean up the criminal justice system's caseload and to transfer petty offences to modes of control that offer the involved person less protection against arbitrary measures than a criminal law suit would (Politoff, 1987). Mass settlements of offences by administrative or financial means are presented as forms of decriminalisation, whereas their punitive character is certainly not less (Hartmann and van Russen Groen, 1994). Hulsman's vision of decriminalisation is subjected to a critical theoretical and empirical enquiry by John Blad (1996).

With the years, Hulsman lost faith that fundamental reform could be realised within current legal structures. John Blad (1996) argues that there is a large continuum in Hulsman's transition from jurist to anti-jurist, when he changes, between 1977 and 1979, the perspective of criminal law as problem-solving institution to criminal law as a social problem. It was not so much Hulsman's observations that changed as the meaning he gave to these observations. He now saw the criminal justice system as a more closed and autopoietic system (a system largely organised according to, and reflecting upon, its own rationale) than before. His aim to achieve a fundamental change in the penal system as a means of increasing social welfare necessitates a change from an internal to an external perspective. Had Hulsman stuck to a system-internal approach when penal policy no longer followed a reductionist course, he would have committed the same betrayal of ideals that he accused the probation service's pen-pushers of. In Hulsman's own perception, the main change lies in a transformation from a top-down vision of reform within the limits of penal rationale to an approach from below, in which the language from the 'life-world' is adopted. This is also the major difference between abolitionism and reductionist agendas. The crucial point of distinction may not be so much the practical goal, but rather the ideological rejection of the penal rationale as such, with its inherent political waves between reduction and expansion. The stiffened penal climate of the 1980s required a more fundamental critique. When repressive and expansionist orientations prevailed, and criminal justice policy was no longer oriented to social welfare, Hulsman concluded that the criminal justice system exists for other than rational reasons, and would therefore be better abolished.

Hulsman rejects the idea that crime consists of any ontological element. It is just a label that is selectively applied to some social problems. These 'crimes' are not fundamentally different from non-criminalised social problems – a contention Hulsman has made from the outset. This distinguishes Hulsman also from Bianchi. Bianchi does not denounce the critique of primary and secondary criminalisation and also deviance, but he does call certain acts 'evil'; the ontological aspect of crime is the immoral character that it shares with many other, non-criminalised acts. For Hulsman, the punitive rationality that blocks the search for solutions begins when a problem is called a 'crime'. The thread in Hulsman's abolitionism, formulated in *Peines perdues* (Hulsman and Bernat de Celis, 1982), is that crime is an inadequate social construction.[5] In this sense, Hulsman has made an important contribution to a reflexive criminology and, indeed, to the decriminalisation of criminology (Nelken, 1994b: 7, 13). Hulsman's abolitionism starts at the level of definition. It does not focus on 'abstract alternatives at the end of the penal tunnel'. He primarily criticises the criminal law vision of reality, which prevents an approach to social problems in anything other than an individualising and punitive way. This shows the strong linguistic basis of Hulsman's abolitionism: other definitions, other categorisations lead to other solutions. This vision does not imply a perspective principally different from before, but the emphasis is surely placed differently, and the expectations of any feasible fundamental reform are drastically lowered. More strongly than before, Hulsman interprets criminal law as a state instrument of social control. Its anonymising and 'funneling' structure creates more problems than it solves. Hulsman even considers it a bigger social problem than crime. As a social and cultural organisation, criminal law is the daughter of scholasticism because it witnesses the same Manichaean vision of morality and a comparable monolithic and absolutist point of orientation (which once came from God and now from the legislator), leading to one last judgement. Hulsman once portrayed the criminal justice system as 'a horse that has ran amok', and then again as 'a colossus with feet of clay'. A trial has a fundamentally non-communicative structure because it does not register what has really happened, but categorises concrete experiences in standard terms oriented at the ideology of the system. The penal reconstruction of reality has, with its central concepts such as crime, guilt and punishment, a paralysing effect on attempts to find the most adequate solution to compensate the victim, or to address underlying social problems and circumstances.

The application of a broader vision of problematic situations from a 'life-world' perspective would imply a recognition of the whole range of already existing informal and semi-institutionalised social reactions. In an adapted civil law structure, aimed at the law of tort, parties are better able to express themselves. In Hulsman's view, the police, judiciary and probation service will perform a socially more useful role in a new setting because they can, once they are no longer hindered by the pressure of further prosecution, better contribute to finding creative solutions oriented at people's real-life situations. Once aimed at social welfare instead of crime control, they can also be more facilitating. This element of Hulsman's abolitionism is elaborated by his staff members Hilde van Ransbeek and Stijn Hogenhuis, and adviser of the Amsterdam police force Frans Denkers. Van Ransbeek studied informal mechanisms of social control in urban and rural settings, Hogenhuis analysed how the police informally contribute to dispute settlement, while Denkers has primarily investigated how people's personal skills in dispute settlement can be stimulated. They argue that civic satisfaction with the police depends more on assistance in solving concrete problems, or even just taking people's personal stories seriously, rather than on its efforts in getting culprits prosecuted and punished.

Hulsman's abolitionism basically implies the abolition of: the conceptualisation and categorisation of crime; pain infliction as an accurate measure of the social hierarchy of values; the projection of damage and harm done to people as a conflict with society; and the dimension of time as a quasi-rational representation of sanctions. According to Hulsman, we have to keep the dominant focus on the offender, and concentrate on means of crime prevention which are not captured in stereotypical crime discourse. Hulsman is a pragmatic abolitionist, for both moral assessments and theoretical elaboration only play a limited role in his work. Hulsman eclectically uses different theoretical insights in an applied fashion, directed at themes of criminal justice politics. Rotterdam philosopher Rolf de Folter placed Hulsman's abolitionism, in view of his non-reductionist approach, in a phenomenological tradition. In order really to understand the problem of 'crime', Hulsman takes us back to the heart of the matter – *zu den Sachen selbst*, as was Edmund Husserl's motto. De Folter (1987: 188, 204) also sees links with post-structuralist theories on normalisation, in which Michel Foucault's work takes a central position. In line with this particular stream of thought, Hulsman argues for a revitalisation of the social matrix, and proposes to bring our ways of dealing with social problems back to their actual lived experience. The epistemological discrepancy between Hulsman's life-world approach and the link with Foucault's post-structuralism remains unresolved.

There is also a strong relation between Hulsman's approach and the social constructionism of Peter Berger and Thomas Luckmann. Hulsman is also notably inspired by Joseph Gusfield's ideas on the culture of social problems and Johan Galtung's distinction between blue (liberal–capitalist), red (socialist) and green (post-material environmentalist) developments in society. Hulsman places his abolitionism in this latter category. He focuses on the organic and small-scale, real-life level of society. Hulsman also gives a rather free interpretation to Habermas' idea of the colonisation of the life-world by a system-rationality. Contrary to Habermas, Hulsman speaks of two different worlds: the world of systems, which is ruled by hegemonic discourse, and the informally structured life-world, which functions rather independently from discursive developments. The life-world's potential as a problem-solving web would, according to Hulsman, increase if it could be 'freed' from bureaucratic regulations from the world of systems.

Criminal justice as a social problem

Even though Bianchi's ethical and depenalising and Hulsman's functionalist and decriminalising approaches are different, both 'black swans' of Dutch criminology have more in common than issues that divide them. It is an interesting phenomenon to observe that both Bianchi and Hulsman, as well as Kempe and Nagel, became more radical as they got older. The radicalisation of Kempe and Nagel's ideas was partly caused by the Second World War. This same experience was the starting-point for Bianchi and Hulsman's thought about crime and punishment. For all four, the 1960s meant another caesura, albeit that for Kempe and Nagel this period came at the end of their career and for Bianchi and Hulsman at the beginning. It is also noteworthy that Nagel was active in the Resistance, and that Kempe, Bianchi and Hulsman were imprisoned and put in concentration camps during the German occupation. For all four, radicalisation followed from disillusionment with system-internal attempts at penal reform. The transition to abolitionism coincided with the end of the reductionist Dutch penal policy at the close of the 1970s.

Neither Bianchi nor Hulsman argues against social control in the typical critical criminological style. They do not see social control as the dominion of the state. They reject the top-down, repressive, punitive and inflexible character of penal control, but advocate bottom-up, integrative and informal forms of social control. The ideas of both Bianchi and Hulsman have, in line with the development of the informal justice debate over the 1980s, been broadly dismissed as unrealistic and sinister. Both share the idea that the translation of social problems into terms of a direct causality between crime and punishment is a major deficit of the penal rationale. Both also agree that even incarceration may be indispensable in some cases, and that civil liberties and human rights need to be guaranteed by some public body.

In order to bring critical criminology a step forward, a number of important questions need to be addressed to the abolitionist perspective. Both Bianchi and Hulsman have, in their own style, given a fundamental critique of the rationale and actual functioning of the criminal justice system. Their negative critique is stimulating, powerful and quite convincing. It is, however, rather awkward that of all the observations about structuralism, macro-phenomenology or indeed emancipatory strategies of penal reform of the 1970s, so little evidence can be found on the abolitionist perspective of the 1980s. It is to be regretted that references to structural limitations of the abolitionist project are largely absent.

A central idea behind Hulsman's thought is that everyday phenomena are more real than theoretical, second-order constructions. This idea, adopted from Peter Berger and Thomas Luckmann, should be rejected because of the partial structural determination of such life-world knowledge which remains too much out of focus. John Blad (1996) argues, however, that also within the paradigm of social constructionism, it is necessary to distinguish the social meaning of phenomena from the mere personal meaning Hulsman tends to rely on. Lode van Outrive (1987) has argued that a dominantly phenomenological approach makes it impossible to see the structural economic and political determination of the particular way social problems are dealt with. The fact that conflicts are taken from their owners (Christie, 1977) is a phenomenon that is not exclusive to law enforcement. It should indeed be seen as one example of the macro-sociological development of the expropriation of labour, social security, education, health care and so on. Consequently, the replacement of criminal law by civil law or informal modes of dispute settlement can, according to van Outrive (1987: 56), only be perceived in terms of a general decentralisation of state power. This implies that the main focus should be on the reduction of the present system. Otherwise, alternatives are bound to be add-ons in the darkening and uncontrollable shadow of Leviathan.

It is often argued that abolitionism is a postmodern and anarchist perspective of criminology. With respect to its rejection of the 'grand narrative' of law and its 'replacement discourse' of smaller narratives of dispute settlement in the life-world, abolitionism is, indeed, a postmodern criminology *avant la lettre*. Hulsman may also be postmodern as far as his theoretical eclecticism and language-games with the concept of crime are concerned, but with his insistence on rational critiques of the penal system, he is very modern. If Bianchi's more intuitive approach is postmodern, this label can hardly be attuned with his political commitment and normative orientation. Some of these 'postmodern' tendencies are rather confusing and problematic. Even if we accept that crime is not a category that reflects on ontological reality, it certainly remains a historical and sociological reality. As long as social problems are criminalised, 'crime' remains a social construction which deserves a specific research attention. With an intuitive approach and theoretical eclecticism, we need to be careful not to build on weak foundations, but with regard to overcoming the ideological purism of the past it should not be judged in solely negative terms, while the inclusion of smaller narratives rightly adjusts the dominance of critical criminology's macro-sociological focus.

There are certainly links between anarchist thought on state control and the abolitionist critique of the penal system, but the two do not necessarily coincide. It is no aim of abolitionists to do away with the state because it has to facilitate social welfare. From the side of the anarchists, Peter Kropotkin is one of the few to defend penal abolition. In general, anarchists do not point their arrows greatly at criminal law. Both Bianchi and Hulsman advocate a reduction of the state's power to punish and propose a wider variety of less repressive and more informal mechanisms of social control, because they put more trust in the reasonableness of people of flesh and blood than in anonymous functionaries and bureaucratic systems. Bianchi's appeal to decentralisation is based on the rationale that because mankind is inclined to all evil and unable to do any good, concentrations of power need to be restricted, so that abuses have less dramatic consequences. Hulsman distrusts bureaucratic systems mainly because of their rampant logic. Once the machine is put in motion, it is hard to change its direction. Individual persons are better able to change direction when circumstances require it.

The positive abolitionist critique of dispute settlement is based on weaker ground than the negative critique of the penal system. Whether we take Bianchi's assensus model or Hulsman's self-regulating mechanisms at life-world level, considerable trust seems to be put in people's capacities to follow ideal structures of communication, by which conflicts can be settled in a rational way. Abolitionists stress the importance of human input in legal procedures, and challenge the dominant focus on technical legality, which excludes non-experts from the process. In order to do justice to this social character, people must first and foremost be enabled to tell *their* story, be listened to, have a say in the process of settlement, be able to question the universality of norms, before any formal element becomes actually relevant.

On a concrete level it seems, however, realistic to assume that people will not always come to an agreement on solutions (even when this may indeed be easier than an agreement on the true nature of the facts) and that someone will probably have to over-rule a sheer endless debate. This raises at least the yet unanswered question of who is going to do this, according to which standards, and how a solution can be advanced without coercion? Abolitionists have not yet come to the point of setting any limits to an ideal-typical perspective of restorative justice. In this respect, Bianchi's alternative, with a mediator in the form of a *praetor*, seems more coherent. This model shows, however, the same fallacies as Hulsman's, namely that it remains unclear what should happen if things go wrong. It is, however, also useful to keep Clara Wichmann's argument in mind that, by always focusing on ultimate consequences, every innovation would be nipped in the bud. As a sensitising concept and a replacement discourse, the positive moment of abolitionism is quite valuable: if only because it challenges the 'nothing works' despair about penal reform without falling back on neo-classical models. It is just not yet thought through to the end.

In pluriform, largely secular societies with a fragmented morality, it seems quite fitting for Hulsman, and really Bianchi as well, to reject the last judgement character of criminal law. It is not always clear what the (central) role of the state as an autonomous party in a conflict should be. The way out that Bianchi, and particularly Hulsman, offer in this respect is, however, far too frivolous. While attacking the criminal justice system precisely for its ritualistic character and punitive symbolism, abolitionists too easily ignore the desire for public affirmation of norms. It may be difficult for abolitionists to accept that particularly vulnerable groups in society have asked for the 'symbolic' support of the penal system, but this problem has to be addressed. It is questionable whether women or ethnic minorities can realistically expect something constructive from penal solutions to their actual problems, but this question leaves the subjective need for a public acknowledgement of their claims untouched. There is an apparent need for moral support or solidarity, an assessment from the state as the embodiment of collective interests. It may be false and superseded, but it is the primary body people can as yet think of. Other forums than those of criminal law, and, indeed, reactions other than punitive ones, may be more suited to fulfil such ritual tasks, but this question still has to be addressed. In Kees van der Vijver's (1993: 183) analysis of the significance of criminal law in the eyes of the general public, it is exactly the negation of such symbolic functions, and of a Durkheimian *conscience collective* as such, that makes abolitionism such an unacceptable option, and why it has provoked such aggressive reactions.

Another problem is that Bianchi and Hulsman both really focus on quite traditional forms of crime, with identifiable offenders and victims. In this way, they reduce social problems to individual concerns, thereby reinforcing a major analytical problem of criminal law, rather than offering any alternative to it. If they accept coercion as an *ultima ratio* (which both ultimately do), who is to control its use and what are the standards of proportionate and subsidiary intervention? Neither Bianchi nor Hulsman rejects the meaning of guarantees, but nor have they given it a particularly high importance in their later work. Particularly in Italy, an orientation towards penal guarantees has therefore been placed against abolitionism. The general guaranteeist argument against abolitionism is that, with the abolition of criminal law, legal safeguards against the state decrease as well, and that the road towards an increasing arbitrariness is opened because no other (legal) system is designed yet which can potentially offer a better, or indeed equal, protection. The abolitionist critique still needs to be elaborated in this respect. Many of these questions can be answered, if the abolitionist debate shifts from a focus on mere practical 'solutions' to a more profound theoretical elaboration. These problems will be elaborated in Chapters 9 and 10.

In The Netherlands there has been a broad, but rather mild and eclectic, reception for critical criminology. Yet all of the most typical Dutch 'schools' – of class and strain, of sociolegal guaranteeism and of abolitionism – follow from national academic traditions which date back several decades. Since abolitionists, in particular, may offer some answers to pivotal questions of the internal, analytical crisis of critical criminology, this perspective will be reassessed in relation to the penal reality of the 1990s.

Notes

1 *Kabouter* means gnome. The name alludes to the 'small is beautiful' ideology and to the ecological character, for *kabouters* are mother nature's little helpers. One of the central figures in Provo, Roel van Duyn, was elected to the Amsterdam city council for Kabouter, where he now (in 1997) represents the Greens.

2 This is not to say that the Dutch secret service BVD did not in those days have a rather obsessive interest in people active in various left-wing groups, notably the Communist party, and such people have indeed regularly encountered problems in finding work or keeping their jobs. Political action which has come closest to 'terrorism' has come from South Moluccans (people from the East Indies who fought on the Dutch side, who were transported to The Netherlands after Indonesian independence and who want to put pressure on the Dutch state to negotiate with the Indonesian government for them to get an independent state).

3 The NVK edited a new introduction to criminology *Tegen de Regels* (*Against the Rules*), drew up guidelines on the ethics of criminological research, and organised meetings on important books or topical issues as well as the national conferences of criminology. The biggest conflict arose when, in 1978, Leiden professor of criminology Wouter Buikhuisen announced a biosocial research project. Journalists (Piet Grijs), professional journals (KRI) and academics (Herman Bianchi) argued strongly against this neo-Lombrosianism. The Leiden department of criminology split in two, and Buikhuisen's project could not be carried out. The NVK was nearly forced to take a position, but felt uneasy about the subject: few members sympathised with Buikhuisen's plans, but it was felt that an academic forum should defend academic freedom. Modest protest letters against the way Buikhuisen was counteracted have been the uneasy compromise.

4 Van Koppen uses this title because the textbook he is referring to appeared on the occasion of Jongman's retirement (Jongman, 1993). By that time, the department had been substantially reduced and is now integrated with the department of criminal law. With the appointment of Willem de Haan as Jongman's successor it is, however, likely that the critical tradition will be maintained.

5 This book is constructed as one large interview with the French journalist Jacqueline Bernat de Celis. The title *Peines perdues* is a pun; it refers both to pains, penalties or troubles which have been in vain, and implies at the same time an invitation to forget about these concepts. There is no English translation of the book, but the most important notions are outlined in Hulsman, 1986.

7

The Radical Penal Lobby in Europe

This chapter analyses the development of the radical penal lobby in Europe and examines its relation to critical criminology. In Chapter 2, the focus on penal reform is, among other things, seen as a consequence of the political commitment of critical criminologists, and motivated by the fact that it offers a good possibility for international comparison. In the last two chapters, we have furthermore seen that studies on the prison system take a central place in European critical criminology. As representatives of the new left, social movements actually encouraged critical criminology's emergence. Willem de Haan (1990: 32) argues in this respect that: 'the dynamism and potential of social movements to identify previously undiagnosed characteristics of, and possibilities within, a given institutional order . . as well as their orientation toward the achievement of novel projects has always been of prime significance for stimulating the sociological imagination.' Social movements are also a central object of study for critical criminologists: (youth) counter-cultures; moral entrepreneurs who lobby for the penal protection of hegemonic 'norms and values'; as well as so-called 'a-typical moral entrepreneurs', like the women's, environmental or anti-racist movements, who use criminalisation as a strategy for emancipatory goals (Scheerer, 1986b). John Braithwaite (1995) devotes a central role to these new social movements in his 'republican criminology' because they sensitise public opinion on crime by 'shaming' harmful behaviour (of the powerful) which previously remained outside the scope of the criminal justice system. Penal pressure groups and prisoners' movements have demonstrated the undesirable consequences of stigmatisation and social exclusion. This provoked criminological research and, to a certain extent, sensitised the public, political and scientific vision of penality. The abolitionist perspective even finds its roots in penal activism.

Another reason to devote a whole chapter to the radical penal lobby is that it forms the social basis of critical criminology's politics from below in respect of the penal question. Prisoners' personal narratives, in particular, reveal a non-discursive and emancipatory knowledge on this theme. There are also interesting personal links between critical criminological forums and the radical penal lobby. The relation between theory and action as such has, however, not so often been an explicit object of study. Because Thomas Mathiesen's work is pioneering in this respect, we will deal with his work first.

Thomas Mathiesen and the abolitionist movement in Norway

Action research should, according to Thomas Mathiesen, be practice-oriented and political objectives should be made explicit. Theory formation should follow from a feed-back process from practical political activity. It should, through a systematic gathering of information, feed new, practical political activity. As Mathiesen (1965) showed in *The Defences of the Weak*, solidarity among prisoners is not self-evident. Therefore, the struggle for prisoners' rights must be organised collectively. For this purpose, Mathiesen co-founded the Norwegian penal pressure group KROM in 1968. Mathiesen's involvement with this movement led him to abolitionism.[1] KROM challenges the penal system's function as an instrument of state control. It consists of (ex-)prisoners and their relatives and left-wing intellectuals. Mathiesen (1974) describes KROM's objective as influencing public opinion on punishment in such a way that, in the long term, the prison system can be replaced by more up-to-date measures, and that, in the short term, all not strictly necessary walls can be torn down.

A central point of Mathiesen's penal action theory is the principle of the 'unfinished' character of alternatives to prison. Mathiesen distinguishes in this respect between (a) positive reforms, which strengthen the penal system; and (b) negative reforms, which are of an abolishing kind. In a politics of negative reform, one needs to operate in a system-foreign structure in order not to be 'defined-in' in hegemonic structures and political discourse, since this would lead to the loss of the different character of alternatives. One should not develop fully elaborated blueprints because, within the current penal rationale, these will lose their restructuring value: 'the finished alternative is finished in a double sense of the word' (Mathiesen, 1974: 13). Mathiesen also warns of the danger of being 'defined-out': one will be ignored as a serious debating partner when criticism cannot be supported by empirical facts, or if macro-political observations can hardly be related to concrete penal questions. Mathiesen calls the position in between the 'competing contradiction', which is the only safeguard against cooption of radical initiatives, and thus against alternatives widening the net of social control. The alternative character of abolitionism lies in a continual adaptation to changing circumstances; it is a 'continually rotating transition to the uncompleted', as is 'the process of life itself' (Mathiesen, 1974: 28). This idea of penal reform between revolution and reformism implies a continual dialectical relation. A final synthesis would imply stagnation.

In 1968, KROM aimed to reform the prison system in cooperation and dialogue with prison authorities. The authorities, however, refused to enter a debate with this prisoners' movement, let alone seriously consider its demands or wishes. According to Mathiesen, this refusal politicised KROM. By engaging in a polemic with the authorities' discourse, KROM opts for a dialectical conflict model. With hindsight, Mathiesen argues that it was precisely the concept of the 'unfinished' that was extremely threatening for the prison authorities because they could not place KROM: were they revolutionaries or reformists? The 'unfinished' is exactly the attempt to overcome this dichotomy: KROM is intentionally both. KROM organises public meetings and annual teach-ins as open seminars about penal policy, and lawyers within KROM bring prisoners' cases before the ombudsman, and select the politically most significant ones (cases of censorship and other infringements of constitutional rights, arbitrary decisions of prison officers and governors, internal rules, working conditions and so on) for publication in the media. In this way, KROM reveals to the general public the hidden penal reality behind closed doors. One of KROM's strongest points is that intellectuals and prisoners cooperate on an equal basis, struggle for the same purposes, and outline the strategic position of the movement together. KROM never uses information it cannot check and only relies on its own sources. With regard to the individual complaints of prisoners, KROM tries to coordinate these actions in order to increase the political effect of each step taken (Mathiesen and Røine, 1975). Next to penal abolition, prisoners' rights is the crucial issue on KROM's agenda. Conflicts about KROM's 'academism' have, none the less, led to the foundation of an affiliated branch for prisoners: SON (*Straffedes Organisasjon i Norge*).

Mathiesen describes KROM's emergence in close connection with the then widely held belief that times would indeed be changing for the better. With the social changes of the 1980s, KROM also changed its position. Mathiesen (1986) reassessed the notion of negative reform and concluded that striving for a moratorium on prison construction now deserved a more prominent place on the agenda. Mathiesen (1990) shows more specifically what changes have taken place within KROM's politics. KROM is now more open to positive reforms. These are no longer solely rejected as net-widening, particularly in the field of juvenile justice. Sometimes they are just indispensable for the improvement of life conditions in total institutions (Mathiesen, 1990). This is an important shift, since the weakest spot of Mathiesen's theory is that it does not indicate how negative reform can be pursued. Because of this, many penal pressure groups following Mathiesen's strategy were forced into defensive positions and concluded that nothing would work. When KROM took a more defensive position, by trying to prevent expansion of the prison system rather than following the original offensive politics of abolition, it also focused more on the criminal justice system as a whole rather than on the prison issue alone. With the elaboration of prisoners' litigation within the European Court in Strasbourg, the human rights focus became increasingly important (Mathiesen 1986, 1990). Even if KROM's actual influence in reducing the use of custody decreases, there is no reason to consider the struggle as useless. Mathiesen compares this with the struggle against fascism or atomic weapons: pressure groups mainly serve to keep sensitivity to certain issues alive. Ninety per cent of all Norwegian prisoners are members of KROM. KROM continues to organise annual three-day conferences (*Synnseter-kongress*) and regular local info-meetings and seminars. It produces a newsletter, *KROM-Nytt*, and publishes its own series of books and consistently comments in national newspapers on topical developments within the field of criminal justice.

The British radical penal lobby

As representatives of the new left, the involvement of British critical criminologists in social action is virtually self-evident. The establishment of the penal pressure group *Radical Alternatives to Prison* (henceforth RAP) in October 1970 was a logical extension to the academic NDC. RAP consisted of a broader group of people than academics and social workers. It included (ex-)prisoners and their relatives, and activists involved in the CND (the campaigning group for nuclear disarmament), the Prison Reform Council and various Christian groups. While the NDC aimed to counter the dominant administrative orientation in criminology, RAP wanted to challenge the reformist orientation of the Howard League for Penal Reform and the National Association for the Care and Resettlement of Offenders (NACRO).

The Howard League had its origins in the struggle against capital punishment from 1866 onwards, and focused, since the abolition of capital punishment, largely on rehabilitation and correction. By 1970, the League was seen to confine itself to minor reformist themes. NACRO, founded in 1966 as a platform for practitioners in social and probation work, was also seen to ignore the wider social significance of penal reform. It took a pragmatic rather than a principled stance towards hegemonic political power relations (Downes and Morgan, 1994: 207). RAP aimed to take a more radical political position, and stressed that prisons cannot rehabilitate and do not house mainly dangerous people who must be locked away in order to protect society, but are indeed mainly filled with petty property offenders for whom more sensible solutions than imprisonment are possible (Ryan, 1978).

In May 1971, RAP began as a working group within Christian Action. Important landmarks in RAP's actions were the involvement in alternatives to bail and to women's imprisonment in 1971 and 1972. With the campaign against the re-establishment of Holloway women's prison and the subsequent publication of *Alternatives to Holloway*, RAP contributed a great deal to making the specific problem of women in detention visible: for example, motherhood, economic dependency, breach and reproduction of gender roles. Together with the Howard League and NACRO, RAP successfully campaigned in 1975 for the abolition of psychiatric control units. Campaigns in the late 1970s were directed at the suspension of shorter sentences and at the creation of opportunities for offenders to restore the damage they have done and to draw up for themselves a plan for their rehabilitation. This latter project, known as the Newham Alternatives Project (NAP), was also meant to challenge the prevailing practice of community service orders in Britain. These are insufficiently oriented to the actual situation of the offender, while the task he or she is to perform hardly offers any possibility to improve social skills (Ryan, 1978; Dronfield, 1980; Sim, 1994). Over the 1980s, RAP contributed to a sharp reduction in the use of custodial sentences for juveniles (Rutherford, 1994b: 287–8).

Though the Howard League and NACRO remained the most powerful penal pressure groups, RAP's more radical but, at the same time, also more client-oriented stance, attracted quite a number of critical probation officers. After increasing opposition from judicial authorities to its locally based alternatives to prison, RAP gradually adopted a more abolitionist course. According to Joe Sim (1994: 269), RAP's abolitionism was a reaction to the emerging authoritarian, populist, Tory law-and-order campaigns and to the penal crisis. Also some seemingly structural miscarriages of British justice provoked a more radical critique.

Whereas many of RAP's medium-term goals were shared by the whole penal lobby, its political outlook was not. RAP adopted the Mathiesian distinction between positive and negative reform and began to publish a journal called *The Abolitionist*. By this time, RAP's position among probation officers (NAPO) became more marginal and it came into conflict with its financial supporter Christian Action (Ryan, 1978; Ryan and Ward 1992: 322). People involved in RAP have, however, not embraced crude abolitionist positions on negative reform point-blank. As Stan Cohen argues in respect of the evaluation of RAP's project in Newham (NAP):

> It is difficult in advance to decide which reforms are . . . 'positive' and hence undesirable because they prop up the system, and which are 'negating reforms' and hence desirable because they expose the contradictions in the system. The NAP story cannot in itself answer this question. It does, however, show the possibilities of achieving genuinely humane as well as potentially negating reforms with the most limited resources. (Dronfield, 1980: 6)

'On 11 May 1972, the national media gathered inside a small public house . . . opposite Pentonville Prison. They listened as Dick Pooley outlined the demands of Preservation of the Rights of Prisoners (PROP), the newly formed British prisoners' union' (Fitzgerald, 1977: 136). According to Mike Fitzgerald (1977: 157), who was not only involved in PROP but was, in the late 1970s, also the NDC's secretary, the establishment of PROP should primarily be seen as a reaction against the brutalising conditions in British prisons, about which very little inside information was known, and as a side-effect of the massive prisoners' strike of 1972 and the following destruction of various prisons during the 1970s. Against this background, PROP set out a Charter of Demands in 1979, signed by some 10,000 inmates in 35 institutions. This charter included the right to unionise; the demand to negotiate with the Home Office about payment for prison labour and the improvement of prison conditions; free prisoners' litigation, without previous approval of the Home Office; the demand that decisions on disciplinary measures and parole are explicitly justified, and the introduction of a right to appeal, and of civil liberties like free communication with the outside world, uncensured correspondence and free choice of medical doctors. In later charters, PROP also argued for a substantial reduction in the prison population and for the right to receive punishment without any further psychiatric or social work interference.

By the 1980s, new reformist pressure groups, such as the Labour Party's Campaign Group for Criminal Justice (1978) and the Prison Reform Trust (1982), emerged. Though not unsuccessful on a legislative level, these groups did not receive much support and trust from prisoners because they were seen to defend prisoners' claims insufficiently within the higher circles of the establishment to which they, unlike PROP, had access. The Home Office was thought to respond only for purely opportunistic reasons: to prevent further disturbances (Ryan, 1983: 47; Downes and Morgan, 1994). In its report to the Committee of Inquiry into the United Kingdom Prison Services of 1979, established after the disorders, PROP reiterated its claims for an immediate opening of the prison administration to public scrutiny, a reduction in the number of prisoners, a moratorium on prison construction, and greater opportunities for education, communication, movement and litigation. These were no longer presented as demands *per se*, but rather as a means to reduce the tensions in British prisons (Taylor, 1981: 142–3).

Despite PROP's more reformist and legal orientation, its direct influence on public opinion and policy was as low as RAP's. The success of both RAP and PROP was of a more indirect and ideological kind. They gave necessary impetus to other campaigning groups to reject an individualising criminal pathology, and to acknowledge the fact that criminal justice also reflects broader power relations (Ryan and Ward, 1992: 327). RAP's critique left its traces within the Howard League; NACRO took up support for alternatives to custody; and the National Council for Civil Liberties (NCCL) increasingly campaigns for prisoners' rights. As we have seen before, the relation between British radical criminologists and legal activism is ambiguous. Within RAP and PROP, the argument for expanding the possibilities of prisoners' litigation was mainly an instrument to achieve decarceration, rather than a goal in itself. Tony Ward (1986: 76) has called the adoption of a justice model by such critical criminologists as Stan Cohen and Mick Ryan 'a noble lie in pursuit of a programme derived from Mathiesen'.

The once-polarised penal lobby now looks more like a varied spectrum of cooperating groups, with just different emphases.

> Compared with the sharp divisions between RAP and the Howard League in the 1970s, the distinction between the radical and the liberal wings of the lobby today seems far more subtle. The degree of consensus between them is shown by the fact that the Prison Reform Trust, Howard League, NAPO, Women in Prison and Inquest all work together (with several other organisations) in the Penal Affairs Consortium, which was founded in 1989, is serviced by NACRO, and lobbies for an agreed programme of reforms. (Ryan and Ward, 1992: 328)

This consortium of 24 different groups is 'a previously unthinkable combination' (Downes and Morgan, 1994: 209).

Though Mick Ryan and Tony Ward argue that both RAP and PROP were almost defunct by the late 1980s, they do not look back with bitter nostalgia. In fact, they offer quite an attractive analysis of why groups such as RAP and PROP dissolved into a more fragmented and less polarised penal lobby.

RAP and PROP were part of the British counter-culture of the early 1970s, when a whole range of marginalised groups oriented themselves towards the revolutionary transformation of society. This political moment passed, and the analysis giving such groups primacy is no longer held in radical circles. RAP, with its rejection of the rehabilitation ideology, could well have played into the hands of the Tories' 'get tough' version of the justice model. The initial distinction between positive and negative reform is now seen to be 'not as helpful as we had first assumed' (Ryan and Ward, 1992: 324). The positive and negative distinction does not address the subtleties and ramifications of particular reforms. 'Reform by its very nature contains both positive and negative possibilities' (Fitzgerald and Sim, 1982: 164). The ultimate idea that nothing works is to be rejected. It is too globalising and has been a major cause of the downward spiral of analytical despair. Tony Ward (1991) argues that struggles around and resistance to penal power are currently better understood through Foucault's (1975c) 'judo model' of action (a tactics in which a minimum of energy is used for defence or polarisation, while constructively bending the opponent's actions into an alternative direction), rather than through Mathiesen's dialectical model of a 'competing contradiction.'

RAP activists came to realise that not all power differentials in society can be traced back to one ultimate source, such as the relations of production; the power men exercise over women is one obvious example. Therefore, Mick Ryan and Tony Ward attribute a large role to the women's movement in the restructuring of the penal lobby in the 1980s. A more subtle analysis of power and domination was reflected within RAP in a more fractured and diverse lobby, with groups like RAP's Sex Offences Working Group, Women against Rape and Women in Prison, who independently organise and articulate their position without rather obligatory references to material forces. This fracturing of the lobby, which also led to the emergence of a number of independent black groups, is not a bad thing; it better reflects the realities and complexities of power and domination. In the 1980s, the Howard League also took more radical positions, notably in the privatisation debate.

Radical penal reform groups in Germany

The development of German radical penal pressure groups cannot be linked as neatly to the AJK as their British counterparts can to the NDC. First, the penal lobby in Germany was much more dispersed: there was little continuity, and initiatives were largely organised at the level of the states (*Länder*) rather than the federation. Secondly, its origins were not in the new left, but rather in the orthodox left. The first German prisoners' union, the *Deutsche Gefangenen Gewerkschaft* (DGG), founded in 1968, dissolved after only one year due to internal quarrels and financial mismanagement before any initiative had been put into practice (Schumann, 1975a: 66–7). In 1969, largely the same initiative was continued under the name of *Gewerkschaft der*

Gefangenen, Verwahrten und Untergebrachten (GGVU) by a number of inmates in Berlin and some sympathisers in society, active in the students' movement. The *Gefangenenrat* saw itself as a proletarian movement, as witnessed by the title of their pamphlet series, *Stimme der Lumpen* (Voice of the Lumpenproletariat) (Engelhardt, 1975). These two groups aimed at the humanisation of detention, and demanded the provision of legal advice and educational programmes to inmates and job schemes after detention, the improvement of contacts with the outside world, and fair wages for prison labour. The GGVU dissolved within two years, largely because too few people were willing and able to organise it, there were no financial resources, and because the group was harassed by the authorities: it was accused of fraud, of diverting children from parental custody and bringing them into contact with criminals, and of contacts with terrorist organisations. A similar thing happened with the rather influential anti-psychiatric group SPK (Socialist Patients' Collective), which was affiliated to a group of Heidelberg psychiatrists. It dissolved in 1971 after accusations about contacts with the *Baader-Meinhof Gruppe* (Engelhardt, 1975; Schumann, 1975a: 67–9).

Karl Schumann (1975a: 70–1) comments on the early phases of the penal reform lobby in Germany:

> One after the other broke up. If one wants to determine the failure of such experiments within the approach of student activists, one might point at two, almost typical, short-comings of Marxist groups in West Germany turning to matters of deviancy and crime: they often endorse a dogmatic analysis which precludes meaningful reference to the actual life conditions of the people; and prefer theoretical discussions over taking care of immediate needs of the suffering groups.

In 1974, a group of academics from Bielefeld organised a meeting with two general trade unions (DGB and ÖTV) in order to investigate how these unions would feel about defending the interests of prisoners.

The Bielefeld group argued, as reasons why trade unions should see this as a part of their task, that most prisoners and ex-prisoners are working-class people; that prisons reproduce inhuman labour conditions; and that the working conditions of prison staff, who are mostly members of the trade union, are also improved if prisoners' living conditions are raised. The unions doubted whether they should take an explicit position with regard to penal reform. Some officials could not see the relation with trade union activities, and others openly rejected the idea because they feared that an association with 'criminals' would be counter-productive for the general aims of trade unions. A compromise could only be reached on further talks about professional education for prisoners. The Bielefeld group drew the following conclusions from the experiences of these first initiatives in the German penal lobby: activities should be concentrated within prison in order not to be carried away by macro-political struggle; they should be strictly legal, in order not to provoke judicial reactions which would damage the initiative; and the struggle for prisoners' rights is to be connected with broader penal reform in order to stress the collective value of individual efforts and to avoid sectarianism (Schumann, 1975b).

In the second half of the 1970s, this group approached AG SPAK, an umbrella organisation of projects for borderline groups, largely financed by the department of youth welfare. AG SPAK, in its turn, had been looking for a reorientation of its welfare activities in prisons. Many members were dissatisfied with its reformist, charity-work orientation. AG SPAK was willing to host a penal reform group, and hoped to concentrate some local and regional activities already existing in this field, such as the action group of the Berlin Environmental Party (*Grüne Alternative Liste Berlin*) on a moratorium on prison construction, comparable initiatives in the states of Hessen (*Initiative für eine bessere Kriminalpolitik*) and Northrhine Westphalia (*Kriminalreform Nordrhein Westfalen*), and prisoners' groups like the *Arbeitskreis Kritischer Strafvollzug*. Around 1980, AG SPAK's penal reform group, the *Kriminalpolitische Arbeitskreis* (henceforth KRAK) was modelled on the Norwegian KROM (Papendorf, 1985: 142). The proletarian *Gefangenenrat Frankfurt* remained outside this 'reformist' framework.

Theoretical feedback on these developments, typical in the case of KROM, has hardly taken place in Germany. The inside story of KROM and KRAK, Knut Papendorf's book *Gesellschaft ohne Gitter* (Society without bars) of 1985, remains largely descriptive and declaratory, and offers few analytical clues. In his introduction to the German translation of Mathiesen's *The Politics of Abolition*, called *Überwindet die Mauern* (Overcome the walls), Karl Schumann connects some practical lessons from recent German attempts at prison activism with the work of Thomas Mathiesen and Michel Foucault. Because of similarities in the underlying philosophy of both about the social functions of the prison system – predominantly serving to discipline the working classes in society – these two authors should be read in connection. Schumann (1979: 16) concludes that the chances of success for political prison activism would increase if not only left-wing media were used for propaganda, but also the so-called bourgeois press; if only absolutely correct and well-argued (not ideologised and exaggerated) information on miscarriages of justice were publicised; and if the most plausible reactions of the system's functionaries were anticipated, countered and de-dramatised in order not to be left empty-handed after official responses.

KRAK did not live 'happily ever after': it was defunct by the mid-1980s. Papendorf (1993: 80–1) argues that KRAK dissolved because the tension between AG SPAK's traditional orientation at rehabilitation and correction, and the radical abolitionist critique of the grassroots groups, could not be resolved – nor could strategies inspired by theoretical considerations of decriminalisation and those of a practical defence of interests in a trade-union model. This led to a schism between 'bourgeois' academics, on the one hand, and 'revolutionary' activists, on the other. The ideological test of abolitionist purity also had a damaging effect on the traditional regionally and autonomously operating activists. KRAK's 'central committee' operated in a totalitarian fashion – by boycotting publications of individual activists presented under the name of KRAK. Papendorf (1993: 80–1) concludes:

Hereby, we have defined the problem, which would haunt KRAK throughout its existence, namely the incapacity to understand KRAK as an autonomous medium or label and to use it in the federal discussion of penal politics. KRAK has always been too heavily theoretical. There has been an increasing amount of discussion on abolitionism, instead of concentrating a bit more on the concrete penal political praxis.

The *Bundesarbeitsgemeinschaft der freien Initiativen – Gruppen in der Straffälligenarbeit* (henceforth BAG), a platform of independent social-work organisations in the penal field, had become involved in penal reform by the 1980s. BAG's first initiatives in this respect were the fight against popular prejudices about crime by giving education on this subject at schools. Because BAG also wanted to distance itself from its traditional individual orientation towards correction and rehabilitation, it contacted KRAK. In 1983, BAG adopted an orientation to radical social work, in which aid was linked with collective interests, and individual cases were used as examples in general information and publicity work. In this way, BAG hoped to prevent social work becoming just another form of social control. Another central aim was the creation of counter-publicity to put the political and media exploitation of the fear of crime into perspective. BAG developed alternative penal policy proposals and, gradually, the social work input was reduced (Bahl, 1993: 167–70).

BAG no longer became involved in practical actions itself but mainly offered an ideological, political frame of reference for social workers and other practitioners. Despite the largely practical orientation of most of its members, it had difficulty putting alternative proposals into practice. BAG's abolitionist focus was largely expressed in 'verbal' activities, such as the de-legitimation of the rationale of punishment, drawing attention in the media to the scandal of miscarriages of justice, the defence of prisoners' constitutional rights, and the possibilities of dealing with criminalised problems in private law suits. Most energy was expended discussing how to escape the ghost of positive reform. BAG primarily aimed to be a network, a think-tank and a vade-mecum, but – with this orientation – BAG gradually entered a dead-end street. Board member Elke Bahl (1993) posed the rhetorical question 'How finished are penal reformers made by the unfinished?' According to Bahl, BAG did, however, contribute to the development of a more critical attitude among probation officers. Besides this, BAG was able to translate reform proposals into political language. For this purpose, contacts were made with the environmental party *die Grünen* (the Greens). The idea was to influence national politics in an abolitionist sense by means of intensive contact with the Greens' parliamentary faction. This political party showed a commitment to an abolitionist-inspired penal policy, but the link with the Greens also resulted in conflictive debates about public safety or sexual violence, which were seen to conflict with the Greens' views on imprisonment. Also, the translation of every single proposal in terms of political feasibility was gradually felt to weaken the competing and contradictory political pressure. With hindsight, both Papendorf (1993: 81) and Bahl (1993: 177) argue that the close contact with the Greens cost more energy than was justified by the results. Gradually, BAG became defunct. Because the prison population was declining anyway, the drive to campaign for its reduction was felt to be less urgent. Problems and anxieties arising from German unification in 1990 also led to inertia. A lack of motivation became apparent, and BAG finally dissolved for financial reasons in 1991 (personal communication from Elke Bahl).

Law-oriented initiatives followed a period of more straightforward political activism. In the early 1980s, an anonymous group of students and 'political prisoners' in Frankfurt drew up a practical handbook for prisoners, with information about their legal and medical position (*Ratgeber für Gefangenen mit medizinischen und juristischen Hinweisen*), which also contained examples of protest letters. A group of radical social workers from Berlin published second and third editions of this *Ratgeber* and asked Johannes Feest and Elke Wegner of Bremen University to check and update the legal information. They became increasingly intrigued by the fact that this book was banned by one prison after another and that, moreover, this ban was confirmed in court after court. They therefore published separate leaflets (*Merkblätter*) on specific legal questions for prisoners. This action gradually resulted in a support project of test cases on penal execution and prisoners' litigation (personal communication from Johannes Feest). The individual legal orientation gained a collective political value by the standard case law emerging from it. By this 'solidarisation-effect', Mathiesen's fears about a 'juridification' of political questions was challenged. Feest and Wegner-Brandt (1993) claim that litigating for concrete demands to normalise specific prison conditions – that is, to see that they are as close as possible to conditions in society – could be a pragmatic strategy towards abolition. In this way, a politics of rights goes hand in hand with a politics of abolition.

The central problem of the German penal lobby was its dispersed character, its theoretical dogmatism and its political sectarianism. Whereas German critical criminologists have opened up interesting perspectives, not many attempts have been made to connect these insights with penal activism. Academically inspired initiatives emerged at a moment when the social and political basis for radical penal reform groups had largely disappeared. One also gets the impression that activists often do not know their own history; the same wheel is invented over and over again, and the same mistakes are continuously made. The later law-oriented projects did not seem to suffer from the problems of their precursors, but the social foundation of these latter groups was smaller.

Michel Foucault and the French penal lobby

Michel Foucault established, together with Jean-Marie Domenach and Pierre Vidal-Naquet, an information group on prisons (*Groupe d'information sur les prisons*, henceforth GIP). At a press conference at GIP's formation on

8 February 1971, in a gloomy chapel beneath the Montparnasse railway station in Paris, Foucault argued:

> None of us can be sure of avoiding prison. Less than ever today. Police control over our day-to-day lives is becoming tighter . . . They tell us that the courts are swamped. We can see that. But what if it were the police who are swamped? They tell us that the prisons are over-populated. But what if it were the population that were being over-prisoned? . . . Little information is published about prisons; this is one of the hidden regions of our social system, one of the dark areas in our lives. This is why, together with a number of magistrates, lawyers, journalists, doctors and psychologists, we have founded a *Groupe d'information sur les prisons*. (Macey, 1993: 258)

The formation of GIP was provoked by a hunger strike of 12 Maoists in the Parisian Santé prison, who wanted to draw public attention to their imprisonment for political reasons. These Maoists brought the radical left and prisoners together. Most of the support for the Maoist action came from students, *Secours rouge* (Red Help) in which Jean-Paul Sartre was also involved, and *Gauche prolétarienne* (Proletarian Left). When riots spread throughout various French prisons, these groups formed a network, together with common prisoners, their relatives and workers (Donzelot, 1975; Lambrechts, 1982: 96). The ultimate purpose of *Secours rouge* and *Gauche prolétarienne* was to unite the prisoners' movement and workers' movement into one revolutionary force. For GIP, the purpose was to show the intolerable practice of the prison system itself. Whether this would ultimately lead to 'the revolution' is another issue. Sometimes these two quite different forms of political commitment clashed. When *Gauche prolétarienne* claimed that this or that action was politically incorrect, that the workers at Renault would not understand the support for prison revolts (the ultimate touchstone for Maoists) or that GIP's speakers were 'insufficiently proletarian', Foucault insisted that 'this is GIP, not *Secours rouge* and not *Gauche prolétarienne*' (Macey, 1993: 264). Foucault did not remain the intellectual outsider in a social movement, but was really the motor of GIP. In his biography of Foucault, David Macey vividly describes how this highly acclaimed professor of the prestigious Collège de France addressed envelopes, made numerous phone-calls, handed out leaflets, wrote pamphlets, organised obscure meetings at his home address and got arrested, while his academic career continued as usual. Nothing in his previous life had prepared him for the coming years.

GIP's main strategy was to collect and publish information about prison conditions as described by prisoners. Their horrifying accounts would speak for themselves: prison is an intolerable institution. In the introduction to a first inquiry in 1971, held in 20 prisons, GIP explicitly argued that: 'It is not up to us to make proposals for reform. We do not dream of an ideal prison. We just want the reality to become known. Public opinion has to be awakened and it should remain awake' (Vingtras, 1972). Questionnaires had to be smuggled in and out of prison because, in France, it is forbidden to collect such information. GIP activists only very gradually gained the sympathy of the queues of visitors, who initially just wanted to see their relatives, but later helped to distribute the questionnaires when GIP was not allowed in. A second inquiry, on the inmates' experience of the legal system and the judiciary, did not really get off the ground, but the initiative was useful to foster and cement links between GIP and radical members of the legal profession. Foucault considered the links with the *Syndicat de la magistrature*, a union of progressive judges established after the events of May 1968, of crucial importance (Macey, 1993: 262).

Because of the involvement of Foucault and other intellectuals, GIP was able to publish the results of its inquiries in the public media – *Magazine Littéraire, le Nouvel Observateur, les Temps Modernes, Esprit,* or *le Monde*. GIP also organised public tribunals, so-called *Comités-Vérité*, where topical penal questions were discussed with the general public. These included the refusal of President Pompidou to pardon two prisoners sentenced to death, and the so-called disclosures of the Toul psychiatrist. With this latter event, the strategy of un-masking prison as an intolerable institution really gained momentum. A psychiatrist from the prison of Toul, Edith Rose, described many denigrating and infantilising 'games' to gain merits for good conduct that she encountered in her practice, as well as many forms of psychological torture executed over the, often mentally weaker, inmates, which not seldom ended in suicide. She also pointed to the frequent use of restraints and the isolation cell; and told of prisoners lying in their own excrement and those who were not allowed to see their own children just because they were not married to the mother. She concluded that so-called 'dangerous recidivists' were actually created by the system itself (Macey, 1993: 275). She revealed these 'secrets' in an open letter to the Inspector General of the Prison Administration, the President of the Republic, the Minister of Justice, and the President of the Order of Physicians. Her letter was widely quoted in the press, published in *La cause du peuple – j'accuse* (the journal of *Gauche prolétarienne*) and reprinted as a paid advertisement in a major national newspaper, *le Monde* (26–27 December 1971). Foucault immediately picked up her message. Not only because it reaffirmed the accounts of prisoners, but also because he saw her report as the political commitment *par excellence* of the specific intellectual – the person who speaks out against the intolerable on the basis of her professional knowledge. Hereby, Foucault implicitly argued against those who think they can speak in the name of someone else – like Sartre or *Gauche prolétarienne*. He stressed the importance of being concrete, and drew a parallel with the Algerian War: 'It was one thing to say that the army was using torture, but quite another to say that Captain X had tortured Y or that so many corpses had been brought out of a particular police station. Doctor Edith Rose was one of those brave enough to take the latter course' (Macey, 1993: 277). Rose herself was forced to leave the prison service. Within the system, her statement was greeted with total silence.

Later, GIP formulated demands such as the right of unrestricted and uncensored information and correspondence, the right of unionisation and association, and of visits by family and political adherents. This task was soon taken over by the prisoners' branch of GIP, the *Comité d'Action des Prisonniers* (henceforth CAP), which was founded in November 1972 by Serge Livrozet. Livrozet did not want to divert CAP from the line set out by GIP, but argued that it was now up to the prisoners themselves to unionise and to continue the demonstrations which had begun behind the walls and on the rooftops (Macey, 1993: 288). CAP had additional demands, such as the abolition of criminal records, deportation, life and death sentences, and eventually the abolition of prisons and remand. It also formulated more modest demands such as the reorganisation of prison labour, the right to reasonable medical and dental care and the right of appeal and of legal defence before the prison administration. *Gauche prolétarienne* questioned the political relevance of such a struggle, but Foucault saw these piecemeal demands as very concrete politics.

> You can say that these demands, and the struggle against the futilities for which prisoners are being punished inside, have no political content. But is it not exactly the crucial acknowledgement, the discovery of all contemporary political movements, that the more everyday things in life, the way in which one eats, the relationship between the worker and his boss, the way in which one loves and how sexuality is repressed, the coercion taking place within the family, the penalisation of abortion – that these are all political? Making all this into an object of collective action, implies at this moment political action. (Lambrechts, 1982: 100)

Next to mobilising public opinion behind these demands, GIP and CAP also tried to show that prison was the symbol *par excellence* of a class society and of class justice. By incarcerating predominantly young people, unemployed and ethnic minorities, it reproduced social inequality. For CAP, 'the chains of prisoners are those of all men who have no power over their lives. They are simply more visible. Prisoners, in the face of attempts by the authorities to isolate them in their struggles, need the support of all rebels. Their anger is yours' (Donzelot, 1975: 113). In Foucault's following analyses, criminal law is seen as a production system of a de-politicised 'economy of illegalisms' by which the useless proletariat is criminalised in order to break workers' solidarity. 'Criminals' are excellent scapegoats to blame social problems on. Public fear about crime is exploited in order to make an omnipotent control apparatus acceptable to the general public. GIP's history showed how deeply internalised the schism between the proletariat and the non-proletarianised masses was. When attempts were made to include prisoners in a broader proletarian movement, the line of distinction with the workers turned out to be too strong. The idea of unionising prisoners alongside workers was also, in France, a failure. The proletarian left was hesitant about such attempts, and the orthodox Communist Party and trade unions were as rejective as in Germany. Foucault concluded that it was therefore a mistake to see prisoners as some kind of substitute proletariat.

Foucault denied having any political goals in his academic work, but if activists felt that his analyses were useful in any way, they were free to use them as tool-kits. On some occasions, Foucault dealt with the question of political strategy in a more explicit way, and sometimes he did this in a highly abstract way, for example when stressing the central role libido plays in revolutionary action: because these are both beyond control, they are the real enemy of fascism (preface to Deleuze and Guattari, 1972). His observations on the 'playful science of judo' are born of discussions with the proletarian left. According to Foucault (1975c), their politics of confrontation is not only very tiring, it is unlikely to be successful if a dwarf (GIP) has to fight a giant (state). In judo strategy, the opponent's actions are not countered front on, but, by stepping aside, the opponent's movement is used as the starting-point for the next phase of action. Stuart Henry and Dragan Milovanovic (1996: 220–1) also use Foucault's metaphor in their idea of the 'social judo' by which a replacement discourse on crime control is created; destructive energy is channelled in a more constructive direction.

GIP had dissolved by 1973 as a result of political and personal exhaustion. It is impossible to say exactly how many people were involved in GIP, but estimates range from a few hundred to thousands (Macey, 1993: 264). CAP took over its objectives and continued till 1980. From that date, prisoners' movements have continued to exist in various prisons, the Parisian *Syndicat autonome de prisonniers de la Santé* being the best established.

In May 1981, a new penal reform lobby was established: *Coordination syndicale pénale* (henceforth COSYPE). Its establishment was motivated by the hardening law-and-order climate in France and the waning recognition of such penological goals as rehabilitation and education, which are frustrated by the very pathological deficiences created by incarceration. COSYPE's objectives are not fundamentally different from those of GIP and CAP. Main areas of attention are the abolition of long-term imprisonment, safety measures and special regimes, the recognition of the right of assembly for prisoners, the support of alternative sanctions and the reduction of the use of custodial sentences. Being related to the *Syndicat de la magistrature*, COSYPE does not orient itself to the masses, the trade unions or the radical left. The struggle against the desocialising effects of imprisonment is fought within the formal democratic arena. The prison department is no longer regarded as the enemy. COSYPE points to the fact that successful reforms, for example the abolition of capital punishment and high-security units or the improvement of prison conditions, have been established in cooperation with such practitioners as police officers, magistrates and social workers. New pressure groups should direct their actions at these people. COSYPE (1983, 1985) defines itself as abolitionist, but argues that this can only be a tentative direction.

The Italian case: prison struggle as class struggle

With the introduction of the critical criminological journal *La questione criminale*, in Bologna on 11 December 1975, a public debate took place on the idea of 'A penal policy of the working-class movement'. The director of the study centre of the Italian Communist Party (PCI), Pietro Ingrao, argued on this occasion that the working class would probably not support the prison struggle on its own initiative. Therefore, an accompanying radical penal lobby to the journal needed to be established within the PCI. 'If *La questione criminale* is to develop a fertile theoretical elaboration, it must also be able to reach the masses. Thus, it needs the mediation of a party such as we intend it, a new mass-party able to give a complete vision of society, and to create a dialectical relationship with hegemonic culture' (Bricola et al., 1975). A penal reform lobby within the PCI has never been established. By this time, prisoners' actions were already taking place under the auspices of a Maoist group, *Lotta continua*, fanned by the left-wing newspaper *Il manifesto* (Guerini and Tagliarini, 1975).

The prison struggle began around 1968 and was, by the penal experts of those days, interpreted as a reflection of a growing class consciousness and new social struggles, in which the penal system was widely seen as an instrument of class domination. Revolts, which took place in many Italian prisons, initially consisted of sheer rebellion, violence and destruction. They served to attract public attention to penal problems like over-crowding, miscarriages of justice and bad sanitary conditions These spontaneous and uncoordinated prisoners' protests marked a first phase in the Italian prison struggle. By the end of 1969, a second phase was heralded, when militants of the extra-parliamentary left, originating in the students' movement, engaged in prisoners' actions. Many of them were imprisoned themselves under anti-terrorist emergency legislation and their comrades supported the actions from within society. This resulted in public statements by the responsible authorities about the serious problems of Italian prisons, as well as the sometimes dubious class-biased politics of the criminal justice administration.

In a third phase, by 1973, 'penal reform becomes the password' (Rauty, 1975: 120; 1976). Prisoners begin to formulate more concrete demands in respect of prison conditions. They first fought for a wide amnesty, while awaiting substantial penal reform. This should include the abolition of preventive detention and of relapse as an aggravating circumstance in the sentencing process; the right to work outside prison on the same contractual basis and for the same wages as 'normal' workers; the right of education, free assembly, free correspondence and other constitutional rights; and the abolition of inhumane practices, such as solitary confinement and straightjackets (Invernizzi, 1975). Penal pressure groups directed themselves more to the individual and tried to create opportunities for prisoners' reintegration into society; this primarily consisted of material aid, such as accommodation, work, contacts and so on.

Some of the demands were granted by the prison reforms of 1975, but these did not stop the rebellion. For prison activists this proved that the main problem was not located within the penal system, but in the social system of marginalisation and exclusion it represents. In 1979, *CONTROinformazione* made an inventory of the many action committees in Italian prisons, and designed strategic theses. These were written in a rather flat, 'workerist' style, in which prisoners are consequently described as *Lumpenproletariat*, and prison authorities as agents of institutional repression or, indeed, as fascists. Giuseppe Mosconi (1978) has analysed this phenomenon as a product of a strategy of social change, which is caught between the rational impulse of reform and the impossibiity of linking this to a broader change in class composition in society. The changing custodial situation after the reforms of 1975 isolated the prison struggle from its intended link with the class struggle. The prison movement declined soon after these reforms.

In search of further explanations for this development, Vincenzo Ruggiero argues that, in the 1970s, Italian pressure groups saw their fight against the penal system largely as a struggle against a central metaphor for the disciplined society. Because prisons are filled with people from lower social classes, incarceration is a metaphor for the social role the proletarian class performs in the labour market. Prison is not primarily meant for prisoners, but for the masses outside: prison is just one link in the chain by which the working class is disciplined.[2] Ruggiero explains the fact that very little material on these initiatives is currently available because much has been destroyed: under anti-terrorist legislation, records of such actions were not the most useful materials to be found with. In addition to his own, *Il carcere immateriale* (Gallo and Ruggiero, 1989), pamphlets of the prisoners' committees were published in journals such as *Assemblea, Critica del diritto* and other non-academic journals. On the whole, however, there is little material left.

Though it still largely consisted of young, unemployed, working-class men, the idea of prison as a disciplining apparatus was abandoned by the 1980s – even by its original supporters. Today, prisoners are merely a metaphor for themselves – deprived of connections with society. The composition of the Italian prison population has also substantially changed. The idea of the 'politically conscious' prisoner can hardly be maintained. Not only did the Italian prison population, after a period of decarceration, double in the two-year period 1991–2, but the number of drug addicts, over this same period, rose from 20 to 60 per cent, and the proportion of prisoners from non-EU countries from 5 to 20 per cent. Traditional public resistance to stiff law-and-order campaigns was broken by the crisis in the left and the glorification of the judiciary in the struggle against the Mafia (Pavarini, 1994: 57). Public belief in possible social change (and thus in penal reform) has collapsed and, albeit to a mere symbolic extent, some 'big criminals' have finally been put behind bars as well, which has made the justice administration politically more acceptable.

The main drive left to reduce the prison population is therefore one of intervention in the drug field. In Italy, the penal lobby currently tends to overlap with pressure groups in the drug field. So, despite its profound political crisis, it cannot really be said, with unwarranted nostalgia, that Italy faces a general decline of commitment to the prison issue. Penal pressure groups played their particular part in a specific historical development, and, currently, a shift of both the focus and the rationale of prisoners' rights and penal reform can be observed.

The prison struggle in Spain as a struggle for democracy

The origins of Spanish penal pressure groups lie directly in the transition to democracy.[3] After the end of the dictatorship in 1975, revolts broke out in many Spanish prisons. Prisoners wanted to attract public attention in order not to be forgotten in the process of democratisation and used the only means they had available: destruction and disobedience. Initially, revolts were violently repressed by special military brigades, *Brigadas antidisturbios*. Underground anarcho-syndicalist (CNT, GRAPO) and Basque and Catalan left-wing separatist groups (*Herri Batasuna, Terra Lliure*) played a central role in the coordination of such action. In the Madrid area, the prisoners' movement was united with social movements of other 'marginalised' groups under Franquism, such as the civil rights movements of women, homosexuals and psychiatric patients. These groups published from 1976 to 1978 a joint bulletin, entitled *¡¡Quienes no han tenido jamás el 'derecho' a la(s) palabra(s) la(s) toman ya!!* Those who never had the 'right' to speak take the word now!!) (Rivera Beiras, 1995: 95–6).

In October 1977, a law (*Ley de amnistía política*) was passed which pardoned political prisoners. In the development of this law, however, various academics and social movements had argued that a distinction between political and common prisoners was, in the Spanish context, largely artificial because many common prisoners were also activists from workers' movements and had been imprisoned for political reasons as well. The limited amnesty was largely interpreted as a means to break the considerable social consciousness and solidarity typical of Spanish prisons. 'Common' prisoners argued that, because of these limited amnesties, public awareness of their situation would soon disappear. In February 1977 they established COPEL (*Coordinadora de los presos españoles en lucha*), whose primary aim was the fight for a full amnesty (Marti, 1977; Bergalli, 1995: 150).

The Spanish parliament (*Cortes*) denied these claims for a full amnesty and again forgot about the prison problem. Destruction in penal institutions, strikes and self-mutilation continued as before, were repressed by the *Brigadas antidisturbios* as before, and the common institutional reaction was, as before, isolation and torture. In society, affiliated support groups initiated a 'solidarity week with the common prisoners'. They organised a conference at the law school of Madrid's Complutense University on 23 February 1977. Intellectuals, including Fernando Savater, Ignacio Berdugo and Carlos García Valdés, here supported the presentation of COPEL's manifesto. It was no exaggerated demand to require that human integrity and human rights be respected (which means the right not to be beaten up in isolation cells); that a just prison reform be carried out; the exploitation of prisoners' work stopped and normal wages paid; more healthy food provided and gifts from relatives allowed; medical services carried out by medical doctors instead of veterinarians; hygienic conditions improved and so on. There was no reaction from the authorities and prison revolts intensified in all Spanish prisons, of which the spectacular escapes from the Madrid Carabanchel prison on 18 July 1977 are the most famous. In this same prison, CNT-member and COPEL-activist Agustín Rueda Sierra, died on 14 March 1978 after he had been beaten up by prison officers. Ten years (!) later, the director, the officers concerned and the medical staff of the prison were found guilty of this event. One week after the event, however, the director general for penitentiary institutions, Jesús Haddad Blanco was killed by a GRAPO attack in Madrid (Rivera Beiras, 1995: 100–1).

After this 'year of the deaths' it became clear that things could not continue in the same way, and that something needed to be done about the prison problem. The media played a significant role in this respect, giving full coverage to the prisoners' actions and motives. Carlos García Valdés, who had one year earlier supported COPEL's claims, was now appointed as the new director general of penitentiary institutions. COPEL had high expectations of him. He began his new job with a series of visits to the most problematic prisons in order to, as he expressed it, personally experience the penal reality, and to make an inventory of the prisoners' demands as regards new prison legislation. He was shocked by the deplorable conditions, the high suicide rate and the immense overcrowding, which he saw as criminogenic factors of the first order. While stressing that within Europe only a few countries had undertaken serious steps to create decent prison regimes, he argued that Spanish prisoners had not asked for golden cages, but had, indeed, really engaged in a struggle for democracy (COPEL, 1978: 69–70). On 26 September 1979, the *Cortes* unanimously accepted the new prison law (*Ley Orgánica General Penitenciaria*), which is, in respect of the recognition of prisoners' rights and democratic prison administration, among the most progressive in Europe. Soon after its introduction, COPEL ceased to exist.

Regardless of the progress made in 1979, not all regulations worked out in practice as they were intended on paper. Esther Giménez-Salinas (1991: 568) argues: 'we have prisoners who, from a material point of view, are in a position typical of a Latin country, while the system and the respect afforded to prisoners' rights reflects that of a Scandinavian country.' Penal reform groups of the 1980s had a different character from COPEL. They largely aimed at the effectuation of legally guaranteed rights and prison conditions. First, various self-help organisations for prisoners and their relatives were established in the different regions of the country. The most active movement was the Basque group *Salhaketa* – the Basque word for denounce. *Salhaketa* originated in a cooperative initiative in 1981 by relatives of common prisoners from the Bassauri prison, lawyers and psychologists. *Salhaketa* denounced the continued violation of prisoners' rights, the malfunctioning of prison surveillance, the lack of alternatives to prison and the penal system as a whole. Prison abolition is an implicit aim at a meta-level, but *Salhaketa* emphasises the massive overcrowding, the high number of unconvicted prisoners awaiting trial, the establishment of support groups for drug addicts, HIV-positive prisoners and prisoners with AIDS, and the way lawyers are often refused admittance to give legal advice to prisoners in case they incite prisoners to subversive behaviour and rebellion.

The terrorism debate is a concern that *Salhaketa* has to deal with in an implicit way because it has perverted – as in Germany, Northern Ireland and Italy – the democratic character of the criminal justice system by the implementation of the so-called anti-terrorist laws, originally meant as emergency laws or decrees against the militant wing of the Basque left-wing separatist party *Herri Batasuna, Euskadi Ta Askatasuna* (Liberation of the Basque Country, henceforth ETA) into the common, national criminal code. Herewith, all kind of offences can be treated according to the more inquisitory regulations meant for terrorists. The inclusion of previously emergency laws and decrees into the national criminal code gives the false impression that they are normal, democratically established laws (Balmaseda Ripero and Carrera González, 1990).[4] Currently, *Salhaketa's* activities also consist of publications, such as a legal handbook for prisoners, *Defenderse en la cárcel* (Defending oneself in prison) of 1989.

Until 1996 probation had no legal status in Spain. There were, however, private non-profit organisations, such as the Catalan *Institut de Reinserció Social* (IRES), which, from 1969, provided social work for prisoners and aimed at their reintegration into society. In cooperation with examining magistrates in Barcelona, they also looked for alternatives to custody for juvenile offenders (for other categories of offenders this was impossible in preliminary phases because of a strict dogmatic interpretation of the principle of legality). Therefore, IRES' popular amendment to the penal code of 1983 to introduce probation was rather complicated. It was rejected on the grounds of cost, but, for the same reasons mentioned in the Italian case, progressive academics were not very enthusiastic about the initiative either (Bergalli, 1992). The struggle for penal reform in Spain largely remains a struggle for legal defence, which, since 1989, has indeed been well organised within a special group of the Barcelona bar (*Grup de presons de la commisió de defensa*). Attempts have been made to establish an equally specialised national platform in the so-called *Servicios de orientación jurídico penitenciario*. *Salhaketa* fired the first shot in this initiative among various regional bar organisations (*Colegios de abogados*) which, by offering free legal advice to prisoners, form an additional pressure group. In Catalonia, an attempt was made to integrate various social and legal movements in the penal field. In 1993, this initiative was raised to a national level in the *Plataforma de integración de movemientos sociales de apoyo a presos/as* (Rivera Beiras, 1994). *Salhaketa* has also taken up a coordinating role in this respect by organising the first national conference of these social movements in the penal field in May 1993. Here, experiences of regional working groups were translated into general questions of strategy.

Policy recommendations to the various groups included the notion that subsidies which imply specific professional or organisational demands are to be rejected; that state funding should only be applied for in concrete projects; that complaints about bad prison conditions are not to be accompanied by requests for alternatives to imprisonment but rather by requests for an improvement of educational and other facilities inside; that sabotage of prisoners' contacts with the outside world by prison administrations should be consequently followed by an official complaint to the supervisory judiciary over the prison system (*Juzgados de vigilancia*) and to the various (para-)legal forums at a European level; that media actions should be initiated to oppose the establishment of extremely large new prisons (so-called *macrocarceles*); and that the extremely high percentage of drug addicts (some 70 per cent) and HIV-positive inmates (some 30 per cent) in Spanish prisons should be stressed because of their particularly deplorable condition, and because of the fact that this puts the whole penal question in a different perspective (*Salhaketa*, 1994: Bergalli, 1995: 164).

In Spain, the fear of abuses of power by state authorities is too great to allow a more flexible legal structure with more discretionary powers and subsequent opportunities for diversion. The choice is really between widening the possibilities of introducing humanitarian reforms, on the one hand, and legally bolting the door to authoritarian developments as much as possible, on the other. Looking at Spain's recent history, it is not surprising that penal activists choose the second option.

The Dutch penal lobby

The Dutch penal lobby consists of some one hundred volunteer organisations.[5] Radical social-work groups, like *Sosjale joenit*, Release Work or JAC, provoked many legal changes over the 1970s. People active in street-corner work, church groups, probation services, and volunteers' victim-aid projects also initiated many actions in the legal field. Groups campaigning in the penal field, such as groups of (ex-)prisoners, relatives of prisoners, of women prisoners, visitors' projects and groups providing practical aid and housing to released prisoners are united in *BONJO (Belangen overleg niet justitiegebonden organisaties* – Interest platform for non-governmental organisations). Some of these received small subsidies from local authorities and from the probation service, while many grassroots organisations were supported by the churches. Another important penal campaigning group of the 1970s consisted of journalists united in the specifically judicial press agency *Argos*, or of the critical journal of the probation service *KRI*. They unearthed and reported on miscarriages of justice, and fulfilled an important role in publicising the activities of the penal lobby.

The Dutch penal lobby emerged in the realm of the new left. Various forgotten groups, who experienced little support from traditional labour organisations, such as minors (*BM*), the mentally ill (*Pandora*), prisoners (*K69*), ethnic minorities, gays and lesbians, squatters, soldiers (*VVDM*) and, most notably, women, organised themselves in order to improve their position.

With the help of progressive collectives of lawyers, free legal-aid shops and professionals' platforms such as The Netherlands Jurists Committee for Human Rights (*NJCM*), these emancipation movements have been quite successful in mobilising the law for their emancipatory purpose (Janse de Jonge et al., 1983).

The Coornhert Liga – *the league of penal reform*

In this context, students organised working groups on criminal justice at various Dutch universities. A conference on sanctioning in 1969 resulted in the establishment of a national students' platform on criminal justice and criminology, called the *Nederlandse vereniging voor strafrecht en criminologie Dirck Volckertsz. Coornhert* (Drogt, 1990). The objectives of this national students' platform were to organise an annual conference and engage, in cooperation with the prisoners' movement, in penal reform. In the spirit of these conferences, a brainstorming evening was initiated in Louk Hulsman's house on the tasks and possibilities of a national league for penal reform. Besides the students, this group consisted of academics and practising lawyers Pieter Herman Bakker Schut, Peter Baauw, Herman Bianchi, Louk Hulsman and Constantijn Kelk. On 3 June 1971 the committee met in an Amsterdam café, to which members of the student platform and the prisoners' movement were also invited. These groups associated in the *Coornhert Liga.*

In its first press release, the *Coornhert Liga* formulated radical penal reform as its central goal. Everybody with a critical attitude towards the criminal justice system was invited to participate. The *Liga* wished to continue the work of Clara Wichmann's CMS, took the British Howard League as its primary organisational example, but felt ideologically closer to the Norwegian KROM because of the prisoners' involvement in its strategies for reform. It hoped to concentrate the existing, latent and diffuse dissatisfaction with the criminal justice system and to transform it into effective action (Bakker Schut et al., 1971: 2). Defence of constitutional rights and civil liberties were stated as the *Liga*'s primary goals. Penal intervention must be limited to those areas which can be rationally motivated as socially indispensable, while law enforcement should be oriented at dispute settlement, and involve minimal damage for all involved parties. Every year, the *Liga* aimed to present an alternative budget to that of the Ministry of Justice. Other objectives were the organisation of conferences and study meetings; the publication of commentaries on miscarriages of justice in the media; the defence of the interests of persons subjected to penal control or victimised by negative attitudes from society in areas where this is insufficiently done by other organisations; and the introduction of changes in education in penal sciences at the universities.

The *Liga* considered the criminal justice system as a major social problem because it tends to hit the most vulnerable groups in society. Decriminalisation, depenalisation, destigmatisation, reducing custody, pleas for independent prisoners' litigation and a qualitative and quantitative improvement in the legal aid system are the *Liga*'s central aims. The *Liga*'s first activities were, next to a series of alternative justice budgets (*Alternatieve justitiebegrotingen*), the publication of a counter-report against the official analysis of the prison riots in Groningen of 1971 and the organisation of a conference on the legitimacy of the criminal justice system in 1972. The *Liga* also distributed a news bulletin, *Plakkaat*, to inform its members of its activities and other relevant issues and events in the sphere of criminal justice. Every more or less progressive lawyer or criminologist became a member of the *Coornhert Liga* in these first years. Press contacts were excellent and the *Liga*'s influence on the public debate on crime was quite considerable. The *Liga* was 'acclaimed with praise by one MP after another' for its critique of the bill on prisoners' litigation: the *Liga* favoured a more comprehensive system of litigation (Franke, 1990: 686).

This success, however, also announced the first crisis: the *Liga* was increasingly depicted as a group of intellectuals, politicians and media figures. 'This type of people' would never be trusted by ex-prisoners and workers. Ex-prisoners felt that the *Coornhert Liga* was too much of a debating club, which did not undertake any concrete action. On the other hand, ex-prisoners were seen to focus merely on frivolities like headed notepaper and micro-power struggles within the *Liga* instead of, indeed, engaging in concrete action (Drogt, 1990: 12–17). The intellectuals and ex-prisoners lost touch. 'The *Liga* does it with words. The "doers" split off in 1972 and continue on their basis-activist path within BWO – the union of law-breakers.' Not without irony, Gerard de Jonge (1990: 249) continues that 'from now on the *Liga* consists of extremely decent people, who for the greater part make a career within the criminal justice system or advocacy.' The *Liga* and BWO have, however, always continued to work together.

Around the mid-1970s a rather quiet period began, in which largely regional initiatives, such as the establishment of judicial complaints bureaux (*Justitiële klachten bureaus*) by law students, were carried out. On a national level, major initiatives included the alternative justice budget, which was now, in explicit Hulsman-style, oriented to welfare instead of penality (Moerland and Kneepkens, 1975); counter-memoranda to penal White Papers of 1976 and 1978; and the 1979 Conference on Diversion. At this conference, the pros and cons of diversion were analysed. Major pros of an early diversion from the penal system are the relative immediateness of the response; the open space it provides for informal dispute settlement; and the prevention of the stigmatising effects of trial and imprisonment. Major cons of the diversion model, and indeed of the introduction of alternatives as such, are the possible increase in social control and the limited legal guarantees for the accused. The *Liga*'s visions of penal reform were now clearly influenced by the ideas of Stanley Cohen, Michel Foucault and Thomas Mathiesen (*Coornhert Liga*, 1980).

The *Liga* only undertook further action in the second half of the 1980s, when virtually the whole political spectrum agreed that we were too soft on crime in the 1970s and that stiff law-and-order campaigns were needed to counter this misguided philanthropy. According to its president of those days, Gerard de Jonge (1990: 247), the *Liga* had now lost faith in internal changes in the criminal justice system and adopted a more explicit abolitionist perspective. An internal policy plan said, however, that 'abolitionism as a vocation implies a merely moral position which cannot be the *Liga*'s objective, for its strategies need to follow rational standards' (*Coornhert Liga*, 1986: 43). The kind of abolitionism defended by de Jonge includes a strong emphasis on legal guarantees and matter-of-fact criticism of new regulations, legislation and White Papers – the negative moment of abolitionism. In relation to this, the *Liga*'s policy document states that 'the danger exists that a specific judicial approach . . . will contribute to the re-legitimation of the deprivation of liberty' (*Coornhert Liga*, 1986: 34). Board member Willem de Haan advocated a 'pragmatic abolitionism', oriented at Stan Cohen's concept of pragmatic moralism, as a future policy, in which the 'politics of bad conscience' plays an important role.

This policy document is a good example of the *Liga*'s ambiguity. Part of the board aligned with concrete legal activism and adopted a guaranteeist perspective, whereas the other half focused on structural, long-term strategies of abolition. De Jonge describes this difference as the tension between the neo-Utrecht and the Rotterdam schools. This seems, however, a strong point rather than weakness because the *Liga* proved to be capable of combining a down-to-earth legal approach with more utopian abolitionist foci in concrete actions. In 1984, the last alternative justice budget appeared – a critique of the dramatic restoration taking place in law-and-order talk, policing, imprisonment and probation (de Jonge et al., 1983). It took six years for the *Liga* to come up with a viable replacement for this illustrious series. In 1989, it began a series of annual *Crimineel jaarboeken* (Criminal yearbooks) in which all legislative, case law and policy activities in criminal justice were examined. This change was necessary because 'the formula of the alternative budgets seemed a little worn out, the points of view were too well known, too predictable, and the annual ritual turning of the alternative prayer wheel, following the opening of the parliamentary year, seemed increasingly non-functional' (de Jonge et al., 1989: 3). Behind this transition from alternative budgets to critical commentaries, of which more volumes have already appeared than of the earlier budgets, a political shift can be observed from an optimistic tone (when changes for the better were still perceived as a realistic possibility) to a more pessimistic one.

In its first alternative justice budgets the *Liga* was an important advocate of alternatives to custody. With hindsight, Gerard de Jonge (1990: 250) argues 'it should be feared the *Liga* contributed to the introduction of a new principal sanction, namely that of performing unpaid labour for public interest [community service order]. The introduction of this overseas product not only led to the expansion of the judicial net, but also to a perversion of the probation service, which became a controller for the prosecution.' Community service is seen as a classic case of co-option and net-widening because it fails to reduce the number of shorter prison sentences which it is meant to replace. Therefore, the introduction of alternatives should, in the present penal setting, be avoided rather than promoted. This diagnosis seems to lead, however, to a vision contradictory to the *Liga*'s claim for alternatives. Though in 1993 an attempt was made to reassess the *Liga*'s autonomous policy proposals in a so-called standpoint series (on drugs, on migration and on alternatives to custody), the *Liga* currently takes a merely defensive position. Its commentaries on recent developments in criminal justice remain increasingly confined to legal critique, while criminological analyses are hardly included.

BWO: the prisoners' union

The main objective of the BWO (*Bond van wetsovertreders*, Union of law-breakers) is the radical reduction of the material and psychological damage inflicted by the criminal justice system upon individual members and particular groups in society. The BWO visits prisoners in order to offer them as practical assistance as possible, and to provide the media and other social movements with inside information. BWO aims to reduce the power of the punishers, with the abolition of the penal system as a final objective. An abolitionist position is motivated by the inability of the penal system to establish any resocialising effects, and by the structurally class-biased approach of the criminal justice system. One of BWO's central activities is the distribution of the journal *BWO-Nieuws*, in which accounts from different prisons, and complaints, questions and poems from prisoners are published. Decisions of various prison complaint committees or new penal regulations are explained in various languages, including Dutch, English, Spanish, Turkish and Arab.

By the end of the 1970s, BWO had received wide publicity for its 'Bajes-manifestaties' – public hearings about the prison system. In the summer of 1979, the broadcasting corporation VPRO enabled BWO to present weekly 'prison reports' (*bajesberichten*) on national radio. These radio programmes gave rise to the establishment of so-called detainees' committees in various Dutch prisons. The unionisation of prisoners had succeeded quite well, but, argued Gerard de Jonge (1994: 261–2), BWO lacked the organisational strength and legal knowledge to give actual support to the prisoners inside. Lawyers filled the gap. They had considerable success in getting the demands of prisoners, for example on the constitutional right to unionise and associate, answered by prison governors. BWO's publicity climax was reached when VPRO radio positioned a crane over the exercise yard of Amsterdam's Overamstel prison (*Bijlmerbajes* in popular parlance) to distribute a BWO publication on prisoners' rights among the prisoners, and to enable them to express their views on live radio. The Amsterdam prosecution service began a preliminary inquiry against VPRO radio, in order to investigate whether there was any risk of prisoners escaping, but it never came to an actual prosecution.

BWO had its heyday around 1980, when it undertook successful actions against the use of beds with restraints for allegedly aggressive prisoners and coordinated actions in the high-security wing of Scheveningen prison (the *bunker* in popular parlance). These campaigns demonstrated the intolerable 'torturous' practices carried out in so-called 'decent' Dutch prisons. The riot of 12 January 1983 in the *bunker* had an exceptionally destructive character – virtually all windows and washbasins were smashed. More typical BWO actions were the demand for proper wages for (obligatory) prison labour, opposition against the high prices in prison shops (operated by a large chain of supermarkets charging much lower prices outside and thus misusing its monopoly position inside) and the struggle for wider contacts with the outside world. With some judicial help, the enlargement of the number of visits was successfully presented as a means of taking rehabilitation seriously.

Around 1980, the State Secretary for Justice invited BWO to participate in negotiations about the future of the prison system. BWO accepted this invitation, but the final 1982 White Paper *Taak en toekomst* (Task and future) did not mention any of BWO's viewpoints – only the distortion of their position that resocialisation does not work. BWO was not so accepted as a representative of prisoners that it had an enforceable right to visit them inside: it depended on the discretion of individual prison governors whether they were allowed in. When in the mid-1980s, the massive prison-building programme actually began, BWO was again excluded from policy discussions. BWO still organised prison hearings, often together with the *Coornhert Liga*, but hardly received any press coverage, with the exception of 1986. The celebration of the hundredth anniversary of the Dutch criminal code was accompanied by wide publicity on everything to do with crime and punishment. A solidarity meeting for a national prisoners' strike which BWO organised in October 1986 in the Amsterdam squatters' bastion Vrankryk (about prison and forced labour) received considerable media coverage, unlike the not very successful strike itself.

The prison struggle became very much a legal struggle. The original BWO initiative in 1982 to publish a 'Prison book' (*Bajesboek*), an accessible legal handbook on prisoners' rights, was elaborated and republished in cooperation with the *Coornhert Liga* in 1988 (de Jonge and Verpalen, 1992). Comparing the German and French experiences, it is worth mentioning that it was never particularly difficult to distribute these books, which also included 'unparliamentary' language and examples of protest and complaint letters. A copy could be found in every prison library. Gradually, BWO abandoned the distinction between positive and negative reform. An orientation towards legal guarantees now seemed more realistic than a rigorous insistence on abolition. A well-established system of legal activism facilitated this process. Gerard de Jonge (1994: 269–70) goes so far as to say that, because the largest BWO successes were achieved in court, it was not worthwhile to put a lot of energy into unionisation as such, particularly as BWO's organisational talents were quite low. De Jonge's observations imply a rather legally biased and instrumental vision of success, which underestimates more indirect success – in sensitising public opinion, practitioners and politicians. De Jonge (1994: 271) argues that the strategy of legal test cases can support prisoners' actions, but does not determine their success. Penal case law is not always equally supportive: prisoners' litigation remains an individualising procedure that can benefit one prisoner at the expense of others, and the sort of complaints that can actually be addressed is limited. Currently, BWO seems to overestimate the emancipatory meaning of prisoners' rights, by disregarding the interests the prison administration has in the maintenance of a reasonably well-functioning system of litigation: it channels tensions in controllable legal ways. The BWO's decision to adopt a legal strategy was pragmatic. The aim is to defend prisoners' interests, and legal rights are a means to do this. BWO opposes (particularly long-term) imprisonment and argues that it is not the role of a prisoners' movement to argue that prisoners should refrain from things that could make life inside a little more bearable. It is, furthermore, doubtful whether there actually is a contradiction between long-term aims, such as abolition, and short-term aims, such as legal defence, argues BWO president Erik van der Maal (personal communication).

With the expansion of the penal system and the decreasing quality of prison regimes, many problems arose immediately after the opening of a large number of new prisons. There were fewer, less experienced staff, visiting regulations became more problematic, working conditions were poorer and so on. These problems became the primary focus in the second half of the 1980s and early 1990s. In this period, however, the union suffered a dramatic loss of members. Personal conflicts within the board and financial irregularities meant that the BWO was virtually defunct by 1993. BONJO took over some BWO activities. In addition, BWO became bankrupt as a result of fraudulent activities by its treasurer. BONJO ironically noted: 'BWO has finally accomplished one of its aims: wide media coverage. Board members curse each other, and in the meantime the purse is empty' (*BONJO Bulletin*, vol. 8, 1994, no. 5, pp. 7–8). A committee of inquiry investigated the irregularities and tried to see which party was supported by the members. In the meantime, the probation service suspended its subsidy to BWO till all irregularities were cleared up.

VOICES: the positive moment in the penal critique

The name VOICES is an abbreviation which, in Dutch, stands for an association for the support of initiatives in the field of crime and society. It wants to support 'real' alternatives to the penal approach to social problems. VOICES was established when the *Coornhert Liga* began to take a more (legal) defensive position and questioned the desirability of alternatives. VOICES has its roots in the probation service. Traditionally, the Dutch probation service has, despite government funding, a fairly autonomous position in the criminal justice system. The service consisted of volunteers and was generally monitored by progressive lawyers or vicars. By the end of the 1960s, most private initiatives were professionalised and fused into a national framework – the ARV. The ARV is still not a fully governmental service, but an independent association of private services with some 1,100 members. In addition to the Ministry of Justice, it has numerous other financial sources:

for example, church and humanist organisations, and a national collection for the probation services among the population. It was a unique feature of the Dutch probation service that the aim to reintegrate offenders into society was really carried by the community. In the 1980s, various civil servants within the various justice(-related) administrations pointed out that society had become less committed to progressive penal politics and that the probation service had lost its credibility. They spoke of a breach of trust with society, which had to be restored by enlarging cooperation with the criminal justice system. The probation service now performs a third task next to providing social work and preparing social inquiry reports, namely monitoring community service orders and other diversion programmes. At the same time, credibility among clients is undermined now that probation officers are seen to have become 'part of the system', and have nothing to offer once prisoners are released.

The disparity between probation managers and field-workers on this theme was a major incentive in the establishment of VOICES. Gradus Wiersma was a central voice in the criticism that the new 'yuppie-managers', who knew little of the content of probation work, disregarded all the volunteers and members who ran the probation services. Wiersma's idea was to establish an alternative probation service directed towards general social work. Under the presidency of Jacquelien de Savornin Lohman, a working group elaborated this objective, and argued that VOICES should also offer something which exceeded the traditional scope of the probation service, namely mediation between victims and offenders. This working group consisted of probation officers, board members of BWO, BONJO, prison parish work, the humanist welfare organisation Humanitas (which offers important facilitating services), national victim-support scheme LOS, as well as prison authorities, defence lawyers, public prosecutors, judges, academics and politicians. In May 1988, VOICES was officially established. Paraphrasing from annual plans of action, VOICES' objectives are: mediation between victim and offender, in order to bring criminalisable conflict situations to a solution before they actually reach court; bringing existing volunteer organisations in the penal field together; restoring the social basis of probation work by the creation of a network of active volunteers who do not have the professional tendency to create needs on the 'market of welfare and happiness'; and changing public opinion by showing that crime can be dealt with better in a compensatory than in a punitive way. VOICES aims to realise its objectives by practical action. Since both are seen to strive for the same goals, professional social workers are thought to fulfil a facilitating role to volunteers. The word 'abolitionism' is rejected for strategic reasons. VOICES' aim is better described as the positive moment in the penal critique by the creation of new realities (practical projects), rather than commenting on existing realities. Its most central projects are the mediation programme *dading* (out-of-court settlement) and the struggle for the admission of volunteer organisations into prison.

The idea of *dading* is that a prosecutor drops the charges when victim and offender agree on a settlement whose content is determined by both parties. The project is based on the idea that victims are better helped by a settlement in a private lawsuit than by penal measures against the offender. *Dading* has functioned in different cities with varying success. Individual prosecutors are willing to cooperate, but *dading* is boycotted by the Ministry of Justice, which only wants to accept forms of mediation within a penal setting. The establishment of a 'visitors' code' for prisons also got off the ground with considerable difficulty. Individual prison governors were willing to cooperate, but the prison department feared losing control and boycotted the code. Next to the management of these initiatives (and some other projects which have scarcely got past the formative stage), VOICES organises annual working conferences so that practitioners in the sphere of criminal justice, welfare and education can experience an alternative scenario of dealing with social problems and conflicts. Working groups prepare reports on youth and employment, the multi-cultural society, alternative drug policy, and probation. As real reform should come from below, one has to be satisfied with very small steps and little successes. Unlike *Coornhert Liga* conferences, which tend to attract a majority of academics and lawyers, VOICES' congresses also attract probation officers and other social workers.

VOICES has not been able to realise all its objectives. Many people are willing to pay a financial contribution, some are also willing to work within actual projects on an *ad hoc* basis, but an insufficient number of volunteers can be mobilised to actually initiate projects and safeguard their continuity. Decentralised activities continue, the board functions within the framework of the welfare organisation Humanitas, annual working conferences are organised, but VOICES has not become the platform it wanted to be. Developments within the probation service were too dramatic to enable committed field-workers (who have to fight for their jobs) to engage very actively in attempts to maintain the social-work component of probation. The victim movement's input became rather marginal after the autonomous volunteer organisations were united in LOS. The idea of supporting public involvement is VOICES's strength in an ideological sense, but it has proved to be its weakness in a practical sense.

Penal activism: some conclusions

We can distinguish two sorts of radical penal pressure groups: prisoners' movements and related grassroots organisations, and penal reform movements initiated by committed lawyers and other intellectuals. Both the type of movement, and the sort of actions engaged in, are related to a country's specific political situation. When prison conditions are more brutal, prisoners' movements are generally stronger and actions have a more militant character. If penal pressure groups are established by academics, this mostly coincides with a relatively democratic and responsive penal climate. A shared goal by all groups is the prevention of suffering and damage caused by detention. Some try to do this by hard action, others by rationally motivated pleas for the abolition of specific parts of the penal system (for example, juvenile detention), whereas a third group primarily supports alternative sanctions. Mostly, these latter two go hand in hand. Generally, one first aims to reduce the prison system and then support other measures. Another generalisable phenomenon is that this latter step is often not made because activists fear to widen the penal net.

We can distinguish four stages in respect of penal activism. A first stage consists of simply drawing attention to bad prison conditions: for example, in the early phases of Southern European prisoners' movements. In a second stage, pressure groups struggle for emancipation and prisoners' rights. This is visible in virtually the whole European penal lobby, albeit not at the same time. A third phase is characterised by consolidation of previous gains. This either follows after important gains have been made (as in Italy and Spain after the establishment of new prison legislation) or when the situation on the penal front is getting worse (as in North-Western Europe in the 1980s). A fourth stage consists of support for alternatives to custody. This was the case in Northern European countries from 1975 to 1979. After that, a return to the third stage can be observed.

Next to the fact that the law-and-order campaigns of the 1980s offered little ground for the introduction of alternatives, this retrograde movement can also be explained by the fact that the alternatives advocated had been implemented in ways other than the penal reformers had intended them. Over this time, the penal struggle was professionalised – notably by lawyers. Mick Ryan and Tony Ward's (1992) analysis in Britain shows that independently operating feminist and black groups, and the emerging privatisation debate, changed the penal lobby. This development can scarcely be observed in other countries. Most continental penal pressure groups reflected very little on these or other 'new' phenomena in the penal sphere, such as 'victimology', crime prevention or organised crime. This neglect may have something to do with the dominant position of lawyers: these issues fall outside their professional scope. This thesis is supported by the fact that critical commentaries on new legal developments are *ad hoc* and case oriented. The social-scientific impulse to raise these issues to a macro-political level is notably lacking. By its dominant focus on a critical following of the criminal justice system the penal lobby has become too defensive to be really innovative.

Prison struggle as class struggle

A central notion in radical penal theories is that the form and purpose of sanctions change in correspondence with state formation and economic developments. Central and Southern European penal pressure groups implicitly reflect these theories. Actual attempts to unionise prisoners along labour lines offer little empirical support for the idea that the penal struggle can be fought as part of the class struggle. Neither in the Latin context nor in Germany has it been possible to mobilise workers for penal reform. The politically conscious prisoner, to whom the class-based penal struggle was oriented, no longer exists and the prison problem has largely become a problem of drugs and foreigners. Political consciousness-raising among prisoners, or indeed penal consciousness-raising within trade unions, was not particularly successful. After 1980, the actions of penal pressure groups were directed less at the masses, and the links with the radical left were loosened. Radical penal pressure groups can be defined as 'successful' if their critique adequately reflects a concrete penal political situation and if other social forces have been influenced in an implicit way. Seen from this perspective, a social movement which is successful in a certain period can, at another moment, be quite outdated. Thus, one should not be nostalgic about its disappearance. The significance of a specific type of pressure group can also fall away once an important part of their claims has been realised in actual politics.

Prison struggle as an exponent of a civilisation process

Next to materialist theories, a central sociohistorical interpretation of penal reform is that changing sanctioning modalities are a product of changing cultural patterns. Herman Franke's book on two centuries of penitentiary developments in The Netherlands, written from an Eliasian perspective, shows a sharp contrast with Foucauldian and Mathiesenian analyses. In Franke's view, it was not the unionisation of prisoners that stimulated penal changes, but rather a so-called offensive of penological civilisation from the side of the bourgeoisie. An increasing respect for the (civil) rights of prisoners led to their gradual emancipation (Franke, 1990). This view is supported by Gerard de Jonge's argument that energy can be better used in the legal defence of concrete demands than in unionisation. If the emergence of penal lobbies is an element in the penal civilisation offensive, their decline in the 1980s is an indication that the process of civilisation has turned around. It seems, however, fair to say that penal pressure groups contribute to increasing sensibilities to the penal question among civilised liberals. In this view, their virtual demise in the 1980s would be partly due to their more modest, realist and pragmatic strategies, for these are less able to touch upon the emotional and normative problems of penality. The *Coornhert Liga*'s labelling in the public media as 'a respectable organisation' (Drogt, 1990: 30) is, in this respect, hardly a compliment.

Increasing sensibilities to a system of legal pain infliction and the questioning of its normative legitimacy are central elements of an abolitionist strategy. Many penal pressure groups have presented themselves as abolitionist. Developments in virtually all countries show that abolitionism may not have had any direct influence on penal policy, but it did touch the right chord among many practitioners working in the penal field. Its alternative visions of restorative justice and of compensating sanctions gave a first impulse to the development of non-custodial sanctions and crime-prevention programmes in many countries, albeit that their practical elaboration made many abolitionists want to forget about this parental role.

The media and the spirit of the times

The role of the media is an important factor in the influence of penal pressure groups. Access to the media differs markedly, and the way in which various groups receive media coverage is notably related to the attitude of the authorities and to the spirit of the times. An important factor in this respect is the participation of notable intellectuals or media figures. When social movements don't reach a wider audience, their influence is limited. In the 1980s, all groups received less media coverage. Public support for strengthened law and order became quite considerable. Many penal pressure groups explicitly motivated their actions in the 1980s by the need to counter these tendencies. In view of the fact that currently prevailing opinions on crime and punishment express little empathy for the social causes of crime or the 'pain' of imprisonment, penal reform may need to start again with the creation of new sensibilities. It seems plausible that the critique of the penal lobby has currently so little appeal because sensibility for the whole issue has disappeared. Perhaps penal reform should therefore start again from scratch: revealing the disqualified knowledge as Utrecht scholar Rijk Rijksen did in 1958, the Toul psychiatrist in 1972, and the Spanish common prisoners in 1977. The strategy of revealing the intolerable practices that take place in prison has proved to be a good way of attracting media attention. If one wants to keep this attention and transform it into a general sensitivity to penal reform, the quality of the information becomes all-important. In all countries, penal reformers stress the importance of their own sources and of publicising them in their own journals. In this respect, Michel Foucault's advice to focus on very concrete issues must be stressed. While mere reiteration of ideology wears out very rapidly, the public media do tend to publish the specific information of penal pressure groups.

Alternatives to prison, negative reform and net-widening

After an idealistic phase, in which critical criminologists supported initiatives to divert cases from the penal system, a pessimist phase emerged in which alternatives, once put into practice, were mainly seen as sinister, uncontrollable, net-widening, mesh-thinning extras which did not reduce the use of custody and, furthermore, made penal control disperse into society. Alternatives to custody were, indeed, only put into practice to a meaningful degree when the fiscal and penal crisis made these sanctions necessary as a cheaper means of expanding the penal system, and when the 'ethics of care' embedded in the welfare state declined. In this infertile ground, Mathiesen's strategy of negative reform became rather ill advised. It led penal reformers to the idea that nothing works, which, in fact, paralysed the radical penal lobby. In the idealist phase, Mathiesen's recommendations were welcome warnings for over-enthusiastic penal reformers, but times changed. Initially, his work responded to a widely felt need for penal reform, but now, not least because there is no concrete example of reform which is only 'negative' and 'system-competitive' (to speak in Mathiesen's terms), penal reformers stand empty-handed.

Maeve McMahon (1992: 222) shows another perverse effect of the net-widening argument. Prison authorities often use it as an argument to terminate potentially reductionist programmes or, indeed, as an excuse to cut back on facilities in prison. If punishment is a just desert, there is little need for decent facilities. If the penal system is, however, to contribute to the re-habilitation of prisoners, this must also be operationalised in a rational system in some way. This acknowledgement heralds a third phase in the critical debate on alternatives to custody. This phase could be called the phase of cautious reaffirmation, in which penal reformers have to become good 'judo players', as Foucault calls it. Penal reformers have to acknowledge that, despite all, the values and principles behind informal justice should be reassessed (Cohen, 1988: 220–3).

From social commitments to a politics of rights

During the 1980s, many social movements adopted a politics of rights. The influence of lawyers on the penal reform lobby is also a product of the legal culture of a particular country. In this respect, Britain is the exception. Here, the language of law and rights only found an audience among critical schol-ars by the end of the 1980s. On the European continent, critical criminologists have been less dismissive of the language of law, and critical forums of lawyers have tried to advance the collective meaning of rights in various ways. Also, Michel Foucault repeatedly stressed the importance of including the *Syndicat de la magistrature* in the prison struggle. In Spain, practising lawyers have played a particularly central role in the penal lobby. The first international penal pressure group, Penal Reform International, founded in November 1989 by the progressive director general of the Dutch prison department in the 1970s, Hans Tulkens, and NACRO president Vivien Stern, also has a strongly legal focus.

In the practical sense, legal activism has an important role to play in the penal lobby. Lawyers are known for their practical skills: they may think less 'profoundly' than sociologists, but they are certainly more clever at finding solutions and compromises. In this sense, they can help to overcome analyt-ical and political despair. An orientation to the defence of gains from the past can, however, easily lead to another form of stagnation, namely that the penal lobby loses its innovative role – its capacity to raise new themes to an analytical and political level.

The dispersal of the penal lobby

Few penal pressure groups on the continent dealt with two pivotal issues in the critical academic debate in Britain: gender and race. Perhaps this point is wrongly made, since it can also be argued that we face a general dispersal of the penal lobby towards one-issue movements. Women's movements and migrants' movements emerged in all European countries, but these hardly dealt with the penal question. Regardless of the question of who raises it, the ethnic question has to be addressed more elaborately in respect of the penal question. Since women only represent a small percentage of the prison population, the relevance of dealing more explicitly with the gender issue is of a different nature. Feminists were the first to visualise the person of the victim.

Within the penal lobby, a simultaneous development can be observed in a close cooperation between different groups and a dispersal of the lobby. In Britain, concrete actions on the prison system are concentrated in the Prison Reform Trust, on non-custodial sanctions in NACRO. In Italy, the penal lobby shifted to the drug field. The drug problem currently seems a central issue as regards penal reform. Many social problems associated with the consumption of illegal drugs are really products of the prohibitionist policy. At the same time, the penal crisis and the legitimacy crisis within the police is also largely caused by the drugs problem. Looking at the catastrophic consequences that the lost war on drugs has had on users, the community and the legal system, a form of legislation would seem only a matter of time. If the international political powers ever come to an agreement on this issue, the limitation of the disturbance of public order will probably be the main motive for legalisation. In combination with the declining influence of health-care agencies on drug policy and the decline of the welfare state in more general terms, it might well be that the penal lobby will in the end find itself in the same uncomfortable position as it did with respect to non-custodial sanctions. After having been among its key advocates, the penal lobby became an opponent once non-custodial sanctions were established. A drug policy which is left to the forces of the market economy is not the same as the controlled policy of normalisation backed up with adequate health-care facilities. Perhaps the time has come to stress these differences more forcefully; for example, by reaffirming the harm-reduction agenda of health agencies, and by stressing that a vision of society in which we actively stimulate a contingent of harmless vegetative outcasts has little to do with any idea one may hold of social justice or indeed of civilisation – this latter argument goes, however, just as well for alcoholism, which is in many aspects an even larger problem.

On another key issue of the 1980s and 1990s, the position of victims of crime, only few penal pressure groups have taken an explicit position. Those groups entering the debate in The Netherlands argued against the dominant professionalisation and judicial cooption of the victim lobby and advocated a more autonomous position of victims of crime in a civil lawsuit. This focus on victims appears unique to the Dutch case, and seems a real opportunity to lift penal reform movements from the odium of being mere interest groups for offenders. The replacement of a predominantly materialist social commitment by a solidarity with victims confronts us, however, with new problems, which will be dealt with in Chapter 10.

The changed position of penal reform movements

Thomas Mathiesen (1990) makes the comparison between the role of penal pressure groups in the current era and the struggle against fascism or atomic weapons: they serve to keep alive the sensibility to these issues and are important impetuses to 'recharge the critical batteries'. The question is whether this is enough, especially if we look at the fact that the social basis of the penal lobby has become quite small. What is the surplus value of a penal pressure group over individual agitation? Institutionalised observers of prisoners' rights, such as appeals committees for prisoners' litigation on a national level, the European Court of Human Rights, the Council of Europe's Committee for the Prevention of Torture and Inhuman or Degrading Treatment or Punishment (CPT), and the *Observatoire international des prisons*, or indeed Amnesty International at a global level, currently fulfil a role that was first performed by penal pressure groups. These groups played an important role in the establishment of such institutional watchdogs. Their current task is critically to observe what actually happens with critiques and recommendations in a national setting, and to sensitise 'new' issues like international policing and migration politics (as the Autonoom Centrum already does in The Netherlands, and State Watch on a European level) or the dispersal of social control by the privatisation of criminal justice agencies. It is ill advised to stick to a defensive attitude. As avant-gardes, social movements must not only analyse new developments, but also visualise alternative realities. The development of such a vision is the objective of the remaining part of this book.

Notes

1 Mathiesen also refers to the Swedish KRUM, founded in 1966, and the Danish KRIM, founded in 1967, but we will only deal with the Norwegian KROM.

2 Information not otherwise referenced is derived from Vincenzo Ruggiero's presentation at the 1990 European Group Conference in Haarlem, The Netherlands, and from personal communications from Ruggiero.

3 The development of Spanish penal pressure groups is elaborately mapped out by Iñaki Rivera Beiras (1993). Information not otherwise referenced is derived from this book.

4 The 'dirty war' of the social democratic authorities against ETA has, over this period of time, led to hit squads (*Grupos Antiterroristas de Liberación*) emerging within various police forces, who have killed at least 26 *Etarras*, (probably) with the consent of high government officials. At the same time, ETA has increasingly killed complete outsiders to the Basque conflict, culminating in the killing of the progressive president of the Spanish Supreme Court, Francisco Tomás y Valiente in February 1996. Also in the Spanish case, the number of people who fight for the defence of the guarantees of a democratic rule of law, the *estado de derecho*, against anti-terrorist laws is much larger than the group of people who support ETA.

5 If other non-governmental campaigning groups in the semi-penal field, such as junkie unions and other pressure groups in the drug field, interest groups of psychiatric patients, prostitutes' unions, volunteer projects for victim aid, ethnic groups, detainees' committees in prison etc. were included, there would be more than 150 different penal pressure groups.

8

What has Happened to Law and Order?

The crisis in critical criminology coincided with a fiscal crisis, an ideological crisis, a crisis in the welfare state, a crisis in the administration of justice and a crisis in the public credibility of government. In the last three chapters, we have encountered various assessments of the internal, analytical crisis in critical criminology. A common factor is that the penal climate of the 1980s led critical criminologists to analytical despair and paralysed penal reformers. The fact that the aetiological side of the new criminology's socioeconomic agenda remained underdeveloped became a particularly pressing analytical problem when the rate of property offences increased sharply in an era of economic growth. The deprivation thesis apparently needed some refinement, but also because credible critical criminological alternatives in this respect remained, by and large, forthcoming, mainstream versions of rational choice and opportunity theses came to flourish. We also touched upon various 'new' problems, such as organised crime, the over-representation of ethnic minorities in street crime, the privatisation of social control and civic feelings of unsafety, which could hardly be addressed by traditional critical criminological analyses that focus on the state as the main actor in social control, and on secondary rather than primary deviance. Ideological purism often led to politically impossible options. Perhaps as a consequence of this, the critical debate on law enforcement shifted in many countries to the legal discipline, and penal reformers also saw law as a more useful tool than sociological conflict models of struggle. If critical scholars did not 'escape' to historical subjects, they fled into hyper-abstract theorising, or adopted frenetic, defensive positions. In order to re-establish critical criminology's relation with current sociopolitical and penal practice, we need to examine first what has actually happened to law and order.

An increased belief in penality

From the mid-1980s on, the following political *leitmotiv* of law and order can be observed in all Western European countries: crime appears to be getting out of hand and society needs to be protected. The 'soft remedies' of the 1970s must be washed away and we need to be tough on crime – which really means tough on 'criminals'. While the belief in penality increased on a rhetorical level, the criminal justice system was in crisis. The media discovered again that crime sells, and politicians used the crime problem for electoral purposes and raised high expectations about an 'achievable safety'. The system could not live up to this media and political pressure, made mistakes and was discredited. With European unification, the economic system shifted from the Rhineland, corporate model to the Anglo-Saxon, competitive model, characterised by unquestioned belief in the regulatory capacities of the market. The general public's image of 'society' seemed to change: once 'the social' was seen as an indispensable embodiment of collective values which prevented social disintegration; now it was merely portrayed as an annoying restraint on individual development. The role of the state subsequently shifted from *a priori* regulation to *a posteriori* control. Modes of crime control followed this tendency.

A growing fear of street crime and a concern for victims were dominant arguments for crime-prevention programmes and for imposing stiffer penalties and 'widening the net' of policing. Next to expansions of general police competences by law, many countries also faced a growth in undercover operations and criminal informants which tended to undermine police accountability. Court delays were followed by the curtailing of legal guarantees in order to create more flexible and efficient criminal procedures. A bifurcation in penal politics coincided with an increasing use of remand and prison sentences beyond the system's actual capacity. Massive prison-building programmes, overcrowding, waiting lists for 'less severe' cases, or actually sending remand prisoners home, marked a custodial crisis in Europe. We currently witness the greatest wave of incarceration for a century, and the problems of crime and punishment are increasingly surrounded by plainly punitive discourse and subsequent policy (Hudson, 1993; Tournier, 1994; Sim et al., 1995; Snacken et al., 1995).

The general picture in Europe may be similar, but the specific social conditions under which the new politics of law and order emerged vary from country to country. In the Italian case, due process came under major pressure from the emergency legislation on terrorism in the 1970s. More than a decade later, public belief in law and order has been increased by Mafia trials and the operation *mani pulite* (clean hands), which aims to stop the large and petty corruption practices which had become a necessity to make Italian bureaucracy actually function (Faccioli, 1984; Pavarini, 1994). Organised crime, fraud and corruption became important problems for virtually all European countries, but the Italian case is the most exemplary in this respect. In Spain, infringements of civil liberties by an authoritarian law on urban security (*ley de seguridad ciudadana*) and by illegal monitoring operations of the secret service CESID, the disclosures about hit squads within various police forces (GAL), and the government's continual attempts to cover up massive corruption scandals, have been major concerns for critical scholars. Concern for the authoritarian tendencies of law and order is expressed in many European countries, but the Spanish case is the most worrying. Britain has the problem of a 'high-handed' police force who have actually created 'evidence' which has put the Guildford Four, the Birmingham Six and the Bridgewater Three behind bars for many years. The Belgian case, as described in Chapter 5, is probably the most dramatic example of a completely failing criminal justice system. It is after all, very rare that huge public demonstrations are held against a court decision, as was the case of the 'White March' in Brussels in October 1996. It is, however, uncertain what the effect of this public pressure on criminal justice will be. It can lead to a more transparent, more democratic system, but it can just as well feed 'get tough' sentiments.

In most countries, critics focus on concrete examples of increased punitiveness in legal practice and analyse these in a case-oriented fashion. In Britain, criminologists have analysed these factors in their socioeconomic and political context (Scraton, 1987; Hall, 1988; Hillyard and Percy-Smith, 1988; Brake and Hale, 1992; Cavadino and Dignan, 1992). Such analyses will be raised here to an international level, though the concrete examples are mainly derived from the Dutch situation. David Downes and Rod Morgan (1994: 183) define the politics of law and order as: 'the public contestation of the dynamics of crime, disorder, and their control'. Key players in this matrix are: 'the major political parties, in particular successive Home Secretaries and their ministerial and opposition teams; senior civil servants who, despite their non-political role, bear crucial advisory responsibilities; pressure and interest groups in the criminal justice field; and the mass-media'. Its implicit ideology is 'not simply the unexceptionable belief that society should be governed by law, and crime effectively controlled. It is a complex if naïve set of attitudes, including the beliefs that human beings have free will, that they must be strictly disciplined by restrictive rules, and that they should be harshly punished if they break the rules or fail to respect authority' (Cavadino and Dignan, 1992: 26). It should be stressed that such a politics is most notably defended within the higher echelons of the justice administration. People involved in the practice of criminal justice at street level (for example, policemen, probation officers, prison warders) are sometimes quite critical of these developments.

'Exploding crime rates' have always been the argument par excellence for advocating harsher punishment, for expanding the role of the police and for putting more emphasis on crime control and less on due process. Such a picture suggests a causal relation between crime rates and law enforcement efforts that is empirically untenable. In the Dutch case, it is, moreover, not clear whether crime rates have actually increased over the past decade. During the 1980s and 1990s, street crime in the most vulnerable urban areas may have taken on a more grim character, but the largest increase in common (property) crime took place in the 1960s and 1970s. Though the fact that this was a period of growing welfare is often used to 'disprove' deprivation theories, it should be noted that even an absolute increase of prosperity at a national level says very little about the relative deprivation of certain sections of society, and, most importantly, that growing rates of common (property) crime coincided with major demographic changes, scaling up, anonymisation, erosion of public space, commercialisation, automation and so on. The often presupposed causal relation between allegedly soft penal reactions and high crime rates cannot be supported by empirical evidence. In The Netherlands, after the war, rising crime rates even coincided with a reductionist penal policy. Periods of penal expansionism tend to reflect most of all a legitima-tion crisis in government (Rutherford, 1986: 64–87; Cavadino and Dignan, 1992: 9–30). When politicians lose their grip on social developments, law and order becomes their main symbol of vigour.

Criminal law also has an important internal dynamics, ranging from new criminalisations, to changes in prosecution priorities, an increasing number of detections and quicker ways of processing cases because of automation or increased efficiency, and indeed the selectivity of the system itself. The penal rationale has also been stirred up by popular metaphors of markets and products (based on a rationale of growth) and hurtles on because of its bureaucratic organisation (what has been put on the rails cannot so easily be put on another track). Moreover, law enforcement is ruled by external polit-ical considerations that have little to do with crime control. The Netherlands have so often been accused of being soft on (particularly drug-related) crime that Dutch politicians have become increasingly concerned about 'what the neighbours may think of us' and have repeatedly tried to present a 'serious' image by enacting more repressive measures. The ensuing 'crime-fighter ethos' did not change the (most notably French) depiction of 'soft' Dutch law enforcement, but it did have very negative consequences for the quality of the Dutch criminal justice system. Police operations in the sphere of organised (drug) crime got so far out of hand, and control over police methods was so badly handled, that it led in 1995 to a parliamentary inquiry *Inzake opsporing* (On Criminal Investigations). The parliamentary committee (van Traa, 1996) concluded that some police methods are incompatible with the democratic rule of law, whereas others require more specific regulation.

Before this parliamentary committee of inquiry reported, critics of the increasingly instrumentalist politics of law and order were widely labelled as moral relativists who did not take crime seriously. This almost became a con-ditioned reflex. Of course, crime is a serious problem. It is, however, a very different question whether severe penal sanctions are a serious answer to these problems. Political pressure for law and order seduced the police to engage in practices they should not have engaged in, and the prosecution and judiciary to allow such practices. Politicians who take the effectiveness of penal solutions for granted raise unwarranted expectations among the general public and thereby contribute to the penal crisis. Looking at the total volume of crime, penal intervention can hardly be more than a symbolic act – in view of the limited number of cases reported to the police, the limited possibilities of detecting crime, low clear-up rates, the (even in the era of automation) lim-ited capacity to process cases, and the poor remedies the penal system has to offer to redress the damage and humiliation experienced. These are all criti-cal criminological insights that are as valid today as they were 20 years ago.

Of all the changes in the criminological field over the past 15 years, the social and cultural criteria for penality have changed most of all. Punitive obsessions are visible not only in the penal sphere. Punitive discourse has been exported to many other areas: social work, welfare and other ad-ministrations, football management, the educational system, civil and administrative law. Everybody who wants to show that he (and sometimes she) is 'serious' uses the power to punish to demonstrate this. Punishment is just 'in' and care is 'out' of fashion, regardless of actual effects. Punishment is no longer aimed at individual lawbreakers. It has become a sign, a symbol, a means to set a frightening example to others. David Garland (1995: 17) reminds us in this respect of the fact that we are moving back to the kind of exemplary punishments Michel Foucault distinguished in his first model of penality (torture) from the era of the absolute monarch:

> though John Major is hardly Louis XV, whenever he or his ministers adopt the posture of being 'tough on criminals', 'condemning more and understanding less', and ensuring that 'criminals are frightened, not the law abiding public' . . . they are deliberately adopting a similar strategy. A show of punitive force against individuals is used to repress any acknowledgement of the state's inability to control crime to acceptable levels.

Towards actuarial justice

Alongside the politics of law and order, a shift in the rationale of criminal justice can be observed. Law enforcement has become one of the political strategies of a risk society – that is, a society that is no longer oriented towards positive ideals, but towards the negative rationale of limiting risk (Beck, 1986). In such a society, solidarity is no longer based on a positive feeling of connectedness, but is expressed in a negative communality of fear. The idea that something good can be done is abandoned, and cost and benefit analyses of how society can be managed in the most efficient way now guide political decision-making. This is portrayed as a shift from idealism to realism. State action is no longer informed by normative principles but by statistical scenarios. The underlying vision of mankind has changed from the accountable citizen to the irresponsible object of control. Breaches of law are no longer judged in terms of culpability but in terms of potential risks to the social order.

Italian legal theorist Filippo Sgubbi (1990) argues in respect of law enforcement that a growing proportion of crime in modern society is treated as a matter of mere transgression, in which attempts to hold an offender morally accountable are replaced by sheer administrative regulation. According to German criminologist Sebastian Scheerer (1986a: 105–6), criminal law is losing its identity, now that it is increasingly characterised by symbolic politics on the rhetorical level and mere administrative support on the practical side. Scheerer (1996) concludes that prison has become a 'dump' for those who are too poor to be punished financially and too much seen as outsiders to be integrated (refugees, East Europeans, asylum seekers), but is at the same time losing its position as the central reaction to the common crimes of the autochthonous population, for whom a wide net of control mechanisms within society, steered by the rationale of security, has become increasingly intrusive. Dutch criminologists Hans Boutellier and Bas van Stokkom (1995) chart the emergence of a policy aimed at community safety in the framework of a risk society whose actual moral order is based on the civic desire for safety and risk reduction. The French journal *Déviance et société* devotes a thematic issue (vol. 19, no. 2) to the growth of the security industry in the realm of the prevention politics of a risk society.

> The new round of 'the end of ideology' game has left its mark in social control systems and ideologies. In the crime control business, we see an ascendancy of managerial, administrative and technocratic styles. The old liberal ideologies (treatment, rehabilitation, social reform) are discredited. The goal is to keep the criminal justice system in reasonable shape. Prison directors are not the 'moral architects' of the early nineteenth century, nor the professionals of the heyday of the treatment ideology; they are just as likely to be accountants. (Cohen, 1994: 72)

Malcolm Feeley and Jonathan Simon (1992, 1994) characterise these developments as the 'new penology' of 'actuarial justice'. The adjective 'actuarial' comes from the insurance industry. Actuaries calculate potential risks and determine insurance premiums accordingly. 'Old' penology is 'rooted in a concern for individuals, and preoccupied with concepts such as guilt, responsibility and obligation, as well as diagnoses, intervention and treatment of the individual offender'. 'New' penology has an actuarial orientation. Crime is a normal phenomenon, and the key problem is how to manage it in the most efficient manner. The answer to this question is a risk calculation 'concerned with techniques for identifying, classifying and managing groups assorted by levels of dangerousness'. The rule of law embodies the core of an old penology; private enterprise has become the metaphor of new penology. 'Old' lawyers were concerned with law enforcement; 'new' administrators of justice are actuaries of a risk society.

> Actuarial justice is nebulous, but it is significant. Actuarial justice involves how we conceive of and talk about crime policy, but it is not an ideology in the narrow sense of a set of beliefs and ideas which constrain action. It involves practices, but is not reducible to a specific technology or set of behaviours. Indeed it is powerful and significant because it lacks a well-articulated ideology and identification with a specific technology. (Feeley and Simon, 1994: 174)

Actuarial justice consists of new models of rationality, new practices and new functions for old forms. 'Their newness lies in their particular combinations and the particular micropractices they are embedded in and the functions which they perform' (Feeley and Simon, 1994: 174). We have already encountered the idea of risk management in the Modern School's orientation towards social defence in the 1880s. During the 1980s, however, this focus on social defence gained another character: it was no longer presented as an explicit legitimation of punishment, but was obscured with pragmatic, managerial discourse which did not deal with questions of legitimacy. Risk, nuisance, efficiency and credibility were the key concepts of this discourse.

Richard Ericson and Kevin Carriere (1994: 102–3) single out three rationales of risk which influence the discourse and practice of actuarial justice. First, there is the negative logic of creating fears of threats and dangers by the construction of suitable enemies. Secondly, there is the idea that the irrational can be controlled by rational means. Now that the ideal of creating a just society has been given up, 'fear becomes a basis for rational action.' And, thirdly, there is the logic of insurance, which is central to the rationalisation of risk. These new rationales of risk also imply new forms of interference in people's private lives. Whereas informal, interpersonal, social control mechanisms were broken down in the 1960s and 1970s, institutional control has been intensified through the recording of personal data in the various, often mutually connected, computer systems of municipal registry offices, housing departments, social services, health services, and the police.

Actuarial tendencies in Dutch criminal justice can be observed both at a discursive level and in penal practice. The government no longer seeks to legitimise its ideological choices with arguments concerning the content of its politics, but presents them merely as inevitable efficiency measures, which find sufficient support in 'public opinion'. Governmental discourse is focused on the technical questions of implementation. A boundless logic of justice and the 'frameless frame' (Peters, 1986) of social-control talk, guided by 'public credibility' and 'limiting nuisance', is reflected in many policy papers of the past decade. In the 1970s, Dutch criminal justice politics became increasingly guided by criminological analyses. In the 1990s, the rationale seems to be the other way around. Political expediency dictates the policy line, and civil servants adopt those criminological studies that are supportive of such proposals and simply ignore those that are not. Stunning examples of such a sheer opportunistic use of criminology can be found in the 1990 White Paper *Recht in beweging* (Law in Motion). This report symbolises the breach with a traditional, more constructive relationship between science and politics (Bovenkerk, 1990; Rood-Pijpers, 1994). In two 1995 policy papers, 'Continuity and Change in Dutch Drug Policy' and 'Old and New Instruments of Law Enforcement', the disdain for criminology is taken even further. Here, serious empirical analyses are included that have nothing to do with the following policy recommendations (Blad and Emmen, 1996; Blom and Blad, 1996). The fact that a wide range of organisational studies on, most notably, the police and the prosecution service, carried out by scholars in social and business administration or, indeed, by private consultancy firms, have actually taken over from (academic) criminological analyses is a key example of the actuarial preoccupation with internal management questions, rather than with sociopolitical ones.

Other actuarial elements included: the fivefold increase in prison capacity over the past 20 years and coinciding 'retrenchment' of the prison system, both of which mark a shift from rehabilitation to selective incapacitation (van Swaaningen and de Jonge, 1995); the shift from a reintegrative to a 'public credibility' discourse on non-custodial sanctions (uit Beijerse and van Swaaningen, 1995); the dominant focus on fighting nuisance in crime-prevention politics (van Swaaningen, 1995); the shift from a health-care approach to the individual to an incapacitating penal approach aimed at fighting nuisance in the drug field (Blom and van Mastrigt, 1994); or the afore-mentioned change in the rationale of probation from providing social work for offenders in the protection of society. Actuarial tendencies can also be observed in the development of a dispersed 'police complex', consisting of general state police, an increasing number of special branches and various private forces (Hoogenboom, 1994), a 'streamlining' of the prosecution service ('t Hart, 1994) and an automation of the judiciary's sentencing politics, in order to increase their efficiency, and the shifted rationale of remand from a means to assure the presence of the accused at trial to a necessary protection of society (uit Beijerse, 1997). The revival of biosocial criminology and risk-profile studies can also be seen in this light. Risk profiles and a person's degree of recidivism are used to detect (potential) offenders, to determine what kind of sanction (custodial or not) an offender can 'handle', and to control prisoners. Records of previous police contacts and school reports of the so-called 'hard core' of juvenile offenders are stored in a database, which can be consulted in order to draw up the 'appropriate' penality. The Central Bureau of Investigations (CRI) collects an offenders' previous records in a so-called Prisoners' Registration and Information Point (GRIP), from which the prison department determines the appropriate level of security measures according to the perceived risk of escape (van Swaaningen, 1996a: 90–2).

Other legal features of actuarial justice include: the shift from a strong emphasis on written law to an orientation towards policy and administrative regulations and the dispersal and expansion of 'penal' legislation into administrative and private law (Hartmann and van Russen Groen, 1994); the increased surveillance of public space and widened monitoring operations, including the private sphere; the penalisation of preparatory acts to a wide range of not specifically mentioned crimes (para. 46 Sr); lower legal standards for the application of means of coercion on anonymous and foreign suspects (paras 61a–c Sv, 67-2 Sv); the obligation to present identification documents in various non-suspect situations (workplace, public transport, football matches); increasingly restrictive immigration laws; and the resurrection of some dead letters in the criminal code to arrest whole groups of people without having to construct an individual suspicion (paras 140 and 435a Sr).[1] These examples embody a form of risk calculation based upon certain presuppositions about what is dangerous to society and upon an ecology of fear. A general fear of the unknown, the foreign, the unconventional is easily presented as a risk factor. This new administration of justice consists of two elements: a rationale of law and order guided by a neo-conservative moralism on crime, and an actuarial rationale led by a managerial approach to law enforcement.

Neo-conservative moralism

Britain's Prime Minister Margaret Thatcher launched a plea for a return to Victorian values. Slightly later, Dutch Prime Minister Ruud Lubbers argued that The Netherlands had become a godforsaken country, whose citizens had lost their sense of norms and values. The policy of the Ministry of Justice should be directed towards an ethical revival in law and order in order to compensate for the moral vacuum which had grown among the population since the 1960s. The people were, in return, invited to carry their own responsibilities in crime control and morally to condemn the anomalies of society. This 'responsibilisation strategy' (Garland, 1995: 8), introduced by the 1985 White Paper *Samenleving en criminaliteit* (Society and Crime), reinforced a moral consensus about the conventional social order. The fact that other morals – concerning environmental awareness, gender relations, the right to self-determination, respect for lifestyles beyond traditional family patterns, the social responsibilities and (financial) integrity of authorities and entrepreneurs, or the protection of vulnerable persons in relations of dependency – have gained importance over this same period of time is largely ignored in this vision of norms and values in decay.

Dutch Minister of Justice Ernst Hirsch Ballin clearly expressed this moralistic appeal in a speech in 1993 to judges in training. According to Hirsch Ballin, the dominant focus on individual rights, rooted in the project of the 1960s, has resulted in a 'mind your own business' mentality, in which a broad aversion to any moralisation of social conflicts has emerged. This tendency has undermined a socially vital, collective sense of norms and values. It has broken down personal moral standards which prevent the individual from committing crimes. Social control is no longer conceivable without normative zest. This has necessitated a re-think in the administration of justice. A one-sided emphasis on legal guarantees should, according to Hirsch Ballin, be understood as a reaction to the more authoritarian, rigid and imperious tendencies in pre-1960s society. At present, however, we witness a reaction among the general population to the far-too permissive state of the recent past. According to Hirsch Ballin (1993), today's citizens no longer fear legal infringements upon their individual rights, but ask for the protection of collective interests against the attacks of criminals. Therefore, a new balance has to be found between the credible enforcement of social norms, on the one hand, and legal guarantees for the individual, on the other.

Margaret Thatcher argued, from her first electoral campaigns, that it was not her but 'the people of Britain who are going to make crime an issue'. The Dutch Minister went even further in this demagogic direction when he actually invited trainee judges to act as moral entrepreneurs and to adapt to the sentiments currently prevailing among the general public. In a *rechtsstaat*, however, judges do not have any political function and should, according to the independent constitutional status of the judiciary, not be led by public sentiment but by professional legal considerations alone. It is alarming that the young judges the minister addressed did not give any rejoinders to his attacks on the allegedly permissive judges of the 1970s, nor to his assumptions of public anxiety about crime, which were merely backed up with statements by 'influential journalists'. The worries of young judges in the 1970s were about class justice and equal rights. Their successors of the 1990s are mainly concerned with efficiency problems of law enforcement and about the increased complexity of legislation (Drayer and Josten, 1993). Other journalists and older members of the judiciary point out that the minister was mixing in affairs that he had nothing to do with. In a democratic *rechtsstaat*, he may have some influence on the general policy of the public prosecutor's office, but the judiciary is an independent power. Ex-prosecutors Hans de Doelder and August 't Hart (1993: 604) asked the minister whether his pleas for simpler procedures implied that procedural mistakes should be accepted and that punishment should be imposed rashly if 'public sentiment' is disturbed.

Stuart Hall (1988) has called the emerging hegemony of crude, middle-class distinctions between the insiders of society (the contented class) and the outsiders (unemployed, criminals and foreigners) the victory of 'authoritarian populism'. It is typified by an increasing xenophobia and a decreasing respect for unconventional lifestyles. Illustrative of the fact that populist sentiments over-rule rational arguments even in the political arena is the fact that drastic, punitive bills are often pushed through parliament overnight after single incidents – a particularly cruel murder, a sensational escape from prison, a gross mistake by the prosecution service. Policy-makers are reluctant to address the general public with analyses that exceed the level of an average talkshow. In accordance with the risk society's vision of mankind, adult people are addressed as children. Hereby, a downward spiral of bigoted simplism is reproduced, in which only truisms are presented, suggesting that political measures are 'inevitable' because 'the market', 'Europe' or 'acute danger of . . .' would require it so. Their introduction is merely a question of 'how?' rather than 'why?' This sloganeering has led to a stream of ill-considered and rushed armchair measures that are unworkable in penal practice.

Democracy implies first and foremost a public space for deviant interpretations. When authoritarian populism permeates parliamentary discourse the idea that 'public opinion' asks for more punitive reactions becomes an axiom rather than a question. It would, indeed, be a democratic problem if 'the people' wanted a stiff politics of law and order and politicians did not respond. It is, however, equally problematic if there is no empirical support for the idea that 'getting tough' on criminals actually helps to bring crime rates down. It is too easy to say that people are just manipulated by the media (of course we are, but not just); many problems are real, some fears are justified, and the demand that something should be done is legitimate. Politicians claim to act according to public opinion, but when they actually propose their measures, they do, as German philosopher Peter Sloterdijk expresses it, not hear one normal word, but the 'administrative twaddle of their own caste'. They live in a 'semantic brothel' (*de Groene Amsterdammer*, 1995, no. 23, pp. 12–14). Sturdy political statements about law and order in the public arena coincide with mere technocratic discussions in parliament. Both gloss over the complexity of such a concept as public opinion.

Increasing support for longer prison sentences, and even capital punishment, coincides with broad public support for community sanctions. This split goes hand in hand with a bifurcation in penal reactions, but a serious analysis of the rationales, aims and expected effects has not been made. A thorough analysis of all the social processes constituting authoritarian populism cannot be made here, though the commercialisation of the media, politics and education, which leads to a focus on the average taste, and in which everything is done to avoid offending public opinion, certainly plays a role. Public opinion studies show that the public demand for more punitive sanctions is closely connected with a low level of actual information; the more deeply one goes into a concrete case, the less the need for pain infliction (van der Laan, 1993). Other research shows that a punitive mentality is related more to a general conformistic, moralistic and ritualistic personality than to concrete visions of crime (Rood-Pijpers, 1988). Decreasing tolerance is not necessarily connected with the threat from 'criminals', but is rather the product of a much more general anomic anxiety which can have various causes: a deterioration in living conditions and lowered expectations; the increasing pace of life which makes people lose track; fear of losing one's 'own' identity in a multi-cultural society; the loss of normative points of orientation after the 'end of ideology'; and the exclusion of problems outside one's own direct experience because of an overdose of incoherent 'information' without analyses. Studies of feelings of insecurity show that punitive reactions are people's first expression of dissatisfaction with their life situation and of a feeling of impotence to change this. They are, however, not primarily reflecting upon crime, and are put in perspective when more concrete questions about possible solutions are posed (Fijnaut et al., 1991). Public opinion is also the product of the manufacture of news. The public image of the seriousness and extent of certain problems corresponds more with media coverage than with the actual caseload of the police and courts. Glossing over such nuances leads to an obscure popular sentiment that is no adequate reflection of public opinion. Such an incoherent pot-pourri of loose opinions should never be used to legitimate policy, or the conformism and material conservatism of the contented class will bulldoze every deviation from middle-class norms and will continue to increase the split in society.

A revival of ideas about civic morality and informal mechanisms of social control from the 1950s announced a shift in the normative debate about the role of the state in the mid-1980s. The citizen whose moral senses were in decay may have been the initial object of complaint, but, by the early 1990s, the morality of the state itself was under attack as well. Despite the government's discourse on morality, plain and elementary decency was increasingly lacking on the side of the authorities. If people are not taken seriously and authorities repeatedly betray their promises, it becomes difficult to trust the conventional order. According to Kees Schuyt (1993), such examples of institutional indifference are also criminogenic. If authorities treat people with contempt, this leads to an indifference about conventional morality that ultimately incites crime. The state developed from a 'politically normative inspired welfare state to a managerially oriented organisational network in which normative standards remain implicit' (Boutellier 1994: 89). According to Hans Boutellier, this is an inevitable process, but it is also a major reason of current legitimation crisis of the state. The 1990 White Paper 'Law in Motion', which is full of notions about the credibility of the criminal justice system, does not refer to such an intrinsic credibility. Legal philosopher Willem Witteveen (1994: 44) poses the question of whether the state still has the moral power to convince people. A government that continually cuts back on public expenditure for the most vulnerable groups in society, and laments from the safe distance of the pulpit that the citizen's sense of civic duties, norms and values is declining, makes it hard for its ethical message to be taken seriously. In Britain, a comparable approach was followed. Lessons in good housekeeping were the major response to people who could no longer afford to pay their bills. Teaching moral values, controlling children, testing the workshy and chasing the cheaters were the strategies of the new coercive state (Hillyard and Percy-Smith, 1988: 204–35). British Tories, as well as the bigger political parties in The Netherlands, hold the expectation that strict law and order will reinforce self-control. When it fails, it is the 'soft school system' and the 'looney left' who are to blame. The state no longer employs all preventive and coercive strategies itself, but leaves it to affiliated private institutions. There are various explanations for the increasing use of punitive symbols by the state, whereas the actual management is increasingly carried out by third parties – local authorities, private enterprise, citizens and so on. After the secularisation process of the 1960s, religious moralising processes were replaced by punitive social control (Braithwaite, 1993b). In this way, the role of criminal justice as a belief system became more important. Consequently, morality now depends more on law than the other way around – the Kantian postulate of law. While the state bestows its worldly power to solve social problems on to third parties, it harks back to para-religious sentiments. Punishment is a ritual that has not yet lost its meaning in late modern times.

Penal business management

Despite the revival of hegemonic moralistic discourse, most actual legal developments have been characterised by managerialism. Principles of due process are replaced by a managerial approach to an efficient procedural order. The quality of law enforcement is interpreted in terms of organisational efficiency. On a rhetorical level, a moralistic 'crime-fighting ethos' has been stirred up, which has, on a practical level, reinforced a one-sided instrumentalist focus on the establishment of an efficient crime-control apparatus. This development is well captured in a nickname given to Dutch Minister Hirsch Ballin: 'Minister for the Restoration of Norms and Moral Indignation in his Additional Function as President of the Board of Governors of Law Incorporated' (*NRC Handelsblad*, 7 April 1993).

Actuarial justice is announced by the increased dominance of policy considerations, notably within the prosecution service. August 't Hart (1994: 117) demonstrates how this policy orientation emerged by the 1970s. On the one hand, the introduction of *beleid* (policy) as pseudo-law was a means of adapting law enforcement to the changing social values of the 1960s without actually having to draw up new legislation. Law will always lag behind social developments and policy can be changed much more quickly. Such an increased policy orientation was, for example, supported by the abolitionist Louk Hulsman. On the other hand, criminal justice officials supported a policy system out of the practical need for standardised guidelines, to set rational and uniform priorities with respect to the offences which are actually to be prosecuted and which are better (conditionally) waived, when the increased number of cases made it impossible to deal with all of them in an equally detailed way. According to 't Hart, this orientation developed by the 1980s into the Weberian *eisernen Käfig*, the iron cage of bureaucracy, in which the public prosecutor changed most of his magisterial role for a mere managerial one. The new metaphor for criminal justice was a company consisting of a number of branches: police, prosecution service, judiciary, probation service, prison system. In a 'redesign' of criminal justice these various branches were to be connected more closely in order to make the company work more efficiently. This process was followed by a whole new idiom. Even in the probation service, one no longer speaks about providing assistance to the offender, but about case management, input trajectories, result-oriented offers, product registration and result measurement. These managerial metaphors were most fiercely advocated by procurator general Dato Steenhuis (Rutherford, 1996: 59–83).

In an era characterised by a celebration of the 'free market', terms and metaphors derived from private enterprise are to be expected. Increasing the efficiency of the police and the prosecution service in order to prevent further expansion of their capacity and to increase the retributive elements of non-custodial sanctions in order to make them more suitable actually to replace prison sentences are not just silly ideas (Steenhuis, 1986; Smits, 1994). Comparing 'production-unit' justice with any other company implies, however, an entirely instrumentalist vision of criminal justice, in which the power-critical dimension of due process has no place. The glossary of control talk of this criminal justice 'company' comes straight from the pages of a management consultancy manual for beginners. The fact that this discourse can be applied to any private enterprise shows little understanding of the specific sociological meaning of public values that are thought to be embodied in the rationale of criminal justice. Dutch Minister of Justice Winnie Sorgdrager (1994: 241) argued in this respect (in her previous position as procurator general): 'Any system that deserves the qualification "due process" will never be able to come up to the mark of some other organisations and their advisers.'

Private enterprise has a public responsibility, to be sure, but in the end is oriented to the maximisation of profit. This will generally coincide with attempts to work more efficiently and to expand the market. It is highly questionable whether metaphors derived from production units are really suitable for criminal justice. If a criminal procedure is made into a penal production process will this imply that the product punishment is to be offered in various tastes appealing to the needs of different consumers? It is, apart from some special design products for very special and affluent consumers, quite unlikely.

Experienced consumers know that market orientations, despite the discourse of diversity, will in practice lead to greater uniformity, especially when cutting costs is the major motivation for the redesign of the company.

The development towards sheer instrumental visions of criminal law, as a means of carrying out government policy, is the end of the line of the Weberian rationalisation process. In this development, bureaucratisation has, according to David Garland (1990: 184), become 'a component of measured and impartial justice'. At the same time, 'the professionalisation of the punitive process has . . . reached a point where professionals have been able to redefine the social meaning of punishment.' As a consequence of this process, the internal rationale of the system has come to determine the way in which social reality is to be interpreted, instead of social reality determining the way the system is to react. This development means that functionalist arguments have overcome normative considerations and principles. Garland (1990: 186) mentions the way in which the rehabilitation principle has declined as an example of this mode of thinking. Rehabilitation is not seen to have failed because it is no longer a valid principle, but because it did not 'work'. Here is the normative fallacy of disproving principles with empirical arguments. Such counter-factual principles remain crucial because they maintain a continuous dialectic between 'are' and 'ought'. They prevent a vicious circle of continually lowering normative points of orientation. A managerial style of law enforcement makes it, however, much easier to carry out a politics of social defence in the context of a traditionally humanitarian working credo of penal practitioners. In a managerial environment, people, whether they are public prosecutors, prison governors or probation officers, tend to act correctly as functionaries of the system. Their personal role, commitment and responsibility to do justice remains outside the criteria of relevance for their behaviour. In such an environment, the human impulse will even be seen as an unprofessional attitude. That is the power of managerialism when ideology is no longer articulated.

The twosome of pragmatic moralism

Moralising and managerial orientations seem contradictory, but on closer observation they need each other badly. With an exclusively functionalist discourse, we touch upon what Garland (1990: 190) calls the limits of the rationalisation process. A moralistic position on crime is therefore a welcome addition to a managerial approach to law enforcement. By adopting a managerial style, administrators of justice are able to reduce complex moral dilemmas to technical and financial questions. Questions of effectiveness can be turned into problems of efficiency. In this way, the Durkheimian notion that punishment is primarily a 'passionate, vengeful reaction, motivated by outraged moral sentiments' can be transmitted to the general public, whereas ultimate problems of conscience – of 'throwing the first stone' – are safely deflected by a simple reference to the system's internal logic. If we are to see criminal justice as an efficient apparatus of crime control, the norms and values on which the system is based should not be disputed too much. Thus, managerialism needs to be accompanied by a homogenising culture of morality (Foqué and Zijderveld, 1994: 311). In penal practice, a moralistic and managerial approach to criminal justice can go together because they touch upon different parts and functions of the system. 'While legislators . . . make some claim to be expressing community feeling, and [judges] will adjust their penal reactions accordingly, the penal administration is not accountable in the same way. Its primary concern is not to express public sentiment but to operate the penal system and harness its resources in the manner it considers most rational and efficient' (Garland, 1990: 187). The coincidence of moralism and managerialism does, however, bring about a paradoxical situation. In practice, it brings forward the same kind of bloodlessness, bleakness, depersonalisation and lack of normative principles and personal sense of responsibility that is, on a rhetorical political level, identified as a major cause of crime on the part of the individual citizen.

A major problem of actuarial justice is that it has no intrinsic boundaries. Its instrumental rationale is a 'frameless frame' (Peters, 1986), which has 'the flexibility of a waterbed' (Rutherford, 1986). Nils Christie (1993) outlines a gloomy picture of what could happen if crypto-religious beliefs about criminal justice, legal management considerations and bureaucratic mechanisms of anonymisation coincide with the profit orientations of private enterprise. If crime control becomes profitable business, Christie argues, the potential of lawbreakers can be expanded *ad libitum* and Western-style gulags will emerge. Notions like risk, fear and suffering have no intrinsic limits, and thus the symbolic display of power to compensate for these feelings may well be equally boundless. The dominance of political objectives in criminal justice also leads to unbounded law enforcement, as does the logic of efficiency. If principles of due process can be violated and more technical equipment is made available to the police, prosecution and judiciary, surely more crimes can be processed. And if planning prison capacity mainly depends on mathematical trend extrapolations, the need for more prisons will continue *ad infinitum*. It can all be done for sure, but does it make sense? Does punishment deter? Does it have any effect on the conditions under which crimes are committed? Is it beneficial for victims or does it at least result in less fear about crime? Where are the normative limits of instrumentalism? And why, indeed, do the enormous costs of penal expansionism play such a limited role, while budgets for vital social provisions are continually cut? These are the real questions that are currently at stake in criminal justice politics. These are also questions that critical criminologists should address.

Actuarial justice and the decline of the welfare state

The emergence of actuarial justice coincides with the decline of the welfare state. The reason why the welfare model fell into crisis in the 1980s lies in its success in the 1970s. The traditional working class is currently quite well off.

Thus, there is a growing majority of people whose personal interests lie in decreasing taxes, while a smaller group of people, who can hardly participate in social life, need good welfare provisions more than ever. Now that this 'one-third society of the masses' can no longer make a fist, the 'two-thirds society of the contented class' is unwilling to pay for such collective services. Not only are the implicit, yet structural, mechanisms of crime prevention of the welfare state abolished, but also a criminogenic split in society is increased. Actuarial justice's rationale of efficiency is inspired by 'free-market' discourse, and so is its logic of risk. The point is not really whether you do harm to society, but whether the balance of the economic costs and benefits of one's behaviour is positive or negative. The shift in the public's attitude to fraud, which went from white-collar criminals to social-security scroungers, is a good illustration of this tendency. The fact that, in The Netherlands, the prosecution of crimes can, since 1984, be 'bought off' with a financial 'transaction' with the public prosecutor's office reinforces the idea that whether or not one can break the law its now negotiable (Blankenburg, 1993: 365). In line with Garland's earlier analyses, a return to the *ancien régime* can also be observed in this respect. The increasing focus on damage instead of breaches of law *per se* is also indicative of this economical rationale (Hoogenboom, 1995: 95). There is nothing new in the acknowledgement that the poor are worse off than the rich when they come into contact with the law, but this historical pattern gains a new dimension under actuarial justice. It is no longer oriented to *a posteriori* judgements of individual behaviour, but to an *a priori* taxation of risks, on which basis appropriate, preventive measures are taken. The economic interpretation of risk implies a boundless logic by which the idea of 'dangerous classes' can be expanded *ad libitum*. In this way, we may end up with discussions about whether going out in the street in winter without wearing a shawl should not be penalised because common colds put such a large claim on public expenditure on health care.

As mechanisms of social exclusion (by penal means or otherwise) also follow economic lines, a new 'dangerous class' consists of people who are unable to consume. Zygmunt Bauman (1995b: 212) analyses how 'welfare provisions have been transformed from the exercise of citizen rights into the stigma of the impotent and the improvident.' People on welfare are subjected 'to ever stricter and ever more humiliating tests, vilified for being a drain on "taxpayer money", associated in the public mind with sponging, reprehensible negligence, sexual laxity or drug abuse'. These potential frauds 'necessitate' new control techniques – the introduction of which may well, by the way, cost 'the taxpayer' more than all the newly discovered social-security frauds will save. At the same time that unmarried single mothers in the United States are denied social benefits and have to send their children to orphanages, legal reforms are introduced that abolish 'the last constraints put on banking activities', 'flexibilise' anti-pollution laws and make 'appeals against company actions more difficult'. Though the 'birth of the Brave New World of deregulation, privatisation, consumer choice – and of the criminalisation of those unable to choose' (Bauman, 1995b: 218) is, in Europe, still curbed by a stronger social-democratic and communitarian tradition, 'we' seem terribly eager to follow the United States in this respect.

The law-and-order campaigns of the 1980s are generally interpreted as a necessary correction of the preceding period of irresponsible permissiveness, in which no one dared to call someone else to account for his or her behaviour. The neo-conservative revolution does, however, also carry the seeds of an increase in crime. In the 1980s, increasing affluence rather than relative deprivation was seen as a main reason for an increase in common crime. A welfare-oriented approach had, indeed, not prevented a steep increase in common crime during the 1960s and 1970s. It is, however, doubtful whether these two phenomena can be linked so easily. The 1960s and 1970s were also the time when baby-boomers were in their adolescence. This demographic fact also determines the boom in juvenile delinquency and in youth welfare institutions. The (in current crime-control discourse) widely criticised, immoral and calculating citizen seems, moreover, very much a product of the utilitarian individualism that followed from the widely celebrated, neo-liberal economic rationale. The judgement of good and bad, of useful and useless in terms of profit, efficiency and output seems to be the core of the problem. Quality is mainly assessed by the logic of 'What good will it do to me?', with 'quick, cheap and a lot of it' as major values. People committing 'welfare crimes' are very law-abiding citizens in respect of the values promoted by TV commercials. The creation of needs for advertising-fetishes means that people feel that they must have certain goods in order to be full members of society. High pressure to compete and achieve in a labour market that is continuously reduced by automation means that people soon feel like failures. Loyal employees are unscrupulously set aside by cunning efficiency plans and reorganisations, while company profits rise. Decreasing government control over and support for private enterprise leads to a 'survival of the fittest'. Companies will only employ personnel who form a small business risk (who are the most healthy and socially acceptable) and who are willing to work and get paid only when the boss needs them. This means that the elderly, the sick, the handicapped, but probably also blacks in a white environment and women (especially if they have children) in a male-dominated environment get sacked, whereas the younger generation has to accept an uncertain position as a 'flexible' and underpaid workforce – commonly known as 'McJobs'.

In accordance with strain theory, tensions between levels of aspiration and the opportunities actually to realise these, lower inhibitions to crime. Willem Bonger's (1932: 113) thesis, that increasing prosperity will cause a decrease in 'crimes of misery' as well as an increase in 'crimes of greed', seems still valid. A growing split in society (between poor and rich, black and white, young and old) results in an increase in 'crimes of misery'. In respect of street robbery, Willem de Haan (1993: xiv) concludes that, because this offence is often committed by people who do not have sufficient means of existence ('illegal' immigrants, junkies, runaways, drop-outs), and is thus rooted in a need to survive, penal measures will not reduce the problem. 'Measures which make the life-conditions of these groups decrease even more . . . will, as a side-effect, bring about an increase in aggressive crime with utilitarian motives. Better results are to be expected from measures . . . which offer people whose decline into hard street crime is imminent a better perspective to integrate into regular society.'

Not only from an aetiological point of view, but also in respect of social control, the unbounded belief in the self-regulating capacity of the market is criminogenic. In order to increase profits, shops have fired staff and carried through efficiency measures by scaling up the size of the store and by automation. This depersonalisation has led to a decrease in informal social control. This loss is compensated for by private policing and techno-prevention – and by consuming, free of charge, the state's 'safety product', by which they pass the costs of their private profits on to the community. A lack of control over shop-owners has, moreover, enabled the rule of the market to change historical city-centres into one big billboard, one commercial succession of fast-food outlets, gambling halls, money-exchange offices and porno- and souvenir-shops. This has created such a gross uniformity in the urban environment that it has become impossible to identify oneself with it – and things like graffiti and vandalism can really come as no surprise. The banking and mail-order businesses are allowed total freedom to seduce people into creating more debts than they will ever be able to pay back. Speculation on the property market has retarded urban renewal. Because many old and derelict houses remained empty for a long time, they attracted crime – and a quickly changing, poorer and poorer composition of the neighbourhood (uit Beijerse and van Swaaningen, 1993).

Economic primacy in the organisation of society is, according to Belgian legal philosopher Koen Raes (1995: 82), also the main cause for subjective feelings of unsafety. A central element in this respect is 'the erosion of anonymous public space'. In order to feel safe, one must perceive the street as normal territory, where one continually meets strangers in an anonymous setting. The way society is currently organised means that we do not have to meet strangers any more. While moving almost exclusively by car, we lock ourselves out of social life; supermarkets have done away with personal contacts in shops and drive-in restaurants are not the most social places; in public buildings we no longer ask a person for directions, but look at signs and monitors; public services are built on the outskirts of cities, so that we can get there more easily by car. Many Western cities are converted into gigantic traffic junctions, and streets and squares into dead parking lots. Thus, public space is colonised by motorised traffic. Consequently, 'the other' becomes a stranger and the city an eerie place. The main causes of subjective unsafety are actively created by an obsession with efficiency.

The modern political 'narratives' of left and right became outdated when the market became a functional substitute for the all-ordaining gods of modernity. The sheer unquestioning belief in the self-regulating capacity of the market means that we can speak of 'free-market theocracy'. The success of this new religion is that it has brought forward an unprecedented uniformity and is none the less associated with freedom. The subsequent success of its politics of law and order is its ability to stir up public anxiety about street crime and its promotion of technical control and policing as major remedies, while few people point to neo-liberalism's efficiency-ridden ideology as a cause of the problem. The primacy of economic interests pushed a concern for social cohesion into the background. This will eventually lead to the disintegration of 'the autonomous social' itself (Donzelot, 1984). The victory of the new right also changed public morality. The concern for crime is strongly moralised, whereas a care for social welfare is de-moralised (Raes, 1995: 88–9). Whether or not the poor can lead a decent life is made dependent again on the philanthropy of the rich. Of course, philanthropic rich are to be preferred over cynical rich, and privately sponsored public services are better than no services at all, but with these mere pragmatic considerations we actually accept a reactionary development. The privatisation of public services implies the bankruptcy of social-democratic morality. It will ultimately lead to a qualitative decrease in social provisions. Those services which do not bring any profit will be abolished, and these may well be exactly those services that the most vulnerable groups in society are dependent on. The welfare state is becoming an insurance state. By this ideological transition, 'misfortune', which would in the past have been covered by collective provisions, will now be seen as people's individual responsibility: if they 'do not bother' (which often means: do not have the money) to insure themselves, it is their 'own fault' if they get into trouble.

It is a great paradox of the current politics of law and order that pleas to increase community spirit have been launched in an era when one public service after another is being privatised. Stimulating community spirit would need to start with the establishment of public services that are not aimed at maximising their own profits. Dutch Minister of the Interior Hans Dijkstal, who is, by the way, a liberal-conservative and not a social democrat, argued that the semi-privatisation (*verzelfstandiging*) of various judicial services 'went too far'. None the less, the privatisation process continues, with the hardly contestable argument for ordinary citizens that in this way state expenditure, which has got out of hand, is cut back. An assembly of the secretary generals of all ministries has, however, called the privatisation of public services an 'escape route' and a 'fashionable trend' which neither makes these services any cheaper nor the state apparatus as a whole any smaller (*NRC Handelsblad*, 19 November 1994). Kees Schuyt (1991) argues that the state has, over the past decade, not only retreated as a public service, but at the same time has actively trampled upon many valuable attainments of the welfare state. The government has become increasingly indifferent about the well-being of its citizens, whose own personal interests have, vice versa, driven away the idea that one has a necessary social responsibility towards the collective. The decline of the welfare state will adversely affect commitment to the state as such.

Both the idea of a risk society, in which people are treated as irresponsible objects of control, and the notion of the severe state of external, punitive social control imply a step backwards in the Eliasian civilisation process. An increased punitiveness may pose as a symbol of strength, but it should be interpreted as a symptom of weak controls and inadequate authority. It should, however, also be emphasised that 'the responsibilisation strategy does not entail the simple off-loading of state functions. Rather it is a new form of governance-at-a-distance, which represents, in this field at least, a new mode of exercising power (Garland, 1995). According to Bob Hoogenboom (1995: 88), the development of crime-prevention politics, by which the classical doctrine of the monopoly of crime control by police and the justice administration is broken and under which label many private security firms found a virtually free market, resembles the opening of Pandora's box. The future of social control is, according to Canadian criminologists Clifford Shearing and Philip Stenning (1987: 322), 'preventative, subtle and apparently non-coercive and consensual. It focuses on categories, requires no knowledge of the individual and employs pervasive surveillance . . . Its order is instrumental and determined by the interests of Disney Productions rather than moral and absolute. And anyone who has visited Disney World knows, it is extraordinarily effective.' The fear of critical criminologists, that authoritarian state apparatuses would create a docile, disciplined proletariat, can be replaced by the notion that today's consumer society and commercial media create docile middle classes, just by numbing them with entertainment, gameshows, soft porn and fashionable clothes and gadgets. This 'Disney order of social control', as Shearing and Stenning call the kind of social control through infantilisation, with a small wink to Stan Cohen, is 'not so Mickey Mouse' at all. Sebastian Scheerer (1996: 333) confirms this analysis for the European situation, but adds that with the current 're-barbarisation' of international relations, Shearing and Stenning's postmodern control state and Nils Christie's (1993) Western-style gulags may well coincide.

Over the past decade, the nature of criminal justice and of social control has changed substantially. If critical criminology is to reconnect with the times, it has to reflect upon a 'new' penal reality of a risk society, where state control is largely operated through the 'responsibilisation' of third parties, and upon a new 'flexible' economy with new 'dangerous classes'. Critical criminology's normative postulate of social justice offers an excellent starting-point for a critique of the major sociopolitical risks that actuarial justice brings about. With respect to its nestling in the risk society, various democratic shortcomings can be observed. The fact that 'the market' determines a large part of the state's actions actually implies that the poor are disfranchised roughly as they were in the nineteenth century, when only those who paid a certain amount of taxes had the right to vote. Those who can fully participate in the consumer society will see their interests sufficiently protected, but who cares about the interests of those who have too little money to spend? A second democratic deficit emerges as a consequence of the privatisation of public services. If not the state itself but representatives of private enterprise are responsible for collective provisions, the possibilities of democratic, parliamentary control decrease. With the semi-privatisation of legal services and the growth of the private security industry, the critical criminological question of 'Who controls the controllers?' becomes particularly pressing.

Another risk of actuarial justice is the erosion of the normative debate. Pragmatic and actuarial considerations can be the only means to a previously defined end. The entrepreneurial state takes them, however, as goals in themselves. The normative basis of certain rules or political choices is obscured by a smoke-screen of formalities and technocratic perils of an organisational kind. This way of government, which empties democratic and social principles of their meaning, marks 'the unbearable lightness of politics'. It is crucial to reveal the gut reaction populism on which this politics is actually based, and to place criminal justice politics in a socioeconomic framework. Looking at the social problems addressed in this chapter, the demand of social justice seems an important normative touchstone of criminal justice politics. This traditional key concept of critical criminology will thus be the focus of the next two chapters.

Note

1 'Sr' stands for Criminal Code and 'Sv' for Code of Criminal Procedure. Paragraph 140 Sr penalises various forms of participation in 'criminal organisations'. The paragraph originates in the prosecution of socialists in the 1890s; in the late 1940s it was used against Indonesian freedom fighters, and suddenly in the late 1980s and 1990s it is used again against squatters and other 'subversive' groups – and against companies involved in the trade in drugs, arms or chemical waste, who cannot be caught under another title. At the occasion of the European Summit in June 1997 in Amsterdam, article 140 was used to keep demonstrators off the streets for two days: over 600 arrests were made although there was no intention to prosecute these demonstrators once the summit was over. Paragraph 435a Sr penalises the wearing of symbols which express a political endeavour. This 'uniform prohibition' was introduced in the 1930s to prevent the parades of Dutch Nazis in uniform. Since the war it had not been used until the Utrecht police discovered it on 4 March 1995 as a means of preventing anti-racist demonstrators – identifiable by anti-Nazi and anarchist signs – from disturbing meetings of the extreme right.

9

'Newer' Criminologies and Social Safety

General developments in criminology

Objects of criminological study often change with the penal climate and scientific fashion. In the 1960s, the general orientation shifted from an aetiologically inspired offender perspective to a social-reaction approach. Partly because models oriented at individual and environmental causes of crime only offered limited explanations, criminologists started to analyse possible criminogenic factors of the criminal justice system itself, such as stigmatisation and secondary deviance. They studied the functions and effects of institutions like the police, the courts and prisons. In the 1980s, the focus changed again. Now social problems (gender- and ethnicity-related problems, drugs, organised and corporate crime, corruption, deterioration of urban areas, breakdown of the community, community safety and so on) were taken as a starting-point. At the same time, the application of theoretical models gained a more loose and eclectic character. As a distinct theoretical project, critical criminology thus became less visible. Of course, a social-reaction approach did not offer 'the' explanation of crime. It was, indeed, necessary for aetiological studies to receive more profound attention again. The subsequent scapegoating of social-reaction theory (mainly the labelling approach) as moral relativism which played down the crime problem seems, however, unjustified. In such portrayals, macro- and meso-sociological analyses are often confronted with a concrete micro-situation to which they do not fit. A sociologically relativist position is, moreover, taken for moral relativism, by which empirical analyses and moral judgements are mixed up. Arguing, at an analytical level, that crime is a social construction, a politically determined label of a certain category of social problem in a certain time and place, does not at all imply that it should not be taken seriously.

It is questionable whether critical criminologists actually have 'played down' the seriousness of crime. This vision seems to be based on a globalisation of some, perhaps over-stressed, 'revolutionary' ideas of a handful of British conflict theorists. It is interesting to note that this stereotyping of critical criminology began as self-criticism by British critical scholars (Young, 1979), and was only at a later stage eagerly taken up and repeated by more mainstream criminologists (van Dijk, 1989; Boutellier, 1993). As an outsider to the British debate, I am loath to challenge Young's scholarly observations, but the situation seems a bit more complex. In the majority of critical criminological studies, glorifications of lawbreakers as 'working-class heroes' and 'rebels with a cause' cannot be found. We must also recall that intellectual distance on the European continent towards deviant sub-cultures was greater than in British neo-Marxist criminology. Seeing deviance as a proto-revolutionary phenomenon implies an individualistic vision of class struggle, whereas it is in a (mainly South) European context always related to organised, collective proletarian action.

Critical criminologists are not value relativists at all, but have indeed pointed to social evils that are largely ignored by the criminal justice system, such as 'male sexualised violence and harassment; various other forms of family violence; corporate and business crime; environmental crime; and crimes of the state or violations of human rights' (Cohen, 1994: 71). The prayer wheel against 'relativistic' criminologists is furthermore oriented to a species that has not been in existence for at least 15 years. An ultimately one-sided empathy for the offender and an equally one-sided attention to the limitations of criminal justice are by no means today's problems. We have already been faced, for quite a long time, with the opposite problem: too little understanding of the specific 'difficult youth' of offenders and over-strained expectations of the criminal justice system. Today, it is mainly 'realists' of the new right who play deviance down. These criminologists perceive crime as something normal, whose causes do not have to be examined, but which just has to be controlled. In criminological theory, 'managerialism is reflected in various neo-classical movements, opportunity theory, rational choice theory and the emergence of the new reasoning criminal. If people cannot be changed and societies cannot be transformed, then theories become less ambitious and lose their critical edge or indeed any social context' (Cohen 1994: 72).

During the 1980s, the position of criminology at Dutch universities became very precarious. Having perhaps grown too fast in the 1970s, criminology departments were now confronted with major cuts – and some were even closed. In response to the tendency within the justice administration to include scientific analyses in policy proposals, a strong accent on acquiring external funds became the main response (van Swaaningen et al., 1992). In order to save their skins, criminologists actually drowned themselves by connecting the very rationale of their existence to an alleged relevance to criminal justice policy. The eagerness with which they jumped into a 'well' of money for research on crime prevention, generated by the 1985 White Paper, 'Society and Crime', marks the start of this process (uit Beijerse and van Swaaningen, 1993: 284–8). Since policy-makers did not seem to share the idea that criminology was terribly useful, and scholars in social and business administration, political science, urban anthropology and, indeed, private accountancy and consultancy firms also discovered the market for crime and punishment, the decline of academic criminology continued. When criminologists connected their fate to a rather flat policy relevance, they suffered more than ever from the utilitarian ethos that had always haunted the discipline. For it does not need any specific criminological expertise to hop from one fashionable policy problem to the next. The criminologist's nightmare that at some point nobody will need him or her any more has actually become a reality. If nearly the whole discipline of criminology slides into an applied fashion, and theoretical and reflexive exercises are no longer done, it is like cutting the roots of the tree on whose branches one is sitting. If specific policy proposals are not examined for their political 'message', and their relation to the postulate of the democratic *rechtsstaat*, or, indeed, to the development of other penal measures; if no serious attention is paid to empirical testing and elaboration of theory; and if the exploration of new horizons only takes place by a simple rejection of (or ignorance about) everything that has gone before, we actually herald the euthanasia of an independent, academic criminology. The future of criminology cannot be built on fashionable *ad hoc* studies swayed by the political issues of the day.

Yet we cannot simply speak of a general swing back to administrative criminology – at least not in the Dutch case – for new distinctions are no longer marked by traditional institutional or thematic contrasts. The contribution from individual academic and 'governmental' criminologists to the public and political debate on law and order is not fundamentally different, and in actual research the differences in subjects, level of reflexivity and theoretical elaboration have largely disappeared. There is still a contrast between a criminology that primarily wants to be 'useful' for policy purposes, and thus circles around the traditional questions of law enforcement, and one that wants to select its subjects and frames of reference autonomously and thus takes a more reflexive attitude towards politics. In Dutch academia, nearly all criminology currently fits in to the first category, whereas the second has nearly disappeared – and has to some extent been taken over by legal philosophy. A key distinction between these two visions of criminology is marked by the interpretation of the concept 'political problem'. In his opening address to the 1992 Conference of The Netherlands Society of Criminology (NVK), State Secretary of Justice Aad Kosto (1993: 17) signalled the remarkable influence of left realism on Dutch criminology, and expressed his approval of the fact that the NVK had chosen the theme 'Crime as a Political Problem' rather than previous orientations to criminal justice as a political problem. Kosto used the notion 'political problem' in a very confined way, namely as a problem to which professional politicians formulate solutions. Criminologists must only provide the empirical 'facts'. According to Rotterdam legal philosophers René Foqué and Jean-Marc Piret (1993: 208), a 'political problem' implies, however, a normative orientation to the *rechtsstaat*. This democratic postulate is now merely treated as a nice idea, which should not hinder efficient law enforcement. In this way, current legal pragmatism is detached from its political and theoretical foundations. Crime has become a policy problem, and is, indeed, no longer a political problem.

The virtual disappearance of normative and reflexive zest is particularly

worrying if we try to answer the question why we actually need specific criminological discipline next to all those other new 'suppliers' in the market of
research on crime and crime control. The surplus value of criminology lies
exactly in showing how specific social problems are labelled as crime problems (in the media, in politics and in actual legislation); how moral questions
of 'good' and 'evil' relate to the social category of 'power' and 'powerless';
and in repeating the obvious – which is to say, showing on the basis of empirical research where certain measures are built on scientific quicksand, which
alternative policy is more appropriate, and, indeed, how often all these 'new'
studies invent the same wheel over and over again. The fact that this reflexive
attitude is badly needed to save criminology as a serious academic discipline
is a strong argument for a retrieval of the critical perspective.

In this context it becomes a poignant question why critical scholars were
actually unable to overcome the crisis of the 1980s? Of course, critical criminologists were not simply pushed off the edge by unscrupulous competitors
in their market, nor were they mere victims of the new right who chased
them out of the political arena and the universities – by new ways of funding
research, the resentment of an old conservative clique who wanted to get even
for the 'injustice' done to them in the 1970s, and the emergence of a yuppie-
generation of university administrators who just wanted to 'sell' the
'university product' and barely understood the principle of academic freedom. These factors all played a significant role, but not a decisive one. The
internal, often highly personalised, ideological fights between realists and
idealists, or Marxists and liberals, were not very fruitful. We have also seen
that many critical criminologists lost their own political commitment in the
so-called 'postmodern condition'. The 'grand narratives' of modernity, such
as progress, rationality and emancipation, have disappeared and the only
thing left now is a plurality of smaller narratives, which all echo their own
rationale of truth. This 'new confusion' has driven many critical scholars to
analytical despair and political defeatism, whereas it made many others
decide to 'go with the flow' of neo-positivism. A small, third group ex-
changed modern hermeneutics for postmodern semiotics.

Partisans of critical theory often criticise postmodernism as a frivolous,
self-satisfied form of indifference. It is seen as a dangerous iconoclastic attack
on rationality, a nihilistic language game and a sociologically undigested
architectural fashion. The postmodern call for difference is just a liberal *cri de
coeur* that obscures power interests (Smaus, 1993). Its radical scepticism is a
mere capitulation to hyper-modern, flexible, neo-conservative economic politics. Critical criminology's impossibilism also finds its roots in the
postmodern condition (Lippens, 1995). John Lea (1994) argues that postmodernism is also 'a bit like criminology, in that it too is best described as an
area, a loose collection of themes, rather than a coherent philosophy'. Like
postmodern scholars, critical criminologists are also particularly fond of
deconstruction, particularly of the grand narrative *par excellence* – law. In
this respect, Lea points to abolitionism, feminism and the labelling approach.
Stuart Henry and Dragan Milovanovic's (1996: ix) attempt to move beyond

postmodernism also seems to be based on this critique. Their plea for a constitutive criminology starts with a rejection of the sceptical postmodern 'obsession with deconstructionism'. Stan Cohen (1990: 31) argues that the main problem of postmodernism is

> not so much that it is politically unrealistic but that its slogans (such as the end of history or the death of rationality) are so intellectually naïve. For most of the world, the old truths of racism, naked injustice, mass starvation and brutal physical repression still apply. In these parts of the world, just to be a sociologist, to state these old truths openly and honestly, is an act of courage and consequence.

Though my assessment of postmodernism's sceptical rejection of all-encompassing master-discourses, and its affirmative plea for more modest, smaller narratives, is less negative, I will not adopt a postmodern position because the modern critical project is worth saving. With respect to its sceptical position on epistemology and causality, postmodernism does not seem to be all that new. Paul Feyerabend's or Imre Lakatos' radical critiques of methodology date back to an era when the word postmodernism was only known to architects, and symbolic interactionists actually deconstructed reality even well before that. I will not go so far back as the Ecclesiastes' lament that everything is in vain and chasing the wind to show that the so-called postmodern condition is as old as the human condition, but suffice it to say that the presumptuous way in which many postmodern scholars discard everything that has been done in the past is actually quite galling. In an era characterised by 'free-market theology' and a glorification of its holy trinity of flexibilisation, automation and globalisation, free-floating observations of 'diversity' and 'complexity' are, furthermore, not the most powerful critiques I can think of. Because questions of crime and crime control are closely related to questions of interpersonal relations, hegemony and the distribution of wealth, both within our Western societies and on a global level, critical criminology's 'old' critiques of interactionism, historical materialism and social justice seem more up to date. On the positive side, postmodern scholars have, for those who are willing to struggle their way through the often high-falutin and impervious idiom, interesting things to say. Yet, a defence of the modern critical project and a postmodern politics of 'reconstruction through replacement discourse' does not necessarily contradict. In Chapter 10, I will try to show how a rational critique of the present criminal justice system, and a 'language of possibility' about how the penal reality can be changed, can well coincide.

Reaffirming critical criminology

In Chapter 5, we concluded that the principle of critical criminology that moral, political and economic questions should not be ignored, but indeed included in social-scientific critique and analysis, is still valid. Its acknowledgement that problems of crime and crime control relate to political choices and priorities (for example, policies on poverty, public health and housing, breaking down informal social control by efficiency measures, feeding xenophobia by moral panics about 'Muslim fundamentalism', double standards on arms traffic, an obsession with certain drugs and so on) is also particularly valuable. We also concluded that the crisis in critical criminology is less profound on the European continent because here the link with interactionism has been better maintained, and the sociopolitical role of law in the protection of normative, democratic values and the most vulnerable groups in society is more readily acknowledged.

Let us recall in this respect what was argued in Chapter 1. Here, the reaffirmation of materialist and interactionist approaches was motivated, first, by the need to counter the trendy trade in criminology which stops its academic development. It is still important to stress which interests steer processes of criminalisation. It is still a powerful way to challenge the (again) increasingly dominant idea that crime differs substantially from other social problems, and subsequently that criminals are a specific type of people – an idea that is gaining ground again with the current revival of biosocial perspectives and certain studies on risk profiling. Related to this is the second argument, namely that the socioeconomic context in which actuarial justice is embedded harks back to old-fashioned, pre-welfare capitalist ideologies, for which various critical social theories can still serve as analytical tools. Social exclusion remains a *basso continuo* in the social causes of crime. Why would it be impossible to use the analytical framework of moral panics oriented at mods and rockers (Cohen, 1972) and 'muggers' (Hall et al., 1978), to the construction of 'junkies' as 'suitable enemies' (Christie, 1986) or a 'new dangerous class' of non-consumers (Bauman, 1995b)?

The third argument to reaffirm critical criminology is the need to counter the 'totalitarian' tendencies of current instrumentalist criminal politics, 'which are a consequence of the ossification of one particular vision, monopolising reality' ('t Hart, 1993). Especially now that law enforcement is moving beyond its classical boundaries of legality, it is crucial to follow the current expansions of the criminal justice system critically, as well as the simultaneous diversion of control tasks to the private sector. The development of crime-prevention projects (which are not necessarily directed at 'crime' in the legal sense of the word and bring people under penal control against whom no legal suspicion is established) is a key example in this respect. It should also be carefully observed that new legislation and police practices in the field of organised crime will not penetrate common criminal law, as special measures in the fight against terrorism did in the late 1970s and early 1980s. The consequences for the rule of law and the social role of the state, and, indeed, for ideas of democratic government in general, need to be accompanied by serious empirical examination. A social-reaction approach also offers an analytical tool to challenge the boundlessness of actuarial justice's instrumentalist rationale. The normative and theoretical impulse of critical criminology should, fourthly, compensate for the empiricist development that is driving academic criminology down a dead-end street. And, fifthly, the crisis in criminal justice makes the need for a perspective that offers an alternative vision of crime and punishment particularly urgent.

Two more recent strands in critical criminology, left realism and neo-abolitionism, respectively reassessed the materialist and the interactionist line in a new political reality. To what extent do these 'newer' criminologies reflect the new penal rationale, what could they add to the debate on crime, criminal justice politics and penality, and, indeed, what could their contribution be to the future of criminology?

Left realism and the social aetiology of crime

Left realism was a child of its time. At the beginning of the 1980s, these critical criminologists started to push forward research which aimed at direct political utility and immediately tangible results in the present social reality. The original orientation to the 'avant garde is translated into that of [the] expert. The point of reference is removed from civil society and relocated in party political discourse. In this context, intellectuals become less engaged with social movements on the ground and more with electoral achievements' (Ruggiero, 1992: 123). In this way, realists wanted to bridge the gap between radical criminology's epistemological critique and policy-supportive empiricism. Two of left realism's founding fathers, Ian Taylor and Jock Young, also stood at the cradle of new criminology in the early 1970s. Why, and to what extent, have they changed their position?

According to Ian Taylor (1981), the rise of Thatcherism and the racial tensions and riots in various English cities in the late 1970s were the main incentives to left realism. Margaret Thatcher and the new right reminded the left of the importance of law and order. There were real problems and something needed to be done. Left realists attempted to recapture the issue of law and order, and remove it from its conservative connotations, by pointing to the socioeconomic causes of crime and by arguing for a genuine, workable and humane social order in order to counter further deterioration in urban life. Even when many common street crimes derive from relative deprivation, they are, argued left realists, also egoistic, sexist, racist – in short, a-social. Crime is no mere expression of class conflict; it is poor against poor and black against black. Ordinary street crimes cause anxiety and irritation within all layers of society, and most notably hit the most vulnerable groups. If the police intervene in these situations, it cannot be sustained that they only defend the interests of the ruling class. In order to distance themselves from 'relativistic', left-idealist positions on this issue, realists used militant book titles, such as *What is to be Done about Law and Order? Losing the Fight against Crime* and *Confronting Crime* (Lea and Young, 1984; Kinsey et al., 1986; Matthews and Young, 1986). According to left realists, it is awkward that socialists claim an important role for the state in many areas of social life, such as education, control over labour relations and welfare, but are hesitant about the state's role in crime control. It seems, however, equally awkward that it is exactly the other way round for neo-conservatives. According to left realists, there are good reasons, different from those of

Thatcher, for criticising the mundane orientations of Britain's educational system. In the education of the working class, considerable emphasis has been put on the improvement of their position in the labour market. The implicit emphasis on individual material values, and consequent marginal intellectual formation, have not been very stimulating in a normative sense, especially when employment prospects were shattered. These issues promoted a crime-prone situation (Taylor, 1981: 123–4).

Left realists challenged the critical criminological assumption that the consensus on penal values among the general public is just an illusion. Basing themselves on their own enquiries, realists argued that it also consisted of real elements. Social reactions do not constitute deviant behaviour, but can reinforce it. The offender is both determined and makes rational choices. He is no latter-day Robin Hood, for he steals *from* rather than *for* the poor. In their field research on feelings of unsafety, realists took up the positivist questions on aetiology and causality that critical criminologists had ignored. After the aetiological crisis, following from the dominant focus on social reactions, they carried out empirical research on crime, and aimed to develop a 'radical victimology'. It has been realism's major theoretical contribution to demonstrate how national victim surveys remain too global. Official statistics suggest, for example, that young men run the greatest risk of being victimised, whereas this is not the case when seen from a qualitative approach at neighbourhood level in central urban areas. Furthermore, many crimes committed by acquaintances or in the domestic sphere are not reported to the police, and thus official statistics give a distorted picture of crime. Psychological consequences of victimisation, such as the fear of going out at night, the powerless feeling of finding the house messed up after a burglary and the subsequent feelings of unsafety in one's own home, problems at work, medical and psychological after-care and so on, are not reflected in official victim surveys.

Instead of adopting a perspective of penal control as a primarily repressive activity of the state, realists put the police forward as a potentially accountable ally of vulnerable groups. The police are given a central role in the fight against the disintegrating consequences of street crime. Because the police are dependent on tip-offs for their clear-up rates, they have a large interest in good relations with the general public. These have worsened because the police focus too much on repression and are therefore, particularly in those areas where community policing is most needed, seen as the oppressor. A democratisation of the police, and their refraining from arbitrary control and under-cover operations, is seen as the main condition for improving these relations. Research that shows that the police can often not do a great deal about social problems, which are both incentives to and consequences of crime, have gradually led realists from a police-centred focus to a multi-agency approach. Neighbourhood Watch schemes were initially applauded but, after empirical evaluation, this enthusiasm has been tempered. Neighbourhood Watch only functions in middle-class communities, which already have relatively good social cohesion; it incites fear of crime rather than diminishes it; and it has no notable effect on the crime problem (Lea et al., 1987: 30).

In The Netherlands, critical criminologists both greeted left realism as an attempt to reformulate political commitments in a new era (Durieux, 1984), and discarded it as a submission to mainstream orthodoxy (Hulsman, 1986). At the end of the 1980s, Willem de Haan and I welcomed the realist incentive to empirical research on the social consequences of crime and to take up socioeconomic aetiological questions. We rejected the realists' adoption of populist 'get tough' discourse, the uncritical use of the concept of crime, the overestimation of the potential of the police, and the neglect of the penal question. These explicit critiques of the realist perspective are, however, quite exceptional. It has been much more common for Dutch criminologists to eclectically adopt some realist insights about victimology, unsafety and crime prevention, without taking notice of the socioeconomic framework in which realists explicitly position their studies. In France, we observed a comparable, implicit approach, albeit more aware of the socioeconomic nestling of both feelings of insecurity and safety politics (Lagrange and Zauberman, 1991). In Belgium, Patrick Hebberecht and his staff (1991) adopted a more explicit left realist perspective in their neighbourhood-oriented research on crime, unsafety and prevention.

Reactions from Germany and Italy were largely negative. Here, realism was discarded as an intellectual wholesale of earlier insights and as a mere opportunistic attempt to attract research funds after the victory of the neo-liberal visions of law and order. According to Henner Hess and Heinz Steinert (1986: 7), realists showed poor insight into political relations when they came up with democratic control over and civic participation in police activities, after the normalising and disciplinary role of the police and the prison system has been so elaborately demonstrated. With this critique, we must recall Nelken's (1994c) distinction between the low public trust in institutions such as the police and the subsequent desire to subject them to a strict hierarchical order on the continent, whereas the British trust 'their' police with much more discretion. In this sense, realism reflects 'some peculiarities of the British' (Ryan and Ward, 1989).

A comparable argument can be made with respect to realism's uncritical stance towards criminalisation. The state power to define crime is, according to left realist John Lea (1987: 36), a mere academic problem: we do not live in an authoritarian state. Most people would consider the vast majority of all offences listed in the criminal code as 'wrong', and in cases of doubt criminalisation will, in our Western democracies, depend on public support. Heinz Steinert (1985: 328) does not share Lea's optimism about the high democratic calibre of Western states, and points to the fact that German *Berufsverbote* (see p. 88) and authoritarian anti-terrorist laws have even been enacted by social democrats. The activities of Spanish social democrats in the field of law and order over the past decade show an even more sinister picture (see pp. 169 and 171). In this respect, we can even pose the more poignant question: even if there is public support for hit squads within the police force, where should this 'fact' lead us? Research shows that people make the most severe judgements when they have the least concrete information and when they are not personally confronted with a problem. Tamar Pitch (1986: 474) argues that one cannot align one's strategies with public opinion without first analysing very carefully how it is constructed. Otherwise, realism will reproduce the same populism as the new right. Many authors also criticised the realists' nearly exclusive focus on common, lower-class street crime, while they left most crimes of the powerful untouched. According to Gaetano de Leo (1986: 457), realists confirm the common-sense notion that crimes are only committed by the lower classes. Policing can, furthermore, hardly be seen as a solution to problems such as sexual violence because it takes place more often in domestic situations than on the street. Many of the causes of street crime which realists point to are structural, socioeconomic problems to which policing is hardly a solution either (Pitch, 1986: 473; Steinert, 1989: 173–9).

The idea that left realism implied a dramatic breach with the past (Scraton, 1987; Smaus, 1993: 87) seems, however, incorrect. There was a fairly logical development. Deviancy theorists, just like realists, accepted crime as a viable concept – they did at least not reject it. Taylor and Young were already advocating a social aetiology of crime in *The New Criminology* of 1973. The next step, via Jock Young's article on working-class criminology of 1975, in which he took issue with moral relativism about crime and an alleged idolisation of deviance, to his conversion to realism by 1979, was not really so great. In fact, left realism even goes back to some of the theoretical roots of critical criminology itself: sometimes the parallels between left-realist analyses and Richard Cloward and Lloyd Ohlin's strain theory of 1960 are particularly striking. By the beginning of the 1980s there were good reasons to take up the left realists' invitation to engage in studies on the causes and impact of crime in working-class communities. There was also a real need to get out of the ghetto of impossible options, as realists suggested, but whether we 'thus' needed to translate our struggle into policy terms remains an open question. There was also good reason to use the concept of crime again, for it represents a sociologically and historically relevant category of behaviour, but whether the notion of deviancy was 'thus' a *reductio ad absurdum*, as Jock Young argued, is not so certain. Carol Smart (1990) provocatively called the realist search for a new master-narrative of explanation 'atavistic'.

The realist incentive to make serious empirical analyses of crime and victimisation at a concrete neighbourhood level should certainly be welcomed. It is, however, unfortunate that this coincided with a neglect of the problem of sanctioning. This was realism's weakest spot. With their focus on the beginning of the 'penal chain' (crime prevention and the police), realists nearly forgot where this chain finally ends: in punishment. There were some global reaffirmations of rehabilitation and non-custodial sanctions (Matthews, 1987: 594) which hardly any well-meaning liberal could oppose. There was a rather implicit plea for a reductionist penal agenda, a rejection of the increasing use of the prison as a dump for borderline cases (Lea and Young, 1984: 266) and a slightly more sophisticated acceptance of the decriminalisation of offences which are both victimless and 'non-problematic' (Lea, 1987: 362). But, because realists implicitly return 'to the common-sense case for the deterrence of crime' through punishment, 'their programme's consequence of increasing punitiveness is typically ignored' (de Haan, 1990: 29–30).

Next to an undisputed contribution to reassessing the critical criminological debate in the social reality of the 1980s, there are also more negative elements to left realism. Its retrospective portrayal of critical criminology as 'left idealism' (Young, 1979; Matthews and Young, 1992) is crude and simplistic. The realist version of criminological history, in which all developments from Cain and Abel onwards logically lead to a left-realist perspective (Young, 1994) is equally unconvincing. The same criticism can be made about the realists' crude portrayal of rising crime rates, which deceivingly suggested a direct relationship between democratic policing and other preventive measures and the reduction of crime. The prominent place of the victim in realist criminology seems, furthermore, rather instrumental, in the sense that he or she remains a cliché which mainly functions as an argument in a left-realist politics of law and order (Young and Rush, 1994: 169). Realists must take care not to waste their energy merely pushing at open doors. Who would not want to take crime seriously and who would not want to do more for the victim? There is hardly any need for a crude reiteration of things that have been repeated by all and sundry for the past decade and a half. Expectations of the police and the criminal justice system have already become more realistic now a multi-agency approach to crime prevention has become the major focus. Recently, realists have also explored the sociocultural context of law and order in a more reflexive fashion (Lea, 1994: Walton and Young, 1997). A more explicit positioning in the normative framework of social justice, and a subsequent critique of the selective way in which realist proposals have been taken up by new 'administrative' criminologists, would be a welcome addition to understanding the real meaning of left realism.

Neo-abolitionism and the critique of penality

'Abolitionists are now regarded as sociological dinosaurs, unreconstituted hangovers from the profound but doomed schisms of the late 1960s, who are marginal to the "real" intellectual questions of the 1990s' (Sim, 1994: 263). As opposed to realism, abolitionism apparently does not fit very well with the spirit of the times. It can, however, hardly be seen as a hangover from the 1960s. As a critique of penality, abolitionism is as old as modern criminal law itself, whereas, in criminology, the abolitionist perspective only reached its heyday in the mid-1980s. In the footsteps of Steven Spielberg, who had a major financial success with dinosaurs, we will reassess, along with Joe Sim, the abolitionist perspective with respect to topical criminological debates.

At various times, Stan Cohen has called the debate between realists and abolitionists the most fruitful in the history of critical criminology. A real debate between the two has, however, hardly taken place. From the realist side, abolitionism is discarded as a mere postmodern variety of left idealism, whereas abolitionists have largely written off realism as criminological simplism steered by political opportunism. None the less, there are good reasons to agree with Cohen (1988: 271):

> As long as all three sides of the crime triangle (offence–offender, victim, and the social reaction-state) are kept in focus, both abolitionists and realists are viable alternatives to mainstream criminology. Each fights against the old enemy: realists concede the existence of the traditional terrain of crime (and fight there for such goals as social justice and democratic control of the police) while simultaneously opening up a front against 'new' crimes; abolitionists are trying to find a different terrain and form of battle altogether.

As abolitionism's major critiques and flaws have already been examined in Chapter 6, we will focus here on the perspective's potential. I will call this continuation of the utopian, interactionist side of critical criminology 'neo-abolitionist'. It is 'neo' because it distances itself from the traditional abolitionist sub-culture of missionaries and true believers, while its rejection of penal institutions is more empirically than morally grounded – and is also less absolute. Its theoretical positions are more reflexive and its political visions less liberal than those of the first generation. Neo-abolitionists accept that 'crime' is a sociological and historical reality, place a stronger accent on its socioeconomic causes and do not see it merely as a conflict between individual victims and offenders. The rosy picture of informal justice is toned down now that empirical studies of alternative sanctions, analyses of deficient legal guarantees in informal settings and, not least, development towards an efficiency-driven privatisation of justice agencies no longer allow for mere romantic visions of justice beyond state control. It is still abolitionist because it rejects the concept of crime as a viable starting-point for actually doing something about conflicts and social problems, and because it rejects penality as the ultimate metaphor of justice. It argues that critical criminology's concept of social control gives too much importance to the repressive role of the state, and counter-balances both the 'nothing works' despair of late 1970s critical criminology as well as the realist resignation to hegemonic crime-control discourse.

The principled rejection of the penal rationale as such, instead of just opposing the wide application of a particular form of punishment, and the incentive to think beyond state-centred visions of social control seem particularly up-to-date insights. With its straightforward critique of the crime and punishment complex, abolitionism requires us to forget about all of criminology's basic concepts. According to Stephan Quensel (1989), abolitionists solved the odd paradox of critical criminology (to consider crime as a biased social construction, while at the same time using it as the key concept in their analyses) by giving it a new direction as an interdisciplinary renaissance in the study of norm formation and social control. This is a challenging epistemological position, but, unfortunately, theoretical and empirical elaboration has so far not been the strongest side of abolitionism. It remains a sensitising perspective, which shows that it is possible to think about questions of crime and punishment without adopting a penal vocabulary. It demonstrates that criminal justice does not play such a central role in social control, that criminology can move beyond functionalist critiques, and that things in the penal field can be changed without waiting for the revolution. More than an anti-criminology (Cohen, 1988: 8; Quensel, 1989: 8), abolitionism seems a liberation criminology (de Haan, 1988).

Next to these elements, the theoretical importance of abolitionism lies in its radical reflection upon insights from the labelling approach and social constructionism.

> It assumes labelling theory's relativism and its insistence on the problematic status of deviant labels – but moves beyond interactional questions of stigma and identity to a historically informed sense of crime as unique form of social control. It assumes the critical school's attack on conventional criminology and its alternative theory of law and the state – but instead of searching for a socialist criminology and crime policy . . . it envisages the eventual abandonment of crime and criminology as viable constructs. (Cohen 1986b: 3)

Abolitionism helps to 'see the limits of jurisprudence for dealing with crime in ways consistent with ideals of social justice' (Hudson, 1993: 14).

As a strategy for reducing reliance on custody, Barbara Hudson (1993: 150–2, 184) considers it to be more realistic and more convincing than the reductionist programme because it challenges the very rationale on which penal solutions are based. Reductionism implies a short-term tactics, which produces, at best, a temporary dip in prison numbers. Abolitionism is a more powerful way to prevent prison from becoming an unproblematised residue for some ultra-dangerous people because it rejects the penal rationale as such. The key issue is not the exclusion of dangerous subjects after the event, but a socially inclusive approach in which the actual creation of dangerous subjects by the system is prevented. Because prisons fail to deliver social justice and let social and personal problems just bottle up (and thereby provoke recidivism), a general ideological shift from exclusion to reintegration is needed. A combination of preventive, compensatory and rehabilitative programmes would be quite generally accepted if punishment were not such a central element in the ideology of criminal justice. According to Hudson (1993: 13), Marxists and penal abolitionists both claim that 'legal justice in a socially unjust society' is impossible. It seems to me, however, that abolitionists argue just about the opposite to Marxists: namely, that social justice can already be facilitated if we are only willing to abandon the penal rationale. The first generation of abolitionists, in particular, has been rather silent about structural conditions for change.

How did abolitionism become a specific branch of critical criminology? A first impulse in this respect was the 'Foucauldian shift' in the critical perspective. The abolitionist critique does not fit so well to a one-dimensional Marxist concept of power, but it adds quite well to the Foucauldian notion of a multi-dimensional, micro-physics of power, which is not localised in one specific group or layer of society, but only exists in relation to something else.

Without denying hegemonic macro-structures of power, someone can be powerful in one situation and powerless in another. A second facilitating factor is that abolitionists continue in the interactionist tradition of critical criminology, which countered the dystopian neo-Marxist tendencies of the late 1970s. 'Abolitionism is an anomaly: although sharing the original deconstructionist impulse, it can hardly be accused of negative scepticism; far from being nihilist, most abolitionists are seen as quaintly optimistic' (Cohen, 1990: 18). The fact that the interactionist orientation within critical criminology remained more vivid in Germany and The Netherlands than in Britain or Italy also explains why abolitionism was more popular in these first two countries. In Italy, with its strong Marxist tradition among progressive intellectuals, abolitionism's negative aspect was adopted, but its positive critique was largely rejected because it carries the danger of expanding the reach of the penal system and, in practice, has mainly led to 'substitutionalism'. In Norway, Mathiesen's Marxist orientation was directed at the negative momentum of abolitionism, whereas Christie's abolitionist reconstructions were communitarian rather than Marxist.

In the mid-1980s, German critical criminologists developed an interesting discourse on abolitionism, as the action perspective between labelling and Marxist theory. Gerlinda Smaus (1986b) connects her combined materialist–interactionist perspective at a theoretical level with an abolitionist criminal justice politics. For Heinz Steinert (1989), the libertarian message of original Marxist thought would lead criminologists to the abolitionist position. Particularly in an era in which critical scholars (left realists) also seemed to hold high expectations of criminal law, while piecemeal reform had become hardly tenable, an abolitionist position seemed nearly self-evident. With respect to the future of critical criminology, Steinert (1984) argues that an abolitionist critique of the criminal justice system is the best guarantee to prevent further penal colonisation of the life-world, and to develop autonomous forms of dispute settlement which force back the penal rationale from below. According to Karl Schumann (1985), abolitionism is the logical political agenda of the labelling approach. Whereas labelling scholars are merely concerned with the understanding of reality and want to make deviant sub-cultures first visible, abolitionists formulate the political conclusions that follow from these analyses. If penal intervention merely stigmatises and thereby incites recidivism, it is a logical conclusion to repel the role of the criminal justice system in favour of less stigmatising mechanisms of social control. 'On the first page of every textbook on deviance and crime is the truth that only the abolitionist movement has taken seriously: the criminal justice system is not the only form of social control' (Cohen, 1988: 228).

From the labelling perspective, abolitionists also adopt the centrality of language as a mechanism of social exclusion, or even of constructing reality. And, like the labelling approach, abolitionism is seen to be idealistic. Dario Melossi (1985: 198) points out that 'in order to characterise as idealistic a theory centred in language, it is necessary to think of language as something which is passively received, as a non-act.' Louk Hulsman still holds the most radical position with respect to this semantic primacy. Instead of crime, he speaks of 'problematic events', thereby avoiding the concept of deviance which has, according to some critics (Sumner, 1994), become untenable. In Germany, the whole debate on idealism versus realism has been pursued within the abolitionist perspective. 'Idealistic' abolitionists are more absolute in their rejection of (penal) sanctions, whereas 'realistic' abolitionists are more practically oriented at diversion and non-custodial sanctions (Haferkamp, 1984). Those accused of being the 'useful idiots' who actually contribute to a hardening of the penal climate rejected this vision as a mock contrast. Haferkamp (1984) suggests a direct political influence which critical criminologists do not have, and runs, moreover, the danger of reaffirming the prison's role as a valid therapeutic institution (Feest, 1984).

The main criticism of the labelling approach was its almost exclusive focus on penal reactions and subsequent secondary deviance. This prevented an adequate analysis of both the causes and the consequences of primary deviance – that is, of the victim's perspective. Abolitionists have taken this critique to heart, and stress the importance of the victim's definition of a problem. They propose a new procedural rationale in which the aggrieved party is liberated from his or her passive role as victim. Deviancy theory's critique of the labelling approach's structural, material deficits has also been adopted by neo-abolitionists. They agree that unemployment, marginalisation and pauperisation strongly affect the chances of those vulnerable to it to come into contact with crime – whether as actor or as aggrieved. The initial liberal notions about the self-regulating capacities of the life-world and about 'diversity' are put into perspective. According to neo-abolitionists, the fact that economic deterioration and crime so often coincide leads to the conclusion that stressing criminality as the core of the problem, and implicitly accepting punishment as the solution for the individual victim, is simplistic. It seems, however, equally pointless to develop (as abolitionists often did) alternatives, without seriously taking into consideration to which problems these alternatives are to respond.

What could be some possible ways forward for abolitionism as a criminological perspective? On the question of punishment, the abolitionist critique is the most clear, powerful and elaborate. Formal sanctions need to be avoided as much as possible by stimulating existing mechanisms of social control in the community and by adequate social politics. If sanctions are to be applied, they need to imply a minimum level of social exclusion and be focused on the compensation of the victim and the integration of the offender into society. The idea that justice is done is not to be symbolised by the ritual of punishment, but rather by the public procedure itself (Christie, 1981; Bianchi, 1994).

Willem de Haan has made an important contribution to a much-needed liberation from the punitive logic of exclusion by introducing the concept of *redress*. De Haan (1990: 102–29) adopts the philosophical principle of generic consistency as a touchstone for the rational justification of punishment. From this perspective, those rights that can be justified by logical necessity are morally superior. Given the (logical and empirical) potential for other ways of dealing more rationally with wrongdoing, punishment cannot *prima facie* be considered as rationally justified. Crime is, moreover, an analytically problematic concept and the straightforward connection with punishment is empirically doubtful. Therefore, de Haan proposes to replace these two concepts by the compound concept of redress. By using the word 'redress', some major analytical problems can be overcome in respect of the conceptualisation of social reactions to what we used to call 'deviance'. 'Redress' includes almost every conceivable reaction to an event: it implies that a response is mandatory without predefining the event; invites analysis of the event before deciding on a proper response; and invokes the consideration of reparative, rational forms of response (de Haan, 1990: 157–8).

Abolitionism is also a powerful replacement discourse. It 'has one great advantage over other critical schools of thought, for it has consistently refused to allow the limits of the debate to be set by "the other side"' (Brants and Silvis, 1987: 146). Herewith it runs, however, the risk of ignoring the 'deeper and more general structures of society', by which it 'will fall prey to the two fallacies of misplaced moralism. The first is the theoretical mistake of assuming that a moral critique of criminal justice can replace scientific analysis. The second is the practical mistake of supposing that to show that abolitionism is right will be sufficient to realise its aim' (Brants and Silvis, 1987: 146). In order to prevent these risks, it would be fruitful to elaborate abolitionism's theoretical foundation. The communitarian debate can help to reflect upon the changing roles of state and community in the abolitionist plea for participatory justice and informal social control in the life-world.

With respect to the political developments outlined in Chapter 8, the communitarian argument is quite paradoxical. On the one hand, it comes close to snug, neo-conservative ideas of a caring community. On the other hand, it criticises coinciding macro-sociological developments such as scaling up, individualisation, commercialisation, expropriation of public space and so on. Chrisje Brants and Jos Silvis (1987: 140) argue that some of the elements of the politics of crime prevention, embedded in the 1985 Dutch White Paper, 'Society and Crime', seem to be based on abolitionist concepts and analyses of criminal justice's dysfunctioning. But, these few nice paragraphs on the community will soon be emptied of their restructured meaning when they are used as an attractive label for the package-deal of the bifurcation of criminal justice, and, slightly later, when they are taken into the realm of the Christian Democrat nostalgic moralism analysed in Chapter 8. The question of how neo-abolitionists are to respond to these analyses with respect to practical questions of crime prevention will be elaborated in the last section of this chapter. The key issue is to adopt the positive message of the communitarian critique, while maintaining a sceptical position on the use of community slogans in the state's strategy of 'responsibilisation'.

A theoretical support sought by abolitionists in this respect is Habermas' (1988) appeal to decolonise the life-world from a criminal justice system which has become derailed into an instrumental medium (Smaus, 1986a).

The tension Habermas observes between systems and life-worlds does not, however, lead him to oppose the role systems play in the life-world *per se*, nor to a rejection of the criminal justice system. He does argue against the degeneration of criminal justice into a state instrument of crime control in which its power-critical dimension is ignored. Next to a rejection of this pre-scribing legal medium which colonises the life-world, Habermas' theories also lead to an alternative vision of law as an institution of procedurally guaranteed dispute settlement, advancing communicative action within the life-world (van der Burg and van Reijen, 1988: 28–9). This theoretical support of the abolitionist replacement discourse on law will be taken up in Chapter 10. Here, we will deal with its 'communitarian' critique. Habermas devotes a more central, social role to the state (and to systems) than the (Anglo-American) communitarians. The communitarian critique of hyper-liberalism shows, however, many similarities with Habermas' critique of (legal) political instrumentalism (van den Brink, 1993; Tweedy and Hunt, 1994: 305). Liberal individualism and political instrumentalism have in common a view of the individual as an isolated entity, rather than as a social being, a *zoön politikon*, who gives his or her individuality shape in relation to his or her environment. Zygmunt Bauman (1995a: 276–7) argues that the notion of 'community', which 'had once been rejected as a constraint' can now not simply be 'hailed as the enabling capacity'. There is a 'clear contradiction between the "com-munity narrative" and the true state of affairs it narrates'. To take a moral stance in this respect means, according to Bauman (1995a: 267), 'to assume responsibility for the Other; to act on the assumption that the well-being of the Other is a precious thing calling for my effort to preserve and enhance it.' This critique finds a criminological counterpart in John Braithwaite's (1995: 279) vision of the liberal conception of freedom. He calls this a 'negative free-dom' because it merely consists of the right to be left alone. Positive freedom 'is defined socially and relationally'. This freedom, which Braithwaite calls 'dominion', requires 'a social world that provides you with an intersubjective set of assurances of liberty'. Thus, the balance of social responsibilities of the hyper-liberal, enterpreneurial state and its individualistic, indifferent citizens we encountered in Chapter 8 has to be reassessed.

John Braithwaite's theories of 'reintegrative shaming' and of 'republican' criminology have much to offer with respect to the elaboration of abolition-ism's 'communitarian' critique.[1] The penal approach stigmatises the actor as a bad person, whereas Braithwaite's (1989) idea of shaming by the victim and the offender's support groups contributes to the offender's reintegration in the community because only the act is disapproved and not the person. Braithwaite's (1993a: 395) 'theoretical bias is that the most important crime control accomplishments of integrated strategies follow from those parts of strategies that react to crime rather in a way that abolitionists would have it (as troubles, problems of living, mistakes, conflicts, as matters for dialogue).' Nils Christie's moralising approach to social control and his appeal to the potentials of the community in this respect seem to have had a particularly strong influence on Braithwaite's work. Braithwaite claims, however, to differ

from abolitionists 'in believing that it is right to shame certain kinds of conduct as criminal in certain contexts' (Braithwaite and Mugford, 1994: 139). In
view of Braithwaite's focus on reintegration, it is unclear why this would be a
crucial difference. A more fundamental point of distinction may be his ultimate acceptance of crime and punishment as viable 'tools', and, indeed, of
the social and institutional status quo. This may well lead to different answers
to such questions as 'Who determines what kind of behaviour is shameful?'
and 'What is the role of the state?'

In Europe, abolitionist visions of dispute settlement have been declared
romantic, nostalgic and outdated; we no longer live in small communities in
which people informally deal with each other's problems in such ways.
Braithwaite contests this critique. He argues that shaming as a form of social
control has increased with the growing interdependencies of modern life.
The level of dependencies has shifted, however, from that of family and
neighbours to more institutional and professional forums. People will always
hate to fail in the eyes of those who really matter to them; that is also the
function of support groups in reintegration hearings. In different circumstances, these can be family, friends, respected colleagues, a political
movement or, indeed, public opinion. Braithwaite (1995: 285) also devotes a
large role in this respect to 'social movement activism'. In Chapter 7, we saw
how the radical penal lobby has sometimes successfully shamed the authorities for maintaining unacceptable prison conditions. Over the past decade,
pressure groups like Greenpeace and Amnesty International have been quite
effective in shaming multi-nationals and governments – with the indispensable help of the media. The issues people actually find shameful have also
changed over time. Few people still speak in moralistic terms about homo-
sexuality, abortion, sex out of marriage, divorce or smoking cannabis (at
least in Holland), whereas moral sensitivity towards spouse abuse, sexual
violence, gender or racial discrimination, fraud and pollution seems to have
increased. When people who have something to lose in society (job, partner,
friends, family) are shamed for such issues, they tend to present themselves as
the 'best boy or girl in class' for some time.

Shaming's reinforcement of self-control is reminiscent of Michael
Gottfredson and Travis Hirschi's general theory of crime. But, unlike these
two North American criminologists, Braithwaite's 'general theory' is not
prescriptive but explanatory. Braithwaite analyses how reintegration ceremonies can strengthen social bonds. Because shaming takes place through
'support groups' of people who care for the offender, social bonds are
restored rather than broken. Braithwaite contrasts these hearings with
Harold Garfinkel's analyses of the degradation ceremonies that are embodied in penal rituals. These label the actor as an outsider and transform an
individual's total identity into one lower in the group's scheme of social
types. Successful reintegration ceremonies should be the opposite of these.
Disapproval is not to be directed at the person but at the act. Referring to
Australian and New Zealand experiments, Braithwaite demonstrates that a
reintegrative approach leads both to more compliance with the law and to

more satisfaction for participants in a hearing rather than in a standard police or court setting.

A second criterion for successful reintegration is the value of what we could call, using old-fashioned terminology, compassion, commitment or empathy. If shaming is to be successful, the people concerned with the disapproval of the act must show that they care, and not act in an emotionless, managerial way (Braithwaite and Mugford, 1994). This acknowledgement implies a major challenge to the effectiveness of the actuarial 'get tough' rationale. On the same lines, Andrew Rutherford (1994a) concludes that the shift from a caring 'working credo' in the penal sphere to a 'managerial credo' will lead to a continuing increase in the number of people excluded from society and to a further decline of compliance with the law. Both Braithwaite and Rutherford expect more positive effects from a 'caring credo'.

Braithwaite's approach also reproduces some flaws of abolitionism and informal justice. It is limited to cases without any dispute over the question of guilt in which cooperative, verbally proficient, individual offenders and victims are willing and able to trust the participants to the ceremony. It offers the offender few safeguards against excessive reactions, and can easily widen the net of social control, leaving the tough cases to criminal justice. It insufficiently acknowledges economic, political and symbolic interests behind criminalisation and the power to punish. It ignores developments in society, in which civil indifference has increased opportunities to commit crime and fears to shame someone, which have actually lowered the social potential for integration ceremonies. It also ignores structural incentives to crime, such as unemployment, ambiguous norms and racism. It holds a vision of a community in which people ultimately have common interests (namely, peaceful coexistence), which ignores the reality of the multi-cultural society in which a large segment is simply denied access to civic participation.

For the idea of reintegrative shaming this criticism may be less fundamental than for the abolitionist perspective, for Braithwaite ultimately accepts the penal rationale, whereas abolitionists want actually to replace all excluding, punitive interventions by reintegrative means of social control. According to Braithwaite, the concept of 'crime' can be useful to reinforce shaming if settlements fail. Being able to say 'Gentlemen, this is a crime we are dealing with' stresses the need for further negotiation. Secondly, the concept of 'crime' marks a border (legality) beyond which behaviour cannot be subjected to shaming ceremonies. Thirdly, the penal 'stick behind the door' safeguards the voluntary character of reintegration ceremonies. Offenders can always walk away, and argue that they prefer a 'normal' penal process.[2] These are all elements that put the positive moment of abolitionism into perspective. Abolitionist strategies of shaming have been primarily directed at intolerable criminal justice practice, and thus at the negative moment, whereas Braithwaite's theory of shaming is focused on crime – as is also the appeal of left realism. In order to create a more powerful basis for abolitionism's positive moment, this focus on crime, or problematic events, will have to be elaborated. This point will be addressed in the following section on community safety.

Shaming is also a useful concept in the abolitionist critique of penality, but in this respect a dimension has to be added to the idea of shaming. Colin Sumner's (1983) concept of 'censure' could well be used as such an addition. Censure points to the productive (in Foucault's sense) social value of labelling and stigmatisation which critical criminologists have generally described in negative terms alone. In relation to the fact that a penal stigma blocks the released prisoner's reintegration into society, it is counter-productive in respect of the prevention of crime. On the other hand, censuring deviance also serves the creation of a Durkheimian *conscience collective*, in the sense that it is a ritual expression of what society holds as wrong, anti-social or problematic. At this point, social censure expresses on a sociological level a comparable moral value as shaming on an individual level. Sumner's analyses show, like those of abolitionists, large similarities with social constructionism. The political dimension of moral questions also necessitates a continuous reflection upon the process according to which 'normality' is construed. The challenge for abolitionism is to maintain Braithwaite's idealistic approach, and combine this with Sumner's scepticism. This is not a simple task, but the key to a solution could be to break the obvious idea that censure is to be accomplished through punishment. The issue of a public affirmation of norms will be taken up again in Chapter 10.

Community safety: a new balance of responsibilities

In modern times, criminal law and social welfare have developed in close connection. For about a century, we can speak of a penal–welfare complex (Garland, 1985). In accordance with modern penology, welfare programmes are aimed at the individual offender. This development reached its peak in the 1970s, when welfare approaches had a major influence on the whole dis-course of criminal justice. After the bifurcation of criminal justice politics in the 1980s, the penal–welfare approach is limited to the 'shallow end' of the system – non-custodial sanctions. In line with new penology, a new welfare intervention in the penal sphere can be observed as well. This is no longer ori-ented at individual offenders, but at social intervention before the criminal law is enforced. It is called a multi-agency approach to crime prevention. The prioritisation of social over penal intervention follows from many crim-inological studies. Within the critical perspective, crime-prevention politics have been most notably promoted by left realists, while abolitionists have, in a less institutionalised way, argued for community solutions to community problems, such as street crime. Realists played a pioneering role in the empir-ical elaboration of the notion of (un-)safety, by initiating various 'crime surveys' in the London boroughs of Islington, Hammersmith and Fulham, in Merseyside and elsewhere. These studies focused on the relation between people's feelings of insecurity and actual risk of victimisation. The analyses were distinguished by neighbourhood profile, social class, gender and race; thus, they were actually victim surveys rather than crime surveys. Abolitionist studies on community safety, carried out in rural areas, middle-sized towns and (working-class districts of) cities like Frankfurt, Rotterdam and Amsterdam, do not start from a crime-oriented perspective, but focus on general problems and annoyances that interviewees volunteer, and analyse the actions people undertake themselves in this respect, rather than the police response.

Crime-prevention projects themselves may even have been subjected to more (evaluation) research than the insecurity they respond to. International comparisons are still rare, but various national studies show a disparity in political visions and practical organisation. In Britain, France, The Netherlands and Belgium there are numerous community safety programmes. In Germany and the Latin countries there are only a few initiatives in the northern provinces. In some countries, the police have been given a central role in crime prevention (Germany), whereas in other countries it is organised by special, local or regional, crime-prevention councils oriented to welfare (France, Italy and Spain). In Britain, the organisational picture is quite opaque. The police seem to play a key role, the actual development of the 'safer cities' politics has been centralised, while local authorities are left to implement so-called 'regeneration' programmes. In Belgium and The Netherlands, initiatives are, ideal-typically, taken by local authorities and social workers, in cooperation with the police and public prosecutor's office, and coordinated on a national level.[3] It is not the purpose of this chapter to describe these concrete projects, but to follow a normative theoretical approach, in which the idea of community safety politics as such is analysed from a perspective of social justice, in which left realism's socioeconomic and abolitionism's destigmatising focus will be integrated.

Many crime-prevention policies consist of situational and actor-oriented prevention, applying notions from opportunity and control theories (uit Beijerse and van Swaaningen, 1993). This approach, which is dominant in The Netherlands, has certain limitations. If attempts are made to prevent crime at a certain location (for example, at railway or tube stations) by limiting opportunities, troublemakers can be chased all through the city. Even when this decreases the total number of crimes, it does not imply that community safety is also improved. When opportunities to steal are limited at a certain place, 'thieves' go somewhere else – to places without cameras, shutters and private-security firms, where door and window furniture is less solid. Herewith, we touch upon a problematic point of the opportunity thesis: the relocation of problems to neighbourhoods with the weakest social cohesion and the lowest level of welfare. In this way, the social division of society is reproduced in the concern for community safety. In this respect, the remark that it is the 'moral success' of crime prevention that 'those who have taken the trouble to take preventative measures are rewarded by a lower chance of victimisation, whereas those who were too lax to do this are being punished' (Willemse, 1995: 46) is plainly cynical. Moreover, the relation between objective victimisation risk and fear of crime is quite contradictory.

Community safety and private security also have a problematic relation in another respect. Metal shutters offer individual shopkeepers some protection against theft, but the iron curtain they impose upon the inner cities makes them look like gloomy ghost towns after closing time. A profusion of roller-shutters, detection gates, cameras and warning signs against pickpockets increases the feeling of 'us against them' rather than creating a sensation of safety. According to Mike Davis (1992), there are, on one side, criminalised 'urban third worlds' of unemployed black youth, policed from the outside, and, on the other, equally militarised zones where the 'incipient gerontocracy of the middle classes' protects its residential 'scanscapes' from the inside. The famous criminographic dartboard of the Chicago School is redrawn according to an 'ecology of fear', emerging from the explosive combination of class, ethnic and generational contradictions.[4] The opportunity thesis implies a war metaphor. Crime is no longer interpreted as a byproduct of social developments, but as a threat to 'the' social order. A strict line is drawn between 'us', the law-abiding citizens, and 'them', the calculating evil-doers. This subjects the politics of crime prevention to an actuarial logic of social defence, whereas from a perspective of social justice it should consist of strengthening people's bonds with society.

Willem de Haan (1989) distinguishes between objective and subjective determinants of unsafety. The first category consists of factors like low levels of employment and welfare, relative deprivation, a high prevalence of violent sub-cultures and low social cohesion. Determining factors of subjective unsafety are the feelings of fear caused by moral panics, previous victimisation, perceived social vulnerability and the idea that the neighbourhood is deteriorating. Also 'plain' information about crime in one's own neighbourhood can increase feelings of unsafety. The 'information paradox' is that, whereas the aim of showing concrete data is to put people's unnecessary fears into perspective, people turn out to be the least afraid if they know little about real risks. Koen Raes (1995: 88–91) has added some more meta-sociological determinants of feelings of unsafety, which are ultimately caused by the 'new obscurity of a naked society'. Daily life has become less familiar and predictable. Many traditions and rituals have become meaningless; in fact, the whole idea of 'meaning' has eroded into a mere functionalist concept. Under the explicit recognition of the socioeconomic determination of this phenomenon, Raes signals the greatest need for regularity, fixed frameworks of interpretation and discipline among the elderly and the traditional working class. The anxiety of the contented class is rather a symptom of their discomfort about the fact that, in spite of liberal ideology, they cannot control their lives, and of their paranoia about potential threats to their personal welfare (Boutellier and van Stokkom, 1995: 104–5). The state can well make an effort to take away some structural determinants of mainly objective unsafety, but decreasing subjective feelings of unsafety can hardly be translated in direct policy terms; they require a more fundamental restructuring of society.

For the establishment of a socially just safety policy, an investigation has to be made into the extent to which the level of social participation determines feelings of unsafety and which other structural components play a role in this respect. In addition, a more differentiated analysis of the question why different groups of people have different subjective feelings of unsafety seems important for the development of a socially just policy on public safety. It needs to be directed to giving people in deprived positions renewed confidence in the social order. The fallacy of control theory is that this belief is taken for granted, whereas we saw in Chapter 8 that the increasing split in society is not exactly helpful in this respect. The idea that the authorities see that everybody has a fair chance in the labour market, can get decent housing at a fair price, and that the opportunities of the 'powerful' to exploit the 'powerless' are curtailed, is fundamental in this respect. 'Dominion requires a highly interventionist state-policy to secure equality-of-liberty prospects . . . that can require minimalism in criminal justice policy alongside interventionism in economic policy' (Braithwaite, 1995: 279–80). Next to this socioeconomic element, social justice also implies a fair chance for people to participate in, and carry real responsibilities for, the organisation of their lifeworld. Here, the premises of crime-prevention politics – and of control theory – can be shared. But, if social participation really is to be a means to increase feelings of safety, the government's new accent on civic responsibility has to be taken more seriously than as just an excuse of the retreating state. A new balance of responsibility between the citizen and the state has to be established.

It is, furthermore, doubtful whether a focus on 'crime' as a motive for intervention will help much to reduce feelings of anxiety and insecurity. Results from interviews in crime-prevention research in the Rotterdam working-class district of Feyenoord show that it is hard to distinguish between crimes as defined in the criminal code and other problems that are as annoying as crime. In all interviews, almost naturally, a connection was made between crime and socioeconomic conditions: these not only facilitate the incidence of crime, but also create an atmosphere in which crime is just one of the elements of daily life (Fijnaut et al., 1991). Crime is used as a label for quite general feelings of anxiety, dissatisfaction and irritation. These feelings are the most common in areas with a high level of social deprivation, and can mostly be traced back to relatively small annoyances and social rather than crime problems: garbage in the streets, broken streetlighting, run-down houses, streets in disrepair, lack of communication with neighbours, unresponsive authorities, and, the rapidly changing composition of the neighbourhood which breaks down community spirit (Hanak et al., 1989; Fijnaut et al., 1991). Crime in the strict, legal sense of the word is undeniably part of the problem, but because tackling the crime problem has such a high place on the political agenda, all misery is translated into a crime discourse. That is the most certain way to receive political attention. In this way, politicians stimulate people to interpret crime as something completely different from any other social problem, instead of acknowledging that the crime problem is an integral part of socioeconomic problems. They also raise unwarranted expectations of criminal justice, which will sooner or later turn against the authorities. If crime-prevention policy is taken into the realm of social justice, the focus needs to be problem rather than crime-oriented, and the responsible authorities need to invest in city sanitation and maintenance, stimulating community activities from below, and creating a facilitating rather than a control-oriented attitude among civil servants.

Later developments in the Dutch politics of crime prevention have been, in fact, quite encouraging in this respect. After the politics of administrative crime prevention (*bestuurlijke preventie*), which was mainly aimed at limiting opportunities by technical prevention and police observation, had functioned for some five years, the social democrat Minister of the Interior Ien Dales announced in 1990 a politics of social renewal (*sociale vernieuwing*). This policy aimed to counteract the increasing social deprivation of various vulnerable groups in society. Initiatives were taken in the field of education, the labour market, urban renewal and neighbourhood building, and the social integration of minimum-income groups. Without engaging here in a discussion to what extent this policy has actually been implemented, it is important to note that in 1993 the politics of social renewal and of administrative crime prevention were brought together in a so-called integral safety policy (*integraal veiligheidsbeleid*) (Rood-Pijpers et al., 1995: 155, 318). The new policy was brought under the supervision of the Ministry of the Interior (the initial crime-prevention policy was coordinated by the Ministry of Justice) and, ideal-typically, it should be directed less to crime and more to public safety.[5] One of the first evaluations of this policy, in the Rotterdam situation, shows, however, that the present politics is (still) largely oriented at monitoring 'risk groups', notably Moroccan youth (Rood-Pijpers et al., 1995). It is too soon to say whether this is just a consequence of the fact that the local coordinators have not yet been able to make the ideological and practical transition from a crime- to a community-safety orientation; that the inclusion of a discourse on social renewal is just needed as window-dressing now that the social democrats are in office again; or that the new policy is well meant but barely understood.

Though it may, in practice, still be dominated by considerations of risk management, there are many reasons for interpreting the idea behind the politics of integral safety as a positive step towards social justice. The major concerns have to do with the ideological (actuarial and managerial) context in which this policy is to be developed. In line with the general Dutch model of social control, the policy of integral safety starts from a presumption of social harmony. Obvious contradictory interests and conflicts are barely considered. Private security firms have, for example, a financial interest in presenting the problems to be as serious as possible, whereas this is not always beneficial to people's feelings of safety. The police and welfare institutions have only limited means. These have often been focused on commercial city centres, whereas the most deprived areas are also deprived in respect of (police and other) concern for community safety. In a politics oriented towards social justice, these tendencies must be countered. If choices have to be made, the authorities should concentrate on the problems of those who cannot adequately protect themselves. The state's care for community safety thus has to be focused on those areas where the structural need of the city's inhabitants is the most urgent (de Haan, 1993: xvi; 1995: 37). It is rather cynical that, with the decline of the welfare state, very normal social politics seems only possible if presented as crime prevention. This process can cause a problematic association of welfare facilities and crime. In this context, the development of integral safety politics can also be interpreted quite differently: socioeconomic measures to fight deprivation in the framework of the politics of social renewal are now brought under the realm of criminal justice. Thus the colonisation of the life-world by a penal rationale increases. Furthermore, the Dutch politics of crime prevention may, on a national level, have become considerably more structural in respect of the objective determinants of unsafety, now that issues like unemployment and other forms of relative deprivation have been taken on board. This aim is, however, incompatible with the actual implementation of this politics at the local level. There are many arguments in favour of this choice – increasing decisiveness and responsiveness being important ones – but at the same time local authorities are quite impotent when it comes to the most structural determinants of community unsafety. Sheer unsolvable problems are moved downwards, while at the same time local authorities receive less money. Thus, national and local politics should be closely geared to one another.

Prevention politics includes a tactics of responsibilisation by which an undisputed morality of safety is produced. The welfare state is transformed into a 'security state' in which everybody, rich and poor, black and white, employed and unemployed, is thought to have the same interest: namely a safe and secure existence (Boutellier and van Stokkom, 1995: 103). The counterpart of playing crime down as a safety problem, among many other inconveniences of urban life, is that various forms of behaviour beyond the threshold of legally defined acts are moralised. This tendency is quite ambiguous because it has no intrinsic boundaries. Therefore, the limits of the reach of prevention programmes need to be more strictly described. Boutellier and van Stokkom's conclusion that moralisation through the criminal justice system is thus to be preferred over moralising crime-prevention projects is, however, ambiguous because penal moralisation is stigmatising and not reintegrative. The problem of a potential boundlessness seems as yet less dangerous than it would be in the realm of actuarial criminal justice, because, ideal-typically, integral safety politics is neither (primarily) oriented at individuals nor at penality. This policy opens, moreover, the possibility of re-moralising the social, facilitating role of the state, which ultimately legitimises its very existence (de Haan and van Swaaningen, 1995).

The 'generalisation of suspicions' by crime-prevention programmes that Boutellier and van Stokkom (1995: 101) fear, must, of course, be prevented. The problem in this respect does not, however, lie in the safety programmes as such, but in the logic of social control in a risk society in which they are embedded. As a type of social reaction, in which people are approached as members of the community and not as outcasts, the different courses, projects and community activities that comprise integral safety politics can be helpful reintegration 'ceremonies'. If safety coordinators can see that something is done about people's general annoyances, succeed in inviting communication and social participation between all social groups, advance the relief of vulnerability, anomie and anxiety, and facilitate the emergence of social networks which counter the unstable composition of deprived neighbourhoods, they are just very welcome. Nor is there anything wrong in indicating people's individual responsibilities in the creating of a safer society. This principle cannot, however, coincide with attempts to homogenise morality and with a dominant preoccupation with control. Particularly in a multi-cultural society, this shows a disrespect for and distrust of people's own norms and values. If people are expected to take up their responsibilities, it implies a respect for the particular ways in which they do this – within the obvious limits of proportionality and a respect for other people. This also implies that a successful civic initiative should not be appropriated by professionals as soon as it is transformed into an institutional project, which mainly serves to expand the welfare market. In her research on civic participation in crime prevention, Olga Zoomer (1993) has indicated how both authorities who offer too little support and those who take over civic initiatives fail to involve people in, and commit them to, care for public welfare, but indeed put them off. Trust in, and financial and other facilitating support for, civic initiatives can, however, reduce anxiety and feelings of insecurity. People must have the idea that there are things they can change by themselves. The Dutch politics of crime prevention is aimed at strengthening people's attachments to society by increasing social control. A politics that begins the other way around, however, seems more logical.

There is a clear paradox between, on the one hand, the vision of safety politics as a means of doing something about social problems associated with crime in a more structural way, and, on the other hand, the risk of 'criminalising' normal social politics, and, indeed, creating a 'punitive city'. As critical criminologists, we should dare to commit ourselves to the first potential, while adopting a sceptical position in respect of the latter risk. Social justice is a crucial normative touchstone in this respect. Whereas actuarial visions of crime prevention accept, or indeed reinforce, a growing split in society, it represents an aetiological and a normative fallacy that needs to be countered in a critical perspective of community safety.

During the 1980s, the materialist and interactionist strands in critical criminology were reassessed by realism and abolitionism. Instead of contrasting these two perspectives, an integrated approach to specific topics in the criminological field seems the best way forward. Crime prevention is an example of a theme that has a central place on today's criminal political agenda where this integration could well be possible. Instead of limiting ourselves to a critique of existing policy, it seems more fruitful to demonstrate that another politics is also achievable. By subjecting this politics to the demands of social justice, we contrast the actuarial discourse of 'efficiency' and 'credibility' with an important counter-value. We will adopt the same 'language of possibility' in the next chapter, where an alternative vision of victim support and legal guarantees will be elaborated.

Notes

1 The word 'republican' may raise wrong associations with the United States' conservative party. The word is actually used after the republicanism of the French Revolution of 1789. Because Braithwaite places a strong accent on state intervention to guarantee its trinity *liberté, égalité, fraternité*, his 'republican theory' seems, in a present-day European context, to come the closest to a social-democratic position.

2 Critique brought forward, respectively, by myself, Willem de Haan and Frank Bovenkerk, and answers by John Braithwaite at an author-meets-critics-seminar at the University of Maastricht, 26 February 1996.

3 I am currently involved in such a comparative research project, which is directed at the *'Città sicure'* project in the Italian region of Emilia Romagna, the *'Seguritat i prevenció urbana'* project in Barcelona, 'regeneration' projects in London, and the *'Veiligheidsbeleid'* in Rotterdam and Ghent.

4 Davis' analysis differs from the Dutch situation in the sense that the deprived areas in Dutch cities consist, alongside many migrant groups, of a large part of the old autochthonous population. In The Netherlands super-protected rich residential areas have emerged, but many autochthonous pensioners also live in the 'urban third worlds' (as far as we can speak in these terms in the Dutch case) and have to cope with a high level of insecurity.

5 Five ministries cooperate: the ministries of the Interior, of Justice, of Welfare and Employment, of Transport and Public Works and of Housing and Environmental Planning. Remarkably absent in this ministerial cooperation on public safety are the ministries of Social Work and Public Health, and of Education, Sciences and Culture, which also have a clear role to play in this respect.

10

The Role of Law and Social Justice

Advocates of actuarial justice and critical criminologists have at least one thing in common: they judge criminal law mainly on its instrumental function and ignore its protective side. Whereas critical criminologists criticise law for this political instrumentalism, advocates of actuarial justice take a mere managerial position. Legal procedures are 'simplified' just to increase the system's efficiency. This neglect of the normative aspects of law warrants an explicit reflection upon the sociological value of legal guarantees in respect of social justice. Because actuarial justice does not deal with questions of legitimation, has no well-articulated ideology and does not consist of a specific set of techniques, a functionalist critique will miss the point. Instead of this traditional critical criminological approach, we will adopt an alternative, normative vision oriented towards legal theory. Whereas it is common in Anglo-Saxon critical criminology to connect empirical analyses with social, political or even moral theory, legal theory remains under-exposed. In a continental European context this orientation is more obvious. This chapter serves to make clear where pragmatic considerations stop making sense, and what the value of counter-factual critique is.

The needs of the victim are often put forward as reason to curtail legal guarantees for the accused. But, do these two necessarily conflict? What kind of intervention would be the most beneficial for the well-being of victims? How would legal procedures look if the victimological impulse is placed into the realm of social justice? Inspired by debates on personal narratives, procedural rationality and human rights, an exploration is made into the limits of law enforcement, the function of law as moral-practical discourse and a moralisation of the social role of the state. The contributions to these themes from 'newer' criminologies, such as neo-abolitionism, feminism, and legal guaranteeism, are discussed and integrated into one constructive, alternative vision. While the concept of social justice was operationalised in Chapter 9 as a socioeconomically fair distribution of the concern for community safety, it will be elaborated here as giving people a fair chance to express their specific vision of a problem they are confronted with, and to participate in the social process of norm formation.

Feminism and the 'victimalisation' of morality

After critical scholars in the 1970s questioned criminology's claim to universality by pointing to its class-blindness, feminists pointed to its gender-blindness.

Feminism also played a key role in raising awareness of a forgotten actor in the field of deviance and social control: the victim. When critical criminologists in the 1970s spoke about victims, they generally referred to victims of society: the underdog, the powerless. These were most notably the victims of stigmatisation and criminalisation by the state – those people whom 'normal' criminologists tend to call 'offenders'. With a research agenda oriented towards secondary deviance (those forms of deviance caused by the social reactions to crime), this is a logical analysis. It is equally understandable that attention to the victims of primary deviance (of crime) has been rather marginal. It does not match very well either with what left realists came to call the Robin Hood vision of crime. Feminism and the women's movement played a crucial role in giving the victim of crime a place on critical criminology's research agenda.

In the original concept of crimes of the powerful, the victims are 'our kind of people' – we who do not own the means of production. The not, or not effectively, criminalised offences were committed by other people – those who possess the means of production. Before some of those managers, bankers and politicians were, in the 1980s, suddenly prosecuted for corporate crime, money-laundering or corruption, blurring the straightforward Marxist picture of criminal law as a mere element of the super-structure of an unjust society, the problem of sexual violence had already complicated it from another perspective. Victims of sexual violence are, structurally speaking, less powerful than their offenders, but this power differential cannot be traced back to economic discrepancies as the ultimate source of domination. Next to Michel Foucault's critique of the micro-physics of power, the feminist critique has been a major force in the reconceptualisation of critical criminological ideas on social control and power.

Feminists have also been quite successful in drawing attention to the practical needs of victims, especially victims of sexual violence. In many countries, victims are now treated more sympathetically by the police, the most sexist formulations of the law have been tempered, victims are better informed about the course of action taken against the offender in their 'case', less painful procedures for bringing the charges, giving evidence and examination of the testimony during court hearings have been developed, and a network of victim support schemes has been established. In criminology, the empirical impulse of victimology has been of major importance. We know much more about the incidence and context of sexual violence, crime statistics have been improved by the introduction of regular victim surveys, and criminological research techniques as well as theoretical perspectives have been refined.

In his study *Solidarity and Victimisation*, Hans Boutellier (1993) even decries the whole 'victimalisation' of our ideas on morality. He argues that the standard of normativity on which penal dogmatics is built can, in a postmodern culture, no longer be uniformly oriented towards religious or social beliefs because these are no longer generally shared. Now that the idea of a collective morality has fragmented, the criminal justice system needs to be

oriented towards a 'victimalised' morality, and can thus only be legitimised by
the services it offers to victims of crime. Boutellier follows Richard Rorty by
arguing that the moral question of 'What is a good life?' has lost its meaning,
and the only sensible normative orientation that is still shared relates to the
question 'Are you suffering?' This is a challenging interpretation of what has
taken place over the past decade, but it also needs some adjustment.
Attention to the marginal position of victims of crime was first raised by the
women's movement and, in the Dutch case, by abolitionists (Bianchi and
Hulsman) and critical criminologists from the Groningen School (Smale).
Also, the *Coornhert Liga* of penal reform argued in the early 1970s for a
national insurance fund for damages caused by crime. Only a decade later, the
victim's interests were institutionalised in criminal-law-oriented victim-support schemes. This is an important acknowledgement because Boutellier
reiterates all the clichés about value-relative abolitionists and other left idealists. It seems, furthermore, reasonable to pose the empirical question of what
benefits a victim could actually gain from a penal procedure – after all,
Boutellier (1993: 31) presents his study as a 'mainly legal sociological analysis'. Less than a quarter of the estimated number of crimes become known to
the police; only one-fifth of these are cleared up; sociocultural, economic and
demographic developments and urban planning are of greater influence on
crime rates than penal intervention; and, at its core, criminal law allows no
other role for the victim than reporting the crime and testifying in order to
establish criminal evidence. The most logical empirical conclusion from
Boutellier's thesis is a plea for a victim-oriented procedural model in a civil
lawsuit. This option is, however, excluded because criminal justice is better
suited to achieving moral atonement.

It is a rather dubious contention to presume a victimalisation of morality
in the postmodern era. Psychologically, most people seem more inclined to
turn away from victims rather than help them: their undeserved suffering
destroys the widely held illusion that in the end good will overcome evil. The
idea of a victimalised morality does not fit postmodern culture, as Boutellier
suggests, because its hyper-liberal morality has produced both a material and
a psychological split between winners and losers. Compassion for junkies,
drifters, winos, the unemployed, industrially disabled, single mothers on welfare, psychiatric patients, 'illegal' immigrants and prisoners is very low. The
question 'Are you suffering?' is not posed to them, nor does it inform our
morality. Such questions are only addressed to those people whom the contented class can identify with. Though people may have become sensitised to
suffering, the suffering of the 'pain' of punishment (both originating in the
Latin word *poena*) seems to have become less visible. Without wanting to
underplay the actual suffering of victims of crime, Boutellier's thesis largely
reflects the spirit of the times in which people anxiously look for victims in
every conceivable situation, in order to be able to demonstrate in every TV
talkshow that they still 'care' for the poor and deprived, while social provisions actually to do something for them are broken down. In these new
indulgence-productions, structural causes of victimisation are studiously

ignored. If you are raped, you are a victim, but if your hotel room on the Costa del Sol does not, despite promises in the travel agent's brochure, have a view over the sea, you use the same label in order to get compensation. Reality television and the popular press peddle the message that we have a 'right' to a life without suffering, without raising the inherent problems and paradoxes of such a position. In this sense, we live, indeed, in an era of universal victimisation, but then the concept of victimalisation has also become meaningless. From a perspective of social justice, it would be more fruitful to place the concept of victimisation within the broader context of social vulnerability.

Whereas Boutellier's thesis of a victimalised morality is derived from empirical analysis, Zygmunt Bauman's (1995a) vision of postmodern morality, which he sees embodied in the responsibility and care for, rather than in the suffering of, 'the other', is of a 'chance-creating', sensitising kind. By arguing that, because in our postmodern culture positive social ideals no longer exist we need to orient ourselves to a morality that is negatively related to the prevention of suffering, Boutellier actually adopts the philosophy of the risk society. With the idea of a victimalised morality, the notion of an 'autonomous social' (Donzelot, 1984) is abandoned. Instead, Boutellier focuses on a negative solidarity of shared fears. Bauman's postmodern morality is more encompassing. It encourages a language of possibility on the necessary reinforcement of 'the social' in order to realise the responsibility and care for the other.

Boutellier's victimalisation thesis also raises important problems with respect to the nature of criminal justice. Continental criminal law is public law because it aims to protect public interests which exceed the interest of individuals, including those of the victim. The legal subject is the offender. He has to account for his deeds to the public prosecutor, who personifies the legal order. The decision a criminal judge has to take is whether the offender is guilty, and which penalty should be attributed accordingly. If victims are given a real voice in court, the nature of the judge's decision becomes fundamentally different. This is particularly problematic with respect to the assessment of the guilt of the offender. By positioning the victimalisation thesis within the realm of criminal law, a functionalist and individualist vision of criminal justice is reproduced, in which the power-critical dimension of due process is marginalised. The practice of 'getting tough' on criminals is presented as 'getting tough' on crime and, indeed, as solidarity with victims. In this way, and by presenting a horrifying picture of the victim's suffering without saying too much about the generally less than happy personal background of the offender, or indeed about the question of 'What is to be done?', the defence of the offender's interests almost becomes something improper, and criminal justice is detached from its guaranteeist nature. If the victim's interest is really to become the principal legitimation of criminal law, this is rather worrying for ideas of proportionality and equality before the law. The needs of victims are, in principle, insatiable, and the question of what needs to happen to the offender cannot be subject to their varied reactions in this respect. This would lead to a situation in which people found guilty of comparable offences could end up with very different sentences. There is no limit to human suffering precisely because it is an emotional question. If rational limits are to be set to subjectively felt suffering in order to formulate some fair and proportionate response, normative standards need to exceed the victim's perspective. The 'victimalisation' of criminal justice does not answer any of these axiological questions.

Emancipation and victimism

Part of the women's movement launched campaigns for a penalisation of rape within marriage, (violent) pornography, kerb-crawling and suchlike. For this reason, Sebastian Scheerer (1986b) calls them 'a-typical moral entrepreneurs'. As opposed to 'normal' moral entrepreneurs, they advocated criminalisation in order to challenge conventional values. This pressure for a social censure of, until that moment hardly recognised, crimes against women is quite understandable. The fact that a part of the women's movement had perhaps 'failed to grasp the difference between reintegrative shaming and stigmatisation' (Braithwaite, 1995: 295) seems mainly caused by the fact that society attributes a central role to criminal justice with respect to the establishment of norms. Criminal law has, however, not been such a terribly important issue for European women's movements. The main issues they have dealt with are birth control and abortion, employment and child care, traditional family structures and role patterns. References to family law, labour law, social-security law, constitutional anti-discrimination paragraphs and pleas for early social intervention to prevent escalation of conflicts were more central than claims for criminalisation. Feminists have quite specific reasons for opposing the way in which criminal justice officials have taken feminist claims 'seriously'. The actual way in which concern for the victim is given shape has forgotten about the initial feminist, or indeed any power-critical, meaning. Victims who resist being pitied (women who do not want to be labelled 'weak'), who argue about more structural causes of victimisation (rape as an ultimate consequence of male hegemony) or who lead a 'suspect' life (single women going out alone at night) cannot count on much compassion. If one wants to gain 'profit' from one's victimisation, one needs to present oneself as the ideal-typical victim, which means 'innocent', vulnerable, helpless, passive and docile. Such role-taking is called 'victimism'. Falling out of this role, by acting too strong, too passionate or too obstinate, raises suspicion about the credibility of a testimony (Verrijn Stuart, 1994). This victimological shift in criminal-law discourse seems primarily inspired by the political interest to find a new legitimation for criminal justice now that the belief in its capacities with respect to conflict solving or crime control has decreased.

The victim has also been used as a new legitimation for social-work interventions, rather than these being services for victims. Should feminists be so pleased with the professionalisation of victim aid, which originated in feminist volunteer work? Both mainstream social work and the penal rationale are based on the premiss 'You have a problem, I am professionally educated to solve problems, so you are dependent on me if you are to overcome your problem.' Analyses of a dependency-creating professionalism in the process of modernisation have become well known through the works of Michel Foucault, Anthony Giddens and Ivan Illich. Systems begin to lead a life of their own, market interests and legitimation strategies of social workers and lawyers generate an internal dynamics, and, in the end, it really does not matter any more whether one is selling soap, justice or aid. Professionals need clients to fill their needs, more than clients need professionals. The end of the victimist line is when people's very identity is derived from a professional recognition of their suffering. If we want to take women as able-bodied persons who can stand up for their own rights, a focus on a liberation from, rather than the creation of, dependencies seems more appropriate.

Many European feminists during the 1980s argued against the identification of women as victims. A key focus on women as victims reinforces the passive and weak image of 'woman', who needs help from the stronger 'man' for her emancipation. For this reason, and because actual court cases reinforced this image, criminal justice was considered an unreliable ally in the struggle for emancipation (uit Beijerse and Kool, 1990; Pitch, 1990; Bergalli and Bodelón González, 1992; Bodelón González, 1993; Verrijn Stuart, 1994). Alison Young and Peter Rush (1994: 169) argue that left realists ignore this point, and use 'the typical victim' in a one-dimensional and rhetorical way without including her or his specific visions and needs in their politics of law and order. For these reasons, some feminists sympathise with the abolitionist perspective: criminal law is shaped by male values of violence and oppression, and in order to represent the female voice a more participatory approach has to be adopted. The relationship with abolitionism has, however, been equally problematic as with realism. The abolitionist distrust of criminal justice may be justified and feminist values may be better represented, but too little attention is paid to the more practical needs of women. Before women can enter the phase of 'postmodern' feminist values, they should be allowed their share of modernity first (Smaus, 1989).

Now that awareness of victimisation has been raised, a move beyond the mere reiteration of moral indignation has to be made. With respect to the question 'What is to be done?', it is necessary to stress the secondary victimisation of victims by criminal law enforcement (when extra suffering is produced in, for example, the establishment of legal evidence). Penal intervention is also painful for a victim. Carefully controlled emotions are stirred up again, whereas there are mostly poor remedies, or no remedies at all, for the most basic problems: regaining your dignity, establishing a satisfactory understanding of what has happened to regain mental peace, and, possibly, some form of redress. It is a serious and open question whether it is always wise to advise victims of emotionally painful events to report a case to the police. In many cases, it may be more important that victims feel supported to tell their story independent of the question of what should happen to the offender. In making this decision, the victim should receive full and honest

information about what she or he can expect from further penal actions. The
central question is how victims can be taken seriously, taking their structurally weak position into account, without breaking down the legal
guarantees for the accused. Concern for victims would, on balance, lead to
the consideration of an independent procedure, guided by the victim's interests, before answering the question of what should happen to the offender.
This point will be elaborated in the following sections.

The sociological value of legal guarantees

We have seen that European penal pressure groups increasingly adopted a
politics of rights. The same holds for other social movements in the 1980s,
such as the women's movement, the environmental movement, the peace
movement and the squatters' movement. And, while many criminologists slid
back into neo-positivist resignation, the normative critique of instrumental
and actuarial visions of law enforcement was taken up by lawyers. This context makes further reflections upon legal guaranteeism particularly
appropriate.

Guaranteeism is mainly a political theory of law, in which the notion that
the rule of law has an independent, power-critical function and may not be
subjected to political expediency is pivotal. In Chapter 6, we saw how
Antonie Peters developed in the early 1970s a sociologised guaranteeism as a
counter-paradigm against the dominant legal functionalism in The
Netherlands. In Chapter 5, we saw how a strictly penal guaranteeism emerged
in the Italian context of the late 1970s, which was marked by an unstable
democratic situation. Here, a strong focus on written law based on the constitution was thought to be a central defence against the autocratic tendencies
of the state's government by decrees and emergency laws. Criminological
reassessments of the concept of crime or ideas about informal justice were
rejected because their flexible character opens the door for arbitrary use by
the state. Therefore, penal guaranteeists stick to a strictly legal definition of
crime and to strict, formal legal procedures. In line with the classical postulate of criminal law, the function of legal guarantees is (a) to protect the
individual citizen against arbitrary state intervention; (b) to see that the
victim is compensated (by redress or, indeed, by retribution) for his or her
damages; and (c) to protect the offender against personal retribution by the
victim or by society.

In the *magnum opus* of Italian guaranteeism, *Diritto e ragione* (Law and
reason), Luigi Ferrajoli (1989) takes issue with the often celebrated North
European pragmatism. Legal pragmatism finds its roots in economic, liberal
utilitarianism. Acts that are considered to be dangerous to 'society' are
mainly those acts that threaten bourgeois hegemony. Social defence is a logical answer to this. Ferrajoli does not argue against pragmatic considerations
as such, but stresses that they must be preceded and bounded by an explicit
normative orientation. Pragmatism is an open road; it can lead us anywhere,

and it can therefore never be a goal in itself. Ferrajoli distinguishes two main directions pragmatic primacy can take. It can lead to a maximisation of utility for the masses, leading to minimal guarantees for the few, but also to minimal suffering of the few, with maximum guarantees against being lynched by the masses. The first option is the dominant functionalism of social defence ideologies, whereas the latter is more in line with the Beccarian and Benthamian idea of the greatest happiness for the greatest number which guaranteeists adopt.

Dario Melossi (1991a) warns that, by embracing penal guaranteeism, we run the risk of 'falling back into the old trap of the naïve lawyer' because sociopolitical problems are individualised and political conflicts reduced to conflicts between the state and the individual. It is, furthermore, doubtful whether legal instrumentalism, against which guaranteeists direct their fire, is indeed so effective in actual practice. Not only guaranteeists, but also critical criminologists, subordinated to the myth of an efficient criminal justice system. Moreover, argues Melossi, guaranteeism does not follow a path of its own, but is merely a polemic which takes place on the path set out by the legislator and by administrators of justice. Other Italian scholars have also criticised the legal positivist tendencies of Ferrajoli's penal guaranteeism (Gianformaggio, 1993). Though a positivist stance seems to be at odds with guaranteeism's conflict model of society, in which law is seen as a means to protect the underclasses against the law of the 'free-market' jungle, specific legal positivism is not just politically short-sighted, as Mclossi (1991a) seems to suggest. A system-internal vision embodies, for example, the political value that law offers protection precisely because it cannot be subjected to political functionalism. Ferrajoli's warnings against pragmatism in law are particularly appropriate with respect to the current actuarial legal culture.

As a normative discourse, guaranteeism opens the possibility of mirroring an empirical reality with counter-factual standards. Dutch legal theorists René Foqué and August 't Hart (1990: 215–40) criticise sociologists for their claim to be able to reveal 'the facts' by empirical methodological tools, their pretensions to make reality visible and controllable and for uplifting 'the social' to a new authority. By subjecting law to the regularity of 'the social', it loses its normative role of setting limits to instrumentalism. Despite the fact that Foqué and 't Hart's legal-theoretical critique mainly refers to positivist sociology, there are good reasons for taking their argument in favour of counter-factual legal thinking seriously.

> The counter-factual dimension of modern political thinking, and legal thinking in particular, as a possibility-facilitating condition for emancipation, can only fulfil this function if the 'imaginary social' is not monopolised by the ideology of one rigid code of interpretation. It should lead to the acknowledgement of the possibility of the other, the unexpected or the not yet anticipated: the utopian. (Foqué and 't Hart, 1990: 146)

When law largely serves instrumental purposes, it also loses, along with its counter-factual character, its critical potential.

Antonie Peters (1976) clearly saw this danger. He never argued, however, that law would thus be a better way of interpreting reality, reconstructing facts or, indeed, advancing social change. Peters (1976) even described law as false consciousness because of the (1) legal preoccupation with relatively marginal problems; (2) de-politisation of conflicts, in which public issues are reduced to private problems; (3) individualisation of social problems, by which collective actions are frustrated; (4) marginalisation of law itself, by its necessarily out-dated view of society; and (5) reification caused by the fact that law has become a professional affair for lawyers, in which public participation is limited. From a feminist side, a critique is added about (6) the gendered character of the law; and (7) its status-quo-reproducing application, especially with regard to a politics of equal rights, in which (8) guarantees for the powerless are countered by a stronger mobilisation of rights of the powerful; as well as (9) the socially negative consequence of a juridification of the life-world by a professional caste of lawyers (Smart, 1989). From the work of Michel Foucault follows, furthermore, that (10) modern legal thinking starts from an ancient understanding of power as one central institution that can be addressed 'personally'. A politics of rights may, moreover, (11) be an attractive strategy for subordinated or disqualified groups to gain a more equal position, but can lead to conservatism once these rights are established. Lastly, (12) the process of juridification of human contact also deprives people of their own capacity for settling disputes. Ultimately, it will lead to a rather fretful, litigious culture, in which no one dares to act autonomously because people always fear being sued.

Legal principles and critical criminology

According to Stan Cohen (1990: 21), a guaranteeist perspective is more ambivalent, but also more realistic than either left realism or abolitionism. Guaranteeists 'allow that justice, legality, the rule of law and rights are shorthand symbols for desired values that hide latent utopian possibilities'. Cohen also (1994: 77) points to 'the meta-theoretical position on formal rights and legality'. Law is 'a plastic medium of discourse'. In the South African apartheid regime, law was on the one hand 'legalised injustice', but it was also 'plastic enough to allow limited victories for the oppressed. Law could be a shield if not a sword.' Chilean lawyer Sergio Politoff (1987: 167) argued in this respect: 'I experienced the destruction of a democratic *rechtsstaat* by a dictatorial regime from very nearby. I currently conclude that those groups who once showed a deep contempt for "bourgeois legality" have now recovered the meaning of these legal guarantees.' There can, according to Cohen (1994: 77), 'be no doubt to anyone working in the human rights movement . . . that the language of formal universal standards has to be defended.' For this purpose, a reflection upon the axiological bases of law is necessary. 'Despite my deep theoretical scepticism about the discourse of pure legality (the a-political model of civil rights), I accept this as the only "realistic" weapon to ensure moral accountability' (Cohen, 1990: 29).

In order to elaborate guaranteeism's contribution to social justice, John

Blad (1994) investigates alternative legal structures. Insights derived from critical criminology and classical principles of criminal law can lead to a qualitative improvement of justice. All classical guarantees of continental criminal law are worth defending – legality, proportionality, subsidiarity, no punishment without guilt, *habeas corpus* (the right of access to a judge), *nemo tenetur se ipsum prodere* (the right not to cooperate), equality before the law, *ne bis in idem* (the right not to be tried twice for the same act) and so on. As far as their realisation is concerned, they need, however, to be subjected to empirical findings. The legal concept of guilt is, for example, put into perspective by various psychoanalytical, Marxist and sub-cultural theories and the principle of equality by the labelling approach and other studies on selectivity. As counter-factual standards, they need, furthermore, to be accompanied by more social, economic and culturally informed principles – just as a second and third generation of social and cultural constitutional rights are added to the classical ones. The judiciary has probably also come to the conclusion that classical legal principles are insufficient, since gradually many new, non-codified principles of a due procedural order have been developed in case law, including the need to justify legal measures carefully and the obligation to keep promises made in earlier phases of the penal process, speedy trial and so on (Cleiren, 1989). Blad (1994: 371) proposes taking a step further and formulates an additional set of principles 'which can be understood as a normative reaction to the critical information derived from social scientific research on the actual functioning of criminal justice'. Alessandro Baratta (1985) argues, vice versa, that developing alternative scenarios for criminal justice follows from critical criminology's perspective of change. Blad starts his search for principles of social justice by adopting those principles of Baratta's (1988) minimal penal law that are explicitly informed by critical criminological insights. These are the principle of culture autonomy and diversity, the primacy of the interests of the victim, and autonomy as regards the articulation of problems and conflicts. He aims to translate some critical criminological insights on procedural rationality and penality into a normative framework of legal principles.

Nils Christie's (1977: 1) famous article 'Conflicts as property' already contains a useful procedural model, consisting of four phases. In the first phase, an enquiry is made into the facts: this phase largely corresponds with the present preliminary investigations of the 'judge of instruction' in continental criminal law. In the second phase, which is largely absent in all criminal justice systems, the needs and interests of the victim are taken care of and an investigation is made into possible ways of redress. In the third phase, a decision is made with respect to the ways in which the offender is to respond, and the question is addressed of whether there is still a need for additional sanctions after attempts at redress. The fourth phase takes care of the offender's needs and interests. Together with Herman Bianchi's (1985, 1994) idea of *assensus*, in which the prosecution has a more mediating and power-equalising role between the parties, this could be a useful procedural principle. The large percentage of offenders who have more than one victim already stresses the need to deal first with the interests of the victim, independently of the question of what should happen to the offender. This new procedural order would be better suited to meeting the needs of the victim, it has the potential to exceed the individual level, and, by giving shape to the idea of law as a public forum, is also suited to facilitating forms of reintegrative shaming. De Haan's idea of redress is taken as a leading principle as far as the social reaction is concerned. Blad (1994: 374) argues, well aware of the limitations of redress in a practical sense, that 'the main thing which needs to be redressed is an active breach of normative expectations'. This normative dimension distinguishes Blad's model from traditional abolitionist ideas of dispute settlement. This negotiating model is, in fact, the most widely applied in cases of white-collar crime. Since the deterrent effect of punishment is related to someone's bonds with society, it would be more likely to threaten those who have a lot to lose, and a more integrative approach could be adopted for the deprived. Because these vulnerable groups still form the criminal justice system's largest clientele, it is – from a perspective of social justice – most urgent to change the punitive rationale here. Legal procedures should first and foremost facilitate and regulate a power-free discourse about redress and reintegration. These notions suggest the need for a more prominent place for the narrative elements of law.

Narratives, feminist jurisprudence and participatory justice

Tamar Pitch (1990: 176) argues that normative thinking about law starts by attributing value to personal experiences. Michel Foucault argued (in respect of prisoners) that speaking on behalf of someone takes away the dignity of that person. Attributing a larger place to personal narratives as constitutive elements of law leads to a more participatory model of justice. The question is how this can be facilitated, without losing sight of the protective elements of law. Looking at the limited number of cases which actually reach court, it is, furthermore, clear that the function of including personal, non-discursive narratives in jurisprudence does not offer 'the' answer to crime or to the concrete needs of victims. It is mainly a reassessment of the sociological role of law in the process of norm-affirmation. The way conflicts are dealt with fulfil an exemplary role in the establishment of a pluriform set of moral points of orientation, which replaces a homogeneous, Durkheimian *conscience collective*. In a Foucauldian style of argumentation, personal narratives give law less of a discursive formation, adjust it to a micro-physics of power and visualise disqualified knowledge. The function of a legal system informed by narrative is to give public meaning to subjectively lived realities. Its non-discursive character confronts the various professional, scientific discourses of truth (produced by penal managerialism) whereas the plural notion of 'narrativity' counters hegemonic consensus models (as the 'homogenised morality' in actuarial justice).

Because law embodies important political values, the axiological debate needs to be pursued. Because substantial legal values are not unambiguous, law is, from a feminist perspective, not just a useful tool, but a quite problematic instrument of change. Law also reflects hegemonic power relations – in labour law, matrimonial law and in criminal law. Thus a politics of rights cannot be adopted without problems. It first needs to be deconstructed. Different stories, reflecting women's lived realities, must find a place. Feminism brought forward fundamental discussions on the concept of rights and justice, especially with respect to the problem of equal and special rights for women. Feminists have not only challenged the content and form of law, but also its place in society as part of the micro-physics of the power to define truth and knowledge. Carol Smart (1989: 138) argues that it is 'almost as hard to be against rights as it is to be against virtue'. The fact that the 'rights of women can always be countered by, most likely stronger, rights of dominant groups' does not lead Smart to reject the idea of rights. 'Rights . . . are depicted as a protection of the weak against the strong, or the individual against the state. No matter how (in-)effective they are in achieving such protections, there is little doubt that a reduction in rights is equated with a loss of power or protection' (Smart, 1989: 143). The notion of equal rights, in particular, has been discarded as uncritical about the gendered concepts of both equality and rights. The inclusion of the power question has brought the idea of equal rights back on the feminist agenda. A plea for equal rights is now interpreted as a means of eliminating structural power differences between men and women. It is still mainly women who occupy themselves with unpaid caring tasks. Therefore, the idea of equal rights only starts to become interesting if the biological and cultural differences in patterns of life and work between men and women (pregnancy, motherhood, education, labour experience) are taken into account (Wentholt, 1991).

The problem of this politics is, however, that women are implicitly portrayed as people in need of extra assistance. As victimism reinforces relations of dependency, feminists cannot limit themselves to legal changes or affirmative action alone. Law has to be embedded in a wider ethics of care in order to limit the risk of resulting in discrimination against women. This acknowledgement brings us to feminist subject philosophy. A major point in this respect is the idea that, in the hegemonic establishment of moral discourse, values like care and empathy are delegated to the private sphere and are thereby excluded from public or political ethics. This latter ethics is dominated by abstract, 'masculine' notions of rights, duties and respect, which outrule more subjective, contextually determined 'feminine' notions of care and empathy. The dominance of abstract approaches to rights results in a morality oriented towards a generalised other, whereas a feminist approach is oriented towards a concrete other (Galenkamp, 1993: 302).

According to Tamar Pitch (1990: 188–91), women are not waiting for mere pity, but for recognition as full persons instead of being only partial persons – victims, minors, mentally ill persons. Therefore, she advocates a politics of difference as social strategy for the Italian women's movement, with a politics of sovereignty as its legal counterpart. The legal postulate tends towards a uniformity of rules, and differences can hardly be reflected. 'Difference cannot but be problematic for legal theory. Having rules depends on there being classes of cases to which those rules apply: legal discourse must be deconstructed so that individual instances can be subsumed within general categories' (Hudson, 1993: 194). Therefore, a feminist politics of rights can, according to Pitch, be better established in a framework of procedural rationality than in a fight over substantial values. In this way, norms are not declared beforehand, but they are actually established through the procedure. With this procedural orientation, class, gender and race bias, and contradictions of interests and values, are subjected to an open, public debate. In a penal approach, they are homogenised by the fiction that the 'ten commandments' of substantive criminal law are unequivocal, that everybody has the same interests and shares the same values, and that a formal technical approach is the best way of solving problems. These axioms make jurisprudence into an ideology (Kerruish 1991). In a procedurally guaranteed normative debate, it becomes clearer to which norms people are really committed and which are not universal. This clarity respects a normative pluralism, and therefore corresponds better with current society than a reticent penal consensus model. Thus, a narrative legal system is currently better suited to fulfilling the symbolic role of criminal justice than norm affirmation. The sociological role of law changes from control of a presupposed consensus to a procedurally guaranteed management of dissensus.

This orientation includes the replacement of a focus on formal legality (the Luhmannian system-internal postulate of legal self-reproduction) with that of a substantial legitimacy of procedural norms. Jürgen Habermas uses this latter concept to argue against Niklas Luhmann's disconnection of procedural rules from their axiological basis. The discussion of neo-abolitionism in Chapter 9 has already pointed to the relevance of Habermas' work in this respect. In his *Tanner Lectures on Human Values*, Habermas (1988) distinguishes between law as an institution, which forms a necessary bridge between the life-world and various social systems by institutionalising moral-practical rationality, and law as a medium, which actually produces and legitimises moral foundations for various social systems and thereby colonises the life-world. According to Habermas, the legitimation of law cannot be guaranteed by a formal procedural rationale alone, but the procedural aspect is an important means of rationalising and institutionalising legal discourse. Without procedural rules or customs we cannot even speak of any substantial legality, as we cannot perceive the life-world without any system. A strictly formal legitimation of law carries the risk of eroding the axiological presuppositions of substantive law and law enforcement. Then, notions of 'decent behaviour' are solely oriented to the norm 'Is it in accordance with the law?' Thus, law becomes a colonising medium, in which personal commitment to normative questions becomes irrelevant and communicative claims in life-world situations are ignored. If the legal system is to reconnect with the life-world, it should facilitate communicative claims. In this sense, Habermas' (1988) *Tanner Lectures* both elaborate his earlier critique of (legal) instrumentalism (Habermas, 1981) and serve as a prelude to alternative concepts of law.

The use of narrative elements (which are kept outside what Foucault calls the professional regime of truth) counters the implicit idea that language is neutral. In order to constitute a vision of law from below, the epistemological status of distinct regimes of truth and knowledge (legal, psychiatric, personal) needs to be reassessed. Feminist subject philosophers argue in this respect that gendered professional concepts such as formal rights and the establishment of an (according to legal standards) objective truth must be replaced by a conscientious search for workable solutions. Thus feminist subject philosophy leads us to a different conceptualisation of penal values, procedures and sanctions. Feminist justice requires a caring, committed, cooperative and creative approach oriented to the concrete other. In an earlier publication, I made an inventory of alternative, feminist visions of justice and penality (van Swaaningen, 1989). Many of these are based on Luce Irigaray's metaphor of masculinity and feminity in law, as a mechanics of the fixed versus a mechanics of the fluent. Thinking in strict schemes, those that have to be followed (the fixed) are seen to embody masculine values. In a feminine approach, strategies are continually adapted to changing circumstances (the fluent). The penal process is full of fixed conditions of necessity. Feminist jurisprudence counters these masculine characteristics of criminal law. The feminist critique shows various parallels with abolitionist visions of justice. The principles of the unfinished and reciprocal change (Mathiesen), assensus (Bianchi), redress (de Haan), the bottom-up approach of social control in the life-world (Hulsman) or pain reduction (Christie) all find their reflection in feminist jurisprudence (van Swaaningen, 1989: 297–8).

This approach also has various consequences for the idea of penality. Feminists have drawn up alternative counter-factual values, oriented towards the ethics of care rather than the primary rationale of punishment. The relation between feminist values and the penal question is, however, complex. Feminist analyses of the way female offenders are to be treated differ substantially from ideas of what an adequate reaction towards rapists would be. Unfortunately, Adrian Howe (1994) does not address this problem in her book on the relation between feminism and penality.[1] She does not deal with an autonomous feminist vision of sanctions but with a feminist critique of penality. In this respect, Howe argues that punitive measures are a logical outcome of coercive processes and modes of socialisation. The role construction of women takes place along the process of normalisation by masculine, military metaphors. In the footsteps of Foucault, she analyses how, in particular, women's imprisonment aims at the creation of docile bodies. The book remains silent on the question of what can be done about this. The intriguing fact that, all over the world, there are indeed very few women in prison could well lead to the hypothesis that female values are crime-stoppers.

Norwegian feminist criminologist Liv Finstad (1990) addresses the question of how the decarceration of sex offenders can be advanced from a feminist perspective. She comes to advocate (in the extreme cases always put forward to demonstrate the impossibility of reactions other than retribution and incapacitation) the development of a less punitive 're-ritualisation' of the

way a victim has to cope with her feelings of revenge, sorrow and injuries as
the most important step in this respect. Tamar Pitch's (1990: 182–3) position
on the Italian law on rape seems to point in the same direction. Because rape
must be legally confronted 'at the very least for its symbolic value', and
because legislation about sexuality is 'an act of censorship rather than an act
of and for freedom', which moreover derives from a masculine hegemony
over legal culture, 'we may decide that . . . we would be better off with as
"light" a law as possible . . . The less detailed such a law the better; the more
spaces it leaves for women's initiatives the better, including, of course, victim-
initiated proceedings in all cases.' This approach fits quite well with the new
procedural order outlined above. What should be done with the offender
(therapy, education, attempts at redress, reintegrative shaming ceremony,
imprisonment) is the next problem. This question should not stand in the way
of first caring for the victim and defending his or her interests.

Human rights as postmodern ethics?

Next to improving people's participation in the formation of social norms,
the protection of the citizen against (abuses of) the state is another crucial element of social justice. This element of guaranteeism, which came under
serious pressure during the ascendancy of actuarial justice, embodies the
democratic quality of a legal system. The protection of human rights is the
most powerful metaphor in this respect. Guaranteeists have elaborated the
substantial political values of the *rechtsstaat*. Once these values are codified,
the fields of law and morality are separated and the focus becomes internal to
the legal discipline. In the Western world, human rights are none the less
often seen as the indissoluble relation between law and morality. Human
rights treaties are subsequently treated as codified morality – thereby coming
close to ideas on natural law. In the political arena, human rights violations
are used as a legitimation for military intervention. Such interventions are
most likely when economic considerations accompany moral indignation. In
light of the United Nations' 'protection' of Muslim enclaves in Bosnia in the
summer of 1995, words about a Western defence of human rights can only be
written with deep embarrassment. This has, in analogy with Jean-Paul
Sartre's vision of the decolonisation process, again revealed the nakedness of
European humanism. But, still, respect for human rights is also a moral standard which has not lost its meaning with the demise of other grand
narratives.

Pressure groups like Amnesty International use human rights as a means of
shaming governments who do not respect them. State Watch critically
observes 'totalitarian' tendencies in 'Fortress Europe' with respect to the
treatment of people from so-called 'third countries', the pressure of the
extreme right on national politics, and the threat of an undemocratic, deeply
interventionist police control based on the fight against terrorism and drugs.
The Council of Europe's Committee for the Prevention of Torture and

Inhuman or Degrading Treatment or Punishment (CPT) has become well known for its critical accounts of various European prison systems. This is all the more important because it shows that human rights violations not only take place in primitive, underdeveloped, dictatorships, far from our civilised shores, but also in Western Europe.

> It is very easy to point to abuses and atrocities in other countries, but it only shows moral blindness and hypocrisy if this critique does not include inhuman practices in one's own environment, and if one does not know how injustice elsewhere relates to injustice here. The real condition of human rights can only become clear if we look at these rights against the background of large structural causes of injustice and denial of human dignity. (Peters, 1983a: 307)

Thus human rights discourse serves two purposes: it relates 'our' problems to global problems, and it controls our legal system.

Human rights are part of wider notions about human dignity. Though violations should always be related to the general standard of life, this principle applies to all situations. If you treat other people as an inferior species, you lower yourself and incite people to lower their moral standards as well. This goes for brutal repression in military dictatorships, but also for the judicially legitimised killings in an increasing number of states in the so-called 'land of freedom'. The government of Alabama is apparently so proud of its history of slavery that it has reintroduced the chain-gang. The creation of an extra security prison system (EBI) in The Netherlands, where prisoners are deprived of basic human contacts, also marks a retrograde move in the process of civilisation. The degree of shameful state behaviour shown in these examples differs substantially, but the implicit disrespect for human dignity, the instrumental rationale of social defence, and the systematic, distancing and emotionless modes of implementation, are comparable. Infringements upon human dignity are often motivated by the argument that soft remedies do not work. A human rights approach leads to the conclusion that such pragmatic primacy cannot be the major consideration in a social *rechtsstaat*. The widely publicised 'credibility' of the criminal justice system has first of all to do with the reciprocity of decent behaviour. The 'moral capital' needed to condemn crime needs to be mirrored in the moral standards applied in law enforcement (Lissenberg, 1989).

The defence of human rights has been part of the critical criminological enterprise since its emergence. Herman and Julia Schwendinger (1975) argue that the infringement of human rights should be the starting-point for a redefinition of crime in the realm of social justice. They want law to be a guardian of human rights. This is an interesting counter-factual exercise in thought, but the actual purpose of perceiving violations of human rights as crimes remains unclear. Over the years, various authors have put question-marks over the Schwendingers' expectations of a penal defence of human rights. Critics have pointed to the contradictory relation that such a radical redirection of the concept of crime has with the specific history and practice of criminal law. The most flagrant violations of human rights, or complicity in these practices, will remain out of reach of criminal justice because economic interests behind the toleration of human rights violations are stronger than questions of morality. The ready supply of military technology to dictatorial countries exemplifies this point.

Alessandro Baratta (1988) connects these ideas on human rights in Western societies with Johan Galtung's theory of structural violence. Many crimes of the powerful are also typical cases of structural violence: precisely because they reflect hegemonic morality they are oppressive for those who are in a structurally weak position. Baratta elaborates the position of the Schwendingers, but doubts whether human rights can be guaranteed within the criminal justice system. A politics of human rights in a criminal lawsuit shows a sharp confrontation between its protective and instrumental sides. Because respect for human rights embodies a central political value of the *rechtsstaat*, human rights should not only be the object of penal protection, but the degree to which the state can actually infringe upon human rights is also the normative touchstone for legitimate penal intervention (Baratta, 1988: 536). This latter perspective is the major line critical criminologists adopt today.

Human rights discourse addresses the question 'Are you suffering?' in a more structural way than the 'victimalisation' of morality. It also informs us that not every 'effective' intervention is legitimate. Critical criminologists such as Stan Cohen (1993) have oriented themselves quite strongly towards human rights over the past decade – in Cohen's case partly because of his involvement in the Israeli peace movement. There is also a theoretical reason for a commitment to human rights, for they have, unlike many other social values, still some political significance. They also 'offend the postmodern preference for plurality, contingency and difference' because they still claim to express a meaningful normative and rather universal standard (Sparks, 1994). Zygmunt Bauman (1995a: 253) interprets human rights, however, in line with postmodern visions of pluralism. 'Cultural pluralism as a permanent condition of mankind' would lead to a 'new rendition of modern "human rights"'. This would put 'paid to the hope that one could get away with cultural crusades and other acts of oppression once normal and proper but today immediately denounced as criminal'.[2] Both in Sparks' and in Bauman's version, human rights can function as a normative touchstone of state ethics. According to Sparks (1994: 6), they sensitise and give meaning to general concepts of justice, rights, discrimination, commonality and so on. The philosophical foundation of human rights as natural rights may have ceased to matter in the postmodern condition, but the culture of human rights continues to matter a lot. In actual politics, questions of sympathy and empathy are of more importance than any theory or empirical fact.

Human rights have, however, also a value as concrete rules: as legal standards and enforceable rights to be used as instruments of litigation (Sparks, 1994: 12). With respect to the value of human rights as rules, Dutch criminologist Peter Bal (1994) argues that their inclusion in criminal law is necessary for a morally just legitimation of the criminal justice system. Ultimately, guaranteeism comes down to the protection of human rights. The present practice of an almost exclusively procedural legitimation of law has pushed aside the question of a substantial legitimacy of law by human rights principles. In the legal-positivist postulate, law and morality are distinct areas. Following Jürgen Habermas, Bal (1994) chooses, however, to interpret law as a moral-practical discourse. Bal concludes that a just legal system continually needs to reflect upon its normative foundations. The alienation from these values of law, and the subsequent adoption of a solely function-alist legal discourse (the notion of *Zweckrationales Handeln* in Habermas' work), paved the way for legal instrumentalism. Bal argues that human rights could give meaning to Habermas' procedural claims embedded in his idea of power-free discourse – intelligibility, true representation of facts, sincerity of commitment and intentionality, and legitimacy of the procedure. As concrete rules, human rights also function as the restricting procedural conditions for a communicative rationalisation of the criminal procedure. Human rights can never be 'achieved' (in the sense that one would reach a point of saying 'Now it is all said and done'): not only because conflicting interests and power differences will always leave one person better able to exercise his or her own rights and violate those of more vulnerable groups, but also for an internal legal reason. In order to protect human rights on a collective level, the human rights of some individuals will sometimes need to be violated. Like Pitch's proposal with respect to women's rights, Bal (1990) proposes a procedural orientation towards human rights to resolve this paradox.

Human rights have a counter-factual character and do not allow for too much political accommodation if they are not to become meaningless (Raes, 1994). Legal and political practice shows that this latter danger is not just hypothetical. Officially acknowledged human rights, as they are, for example, codified in the European Convention of 1950, can sometimes also erode the value of national guaranteeist principles. Hans de Doelder (1991) relates the increased importance of the rulings of the European Court of Human Rights in Strasbourg to 'simplifications' of Dutch procedural law and the decreasing quality of legal justifications in case law. The time we were holier than the Pope is over. National legal values or principles are hardly applied any more: if methods of investigation do not conflict with the European Convention on Human Rights, it is okay. Thus, codified human rights function both as the minimum standard of what we have to live up to, but also as the maximum guarantee that is really necessary. If national legislation is more 'protective', this surplus is abolished by new bills. Antonie Peters (1983a: 307) indicates, furthermore, how ironic it is to see that, in an era of structural unemploy-ment, the 'right' to employment is constitutionally recognised in The Netherlands. What does such a right mean? 'It is an insult to the unem-ployed . . . human rights should never . . . induce complacency.' Such an inflated use of human rights cannot be the reason for their codification.

The Universal Declaration of 1948, which also contains economic, social and cultural rights, has a status different from the European Convention of 1950. While international treaties and national constitutions contain human rights as rules, the Universal Declaration is a moral standard that reflects a human rights culture. The claimed universality of human rights is criticised from many sides. The main points are that they would be Euro-centric, fail to address power questions and offer too little indication of how human rights can be effectuated. Zygmunt Bauman's (1995a) postmodern redefinition of human rights as the right of cultural pluralism could follow from such analyses. Richard Sparks (1994: 13) sticks to the modern vision of universalism: 'whereas human happiness is notable for its diversity, misery is characterised by its unity.' Thus, a plea for a more normative discourse on social justice and human rights is at odds with the postmodern condition as it claims some universal validity. As Aristotle argued in his *Nicomachean Ethics*, questions of morality do not allow for too much precision. This puts the modern 'rationalisation' of human rights into perspective. Following Aristotle, it would be better not to refine their meaning too much. Over-detailed drafting is a major cause of an inflated interpretation of human rights treaties. More generally, a counter-factual approach makes the narrative culture of human rights more suitable as replacement discourse. Those who advocate the detailed drafting of human rights as specified legal paragraphs overestimate the functional importance of law and demand too much of the possibilities of a politics of human rights. After a long series of United Nations (and other) 'peace-keeping' interventions, it seems realistic to argue that, ultimately, the respect for human rights depends on goodwill – especially on the goodwill of the contented class towards the deprived. This goodwill can be facilitated by a politics of shaming oriented towards the culture of human rights.

Of course, 'it is intellectually and rhetorically much more comfortable to draw up a stern libertarian story or to claim the most broad spectrum of rights, than timidly pointing at the fact that many rights would remain dead letters if there were no duties (of others but also of oneself) included' (Raes, 1992).There are many good reasons to connect the debate on human rights with a discourse of human responsibilities. Rights can only be effectuated if people feel morally committed to them. Koen Raes calls this the interdependency of human rights and moral responsibility. This necessarily implies a commitment to collective interests – in the same way that John Braithwaite's (1995) idea of 'dominion' implies a policy securing equality of liberty prospects. A commitment to collective values and the acceptance of the idea of an 'autonomous social' (Donzelot, 1984) are necessarily reciprocal to a claim for rights. Such a civic commitment presupposes a caring state, responsible for good public provisions: education, welfare, housing, transportation and so on. Private enterprise can perfectly well carry out some of these tasks. The state has, however, the task of seeing that public facilities do not become profit-ridden, that rich and poor have an equal share of them, and that employers maintain the social rules that the labour market has to obey. On these criteria, the post-welfare, entrepreneurial state fails, and is thereby losing its legitimacy. In this sense, the materialisation of human rights becomes a positive measure for intervention. Raes (1992) also poses the question of how far our responsibility goes: does it stop at the neighbour's door, or does the West also have a responsibility for the Third World, for people suffering from repressive regimes, for our natural environment, for future generations? How far can such responsibilities go before they become mere lip-service to stilted principles?

Human rights can only be perceived as universal as far as their counter-factual value, to set limits to pain, to human-created suffering, is concerned. The main theoretical value for critical criminology lies in the political culture of human rights as a sensitising concept. Their concrete application as an incentive to take up social responsibilities is strongly dependent on the specific socioeconomic context in which they are to be implemented. They counteract a misunderstood relativism in respect of collective values. As rules, they counteract a solely procedural legitimation of law and offer a substantial, normative standard against which the legitimacy of various social reactions can be measured. According to Antonie Peters (1983a: 319), the main importance of human rights brings us back to their original meaning in the French Revolution: they express a striving for emancipation. If this struggle

> remains limited to the legal and political sphere, it can easily become a substitute for real emancipation . . . Social justice is subjected to economic development or economic restoration, with the suggestion that if it goes better economically, there is also more justice to distribute. In the meantime, everybody in the still relatively affluent and politically stable West gets more rights in the politically and economically harmless expressive sphere of free-floating chatter and sexual pleasure. Whereas human rights were initially intended to enable people to participate fully in the way social life is given shape, they now deteriorate into the right to consume society's products. In this fatal way, human dignity is being threatened. Therefore I think we should fight for human rights in their original meaning. (Peters, 1983a: 321)

Guaranteeism can easily slide into a mere conservative, defensive mode once specific rights are established. In the actuarial vision of justice, its procedural discourse falls outside the hegemonic frame of reference. In order to safeguard guaranteeism's incentive to penal reform, reflections upon substantial, axiological questions are indispensable. Whereas penal procedural safeguards presuppose a homogeneous set of norms and values, an alternative procedural orientation, informed by feminist and abolitionist visions of justice, serves actually to establish more pluriform standards of morality. In this way, guaranteeism offers an up-to-date normative counter-discourse to actuarial justice's monopolisation of visions of legal practice.

Notes

1 Howe (1994: 227) argues that my own article mentioned above (van Swaaningen, 1989) 'does not provide any persuasive reasons for abandoning the use of criminal sanctions against violent men'. My answer is that it was not the aim of the article to present such reasons. It tried to show alternative visions of justice, inspired by feminist philosophy. Furthermore, though I do think the punitive character of sanctions should be minimised for it carries many negative counter-effects, empirically as well as morally, I do not want to argue that the imprisonment of violent men would be wrong in principle. It is just not the primary 'proof' that 'justice is done'.

2 Because it is a minimal and legalistic standard morality, the popularity of human rights discourse in the Western world is also interpreted as an expression of postmodern liberalism. In Western welfare states, a respect for human rights is too minimal a standard. Here, a critical project would need to be more encompassing (Lippens, 1995: 59).

11

Conclusion

Theoretical conclusions

Limits to instrumentalism

Throughout this book, from the Modern School of integrated penal sciences at the beginning of this century to the actuarial approach of justice at the end of it, warnings of an instrumentalist legal discourse without clear normative limits have been a *leitmotiv*. Without an explicit formulation of inherent principles, goal-oriented programmes are vulnerable to being absorbed by totalitarian politics. A key argument of the scholars who, in the decade before the Second World War and the one following, warned against authoritarian developments is that, in a democratic society, individuals may not be used for political purposes but should only be punished because they have violated a specific rule. The political situation of the 1930s cannot be compared too closely with that of the 1990s. John Braithwaite contrasts the growing authoritarianism of the 1930s with today's hyper-liberalism, but, following Nils Christie's (1975) analyses of the relation between the 'tightness' of the social web and a society's level of violence, he also observes a common danger: 'societies in which the group is everything (the individual is engulfed) as well as societies of rampant individualism (the individual is isolated) risk endemic violence' (Braithwaite, 1995: 282). In the first situation, social control is based on a permanent threat of violence; in the latter, 'Mickey Mouse' takes the insiders of society smilingly by the hand in order to control their movements, while he creates 'gulags' for the outsiders (Shearing and Stenning, 1987; Christie, 1993; Scheerer 1996). Similarities can be observed between the present culture of actuarial policy (marked by risk profiling, police and technical observation, and a bifurcated sanctioning politics ranging from educational courses to selective incapacitation) and the Modern School's focus on measures beyond the principle of legality, its categorisation of offenders according to their perceived ability to reform and the development of general prevention into a kind of public re-education. A common orientation towards social defence, an alleged 'need' to correct the misguided philanthropy of preceding decades, an authoritarian populism about law and order in the mass media and in politics, and the success of right-wing nationalists (of which the French *Front National*, the Austrian *Freiheitlichen* and the Belgian *Vlaams Blok* are beginning to get a grip on actual government) to feed intolerance towards 'foreigners' among the population and push the authorities to enact a stiff (anti-)migration policy, make the comparison all the more worrying.

The question of whether instrumentalist politics are motivated by notions of efficiency or by a more benign functionalism aimed at social welfare may be less significant than one might wish. Initiatives launched with good intentions can work out disastrously (Cohen, 1985). At the core, the abolitionist project suffers, with its focus on informalism, from the same immoderation and political naïvety as the project of the Modern School. Without an explicit normative foundation for its points of departure and clear legal safeguards that can put limits to social control, both perspectives are vulnerable to being used for any political goal. Measures taken in the spirit of the Modern School in the 1920s, the proposals about alternatives to custody of the 1970s and those on crime prevention in the present era really confront us with the same dilemma. On the one hand, they open the door to practices that can't be controlled, but they also offer progressive incentives to penal reform. In this book, the inclusion of modern insights on the penal system is, with some caution, judged positively. Along the same lines, ideas on non-custodial sanctions and crime prevention are also carefully reaffirmed. The same holds true for the related dilemma between formal and informal justice. Romantic visions of informal justice and reflexive law are unjustified because they leave too much room for uncontrollable power interests. Yet the danger of (over-)stressing the formal aspects of law leads to unworkable situations, stagnation and a complete dependency on professionals and bureaucrats. In this way a system is created in which personal responsibility and professional ethics are marginalised and subjected to a bureaucratic rationale where one is just an anonymous functionary of the system, carrying out the orders of superiors. This warrants a new reflection on informal justice. In Chapter 10, I tried to save the advantages of informal justice without reproducing the disadvantages.

Human rights can function as a moral standard which sets limits to purely instrumentalist law enforcement, while leaving enough space for normative pluralism in a democratic society. Questions of morality cannot be answered in a detailed way, without imposing a false consensus. Human rights are global enough to avoid this danger. As concrete rules, they embody a formalised ethical threshold beyond which legitimate state intervention cannot go. If the state lowers its standards of morality and subjects those standards to a rationale of efficiency, we fall into a downward spiral of violent despair, a never-ending penal arms race between 'criminals' and law enforcers. A human rights culture also encourages positive state intervention, by specifying the social provisions needed to realise such rights. The more detailed questions of morality become, the more procedural the orientation needs to be. Law as a moral-practical discourse is more a procedurally guaranteed management of dissensus than the control of a fictitious consensus. This position does justice to the cultural and moral pluralism of present-day society, without sliding down into the moral minimalism of actuarial justice.

The point is not to reject functionalist considerations altogether, but to subject them to a normatively motivated programme of action. Functionalist arguments cannot be treated as principles with an intrinsic value, but they can be a means of achieving certain pre-formulated goals. This position comes close to the moral pragmatism Stan Cohen (1985: 252–3) put forward as an answer to the question of what is to be done. The 'moral' element affirms values as doing good and doing justice. 'The "pragmatic" element stands against all forms of premature theoretical and political closure, all quests for cognitive certainty which rule out certain solutions as being conceptually impure or politically inadmissible.' Guaranteeism reflects a moral pragmatic position on legal functionalism. In this context, social justice remains a powerful concept for critical criminology. The elaboration of this traditional critical ideal with respect to community safety and human rights demonstrates the need for a stronger orientation towards the state's social, facilitating role – which is also its ultimate legitimation. This acknowledgement points in the opposite direction from the prevailing preference of politicians to let even the availability of public services be increasingly determined by the interests of the private sector. The elaboration of social justice with respect to the needs of victims and the participatory character of law as a democratic institution of norm affirmation shows a sharp contrast with current technocratic approaches to law enforcement.

Legal guarantees need to be defended as they embody the democratic calibre of the state. A major value of the *rechtsstaat* is to put normative limits to an instrumental focus on social defence. It demonstrates the significance of counter-factual, sensitising principles in the process of social change. As a mere defensive perspective, however, guaranteeism falls short in its contributions to penal reform. If community safety is to be improved, and the conclusions from criminological analyses of the social causes of everyday crime are followed in a structural politics of crime prevention, these developments cannot be judged in negative terms just because interventions would exceed the principle of legality. Normal social politics are not to be bound by legality, but when interventions imply the control of specific individuals such safeguards become necessary. This distinction needs to be made. In order to follow social interventions critically the social-reaction perspective is reassessed. This approach is more powerful if it is guided by the social values that underlie legal principles.

Tolerance can be carefully reaffirmed as a means of social control. We saw in Chapter 2 that this mode of social control has various shortcomings – paternalism, bargaining with principles, uneasy compromises, élitism, loss of credibility and so on. Yet we also saw that, in the Dutch case, it has worked out as a balance by which stagnation and polarisation in government and social reform can be overcome in a rather pragmatic way. It gives deviations from the standard of normality a relatively large latitude. In this latter sense, it is in line with the rationale of minimal penal law and with the idea that a not too detailed legislation is needed in order to leave room for narrative elements (Baratta, 1988; Pitch, 1990: 183). There is also no reason to contest

John Braithwaite's (1993a: 396) argument that 'persuasion is cheaper; persuasion is more respecting of persons and of their freedom, being based on dialogue rather than coercion; and "defiant" reactions that exacerbate crime are more likely when deterrent threats are the port of first call.' In order to prevent a sheer pragmatic wheeling and dealing with social conflicts, the normative principles on which a politics of tolerance is based (respect for diversity, cultural autonomy, protection of public health) should, again, accompany sheer functionalist discourse. In this respect, 'criteria for toleration' are complementary to criteria for criminalisation (Hulsman, 1972).

Reassessing critical criminology's analytical tools

The first part of this book showed that the widely shared view that, before the 1960s, all criminologists held a pathological, psychological or administrative focus on the correction of offenders is incorrect. This picture does not do justice to the precursors of critical criminology of those particular times. The globalising picture of criminology as a discipline that (implicitly) serves law-and-order interests did, however, offer critical criminologists of the 1960s and 1970s a welcome basis to announce a new start: get rid of the auxiliary role of law enforcement and establish an autonomous agenda. In a similar way, Chapters 5–8 showed how the view that critical criminologists were naïve and idealistic as regards penal reform, and irresponsible as regards the negative social consequences of crime, is equally incorrect. In the 1960s, the focus 'had to' shift from an individualising aetiology to the role institutions of social control play in the amplification of deviance because this had hardly been done before and the old aetiological theories had become worn out as explanatory models. Ideas on crime as a latent resistance to unequal social relations did not have such a prominent place in critical criminology as has often been suggested, and critical scholars were actually quite nuanced and realistic about penal reform. Restrospective simplifications of such youthful lapses have, however, offered the idealistic generation of the 1960s an ideological common ground to become more 'realistic' now that they have come of age, and to announce, by the 1980s, yet another new start for criminology: get rid of moral relativism and establish an agenda in which crime is taken seriously.

Critical voices of the 1960s sensitised such social values as the equal distribution of wealth, respect for different lifestyles, women's emancipation and the right of self-determination. In this context, critical criminologists sensitised new criminological themes: from sexual and family violence, corporate and environmental crime, to violations of human rights and other crimes of the state. These themes were empirically elaborated in the 1980s. In this sense, much of the critical project has been incorporated into general criminology. The innovating role of critical criminology in this respect should be stressed. The fact that most empirical studies in these areas are not supportive of a stiff penal approach confirms, moreover, the basic contentions of critical criminology. The actual political consequences drawn from the debates on rape, child abuse or organised crime are quite another story. This is, however, the objective of political critique, and it is not part of critical criminology's role actually to raise awareness of these themes.

Most critical criminological concepts are not so much superseded as in need of a new content. By using the word 'deviance', critical criminologists probably contributed to the commonplace that they did not take crime to be a serious problem. This has, however, more to do with a conflict-theoretical interpretation of deviance, and with the political conclusion the reader wants to put on it, than with the analytical concept as such. There are, however, other problems connected with the concept of deviancy. Postmodern scholars raise important questions in this respect. If there are no more leading ideologies and beliefs, can we still speak of deviance in the way we used to do? 'Deviant from what?' becomes the obvious question. Empirical studies on corporate and organised crime, fraud and corruption have, furthermore, empirically shown the untenability of a sharp distinction between the nasty underworld and decent upperworld. Many property crimes are, moreover, extrapolations rather than deviations from the hegemonic social 'norms' of 1990s Western society: individualistic hedonism, turning a quick buck, a maximum exploitation of resources and so on. Hate crimes of rape, queer-bashing or racism are first of all symbolic reaffirmations of white, male supremacy rather than breaches of the hegemonic social order. On the other hand, the closure of the whole debate on deviance (Sumner, 1994) seems premature because postmodernism, and, notably, related feminist theories, have given a new dimension to deviance by opening a debate on 'otherness' and cultural pluralism. Critical criminologists have tried to complete labelling analyses with a macro-sociological power dimension. Thus, more detailed attention should be given to the politically determined standard of normality against which deviance is measured. This notion is well expressed by the concept of censure (Sumner, 1983). It allows a set of alternative standards of what would be a justified censure of behaviour and what would not.

The same can be said about the predominantly negative idea critical criminologists hold of social control. No society can function without some form of social control. It seems of little use to keep debating about a need for more or less social control. It is more fruitful to ask what *sort* of social control we want – preventative, integrative, corrective, punitive, repressive. It also seems more challenging here to draw up alternative standards instead of just offering a negative critique. Willem de Haan's concept of redress can function as a principle that captures the traditional twofold relation between crime and punishment. The question of what can be done for victims of crime, or how community safety can be improved, show that a strong focus on crime can be quite deceiving with respect to possible solutions. Crimes can consist of structural socioeconomic problems, minor social problems, conflicts or attacks. Reactions are to be differentiated accordingly. In practice, good social politics or good sociopsychological assistance, independent of any steps to be undertaken towards actual offenders, may sometimes be all that is realistically possible, while these measures can also restore normative expectations. If crime finds its basis in a conflict between identifiable (groups of) people, mediation ought to be the first step. Only if serious attempts in these areas have failed, should more coercive approaches come into the picture. Within this scale of reactions, sanctions aiming at redress are to be preferred over predominantly punitive ones because these are more beneficial for victims and they cause the least damage to offenders while inviting them to take up their responsibilities.

The state-centredness of critical criminology misses the central point in present-day society. The vision of the state as a omnipotent repressive apparatus has been largely superseded. Social control is decentralised, or fragmented, depending on the vocabulary one prefers to use. In the new entrepreneurial state's strategy of transferring its own responsibilities to quangos, private enterprise and individual citizens, social control is increasingly left to the private sector. Social control also gains a fundamentally different character because information technology facilitates an increasingly invisible and dispersed, but very tight and deeply interventionist, control industry. The privatisation of social control sheds a completely different light on questions of accountability and on the place of normative considerations in law enforcement. Without proposing a return to the previously criticised, paternalistic and interventionist welfare state, critical criminologists might do better to invite the state to intervene more rather than less. Again, the question is rather 'how' than 'whether'. The section on community safety (see Chapter 9) concluded with a re-moralisation of the state's role with respect to social welfare. The critique of the repressive and paternalistic sides of the state is still valid, but it cannot be the whole story. Criticising an entrepreneurial state while, at the same time, advocating a facilitating state that embodies collective values and social services may seem paradoxical. Empirical analyses are, however, quite supportive of such a twofold position. Both a state that incorporates civic initiatives and reformulates them according to its own logic, and a state that offers too little support, alienate people from collective interests (Zoomer, 1993).

The concept of net-widening has been quite damaging as a contribution to penal reform. Should we better forget about this concept? The answer is again negative; it is still important to stress that non-punitive reactions to crime should be *instead of* rather than *additional to* imprisonment, but again the argument should not stop here. Current non-custodial sanctions are certainly no 'real' alternatives to imprisonment and they do widen the net. But, now they are widely used in penal practice this can no longer be an argument to reject them. It should be stressed that real alternatives to custody start with a different way of approaching problems from the outset. A penal process predetermines punitive outcomes in whatever shape they may appear. Along the same lines as the net-widening argument, Michel Foucault (1975a) demonstrated how the introduction of the prison sentence led to a 'great incarceration'. This seems, however, hardly an argument to stick to corporal punishment. Existing non-custodial sanctions should now also be judged on their own merits. At this point we cannot engage in a balanced discussion in favour of or against non-custodial sanctions. We should, however, pay serious attention to the political context in which penal reformers have to operate. At present, the development of non-custodial sanctions is the only penal debate not yet primarily aimed at repression, and it has gained wide public support. Arguing now against these sanctions and sticking to a politics of negative reform leaves the political space open to forces which want to increase the retributive elements in the tasks an offender with a non-custodial sanction has to fulfil, and alienates a relatively important lobby in the opposition to the further expansion of the prison system: probation officers. It is important to retain their commitment to penal reform by stimulating the few idealist forces still left in penal practice. The main concern is now the particular way in which non-custodial sanctions currently develop. There is a risk that they may develop in a primarily retributive direction, which is likely to limit their reintegrative potential. Their increasingly bureaucratic and result-oriented implementation may well decrease educational effects, which are most likely to follow from a personal approach and human contact. And their current control, without enforceable legal guarantees, hardly offers any serious safeguard against abuses (uit Beijerse and van Swaaningen, 1994). These problems form the context in which the net-widening argument is to be placed at this moment.

New orientations for penal reformers

These observations about the concept of net-widening bring us to the relation between critical criminological insights and penal reform. After a phase of impossibilism, in which the net-widening argument became a dogma, criminological concern for penal reform became rather marginal. Critical legal scholars remained more loyal to this topic, but they mainly reacted from defensive positions. The resort to a politics of rights is an example of this tendency. In the context of the attacks on the democratic values of the social *rechtsstaat* in the actuarial model of justice, penal reformers now try to save as many gains as possible from previous decades. If their sensitising role in the public debate is not to run out, penal reformers should set themselves more comprehensive goals.

First, penal reformers' primary attention should be given to human rights discourse. Disclosures about human rights violations (at police stations, in prisons), which are likely to receive media coverage, form a sufficient strategy to shame the entrepreneurial state, and human rights treaties offer critical lawyers new tools. Human rights should, however, not only be used in a merely instrumental way. The inflation of human rights as concrete legal rules led to deceptive appearances. We should, moreover, be aware of the fact that law can also polarise conflicts. If penal authorities are relatively cooperative, the model of negotiations *entre nous* is a more pragmatic option (de Jonge, 1994: 269–72). Using the culture of human rights as a strategy of shaming, and publicising the ways in which the state neglects its social role, is probably more effective in a less responsive political culture. This could also be a way to stimulate new sensibilities about the penal question.

A second role for critical criminology in the fight for penal reform would be to link the case-wise approach of lawyers with broader political developments. By looking for the loopholes in law-and-order politics, state initiatives can be bent in a progressive direction. Barbara Hudson (1993: 179) shows how the primacy of punishment can be challenged in relative accordance with administrative interests. Policy options such as crime prevention, reductionism, selective abolitionism and a new rehabilitation agenda are very relevant in the light of 'the persistence of overcrowding and eruptions of serious disorder in prisons', and of the gradual acknowledgement that 'more of the same' is extremely costly, does not counter rising crime rates, and is reinforcing the ethnic and socioeconomic split in society.

Thirdly, penal-reform activities also need to be adapted to changes in the penal rationale itself. Imprisonment is based on a penal philosophy of individual guilt. This guilt first needs retribution, and then the perpetrator is to be prepared for his return to society. This focus on the individual can be answered by ethical and functionalist critiques: the retribution of one pain by another does not show much civic responsibility, and prisons do not rehabilitate. At present, crime control is oriented towards society, and in the actuarial approach the person of the offender has become quite irrelevant. The main point in this process is risk calculation and safety management. Consequently, penal reformers should also widen their scope. Their main argument about the rehabilitation of lawbreakers – by which a safer society may implicitly follow – finds less favour among the general public. The argument thus needs to be directed to how moves for reform could increase public safety. Imprisonment is not very successful for this purpose because of its deskilling and stigmatising rationale of exclusion from society, and its nearly always temporary character: whatever the level of incarceration may be, there will always be more 'evil-doers' on the street than behind bars. It is the continuing task of penal reformers to repeat this obvious fact. The adoption of the hegemonic discourse of 'protecting society' is comparable with the earlier use of prisoners' rights discourse as a 'noble lie' to advance more radical reform (Ward, 1986).

A fourth significant shift in criminal justice is the retreat of the state as a social service, and the increasing influence of the private sector. Here we should not only consider the privatisation of prison management, but also of private policing and the whole security industry which has risen in the area of crime prevention. More fundamental than the question of whether prisoners are better or worse treated by the private sector or by the state are questions with respect to the accountability of crime control. The privatisation of criminal justice agencies raises questions about the legitimation of punishment that we have only just begun to realise. Which forces will steer crime control if imprisonment as we know it now is superseded as the centrepiece of criminal justice, and, indeed, if state control over penal developments is itself slowly decreasing?

A fifth issue which has received too little attention is the irrational side of punishment. Trained as intellectuals are in reasonable, realistic and polite debate, their arguments may also have been too rational and functional. Perhaps because penal reformers have forgotten that punishment is mainly an emotional, vengeful reaction, a public symbol of rejection regardless of any concrete effect, their arguments have not convinced the general public. By speaking about a derailment of the rule of law and of legal guarantees, or expressing dismay about worsening prison conditions, penal reformers are more and more addressing only a small group of insiders. They have to realise this and speak in other terms. The popular desire for punitive symbols of vigour has become particularly strong. Imprisonment is a powerful metaphor of vigour in the current control state that has replaced the caring welfare state. If the use of custody is to be reduced, an acceptable answer to these irrational, symbolic elements needs to be found as well. This may be the most difficult of all. In this respect it seems more crucial to challenge public opinion and the political arena on such general themes as the ethics of the state, rather than try to influence practitioners. The latter may be more 'effective' in the short term and on a practical level, but if the general public remains unaware of the rationale of a certain practice it will ultimately lower people's confidence in justice. The appeal to strengthening the narrative elements of law (in order to make law a less technocratic trade and to reflect society's cultural and moral pluralism) is an attempt to increase public understanding and concern for the problems of crime.

Action needs to be taken with respect to the concrete issues mentioned in the conclusions to Chapter 7 (the drug problem, the position of the victim, the role of the media, lawyers and the avant-garde), as well as the later mentioned macro-sociological developments in the penal field (actuarial justice, retreat of the state, revival of punishment as symbol of vigour). Penal reform lobbies should not only be just lawyers' organisations. A predominantly legal orientation focuses on the level of concrete cases and parliamentary or court decisions, rather than on the sociological analyses of all these developments together. This latter level is fundamental if we are to get an idea of the direction in which penal reform is going. It would probably be more convincing to the general public if the basic critique of individual cases could be placed in an overall picture. Then, all those cases and decisions would no longer stand by themselves, but represent a new vision of criminal justice.

Once these guiding principles and general orientations have been formulated, it will be time to develop an order of activities at various levels of the penal system. Prisoners' rights are extremely important, but their effectuation stands or falls with the ability to do something about the problems of overcrowding and penal expansionism which have become endemic in many European countries. The prime focus thus needs to be on these issues. Experience in the United States, where about eight times as many people are imprisoned as the European average, and where the 'three strikes and you are out' politics perfectly demonstrates the rampant logic of prison's alleged incapacitating function, shows it does not make much sense to keep on building more prisons if the aim is to create a safer society. The moral and functional failure of the United States' 'get touch' policy is the best example to show we must think in other directions. A major part of the attention of penal reformers should therefore be on sentencing trends and policies, and on a politics in which non-custodial sanctions and crime-prevention programmes actually decrease the number of prison sentences. That is why the potential for reform currently lies more in the community than in the prison system. Here, the political debate is still relatively open. It may well be more possible to influence public opinion and policy-makers in this relatively new field than in the traditional penal area.

The debate on penal reform has centred for too long around rehabilitation and non-custodial sanctions (pro and contra), whereas penal reformers have still hardly addressed more recent debates on crime prevention, public safety and the social consequences of the privatisation of social control. Penal reformers should not forget their classical themes, but, in the present political climate, they should primarily advocate a new balance of responsibilities between the individual and society. The individual is to be held responsible for the suffering he or she causes to other people, but it is society's responsibility to do its utmost to see that people are not brought to a position in which the restraint on doing harm is lowered. That is a question of social justice.

Objectives for critical criminologists

The issues raised above are also addressed in critical criminology's demand for political commitment. The following observations can be made about its future as a theoretical perspective. A first point is to break the power of the hegemonic discourse on crime in such a way that it not only reaches its own parish, but, indeed, those people who are not convinced already. Though a critique of ideology remains an important task, one's own ideological positions should not be presented as empirical analyses. Critical criminologists should first of all be good researchers. In this sense, I am not too unhappy about the demise of the 'grand truths' of the 1970s and about the eclectic adoption of smaller narratives. It has made critical criminologists, such as left realists and neo-abolitionists, deal with more concrete subjects and has brought them to more serious empirical studies. These can show the limits of law-and-order politics in controlling crime by, for example, exposing the structural causes of crime or the low percentage of crimes the criminal justice system actually deals with, or by demonstrating, with empirical data on the increasing number of poverty crimes, that certain socioeconomic developments are criminogenic. Critical criminologists should also indicate alternative ways of dealing with criminalised problems and conflicts. Though concrete 'blueprints' for an alternative prevention policy, procedural rationale or sanctions should not be shunned, the main value of such a language of possibility lies in challenging prevailing truisms on crime and crime control. The direct influence of criminological research on criminal justice politics cannot be overestimated. Particularly if criminological analyses point in a different direction from prevailing policy orientations: 'oppositional discourse is as constitutive of existing reality as is supportive discourse' (Henry and Milovanovic, 1996: 204). Instead of trying to convince policy-makers with rational arguments, it seems more realistic to start from the position that political decisions are not grounded in rational considerations or scientific research, but in sentiments, party ideology and political expediency. Therefore, critical criminologists should focus on visualising alternative realities, breaking hegemonic stereotypes and implicitly sensitising public opinion. Chapters 9 and 10 are a contribution to this endeavour.

Secondly, a closer liaison between criminologists and legal scholars is crucial with respect to both the normative and the idealistic elements of critical criminology. Particularly over the past 15 years, legal tools have been used frequently to translate political commitments. After many social movements adopted a politics of rights, critical criminologists also abandoned the traditionally dismissive attitude towards the language of rights – as something belonging to an élitist, anachronistic, ideological or, indeed, irrelevant superstructure. Criminology emerged at the end of the nineteenth century to save criminal law from certain death as doctrinalism, a system that had lost touch with social reality. At present, normative legal theory seems, in return, necessary to save criminology from an entirely utilitarian ethos. In the mere technical sense, both disciplines have their own methodology and frames of reference, but when it comes to the fundamental questions (and to the very practical questions of implementation) criminal law and criminology are increasingly studied together. The precursors of criminology would not have foreseen the drastic change in relations between criminal law and criminology over a century.

The current, more positive attitude to the protective side of law among Anglo-Saxon critical criminologists is particularly remarkable since an orientation to the legal field here is, historically, rather alien. Left realists discovered, in the wake of the new social movements, that taking rights seriously is the only thing that remains for the left now that passionate political action from the bottom is no longer expected (Donzelot, 1984). Though the Schwendingers' (1975) politics of human rights hardly demonstrated a specifically legal vision, it did create a common ground for the later influence of critical legal observations on human rights within critical criminology. By this rediscovery of law, the gap between Anglo-Saxon and continental European critical criminology is gradually being closed. The epistemological lessons of this development still need to be made more explicit. A counter-factual way of thinking, using principles as normative touchstones, can show the limits of 'values' such as pragmatism, efficiency or utility. Had such considerations determined our past, no cathedrals or majestic city squares would have been built, no paintings or sculptures created, no music or poetry written, and no democracy established. We should be pleased that our ancestors were guided by less utilitarian considerations. By taking means for goals, current politicians ignore the 'useless' (that is, unquantifiable) aspects that determine people's satisfaction with their life-world. This resembles the positivist's pre-occupation with methodological questions, while he or she ignores the complexity of social reality, or the visions of society and of mankind behind certain theories, because these do not fit into a neat scientific model. By explicitly formulating a normative framework, such as social justice, critical scholars prevent the agenda being set by hegemonic policy discourse. In order to envisage new ways and an alternative structure of relevance, a more pro-active, sensitising approach seems to be more fruitful than to keep trying to challenge hegemonic stereotypes about crime and punishment with reactive and defensive arguments.

Thirdly, the future of critical criminology in a theoretical sense lies in its reflection upon concrete social problems. The idea of being 'loyal' to one par-ticular theory and analysing everything from that perspective has been superseded. Different theoretical frames of reference can be used to address the questions for which they are the most suited. If research is done in a more eclectic way and a wider variety of criminological perspectives is used to analyse different problems, the epistemological level becomes increasingly important in order to prevent complete fragmentation of the discourse. At this level, the normative impulse of social justice is necessary to break the assumed notions of actuarial justice, and to stress that different visions of crime control are ultimately based in a political confrontation of values and views of society. Normative orientations also need to be made more explicit because analytical despair, political defeatism and alleged moral relativism have proved to be the near death-blow of critical criminology. Before the mid-1980s, it was generally thought that the defence of norms and values was the domain of the right, while the left defended a relativist vision of moral-ity. A paradigm of change such as critical criminology can, however, hardly be perceived without making the directive impulses explicit. Critical crim-inologists had little to say to the penal actuaries who argued that they had done exactly what critics had asked them, namely to create as objective (namely technical) a criminal justice system as possible. The question of why automation and bureaucratisation are no adequate answers to the ideology-reproducing functions and selectivity of criminal law could not be answered in a satisfactory way.

Nils Christie (1981: 10) argued: 'Moralism within our areas has for some years been an attitude or even a term associated with protagonists for law and order and severe penal sanctions, while their opponents were seen as floating in a sort of value-free vacuum. Let it therefore be completely clear that I am also a moralist. Worse: I am a moral imperialist.' With the so-called frag-mentation of morality in postmodern culture, the question of what our ethics are currently based upon may have become increasingly difficult to answer, but it has also become all the more pressing. We assessed a 'victimalised' morality (Boutellier, 1993) as too minimal because it contains so many ele-ments of the negative solidarity of shared fears that also marks the risk society. A morality oriented towards concern and responsibility for the 'con-crete other' (Bauman, 1995a) offers more potential for a replacement discourse of social justice. Reassessment of the sociological value of legal safeguards and a culture of human rights, participatory justice, and narrative procedural structures facilitating moral-practical discourse, attempts to formulate a critical, pluriform vision of morality that fits current culture. This exploration also demonstrates how the real questions of criminal justice and crime control are avoided by technocratic discourse and how it implicitly reinforces a social and moral consensus based on values and visions of a society that no longer exists.

Particularly when they are not aimed at the authorities but at individuals, moral appeals are often associated with reactionary or crypto-religious connotations – duty, shame or sin. These moral concepts can, however, not be ignored because they are part of the popular mythology of crime and punishment. Stan Cohen (1979) also indicated the profoundly moralistic intent of deviancy theory itself. In order to stress the individual's responsibility, he argued for the reintroduction of 'old concepts' like guilt, justice and tolerance. John Braithwaite's (1989) ideas on reintegrative shaming give a new sociological relevance to these notions. We can also use words that sound more progressive, such as solidarity, commitment and sensibility, but Braithwaite has touched upon an important point. Next to his positive focus on possible options, Braithwaite's analyses also show that norms are not static but flexible. The development of norms depends on the question of whether or not their substantial content is challenged. A sheer technical orientation to procedural legitimacy alone will not advance a development of norms, but rather lead to a procedural avoidance of norms which ultimately erodes their whole meaning. If law is not oriented towards axiological questions, but at analyses of costs and benefits, it actually invites fraud and deceit. Braithwaite also reinforces the critical criminological argument about the major shortcomings of punitive control: stigmatisation and exclusion prevents a prisoner's reintegration into society, and the possibility of his developing crime-preventive bonds. In that sense, criminal law itself is a major incentive to crime.

Fourthly, it has already been argued that it is not very fruitful for critical criminologists to consider the state merely as an instrument of repression or paternalistic care. Here we will take one step further. Because negativism and suspicion in this respect had nearly become conditioned reflexes, the critique of critical criminology became so global and predictable that it could no longer be taken seriously. It is doubtful whether the overall macro-sociological orientation of critical criminology was so fruitful. This contention does not imply a simple return to analyses at a micro- and meso-level, or to models of society as caring communities of family and neighbours. There is, however, a need to study justice at a community level – not only because many crime-prevention policies are directed at the community, but also because, with some sociological imagination, it may even be possible to give the whole notion of 'community' a new meaning. A community can be a student, political or professional organisation, a social movement, an ethnic or neighbourhood group, a sporting club or a circle of people communicating on the Internet. Ideas on reintegrative shaming, participatory justice and on pluriform morality rooted in smaller narratives all start from such new ideas of community. The alternative (legal) forums guided by such principles should have equally strong symbolic functions as criminal law, without reproducing the negative (disintegrating, technocratising, stigmatising, excluding) aspects of the penal approach. Such 'communitarian' positions on social control are worthy of a careful reaffirmation – careful because, unlike most communitarian philosophies, critical criminology is not confined to a plea for more community control, but indeed stresses the social task of the state as well. Communitarian ideas can, however, be reaffirmed because 'it still makes sense to look for more humane, just, and workable alternatives to the criminal justice system's mechanisms of apprehension, judgement, and punishment. It still makes sense to say that mutual aid, good neighbourliness, and real community are preferable to the solutions of bureaucracies, professionals, and the centralised state' (Cohen, 1988: 223).

Fifthly, an appeal should be made for academic credibility and integrity. In his nightmare scenario of penal developments in the Western world, Nils Christie (1993: 159–73) pointed to the historical importance of science as a rational legitimation of the most frightening politics of social defence – that of the Nazis. It was intellectually frightening because a completely inhumane philosophy was carried out in an extremely systematic way, through very rational laws of efficiency. It is not coincidental that the end of modernity has been situated in Auschwitz. Stephan Quensel tried to draw some lessons from the criminological 'complicity' in the development of the Nazi's law-and-order politics. In his opening address to its 1988 Congress in Hamburg, Quensel (1989: 2) reminded his audience of the dubious political history of the International Society of Criminology. He concluded from this development that, because criminology is such a dated and politically bound discipline, which always has a partial responsibility for traditional visions and myths about the 'crime problem', the 'positivist innocence' with which criminologists think they can retire to 'pure science' is untenable. The Beckerian question 'Whose side are we on?' is as valid today as it was 60 or 30 years ago, and criminologists should continue to repeat the obvious: the truism about crime and crime control for the criminologist can still offer a new insight to the general public.

Critical criminology may have suffered from a sometimes unreflexive political correctness, yet this is not the problem of today. Taboos about issues related to race or gender hardly seem to exist any more and genuine solidarity with vulnerable groups is widely portrayed as a pathetic relic from the past. At present, a possible ideologism is not a problem for social critics, but rather for today's 'administrative' criminologists. Looking at current academic casualness, it seems as though there was never any struggle over positivism. Under the notion of value-free research, hegemonic concepts, presuppositions and definitions of a problem are adopted as of old as if they were given facts. Questioning common beliefs and dominant conceptualisations is again called 'ideological', whereas implicitly adopting them and focusing on derived variables is again seen as 'pure science'. Critical scholars should not make the old mistake of rejecting positivism altogether. Positivism has its values, but its explanatory power is limited: central epistemological questions remain unanswered while it focuses on images of the status quo rather than exploring new visions. Critical scholars should seriously deal with positivism, while stressing that all those value-free, methodologically sound analyses are surrounded by at least four value-bound, subjective moments: (a) the choice of the subject (do you study 'problematic groups' or a 'problematic society'?); (b) the implicit ideology of a chosen model (many mainstream theories take for granted the idea that personal, utilitarian motives guide every human act); (c) the choice of which variables to include and which to leave out (or how problems of operationalisation can reduce the complexity of reality to an unacceptable degree); and (d) the conclusions one draws from the analyses (are they the only possible conclusions, or do the same analyses also allow for other conclusions?). This latter point becomes particularly tricky if conclusions are accompanied by (policy-)recommendations – whether or not these are actually supported by the data.

In the current result-oriented professional context, it is unlikely that really innovative studies will emerge. If scientific progress is to be made, existing boundaries need to be challenged and new ways have to be explored. Not all of these new ways will, however, generate success and thus the cautious researcher, who must produce a certain output in a limited time, will avoid such risks and remain on the safe side. Without intellectual scepticism, without taking up research whose outcome is not guaranteed from the outset, and without lifting concrete empirical studies to a higher level of abstraction, criminology will be unable to make any theoretical progress. It will consequently fall short in creating explanatory models and innovative frames of reference and will subsequently become superfluous. Stan Cohen (1990: 28–9) described the triple loyalty of the critical criminologist as: 'first, an overriding obligation to honest intellectual enquiry itself (however sceptical, provisional, irrelevant and unrealistic), second, a political commitment to social justice, but also (and potentially conflicting with both) the pressing and immediate demands for short term humanitarian help. We have to appease these three voracious gods.' The future of critical criminology lies in its ability to offer new impulses at these three levels.

References

Adorno, Theodor W. (1950) *Studien zum autoritären Charakter*. Frankfurt am Main: Suhrkamp (1973 edn).

Adorno, Theodor W. (1969) Zur Logik der Sozialwissenschaften, in Adorno et al., *Der Positivismusstreit in der deutschen Soziologie*. Berlin: Luchterhand.

Ahearne, Mike (1994) *Beccaria: a Suitable Case for Reconstruction*. Middlesex: Middlesex University, Centre for Criminology.

AJK (*Arbeitskreis Junger Kriminologen*) (ed.) (1974a) *Kritische Kriminologie: Positionen, Kontroversen und Perspektiven*. Munich: Juventa.

AJK (*Arbeitskreis Junger Kriminologen*) (1974b) Zu einem Forschungsprogramm für die Kriminologie: Ergebnisse der Klausurtagung des AJK im August 1973, *Kriminologisches Journal*, 6: 241–59.

Akers, Ronald L. (1997) *Criminological Theories*, 2nd edn. Los Angles: Roxbury.

Althoff, Martina (1995) Die Entdeckung der Kategorie 'Geschlecht': ein Überblick über die Auseinandersetzung mit dem Geschlechtsverhältnis im Kriminologischen Journal, *Kriminologisches Journal*, 28 (5th Beiheft): 77–94.

Ancel, Marc (1954) *La défense sociale: un mouvement de politique criminelle humaniste*. Paris: Cujas.

Ancel, Marc (1964) Défendre la défence sociale?, *Revue de science criminelle et de droit comparé*, p. 206.

Ancel, Marc (1967) La protection des droits de la personne dans le procès pénal et les doctrines de la défense sociale, *Revue de science criminelle et de droit comparé* (suppl.): 7–11.

Andrés Ibáñez, Perfecto (ed.) (1978) *Política y justicia en el estado capitalista*. Barcelona: Fontanella.

Bahl, Elke (1993) Wie fertig macht das Unfertige?, in Papendorf and Schumann (eds), pp. 167–79.

Bailey, Roy and Young, Jock (eds) (1973) *Contemporary Social Problems in Britain*. Farnborough: Saxon House.

Bakker Schut, Herman, Pieter et al. (1971) *Coornhert Liga: alternatieve justitiebegroting 1972*. Deventer: Kluwer.

Bal, Peter (1990) Procedurele rationaliteit en mensenrechten in het strafproces, *Recht en kritiek*, 16: 259–79.

Bal, Peter (1994) Wat draagt Habermas bij tot de ontwikkeling van een discours-theorie van het straf(proces)recht?, *Recht en kritiek*, 20 (2): 152–69.

Balmaseda Ripero, Juana M.ª and Carrera González, M.ª José (1990) Salhaketa: support association to Euskadi prisoners, Paper presented at the XVIIIth Conference of the European Group for the Study of Deviance and Social Control, Haarlem, The Netherlands, 7 September.

Baratta, Alessandro (1980) Strafrechtsdogmatik und Kriminologie: zur Vergangenheit und Zukunft des Modells einer gesamten Strafrechtswissenschaft, *Zeitschrift für die gesamte Strafrechtswissenschaft*, 92 (1): 107–42.

Baratta, Alessandro (1982) *Criminología crítica y crítica del derecho penal*. Madrid: Siglo Veintiuno (Spanish edn 1986).

Baratta, Alessandro (1985) Die kritische Kriminologie und ihre Funktion in der Kriminalpolitik, *Kriminalsoziologische Bibliographie*, 49: 38–52.

Baratta, Alessandro (1988) Prinzipien des minimalen Strafrechts: eine Theorie der Menschenrechte als Schutzobjekte und Grenze des Strafrechts, in Günther Kaiser (ed.).,

Kriminologische Forschung in den achtziger Jahren. Schriftenreihe vol. 35, no. 2. Freiburg: Max Planck Institut.

Baratta, Alessandro (1990) No está en crisis la criminología crítica, in Mauricio-Martínez, *Qué pasa en la criminología moderna.* Bogotá: Temis.

Bauman, Zygmunt (1995a) *Life in Fragments: Essays in Postmodern Morality.* Oxford: Blackwell.

Bauman, Zygmunt (1995b) The strangers of the consumer era: from the welfare state to prison, *Tijdschrift voor Criminologie,* 37 (3): 210–18.

Beck, Ulrich (1986) *Risk Society: towards a New Modernity.* London: Sage (English edn 1992).

Becker, Howard S. (1967) Whose side are we on?, *Social Problems,* 14: 239–47.

Behr, Claus-Peter, Gipser, Dietlinde, Klein-Schonnefeld, Sabine, Naffin, Klaus and Zillmer, Heiner (1981) The use of scientific discoveries for the maintenance and extension of state control: on the effect of legitimation and utilization of science, in Brusten and Ponsaers (eds), pp. 95–120.

Beijerse, Jolande uit (1997) *Gevangenschap in afwachting van . . .?* forthcoming thesis, Erasmus University Rotterdam.

Beijerse, Jolande uit and Kool, Renée (1990) The traitorous temptation of criminal justice: deceptive appearances? The Dutch women's movement, violence against women and the criminal justice system, in Rolston and Tomlinson (eds), pp. 253–74.

Beijerse, Jolande uit and Swaaningen, René van (1993) Social control as a policy: pragmatic moralism with a structural deficit, *Social and Legal Studies,* 2: 281–302.

Beijerse, Jolande uit and Swaaningen, René van (1994) De zachte krachten zullen zeker winnen op 't eind: een op de praktijk gericht strafrechthervormend perspectief op alternatieven voor detentie, in Verpalen (ed.), pp. 23–50.

Beijerse, Jolande uit and Swaaningen, René van (1995) Publieke geloofwaardigheid: een gevaarlijk beleidsargument in een rechtsstaat: het beleid rond alternatieve sancties als voorbeeld, in John Blad, Tineke Cleiren, Jaap van der Hulst, Erik Koopmans, Paul Mevis and Wouter Bos (eds), *Met recht op de vlucht.* Arnhem: Gouda Quint, pp. 1–10.

Beirne, Piers (1993) *Inventing Criminology.* New York: State University of New York.

Beleza, Teresa Pizarro (1987) A moderna criminologia e a aplicação do dereito penal, *Revista Jurídica,* pp. 39–68.

Bemmelen, Jacob M. van (1935) Het juridisch jaar 1934, in *Weekblad van het Recht,* no. 12849.

Bemmelen, Jacob M. van (1942) *Criminologie: leerboek der misdaadkunde aan de hand van nederlandse gegevens en onderzoekingen.* Zwolle: Tjeenk Willink (1948 edn).

Bemmelen, Jacob M. van (1955) De psychologie en de begrippen van opzet en schuld, in Jacob M. van Bemmelen, *Op de grenzen van het strafrecht.* Haarlem: Tjeenk Willink.

Bergalli, Roberto (1980) Origen de las teorías de la reacción social: un aporte al análisis y crítica del Labelling Approach, in UAB, pp. 49–96.

Bergalli, Roberto (1992) Resocialización y medidas alternativas: extravíos conceptuales, políticas sinuosas y confusiones piadosas en la práctica penitenciaria de España y Catalunya, in Associació Catalana de Juristes Demòcrates (ed.), *Política penitenciaria y doctrina oficiál: la intolerante resistencia a la crítica.* Barcelona: ACJD, pp. 17–38.

Bergalli, Roberto (1995) The Spanish attempt to build a democratic criminal justice system, in Ruggiero et al. (eds), pp. 149–68.

Bergalli, Roberto and Bodelón González, Encarna (1992) La cuestión de las mujeres y el derecho penal simbólico, *Anuario de Filosofía de Derecho* (Madrid) 9: 43–73.

Bergalli, Roberto, Bustos Ramírez, Juan and Miralles, Teresa (1983) *El pensamiento criminológico,* vol. 1: *Un análisis crítico.* Barcelona: Península.

Bianchi, Herman (1951) Recht en vergelding, *De Vlam,* 9 June, p. 8.

Bianchi, Herman (1956) *Position and Subject-matter of Criminology: Inquiry concerning Theoretical Criminology.* Amsterdam: North Holland.

Bianchi, Herman (1958) *Waar en waarom misdaad.* Amsterdam: Noordhollandsche Uitgeversmij.

Bianchi, Herman (1960) *De strafrechter en de bescherming van de samenleving.* Amsterdam: Calvinistische Juristen Vereniging.

Bianchi, Herman (1961) *Strafsancties en geestelijke volksgezondheid.* Amsterdam: Noordhollandsche Uitgeversmij.

Bianchi, Herman (1964) *Ethiek van het straffen.* Nijkerk: Callenbach.

Bianchi, Herman (1967) *De vliegengod: opstellen over gezag, recht en orde.* Alphen a/d Rijn: Samsom.

Bianchi, Herman (1971) *Stigmatisering.* Deventer: Kluwer.

Bianchi, Herman (1974a) Goevernementele en non-goevernementele kriminologie; een meta-probleem, *Nederlands Tijdschrift voor Criminologie,* 16: 201–17.

Bianchi, Herman (1974b) Naar een nieuwe fenomenologische kriminologie, *Nederlands Tijdschrift voor Criminologie,* 16: 97–112.

Bianchi, Herman (1974c) York en Florence: op weg naar een nieuwe criminologie (?), *Nederlands Tijdschrift voor Criminologie,* 16: 3–17.

Bianchi, Herman (1975a) Social control and deviance in The Netherlands, in Bianchi et al. (eds), pp. 51–9.

Bianchi, Herman (1975b) Strukturalistische kriminologie?, *Nederlands Tijdschrift voor Criminologie,* 17: 265–78.

Bianchi, Herman (1976) De radicale criminologen en Bonger, *Tijdschrift voor Criminologie,* 18: 202–9.

Bianchi, Herman (1979) Openingen naar een makro-fenomenologie, in de Folter (ed.), pp. 24–36.

Bianchi, Herman (1980) *Basismodellen in de kriminologie.* Deventer: Van Loghum Slaterus.

Bianchi, Herman (1985) *Gerechtigheid als vrijplaats: de terugkeer van het slachtoffer in ons recht.* Baarn: Ten Have.

Bianchi, Herman (1994) *Justice as Sanctuary: Toward a New System of Crime Control.* Bloomington, Ind.: Indiana University Press.

Bianchi, Herman, Simondi, Mario and Taylor, Ian (eds) (1975) *Deviance and Control in Europe.* London: Wiley.

Bianchi, Herman and Swaaningen, René van (eds) (1986) *Abolitionism: Towards a Non-repressive Approach to Crime.* Amsterdam: Free University Press.

Birkmeyer, Karl von (1907) *Was lässt von Liszt vom Strafrecht übrig: eine Warnung vor der Modernen Richtung im Strafrecht.* Munich: Beck.

Blad, John R. (1994) Strafrecht als integratief project, in Foqué et al. (eds), pp. 357–77.

Blad, John R. (1996) *Abolitionisme als strafrechtstheorie: theoretische beschouwingen over het abolitionisme van L.H.C. Hulsman.* Arnhem: Gouda Quint.

Blad, John R. and Emmen, Mieke (eds) (1996) *Rechtshandhaving en sancties: reactie op het rapport van de commissie Korthals Altes.* Amsterdam: Coornhert Liga standpunt no. 3.

Blad, John R., Mastrigt, Hans van and Uildriks, Niels A. (eds) (1987a) *The Criminal Justice System as a Social Problem: an Abolitionist Perspective,* Liber Amicorum Louk Hulsman, parts I and II. Rotterdam: Jur. Inst. EUR.

Blad, John R., Mastrigt, Hans van and Uildriks, Niels (1987b) Hulsman's abolitionist perspective, in Blad et al. (eds), pp. 5–19.

Blankenburg, Erhard R. (1993) Het einde van de tolerantie in Nederland?, in Nijboer (ed.), pp. 361–5.

Blankenburg, Erhard R. and Bruinsma, Freek (1991) *Dutch Legal Culture.* Deventer: Kluwer.

Blankenburg, Erhard R., Steinert, Heinz and Treiber, Hubert (1980) Empirische Rechtssoziologie und Strafrechtsdogmatik – die Beliebigkeit von Ergebnissen empirischer Sozialforschung für die strafrechtsdogmatische Diskussion am Beispiel der von Juristen geführten Debatte zum Ladendiebstahl, in Lüderssen and Sack (eds), pp. 396–429.

Block, Alan and Chambliss, William J. (1981) *Organizing Crime.* New York: Elsevier.

Blom, Tom and Blad, John R. (1986) Van drugsbeleid naar drugbeleid: het primaat bij justitie, in Lex van Almelo, John Blad, Jacco Boek, Cecilia Boor, Pieter Ippel and Pieter Wiewel (eds), *Coornhert Liga crimineel jaarboek 1996.* Nijmegen: Ars Aequi Libri, pp. 19–34.

Blom, Tom and Mastrigt, Hans van (1994) The future of the Dutch model in the context of the war on drugs, in Leuw and Haen Marshall (eds), *Between Prohibition and Legalization: the Dutch Experiment in Drug Policy.* Amsterdam: Kugler, pp. 255–83.

Bodelón González, Encarna (1993) Les amistats perilloses: les dones i les estratègies de criminalizació, *Revista Demà,* no. 17.

Bokos, Vassilis, Koulouris, Nikos, Strathoulopoulou, Eugenia, Tsironis, Gregory, Vidali, Sophie and Zaphiropoulou, Eleni (1992) Prisoners' struggle, governmental manoeuvres, and social inertia in the '90s: the neutralization of abolitionist tendencies and the intervention of criminologists – the Greek case, *Chronika* (criminological journal of the University of Thrace), 5: 133–45.

Bonger, Willem A. (1905) *Criminality and Economic Conditions*. Boston: Little, Brown (English edn 1916).

Bonger, Willem A. (1909) Cesare Lombroso, reprinted in Bonger (1950), pp. 3–13.

Bonger, Willem A. (1911) Misdaad en socialisme, reprinted in Bonger (1950), pp. 83–121.

Bonger, Willem A. (1922) *Over de evolutie der moraal*. Amsterdam: Ontwikkeling.

Bonger, Willem A. (1932) *Inleiding tot de criminologie*. Haarlem: Bohn.

Bonger, Willem A. (1934) *Problemen der democratie: een sociologische en psychologische studie*. Groningen: Noordhoff.

Bonger, Willem A. (1935) Het 'nieuwe' strafrecht, *Rechtsgeleerd Magazijn*, 54: 236–66.

Bonger, Willem A. (1936) De criminologie in het Tijdschrift voor Strafrecht 1886–1936, reprinted in Bonger (1950), pp. 121–33.

Bonger, Willem A. (1939) *Ras en misdaad*. Haarlem: Tjeenk Willink.

Bonger, Willem A. (1950) *Verspreide geschriften I*. Amsterdam: Arbeiderspers.

Boogaart, Hilde van den and Seus, Lydia (1991) *Radikale Kriminologie: die Rekonstruktion zweier Jahrzehnte Wissenschaftsgeschichte Großbritanniens*. Pfaffenweiler: Centaurus.

Boutellier, Hans J.C. (1993) *Solidariteit en slachtofferschap: de morele betekenis van criminaliteit in een postmoderne cultuur*. Nijmegen: Socialistiese Uitgeverij.

Boutellier, Hans J.C. (1994) De zorgzame staat: over het morele motief in overheidsbeleid, *Justitiële Verkenningen*, 20 (6): 85–101.

Boutellier, Hans J.C. and Stokkom, Bas van (1995) Consumptie van veiligheid: van verzorgingsstaat tot veiligheidsstaat, *Justitiële Verkenningen*, 21 (5): 96–111.

Bovenkerk, Frank (1990) Justitie en criminologie verdienen beter, *Tijdschrift voor Criminologie*, 32 (4): 278–83.

Box, Steven (1971) *Deviance, Reality and Society*. London: Holt, Rinehart and Winston.

Braithwaite, John (1989) *Crime, Shame and Reintegration*. Cambridge: Cambridge University Press.

Braithwaite, John (1993a) Beyond positivism: learning from contextual integrated strategies, *Journal of Research in Crime and Delinquency*, 30 (4): 383–99.

Braithwaite, John (1993b) Shame and modernity, *British Journal of Criminology*, 33: 1–18.

Braithwaite, John (1995) Inequality and republican criminology, in John Hagan and Ruth D. Peterson (eds), *Crime and Inequality*. Palo Alto: Stanford University Press, pp. 277–305.

Braithwaite, John and Mugford, Stephan (1994) Conditions of successful reintegration ceremonies, *British Journal of Criminology*, 34 (2): 139–71.

Brake, Mile and Hale, Chris (1992) *Public Order and Private Lives: the Politics of Law and Order*. London: Routledge.

Brants, Chrisje and Silvas, Jos (1987) Dutch criminal justice and a challenge to abolitionism, in Blad et al. (eds), pp. 133–48.

Bricola, Franco (1975) Politica criminale e politica penale dell' ordine pubblico, *La questione criminale*, 1 (2): 221–88.

Bricola, Franco, Sbricolli, Mario, Neppi Modona, Guido, Seppilli, Tullio and Ingrao, Pietro (1975) Per una politica criminale del movimento operaio, *La questione criminale*, 1 (3): 485–514.

Brink, Bert van den (1993) Jürgen Habermas: gemeenschapsdenken, maar dan anders, in van Klink et al. (eds), pp. 111–22.

Bruinsma, Gerben, Leuw, Ed, Lissenberg, Ellie and Vliet, Annelies van (eds) (1987) *Vrouw en criminaliteit*. Meppel/Amsterdam: Boom.

Brusten, Manfred and Ponsaers, Paul (eds) (1981) *State Control on Information on the Field of Deviance and Social Control*, Working Papers in European Criminology no. 2, Wuppertal/Louvain: EGSDSC.

Buikhuisen, Wouter (1965) *Achtergronden bij nozemgedrag*. Assen: Van Gorcum.

Buitelaar, Wout and Sierksma, Rypke (1972) *Gevangen in de gevangenis: beschouwingen over gevangenis, misdaad en maatschappij*. Meppel: Boom.

Burg, Wibren van der and Reijen, Willem van (1988) De plaats van de 'Tanner Lectures' in het oeuvre van Jürgen Habermas, in Habermas (1988), pp. 9–47.

Cavadino, Michael and Dignan, James (1992) *The Penal System: an Introduction.* London: Sage.

Christie, Nils (1975) *Hvor tett et samfunn?* Oslo: Universitetsforlaget.

Christie, Nils (1977) Conflicts as property, *British Journal of Criminology,* 17 (1): 1–19.

Christie, Nils (1981) *Limits to Pain.* Oxford: Martin Robertson.

Christie, Nils (1986) Suitable enemies, in Bianchi and van Swaaningen (eds), pp. 42–54.

Christie, Nils (1993) *Crime Control as Industry: Towards Gulags Western style?* London: Routledge.

Ciacci, Margherita and Simondi, Mario (1977) Un courant novateur de savoir criminologique: l'experience de l'EGSDSC, *Déviance et société,* 1 (1): 109–17.

Cleiren, Tineke P.M. (1989) *Beginselen van een goede procesorde.* Arnhem: Gouda Quint.

Cohen, Lawrence E. and Machalek, Richard (1988) A general theory of expropriative crime: an evolutionary ecological approach, *American Journal of Sociology,* 94 (3): 465–501.

Cohen, Stanley (ed.) (1971) *Images of Deviance.* Harmondsworth: Penguin.

Cohen, Stanley (1972) *Folk Devils and Moral Panics: the Creation of Mods and Rockers.* London: MacGibbon and Kee.

Cohen, Stanley (1979) Guilt, justice and tolerance: some old concepts for a new criminology, reprinted in Cohen (1988), pp. 114–46.

Cohen, Stanley (1981) Footprints in the sand: a further report on criminology and the sociology of deviance in Britain, reprinted in Cohen (1988), pp. 67–92.

Cohen, Stanley (1985) *Visions of Social Control: Crime, Punishment and Classification.* Cambridge: Polity Press.

Cohen, Stanley (1986a) Community control: to demystify or to reaffirm?, in Bianchi and van Swaaningen (eds), pp. 127–32.

Cohen, Stanley (1986b) Editorial, *Contemporary Crises,* 10 (1): 3–4.

Cohen, Stanley (1987) An interview with Maeve McMahon and Gail Kellough, *Canadian Criminology Forum,* 8, no. 2.

Cohen, Stanley (1988) *Against Criminology.* New Brunswick: Transaction.

Cohen, Stanley (1990) *Intellectual Scepticism and Political Commitment: the Case of Radical Criminology.* Amsterdam: Bonger Institute UvA.

Cohen, Stanley (1993) Human rights and crimes of the state: the culture of denial, *Australian and New Zealand Journal of Criminology,* 26: 97–115.

Cohen, Stanley (1994) Social control and the politics of reconstruction, in Nelken (ed.), pp. 63–88.

Cohen, Stanley and Taylor, Laurie (1972) *Psychological Survival: the Experience of Long-term Imprisonment.* Harmondsworth: Penguin.

Cohen, Stanley and Taylor, Laurie (1975) From psychopaths to outsiders, in Bianchi et al. (eds), pp. 3–33.

Cooper, Andrew, Hetherington, Rachael, Baistow, Karin, Pitts, John and Spriggs, Angela (1995) *Positive Child Protection: a View from Abroad.* Lyme Regis: Russell House.

Coornhert Liga (1980) *Rechtsomlegging.* Utrecht: Ars Aequi.

Coornhert Liga (1986) Toekomstig beleid, in *Plakkaat; bulletin van de Coornhert Liga,* August.

COPEL (1978) *Rebelión en las carceles.* Donostia/San Sebastián: Hordago.

COSYPE (1983) Mouvement des prisonniers: une nouvelle donne en Justice, *Journal du syndicat de la magistrature,* pp. 3–5.

COSYPE (1985) Pour le congrès sur l'abolition de la prison. Unpublished paper given at the 1985 International Conference on Prison Abolition, Amsterdam.

Currie, Elliot (1992) Retreating, minimalism, realism: three styles of reasoning on crime and drugs in the United States, in John Lowman and Brian MacLean (eds), *Realist Criminology.* Toronto: University of Toronto Press. pp. 88–97.

Currie, Elliot (1996) *Is America Really Winning the War on Crime and Should Britain Follow its Example?* London: NACRO.

Davis, Mike (1992) Beyond *Blade Runner:* urban control and the ecology of fear, *Open Magazine,* 23 (28): 1–21.

Deleuze, Gilles and Guattari, Félix (1972) Anti-oedipus: Capitalism and Schizophrenia. Minneapolis: University of Minnesota Press (English edn 1983).

Dijk, Jan J.M. van (1981) Verschillen en overeenkomsten tussen praktische en academische criminologie, Justitiële Verkenningen, 7: 3–24.

Dijk, Jan J.M. van (1989) Penal sanctions and the process of civilization, International Annals of Criminology, 27: 191–204.

Dijk, Jan J.M. van, Haffmans, Charles, Rüter, Frits, Schutte, Julian and Stolwijk, Simon (eds) (1986) Criminal Law in Action: an Overview of Current Issues in Western Societies. Arnhem: Gouda Quint.

Doelder, Hans de (1991) Een toekomstvisie op ons gerechtelijk vooronderzoek, Nederlands Juristen Blad, 9: 353–9.

Doelder, Hans de and Hart, August 't (1993) Vertrouwenscrisis, Nederlands Juristen Blad, 68 (16): 604.

Donzelot, Jacques (1975) The prison movement in France, in Bianchi et al. (eds), pp. 109–15.

Donzelot, Jacques (1984) L'invention du social: essai sur le déclin des passions politiques. Paris: Fayard.

Downes, David (1988a) Contrasts in Tolerance: Post-war Penal Policy in The Netherlands and England and Wales. Oxford: Clarendon Press.

Downes, David (1988b) The sociology of crime and social control in Britain 1960–1987, in Rock (ed.), pp. 45–57.

Downes, David and Morgan, Rod (1994) 'Hostages to fortune'? The politics of law and order in post-war Britain, in Maguire et al. (eds), pp. 183–232.

Downes, David and Rock, Paul (eds) (1979) Deviant Interpretations: Problems in Criminology. Oxford: Clarendon Press.

Downes, David and Rock, Paul (1988) Understanding Deviance: a Guide to the Sociology of Crime and Rule Breaking. Oxford: Clarendon Press.

Drayer, Elma and Josten, Marc (1993) Hirsch Ballins boodschap: jonge rechters reageren lauw op de tijdgeest, Vrij Nederland, 54 (14): 22–5.

Drogt, Annemieke (1990) Het ontstaan en de ontwikkeling van de Coornhert Liga: heeft de Coornhert Liga invloed gehad op het strafrechtelijk klimaat in Nederland? Unpublished thesis, Utrecht: Willem Pompe Instituut voor Strafrechtswetenschappen.

Dronfield, Liz (1980) Outside Chance: the Story of the Newham Alternatives Project. London: RAP.

Duff, Antony, Marshall, Sandra, Dobash-Emerson, Rebecca and Dobash, Russell P. (eds) (1994) Penal Theory and Practice: Tradition and Innovation in Criminal Justice. Manchester: Manchester University Press.

Durieux, Hugo (1984) Op zoek naar een linkse law and order politiek, KRI, 14, no. 3.

Engelhardt, Knut (1975) Neue Perspektiven der Gefangenenbewegung, Kritische Justiz, 4: 357–70.

Ericson, Richard and Carriere, Kevin (1994) The fragmentation of criminology, in Nelken (ed.), pp. 89–109.

European Group for the Study of Deviance and Social Control (1975) Manifesto, Crime and Social Justice, 2: 47.

Faccioli, Franco (1984) Il sociologo e la criminalità: riflessioni sulle origini della criminologia critica in Italia, Dei delitti e delle pene, 1 (1): 602–42.

Falandysz, Lech (1991) Abolitionism between necessity and utopia, Lasocik et al. (eds), pp. 16–20.

Faugeron, Claude (1981) Les conditions de la recherche en sociologie de la déviance et du contrôle sociale en France, in Brusten and Ponsaers (eds), pp. 130–9.

Feeley, Malcolm and Simon, Jonathan (1992) The new penology: notes on the emerging strategy of corrections and its implications, Criminology, 30 (4): 449–74.

Feeley, Malcolm and Simon, Jonathan (1994) Actuarial justice: the emerging new criminal law, in Nelken (ed.) pp. 173–201.

Feest, Johannes (1984) Kritik des 'realen Abolitionismus', Kriminologisches Journal, 16: 229–31.

Feest, Johannes and Wegner-Brandt, Elke (1993) Musterprozesse um 'Musterbegründungen', in Papendorf and Schumann (eds), pp. 195–214.

Ferrajoli, Luigi (1983) Il caso '7 aprile'; lineamenti di un processo inquisitorio, *Dei delitti e delle pene,* 1 (1): 167–205.

Ferrajoli, Luigi (1989) *Diritto e ragione: teoria del garantismo penale.* Bari: Laterza.

Ferrajoli, Luigi and Zolo, Danilo (1977) Marxismo e questione criminale, *La questione criminale,* 3 (1): 97–133.

Fijnaut, Cyrille J.C.F. (1979) *Opdat de macht een toevlucht zij? Een historische studie van het politie-apparaat als politieke instelling.* Antwerpen: Kluwer.

Fijnaut, Cyrille J.C.F. (1984a) Die Fiktion einer integrierten Strafrechtswissenschaft gegen das Ende des vergangenen Jahrhunderts, *Zeitschrift für die gesamte Strafrechtswissenschaft,* 96 (1): 135–70.

Fijnaut, Cyrille J.C.F. (1984b) G.A. van Hamel: een behoudend strafrechtshervormer, *Delikt & delinkwent,* 14 (1): 8–24.

Fijnaut, Cyrille J.C.F. (1986a) *Verleden, heden en toekomst van de geïntegreerde strafrechtsweten-schap.* Arnhem/Antwerp: Gouda Quint/Kluwer.

Fijnaut, Cyrille J.C.F. (1986b) Het Leidse strafrechtelijke en criminologisch instituut, in ter Hoeven et al. (eds), pp. 75–87.

Fijnaut, Cyrille J.C.F. (1986c) In de klem der verdeeldheid, in J.P. Balkema (ed.), *Gedenkboek 100 jaar wetboek van strafrecht.* Arnhem: Gouda Quint, pp. 125–56.

Fijnaut, Cyrille J.C.F., Moerland, Hans and Beijerse, Jolande uit (1991) *Een winkelboulevard in problemen: samenleving en criminaliteit in twee Rotterdamse buurten.* Arnhem: Gouda Quint.

Fijnaut, Cyrille J.C.F. and Spierenburg, Pieter (eds) (1990) *Scherp Toezicht: van Boeventucht tot Samenleving en Criminaliteit.* Arnhem: Gouda Quint.

Finstad, Liv (1990) Sexual offenders out of prison: principles for a realistic utopia, *International Journal of the Sociology of Law,* 18 (2): 157–77.

Fiselier, Jan P.S. (1976) Bonger over vermogenscriminaliteit, *Nederlands Tijdschrift voor Criminologie,* 18: 160–73.

Fitzgerald, Mike (1977) *Prisoners in Revolt.* Harmondsworth: Penguin.

Fitzgerald, Mike and Sim, Joe (1982) *British Prisons.* Oxford: Blackwell.

Fitzpatrick, Peter and Hunt, Alan (eds) (1987) *Critical Legal Studies.* Oxford: Blackwell.

Folter, Rolf J. de (ed.) (1979) *Fenomenologie, kriminologie en recht.* Assen: Van Gorcum.

Folter, Rolf J. de (1987) *Normaal en abnormaal: enkele beschouwingen over het probleem van de normaliteit in het denken van Husserl, Schütz en Foucault.* Groningen: Historische Uitgeverij.

Foqué, René M.G.E. (1995) Het gedoogbeleid en de opportuniteit van de rechtsstaat, *Justitiële Verkenningen,* 21 (8): 48–64.

Foqué, René M.G.E. and 't Hart, August C. (1990) *Instrumentaliteit en rechtsbescherming; grond-slagen van een strafrechtelijke waardendiscussie.* Arnhem/Antwerp: Gouda Quint/Kluwer.

Foqué, René M.G.E. and Piret, Jean-Marc (1993) De moderniteit van het strafrecht en de figuratie van het algemeen belang, in Nijboer (ed.), pp. 207–18.

Foqué, René M.G.E. and Zijderveld, Anton (1994) De kwetsbare rechtsstaat; over de ruimte van recht en macht in een pluralistische cultuur, in Foqué et al. (eds), pp. 291–316.

Foqué, René M.G.E., Ladan, Rudolph, Rood-Pijpers, Elly B.M. and Zijderveld, Anton (eds) (1994) *Geïntegreerde rechtswetenschap.* Arnhem: Gouda Quint.

Foucault, Michel (1975a) *Discipline and Punish: the Birth of the Prison.* New York: Vintage (English edn 1979).

Foucault, Michel (1975b) Prison talk: an interview with J.J. Brochier, in Colin Gordon (ed.), *Michel Foucault Power/Knowledge.* London: Harvester (English edn 1980), pp. 37–54.

Foucault, Michel (1975c) Sur la selette: entretien avec J.L. Ezine, *Les nouvelles littéraires,* 17 March 1975, p. 3.

Franke, Herman (1990) *Twee eeuwen gevangen: misdaad en straf in Nederland.* Utrecht: Spectrum.

Frenkel, Frits E. (ed.) (1966) *Provo: kanttekeningen bij een deelverschijnsel.* Amsterdam: Polak and Van Gennep.

Galenkamp, Marlies (1993) Seyla Benhabib: feitelijke inbedding en liberale distantie, in van Klink et al. (eds), pp. 297–310.

Gallo, Ermanno and Ruggiero, Vincenzo (1989) *Il carcere immateriale.* Torino: Sonda. (Summarised in English as 'The immaterial prison: custody as a factory for the manufacture of handicaps', *The International Journal of the Sociology of Law,* 19 (3): 273–91.

Galtung, Johan (1977) *Imperialismus und Strukturelle Gewalt: Analysen über abhängige Reproduktion.* (German edn by Dieter Senghaas) Frankfurt am Main: Suhrkamp.

Garland, David (1985) *Punishment and Welfare: a History of Penal Strategies.* Aldershot: Gower.

Garland, David (1988) British criminology before 1935, in Rock (ed.), pp. 1–18.

Garland, David (1990) *Punishment and Modern Society: a Study in Social Theory.* Oxford: Oxford University Press.

Garland, David (1992) Criminological knowledge and its relation to power: Foucault's genealogy and criminology today, *British Journal of Criminology,* 32 (4): 403–22.

Garland, David (1994) Of crimes and criminals: the development of criminology in Britain, in Maguire et al. (eds), pp. 17–68.

Garland, David (1995) The decline of the rehabilitative ideal? Rethinking recent penal history. Paper presented to a Howard League Seminar in Edinburgh Prison, 22 February 1995.

Gianformaggio, Letizia (ed.) (1993) *Le ragioni del garantismo: discutendo con Luigi Ferrajoli.* Torino: Giappichelli.

Giménez-Salinas i Colomer, Esther (1991) Spain, in Dirk van Zyl Smit and Frieder Dünkel (eds), *Imprisonment Today and Tomorrow: International Perspectives on Prisoners' Rights and Prison Conditions.* Deventer: Kluwer, pp. 567–98.

Gottfredson, Michael and Hirschi, Travis (1990) *A General Theory of Crime.* Stanford: Stanford University Press.

Gouldner, Alvin (1970) *The Coming Crisis in Western Sociology.* New York: Basic Books.

Gradisen, Willem (1988) Het congres te Berlijn in 1935: een confrontatie met het nationaal-socialistische strafrecht, *Recht en kritiek,* 14 (4): 364–80.

Groenhuijsen, Marc S. and Landen, Dirk van der (eds.) (1990) *De moderne richting in het strafrecht: theorie, praktijk, latere ontwikkelingen en actuele betekenis.* Arnhem: Gouda Quint.

Guerini, Umberto and Tagliarini, Francesco (1975) Esigenze di politica criminale e dibattito elettorale, *La questione criminale,* 2: 339–51; 3: 517–33.

Gunning, Marjet, Kelk, Constantijn and Schuyt, Kees (1993) Voorwoord, in Peters (ed.), pp. 5–8.

Gunther Moor, Lodewijk and Leuw, Ed (eds) (1978) *Beslissingsmomenten in het strafrechtelijk systeem.* Utrecht: Ars Aequi.

Haan, Willem J.M. de (1988) Bianchi's bevrijdingscriminologie: een terreinverkenning in het spanningsveld tussen links realisme en utopisme, in van Swaaningen et al. (eds), pp. 57–77.

Haan, Willem J.M. de (1989) *Structurele determinanten van onveiligheid.* Den Haag: Sdu.

Haan, Willem J.M. de (1990) *The Politics of Redress: Crime, Punishment and Penal Abolition.* London: Unwin Hyman.

Haan, Willem J.M. de (1991) Abolitionism and crime control: a contradiction in terms, in Stenson and Cowell (eds), pp. 203–18.

Haan, Willem J.M. de (1993) *Beroving van voorbijgangers.* The Hague: Ministry of the Interior.

Haan, Willem J.M. de (1995) Integrale veiligheid: beleidsvernieuwing of beleidsvervaging?, *Justitiële Verkenningen,* 21 (5): 25–48.

Haan, Willem J.M. de and Swaaningen, René van (1995) Integrale veiligheid en justitiële moralisering: een reactie, *Justitiële Verkenningen,* 21 (8): 89–92.

Habermas, Jürgen (1968) Erkenntnis und Interesse, in *Technik und Wissenschaft als Ideologie.* Frankfurt am Main: Suhrkamp, pp. 146–64.

Habermas, Jürgen (1973) *Legitimationsprobleme im Spätkapitalismus.* Frankfurt am Main: Suhrkamp.

Habermas, Jürgen (1981) *Theorie des kommunikativen Handelns,* 2 vols. Frankfurt am Main: Suhrkamp.

Habermas, Jürgen (1988) *Recht en moraal; twee voordrachten* (in English as *The Tanner Lectures on Human Values*). Kampen/Kapellen: Kok Agora/DNB Pelckmans.

Hacking, Ian (1981) How should we do a history of statistics?, *Ideology and Consciousness,* pp. 33–42.

Haferkamp, Hans (1984) Herrschaftsverlust und Sanktionsverzicht; kritische Bemerkungen zur Theorie des starken Staates, der neuen sozialen Kontrolle und des ideellen Abolitionismus, *Kriminologisches Journal,* 16: 112–31.

Hall, Stuart (1988) *The Hard Road to Renewal: Thatcherism and the Crisis of the Left.* London: Verso.

Hall, Stuart, Critcher, Chas, Jefferson, Tony, Clarke, John and Roberts, Brian (1978) *Policing the Crisis: Mugging, the State, and Law and Order.* London: Macmillan.

Hamel, Gerard A. van (1880) *De grenzen der heerschappij van het strafrecht.* Amsterdam: Van Kampen.

Hamel, Gerard A. van (1890) De tegenwoordige beweging op het gebied van het strafrecht, in *Verspreide opstellen.* Leiden: Brill, 1912, vol. 1, pp. 523–51.

Hanak, Gerhard, Stehr, Johannes and Steinert, Heinz (1989) *Ärgernisse und Lebenskatastrophen; über den alltäglichen Umgang mit Kriminalität.* Bielefeld: AJZ.

Hart, August C 't (1993) *Totale instituties en het totalitaire.* Arnhem: Gouda Quint.

Hart, August C 't (1994) *Openbaar Ministerie en rechtshandhaving: een verkenning.* Arnhem: Gouda Quint.

Hartmann, Arthur and Russen Groen, Peter van (1994) Van strafrecht naar bestuursstrafrecht: de derde decriminaliseringsgolf?, in Moerings (ed.), pp. 145–63.

Hattum, W.F.C. van (1975) Afschaffing van de gevangenisstraf, *Balans,* 8: 29–33.

Hebberecht, Patrick (1984) De kriminologische wetenschap en de studie van de primaire kriminaliseringsprocessen: een overzicht en bespreking van het theoretisch en empirisch onderzoek van de primaire kriminaliseringsprocessen. Unpublished thesis, University of Ghent.

Hebberecht, Patrick, Hofman, Hans, Philippeth, Koen and Colle, Peter (1991) *Een buurtgericht onderzoek naar criminaliteit, onveiligheid en preventie.* Bruges: Vandenbroele.

Heerikhuizen, Bart van (1987) *W.A. Bonger: socioloog en socialist.* Groningen: Wolters Noordhoff.

Heide, Jack ter (1965) *Vrijheid: over de zin de straf.* The Hague: Bert Bakker.

Henry, Stuart and Milovanovic, Dragan (1996) *Constitutive Criminology: Beyond Postmodernism.* London: Sage.

Hess, Henner and Steinert, Heinz (1986) Kritische Kriminologie: zwölf Jahre danach, *Kriminologisches Journal,* 18 (1): Beiheft, 2–9.

Hess, Henner, Moerings, Martin, Pass, Dieter, Scheerer, Sebastian and Steinert, Heinz (1988) *Angriff auf das Herz des Staates; soziale Entwicklung und Terrorismus.* Frankfurt am Main: Suhrkamp.

Hillyard, Paddy and Percy-Smith, Janie (1988) *The Coercive State: the Decline of Democracy in Britain.* London: Fontana.

Hirsch Ballin, Ernst M.H. (1993) Normhandhaving en rechtsbescherming. Lecture to the Congress of Judges in Training, The Hague, 1 April 1993 (elaborated version published as 'Publieke Moraal en Recht', *Justitiële Verkenningen,* 19 (2): 9–28).

Hirst, Paul Q. (1975) Marx and Engels on Law, Crime and Morality, and Radical deviancy theory: a reply to Taylor and Walton, in Taylor et al. (eds), pp. 203–32, 238–44.

Hoefnagels, G. Peter (1969) *Beginselen van criminologie.* Deventer: Kluwer. (In English as *The Other Side of Criminology: an Inversion of the Concept of Crime.* Deventer: Kluwer, 1973).

Hoefnagels, G. Peter (1975) Criminologie, fenomenologie en de Utrechtse School, *Nederlands Tijdschrift voor Criminologie,* 17: 3–14.

Hoefnagels, G. Peter (1977) *Rituelen ter terechtzitting.* Deventer: Kluwer.

Hoeven, Guus J.A. ter, Overeem, Ruurd, Hogenhuis, Stijn F.H.M. and Rood-Pijpers, Elly B.M. (eds) (1986) *Bezonnen Hoop.* Zwolle: Tjeenk Willink.

Hoogenboom, Bob (1994) *Het politiecomplex: over de samenwerking tussen reguliere politie, bijzondere opsporingsdiensten en particuliere recherche.* Arnhem: Gouda Quint.

Hoogenboom, Bob (1995) Pandora's doos: tien jaar SeC en particuliere beveiliging, *Justitiële Verkenningen,* 21 (3): 88–101.

Howe, Adrian (1994) *Punish and Critique: Towards a Feminist Analysis of Penality.* London: Routledge.

Hudson, Barbara A. (1993) *Penal Policy and Social Justice.* Basingstoke: Macmillan.

Hulsman, Louk H.C. (1965a) *Handhaving van recht.* Deventer: Kluwer.

Hulsman, Louk H.C. (1965b) Strafrecht en gerechtigheid, *Te Elfder Ure,* 12 (2): 60–5.

Hulsman, Louk H.C. (1967) Frustratie en justitie, in *Overheid en frustratie.* Deventer: Kluwer, pp. 63–77.

Hulsman, Louk H.C. (1968) Links en rechts in het recht, in H.G.M. Derks (ed.), *Anatomie van links*. Amsterdam: Polak & van Gennip.

Hulsman, Louk H.C. (1969) Straftoemeting, in Ch.J. Enschedé, L.H.C. Hulsman and G.E. Langemeijer (eds), *Straf*. Baarn: Bosch & Keunig, pp. 61–119.

Hulsman, Louk H.C. (1971) Reclassering en strafrecht, in F. van Rossen (ed.), *Menswetenschappen*. Amsterdam: Psychiatrisch Juridisch Gezelschap, pp. 64–79.

Hulsman, Louk H.C. (1972) Kriteria voor strafbaarstelling, in Eric André de la Porte (ed.) *Strafrecht terecht? Over dekriminalisering en depenalisering*, Baarn: Anthos, pp. 80–92.

Hulsman, Louk H.C. (1975) Défense sociale nouvelle et critères de décriminalisation, in *Aspects nouveaux de la pensée juridique: recueil d'études et hommage à Marc Ancel, II*. Paris: Pedone, pp. 19–33.

Hulsman, Louk H.C. (1986) Critical criminology and the concept of crime, in Bianchi and van Swaaningen (eds), pp. 25–41.

Hulsman, Louk H.C. and Bernat de Celis, Jacqueline (1982) *Peines perdues: le système pénal en question*. Paris: Le Centurion. (In Dutch as *Afscheid van het strafrecht: een pleidooi voor zelfregulering*. Houten: Wereldvenster, 1986.)

Hulsman, Louk H.C. and Nijboer, Hans F. (1993) Criminal justice system, in Jeroen Chorus, Piet-Hein Gerver, Ewoud Hondius and Alis Koekkoek (eds), *Introduction to Dutch Law for Foreign Lawyers*. Deventer: Kluwer, pp. 309–58.

Humphries, Drew (1974) Report on the conference of the EGSDSC, *Crime & Social Justice*, 1: 11–17.

Hunink, Maria, Kloosterman, Jaap and Rogier, Jan (eds) (1979) *Voor Arthur Lehning*. Baarn: Het Wereldvenster.

Iani, Luca (1994) La criminologia critica in Italia: origini, sviluppi e prospettive future. Unpublished 'laurea' thesis, Rome: Facoltà di psicologia, Università La Sapienza.

Invernizzi, Irene (1975) Class struggle in the prisons: practical and theoretical problems, in Bianchi et al. (eds), pp. 129–32.

Janse de Jonge, Han (1985) David Simons, (1860–1930): advocaat van vrijheid en humaniteit, *Delikt en delinkwent*, 15: 306–26.

Janse de Jonge, Han (1991) *Om de persoon van de dader: over straftheorieën en voorlichting door de reclassering*. Arnhem: Gouda Quint.

Janse de Jonge, Han, Prakken, Ties and Roos, Theo de (1983) Action and law in The Netherlands, *Contemporary Crises*, 7: 113–33.

Janssen, Otto and Swierstra, Koert (1980) *Heroïnegebruikers in Nederland: een typologie van levensstijlen*. Groningen: Kriminologies Instituut RUG.

Jones, Trevor, MacLean, Brian and Young, Jock (1986) *The Islington Crime Survey: Crime, Victimisation and Policing in Inner-city London*. Aldershot: Gower.

Jonge, Gerard de (1990) De Coornhert Liga: een beschaafd luisje in de pels van justitie, *Proces*, 69 (9): 242–50.

Jonge, Gerard de (1994) *Strafwerk: over de arbeidsverhouding tussen gedetineerden en Justitie*. Breda: Papieren Tijger.

Jonge, Gerard de and Verpalen, Rino J.M. (1992) *Bajesboek: handboek voor gedetineerden en ter beschikking gestelden*. Breda: Papieren Tijger.

Jonge, Gerard de, Knap, Job, Michel, Marijke, Mols, Gerard, Rombouts, Petra, Simons, William, Verpalen, Rino, Verrijn Stuart, Heikelien, Vries, Teun de and Vrijdaghs, Constance (1983) *Alternatieve Justitiebegroting 1984*. Maastricht: Coornhert Liga.

Jonge, Gerard de, Mols, Gerard and Vliet, Annelies van (eds) (1989) *Coornhert Liga crimineel jaarboek 87–88*. Breda: Papieren Tijger.

Jongman, Riekent W. (ed.) (1978) *Klasse-elementen in de rechtsgang*. Groningen: Kriminologies Instituut.

Jongman, Riekent W. (ed.) (1993) *De armen van vrouwe justitia: sociale positie, criminaliteit en justitiële reacties*. Nijmegen: Ars Aequi.

Jongman, Riekent W. and Timmerman, Harrie (1985) Criminaliteit als verzet: motivatie en remmingen, *Tijdschrift voor Criminologie*, 27: 303–19.

Jongman, Riekent, Drost, Thea and Schilt, Taco (1977) Het klasse-effect; verschuiving van de discusie naar methodologische strijdpunten, *Nederlands Tijdschrift voor Criminologie*, 19: 165–82.

Kaiser, Günther (1976) Was ist eigentlich kritisch an der 'kritischen Kriminologie'?, in G. Warda et al. (eds), *Festschrift für Richard Lange zum 70. Geburtstag*. Berlin: de Gruyter, pp. 521–39.

Kalmthout, Anton van (1990) De moderne richting en het Nederlandse sanctiestelsel, in Groenhuijsen and van der Landen (eds), pp. 195–221.

Kelk, Constantijn (1978) *Recht voor gedetineerden: een onderzoek naar de beginselen van het detentierecht*. Alphen a/d Rijn: Samsom.

Kelk, Constantijn (1988) Bianchi's belligerente bespiegelingen over strafrecht en penologie, in van Swaaningen et al. (eds), pp. 33–57.

Kelk, Constantijn, Moerings, Martin, Jörg, Nico and Moedikdo, Paul (eds) (1976) *Recht, Macht en Manipulatie*. Utrecht: Spectrum.

Kempe, Ger Th. (1947) *Misdaad en wangedrag voor, tijdens en na den oorlog: opstellen over criminologie*. Amsterdam: Querido.

Kempe, Ger Th. (1950) *Schuldig zijn*. Utrecht: Dekker & van de Vegt.

Kempe, Ger Th. (1952) Criminologie in existentialistische doorlichting, *Tijdschrift voor Strafrecht*, 61: 166–86.

Kempe, Ger Th. (1963) De criminoloog en het werk van de strafrechter, *Tijdschrift voor Strafrecht*, 62: 279–92.

Kempe, Ger Th. (1964) Recensie Ethiek van het straffen, *Maandblad voor berechting en reclassering* 43: 194–5.

Kempe, Ger Th. (1967) *Inleiding tot de criminologie*. Haarlem: Bohn.

Kempe, Ger Th. (1968a) Franz von Liszt en de criminologie, *Mededelingen KNAW*, 31 (3): 64–83.

Kempe, Ger Th. (1968b) Herdenking Willem Petrus Joseph Pompe 10 maart 1893–26 juli 1968, *Jaarboek KNAW 1968–1969*. Amsterdam: Noordhollandsche Uitgeversmij.

Kempe, Ger Th. (1975) De publieke opinie en de strafrechter in de laatste halve eeuw; enkele inleidende opmerkingen, in *Dilemma's in het hedendaagse strafrecht*. Utrecht: Ars Aequi, pp. 5–22.

Kempe, Ger Th. (1976) Uitvoerder of kruisvaarder?, in Kelk et al. (eds), pp. 47–66.

Kerchove, Michel van de (1987) *Le droit sans peines: aspect de la dépénalisation en Belgique et aux États-Unis*. Brussels: Publications des Facultés Universitaires Saint Louis, no. 41.

Kerner, Hans-Jürgen and Schumann, Karl F. (1974) Einführung zum kritischen Kriminologie: zur Grundlegung eines kritischen Ansatzes in der Kriminologie, in AJK (1974a), pp. 7–14.

Kerruish, Valerie (1991) *Jurisprudence as Ideology*. London: Routledge.

Kinsey, Richard, Lea, John and Young, Jock (1986) *Losing the Fight against Crime*. Oxford: Blackwell.

Klink, Bart van, Seters, Paul van and Witteveen, Willem (eds) (1993) *Gedeelde normen?: gemeenschapdenken en het recht*. Zwolle: Tjeenk Willink, pp. 111–22.

Koppen, Peter J. van (1994) Groninger zwanezang, *Tijdschrift voor Criminologie*, 36 (3): 264–71.

Kosto, Aad (1993) Proloog, in Nijboer (ed.), pp. 17–25.

Laan, Peter H. van der (1993) Het publiek en de taakstraf: een maatschappelijk draagvlak voor de taakstraf, *Justitiële Verkenningen*, 19 (9): 89–110.

Lagrange, Hugues and Zauberman, Renée (eds) (1991) L'insécurité urbaine et les politiques local, *Déviance et société*, 15, no. 3 (special issue).

Lambrechts, Mark (1982) *Foucault: excerpten en kritieken*. Nijmegen: Socialistiese Uitgeverij.

Lapis, Teresa (1981) The political economy of the development of Italian criminology, in Brusten and Ponsaers (eds), pp. 155–76.

Larrauri i Pijoan, Elena (1991) *La herencia de la criminología crítica*. Madrid: Siglo Veintiuno.

Larrauri i Pijoan, Elena (ed.) (1994) *Mujeres, derecho penal y criminología*. Madrid: Siglo Veintiuno.

Lasocik, Zbigniew, Platek, Monika and Rzeplinska, Irena (eds) (1991) *Abolitionism in History: on Another Way of Thinking*. Warsaw: Uniwersytetu Warszawskiego.

Lea, John (1987) Left realism: a defence, *Contemporary Crises*, 11 (4): 357–70.

Lea, John (1994) Criminology and postmodernity. Paper presented to the Common Study Programme on Criminal Justice and Critical Criminology, Barcelona, November.

Lea, John and Young, Jock (1984) *What is to be Done about Law and Order? Crisis in the Eighties.* Harmondsworth: Penguin.

Lea, John, Matthews, Roger and Young, Jock (1987) *Law and Order: Five Years on.* London: Middlesex Centre for Criminology.

Léauté, Jacques (ed.) (1959) *Une nouvelle école de science criminelle: l'école d'Utrecht.* Paris: Cujas.

Leo, Gaetano de (1986) Il crimine come problema e la sua spiegazione; nuovo realismo e oltre, *Dei delitti e delle pene,* 3: 453–68.

Leo, Gaetano de and Salvini, Alessandro (1978) *Normalità e devianza: processi scientifici e istituzionali nella costruzione della personalità deviante.* Milano: Mazzota.

Lilly, J. Robert, Cullen, Francis and Ball, Richard A. (1989) *Criminological Theory.* London: Sage.

Lippens, Ronny (1995) Verhalen uit de oude doos; enige beschouwingen over kritische criminologieën en de verdoezelde nood aan hernieuwde utopische visies, *Recht en kritiek,* 21 (1): 38–61.

Lissenberg, Ellie (1989) *Verlagen en verheffen.* Alphen a/d Rijn: Samsom.

Liszt, Franz von (1905) Der Zweckgedanke im Strafrecht, in *Strafrechtliche Aufsätze und Vorträge.* Berlin: Gutentag.

Lüderssen, Klaus (1980) Kollektive Zurechnung – individualisierende Haftung: ein Grundwiderspruch der modernen Kriminalpolitik?, in Lüderssen and Sack (eds), pp. 737–52.

Lüderssen, Klaus and Sack, Fritz (eds) (1980) *Einleitung zu Vom Nutzen und Nachteil der Sozialwissenschaften für das Strafrecht.* Frankfurt am Main: Suhrkamp.

Lyotard, Jean François (1986) *Le postmoderne expliqué aux enfants: correspondance 1982–1985.* Paris: Galilée.

Macey, David (1993) *The Lives of Michel Foucault.* London: Hutchinson.

Machielse, Ad J. (1979) Défense sociale, *Tijdschrift voor Criminologie,* 21 (2): 67–82.

McMahon, Maeve W. (1992) *The Persistent Prison? Rethinking Decarceration and Penal Reform.* Toronto: University of Toronto Press.

Maguire, Mike, Morgan, Rod and Reiner, Robert (eds) (1994) *The Oxford Handbook of Criminology.* Oxford: Clarendon Press.

Marcuse, Herbert (1969) *An Essay on Liberation.* Boston: Beacon Press.

Marti, Oriol (1977) La COPEL: história de una lucha silenciada, *El Viejo Topo,* 13: 35–8.

Mathiesen, Thomas (1965) *The Defences of the Weak: a Social Study of a Norwegian Correctional Institution.* London: Tavistock.

Mathiesen, Thomas (1974) *The Politics of Abolition.* Oslo: Universitetsforlaget.

Mathiesen, Thomas (1986) The politics of abolition, *Contemporary Crises,* 10 (1): 81–94.

Mathiesen, Thomas (1990) KROM: Norwegian association for penal reform. Paper presented at the 18th Annual Conference of the European Group for the Study of Deviance and Social Control, Haarlem, The Netherlands, 7 September.

Mathiesen, Thomas and Røine, Wiggo (1975) The prison movement in Scandinavia, in Bianchi et al. (eds), pp. 85–97.

Matthews, Roger (1987) Decarceration and social control: fantasies and realities, in John Lowman et al. (eds), *Transcarceration: Essays in the Sociology of Social Control.* Aldershot: Gower.

Matthews, Roger and Young, Jock (eds) (1986) *Confronting Crime.* London: Sage.

Matthews, Roger and Young, Jock (1992) Reflections on realism, in Young and Matthews (eds), pp. 1–23.

Melossi, Dario (1985) The crisis in critical criminology: toward a grounded labeling theory, *Criminology,* 23: 193–208.

Melossi, Dario (1990) *The State of Social Control: a Sociological Study of Concepts of State and Social Control in the Making of Democracy.* Cambridge: Polity Press.

Melossi, Dario (1991a) Ideologia e diritto penale; garantismo giuridico e criminologia critica come nuove ideologie della subalternità?, *Dei delitti e delle pene,* 1: 15–35.

Melossi, Dario (1991b) Weak Leviathan and strong democracy: or two styles of social control. Paper presented at the Law and Society Conference in Amsterdam, 26–29 June.

Melossi, Dario (1996) Social control in the new Europe. Paper given at the Crime and Social Order Conference at the University of Manchester, 7–10 September.

Miralles, Teresa and Muñagorri, Ignacio (1982) State control and internal security in Spain 1978–1981, in Squires and Hillyard (eds), pp. 161–87.

Moedikdo, Paul (1974) *Sociologie en recht: over hedendaagse opvattingen betreffende het strafrecht en hun maatschappelijke betekenis.* Meppel: Boom.

Moedikdo, Paul (1976) De Utrechtse school van Pompe, Baan en Kempe, in Kelk et al. (eds), pp. 90–155.

Moerings, Martin (1977) *De gevangenis uit, de maatschappij in: de gevangenisstraf en haar betekenis voor de sociale kontakten van ex-gedetineerden.* Alphen a/d Rijn: Samsom.

Moerings, Martin (1983) Protest in The Netherlands: developments in a pillarised society, *Contemporary Crises,* 7 (2): 95–113.

Moerings, Martin (1989) Terrorisme: een serieus probleem voor Nederland?, *Tijdschrift voor Criminologie,* 4: 357–78.

Moerings, Martin (ed.) (1994) *Hoe punitief is Nederland?* Arnhem: Gouda Quint.

Moerland, Hans and Kneepkens, Manuel (1975) *Welzijn en justitie: alternatieve justitiebegroting Coornhert Liga 1976.* Utrecht: Ars Aequi.

Mooney, Jayne (1996) Violence, space and gender in a European context. Paper presented to the Crime and Social Order Conference at the University of Manchester, 7–10 September.

Mosconi, Giuseppe (1978) Diritto ed istituzioni tra razionalizzazione e lotta di classe, *La questione criminale,* 4 (1): 177–95.

Nagel, Willem H. (pseudonym J.B. Charles) (1953) *Volg het spoor terug.* Amsterdam: De Bezige Bij.

Nagel, Willem H. (1956) *Het strafrecht en de onmens.* The Hague: Bert Bakker.

Nagel, Willem H. (1958) Sociologische criminologie, *Sociologisch Jaarboek,* 12: 58–109.

Nagel, Willem H. (pseudonym J.B. Charles) (1962) *Van het kleine koude front.* Amsterdam: De Bezige Bij.

Nagel, Willem H. (1965) *Het voorspellen van krimineel gedrag; een rapport uitgebracht aan het Ministerie van Justitie.* The Hague: Staatsuitgeverij.

Nagel, Willem H. (1974) Politiek en kriminologie, in G. Peter Hoefnagels (ed.), *Waarde, macht, kriminologie – studium generale Rotterdam,* no. 3. The Hague: Martinus Nijhof, pp. 3–24.

Nagel, Willem H. (1975) De Dialektiek; 'jouw vrijheid/mijn vrijheid' in de nationale rechtsorde en in de 'orden' van de subkulturen, in J. Th. J. van den Berg (ed.), *Praesidium Libertatis.* Deventer: Kluwer, pp. 167–77.

Nagel, Willem H. (1976) De tijd en de kriminoloog, re-published in *Het betrekkelijke van kriminaliteit.* Alphen a/d Rijn: Samsom, 1977.

Nagel, Willem H. (1981) De nieuwe Utrechtse School, in A. Justine Bins (ed.), *Beginselen; opstellen over strafrecht aangeboden aan G.E. Mulder.* Arnhem: Gouda Quint, pp. 207–25.

Naucke, Wolfgang (1982) Die Kriminalpolitik des Marburger Programms 1882, *Zeitschrift für die gesamte Strafrechtswissenschaft,* 94: 525–64.

Nelken, David (ed.) (1994a) *The Futures of Criminology.* London: Sage.

Nelken, David (1994b) Reflexive criminology?, in Nelken (ed.), pp. 7–42.

Nelken, David (1994c) Whom can you trust? The future of comparative criminology, in Nelken (ed.), pp. 220–43.

Neppi Modona, Guido (1976) Appunti per una storia parlamentare della riforma penitenziaria, *La questione criminale,* 2: 319–72.

Nijboer, Jan A. (ed.) (1993) *Criminaliteit als politiek probleem.* Arnhem: Gouda Quint.

Opp, Karl-Dieter (1972) Die 'alte' and die 'neue' Kriminalsoziologie; eine kritische Analyse einiger Thesen des labeling approach, *Kriminologisches Journal,* 4: 32–52.

Outrive, Lode van (1978) *De gevangenis: een systeem of drift.* Leuven: Davidsfonds.

Outrive, Lode van (1987) Hulsman's Abolitionism; the great reduction, in Blad et al. (eds), pp. 53–67.

Papendorf, Knut (1985) *Gesellschaft ohne Gitter: eine Absage an die traditionelle Kriminalpolitik.* Munich: AG SPAK.

Papendorf, Knut (1993) Ausgrabungen aus der bundesrepublikanischen aboli(tioni)stischen Frühzeit, in Papendorf and Schumann (eds), pp. 65–84.

Papendorf, Knut and Schumann, Karl F. (eds) (1993) *Kein schärfer Schwert, denn das für Freiheit streitet! Eine Festschrift für Thomas Mathiesen.* Bielefeld: AJZ.

Pavarini, Massimo (1985) Il sistema della giustizia penale tra riduzionismo e abolizionismo, *Dei delitti e delle pene,* 3 (3): 525–53.

Pavarini, Massimo (1994) The new penology and politics in crisis: the Italian case, *British Journal of Criminology,* 34: 49–61 (special issue).

Pavarini, Massimo (1995) Note sulle concezioni amministrative e tecnocratiche della penalità, *Dei delitti e delle pene,* 2nd series, 4 (3): 157–67.

Peters, Antonie A.G. (1972) Het rechtskarakter van het strafrecht, reprinted in Peters (1993), pp. 15–34.

Peters, Antonie A.G. (1976) Recht als vals bewustzijn, reprinted in Peters (1993), pp. 239–64.

Peters, Antonie A.G. (1979) Recht als project, reprinted in Peters (1993), pp. 265–88.

Peters, Antonie A.G. (1983a) Rechten van de mens: emancipatie van de mens, reprinted in Peters (1993), pp. 305–21.

Peters, Antonie A.G. (1983b) In memoriam professor mr W.H. Nagel, *Tijdschrift voor Criminologie,* 25: 161–72.

Peters, Antonie A.G. (1986) Main currents in criminal law theory, in van Dijk et al. (eds), pp. 19–36.

Peters, Antonie A.G. (1990) Strafrecht en beleid: de constitutionele dimensie, in Fijnaut and Spierenburg (eds), pp. 211–25.

Peters, Antonie A.G. (1993) *Recht als kritische discussie.* Arnhem: Gouda Quint.

Pisapia, Gianvittorio (1978) *Contributo ad un'analisi sociocriminologica della devianza.* Padua: CEDAM.

Pit, Klaas (1984) Clara Gertrud Wichmann, 1885–1922: de ontwikkeling van haar maatschappij-filosofische en politiek-theoretische denkbeelden vanaf 1916. Unpublished manuscript, Hilversum.

Pitch, Tamar (1975) *La devianze.* Florence: La Nuova Italia.

Pitch, Tamar (1983) Adequacy or obsolescence of the notion of deviancy, in Squires and Hillyard (eds), pp. 5–9.

Pitch, Tamar (1986) Viaggo attorno alla 'criminologia': discutendo con i realisti, in *Dei delitti e delle pene,* 3: 469–88.

Pitch, Tamar (1990) *Limited Responsibilities; Social Movements and Criminal Justice.* London: Routledge (English edn 1995).

Pitch, Tamar, Faccioli, Franca, Pia, Maria, Casarini, Maria, Trasforini, Antonietta and Graziosi, Marina (1983) Donne, devianza e controllo sociale, *Dei delitti e delle pene,* 1 (1): 91–166.

Pitts, John (1994) What can we learn in Europe? *Social Work in Europe,* 1 (1): 48–53.

Plack, Arno (1974) *Plädoyer für die Abschaffung des Strafrechts.* Munich: List.

Politoff, Sergio I. (1987) Decriminalisering en rechtsbescherming in wisselende contexten, *Recht en kritiek,* 13: 159–70.

Pompe, Willem P.J. (1928) *De persoon des daders in het strafrecht.* Utrecht: Dekker & van de Vegt.

Pompe, Willem P.J. (1940) Het eerste internationale congres voor criminologie te Rome 3–8 october 1938, *Tijdschrift voor Strafrecht,* 50: 131–60.

Pompe, Willem P.J. (1954) De misdadige mens, *Tijdschrift voor Strafrecht,* 62 (1): 152–71.

Pompe, Willem P.J. (1957) De mens in het strafrecht, *RM Themis,* 2: 88–109.

Pompe, Willem P.J. (1963) *Strafrecht en vertrouwen in de medemens.* Utrecht: Dekker & van de Vegt.

Pompe, Willem P.J. (1965) Recensie van Ethiek van het straffen, *Mens en maatschappij,* 40: 74–7.

Quensel, Stephan (1989) Krise der Kriminologie: Chancen für eine interdisziplinäre Renaissance?, *Kriminalsoziologische Bibliographie,* 16 (62): 1–31.

Radzinowicz, Leon (1966) *Ideology and Crime: a Study of Crime in its Social and Historical Context.* London: Heinemann.

Raes, Koen (1992) Grondrechten en sociale solidariteit: notities over de interdependenties tussen mensenrechten en morele verantwoordelijkheid, *Recht en kritiek,* 18 (2): 102–25.

Raes, Koen (1994) Contrafacticiteit en geldigheid: Habermas' discursieve rechtstheorie, *Recht en kritiek,* 20 (2): 93–110.

Raes, Koen (1995) De naakte samenleving; pleidooi voor een onpersoonlijke maar vertrouwde publieke cultuur, *Justitiële Verkenningen,* 21 (5): 62–95.

Rauty, Raffaele (1975) Introductory note to the prison revolts in Italy, in Bianchi et al. (eds), pp. 115–24.

Rauty, Raffaele (1976) Lotte carcerarie e problemi dell'informazione e delle riforma, *La questione criminale,* 2 (2): 471–88.

Reiwald, Paul (1947) *Die Gesellschaft und ihre Verbrecher.* Zürich: Pan.

Rijksen, Rijk (ed.) (1958) *Meningen van gedetineerden over de strafrechtspleging.* Assen: Van Gorcum.

Rivera Beiras, Iñaki (1993) La devaluación de los derechos fundamentales de los reclusos; la cárcel, los movimientos sociales y una cultura de la resistencia. Unpublished thesis, University of Barcelona.

Rivera Beiras, Iñaki (1994) El derecho de defensa y asisténcia letrada de los reclusos: ¿otro derecho de segunda categoría? Unpublished paper presented to Barcelona bar, 11 March.

Rivera Beiras, Iñaki (ed.) (1995) *La carcel en el sistema penal: un análisis estructural.* Barcelona: Bosch.

Robert, Philippe (1973) La sociologie entre une criminologie de passage à l'acte et une criminologie de la réaction sociale, *Année Sociologique,* 24: 441–504.

Robert, Philippe and Outrive, Lode van (eds) (1993) *Crime et justice en Europe: état des recherches, évaluations et recommandations.* Paris: L'Harmattan. (In English as *Research, Crime and Justice in Europe: an Assessment and Some Recommendations,* co-edited by Tony Jefferson and Joanna Shapland. Sheffield: Centre for Criminological and Research, 1995).

Rock, Paul (ed.) (1979) *A History of British Criminology.* Oxford: Oxford University Press.

Rock, Paul (ed.) (1994) *History of Criminology.* Aldershot: Dartmouth.

Rogier, Jan (1979) Aspecten van het weekblad De Vlam, in Hunink et al. (eds), pp. 377–419.

Röling, B.V.A. (1940) Boekbespreking, *Rechtsgeleerd Magazijn,* pp. 455–7.

Röling, B.V.A. (1942) Het criminologische werk van prof.dr. W.A. Bonger, *Tijdschrift voor Strafrecht,* 52: 89–114.

Rolston, Bill and Tomlinson, Mike (eds) (1986) *The Expansion of European Prison Systems.* Working paper no. 7, Belfast: EGSDSC.

Rolston, Bill and Tomlinson, Mike (eds) (1989) *Justice and Ideology: Strategies for the 1990s.* Working paper no. 9, Belfast: EGSDSC.

Rolston, Bill and Tomlinson, Mike (eds) (1990) *Gender, Sexuality and Social Control.* Working paper no. 10, Belfast: EGSDSC.

Rood-Pijpers, Elly B.M. (1988) *Mensen over misdaad en straf.* Arnhem: Gouda Quint.

Rood-Pijpers, Elly B.M. (1994) De plaats van strafrecht en criminologie in Recht in Beweging, in Foqué et al. (eds), pp. 317–39.

Rood-Pijpers, Elly B.M., Rovers, Ben, Gemert, Frank van and Fijnaut, Cyrille J.C.F (1995) *Preventie van jeugdcriminaliteit in een grote stad.* Arnhem: Gouda Quint.

Roos, J.R.B. de (1902) Het vijfde congres voor crimineele anthropologie, *Tijdschrift voor Strafrecht,* 12: 336–8.

Roos, J.R.B. de (1911) De ontwikkeling der crimineele aetiologie en hare betekenis voor de theorie en de practijk van het strafrecht, *Tijdschrift voor Strafrecht,* 22: 277–301.

Roshier, Bob (1989) *Controlling Crime.* Milton Keynes: Open University Press.

Ruggiero, Vincenzo (1992) Realist criminology: a critique, in Young and Matthews (eds), pp. 123–40.

Ruggiero, Vincenzo (1995) Flexibility and intermittent emergency in the Italian penal system, in Ruggiero et al. (eds), pp. 46–70.

Ruggiero, Vincenzo, Ryan, Mick and Sim, Joe (eds) (1995) *Western European Penal Systems: a Critical Anatomy.* London: Sage.

Ruller, Sibo van (1988) Ideeën over misdaadbestrijding in de jaren dertig, *Tijdschrift voor Criminologie,* 30: 98–110.

Rutherford, Andrew (1986) *Prisons and the Process of Justice.* Oxford: Oxford University Press.

Rutherford, Andrew (1994a) *Criminal Justice and the Pursuit of Decency.* Winchester: Waterside.

Rutherford, Andrew (1994b) Abolition and the politics of bad conscience: a response to Sim, in Duff et al. (eds), pp. 285–91.

Rutherford, Andrew (1996) *Transforming Criminal Policy: Spheres of Influence in the United States, The Netherlands and England and Wales during the 1980s.* Winchester: Waterside.

Ryan, Mick (1978) *The Acceptable Pressure Group: Inequality in the Penal Lobby – a Case Study of the Howard League and RAP.* Farnsborough: Saxon House.

Ryan, Mick (1983) *The Politics of Penal Reform.* London: Longman.

Ryan, Mick and Ward, Tony (1989) Left realism against the rest revisited, or some particularities of the British, in Rolston and Tomlinson (eds), pp. 146–60.

Ryan, Mick and Ward, Tony (1992) From positivism to postmodernism: some theoretical and strategic reflections on the evolution of the penal lobby in Britain, *International Journal of the Sociology of Law,* 20: 321–35.

Sack, Fritz (1969) Kriminalität, vol. 12 of René König (ed.), *Handbuch der empirischen Sozialforschung.* Stuttgart: Ferd. Enke Verlag (1978 edn), pp. 227–309.

Sack, Fritz (1972) Definition von Kriminalität als politisches Handeln: der labeling approach, *Kriminologisches Journal,* 4: 3–31.

Sack, Fritz (1975) Die Chancen der Kooperation zwischen Strafrechtswissenschaft und Kriminologie – Probleme und offene Fragen, in Klaus Lüderssen and Fritz Sack (eds), *Seminar: Abweichendes Verhalten II, die gesellschaftliche Reaktion auf Kriminalität I.* Frankfurt am Main: Suhrkamp, pp. 346–85.

Sack, Fritz (1988) Wege und Umwege der deutschen Kriminologie in und aus dem Strafrecht, in Helmut Janssen, Reiner Kaulitzky and Raymond Michalowski (eds), *Radikale Kriminologie: Themen und theoretischen Positionen der amerikanischen Radical Criminology.* Bielefeld: AJZ, pp. 9–34.

Sack, Fritz (1994) Conflicts and convergences of theoretical and methodological perspectives in criminology, *European Journal of Crime, Criminal Law and Criminal Justice,* 1: 2–17.

Salhaketa (1989) *Defenderse en la cárcel: guia de recursos jurídicos para personas presas y detenidas en la comunidad Vasca y Navarra.* Vitoria/Gasteiz: Gobierno Vasco/Eusko Jaurlaritza.

Salhaketa (1994) *Situación carcelaria: nuevas repuestas de los movemientos sociales – conclusiones de los primeros encuentros.* Internal pamphlet, Vitoria-Gasteiz.

Savornin Lohman, Jacquelien (Soetenhorst) de (1975) *Kwaad dat mag? Strafrechtspleging tussen traditie en vernieuwing.* Rotterdam: Universitaire Pers.

Scheerer, Sebastian (1986a) Limits to criminal law?, in Bianchi and van Swaaningen (eds), pp. 99–112.

Scheerer, Sebastian (1986b) Atypische Moralunternehmer, *Kriminologisches Journal,* 18 (1): Beiheft, 133–55.

Scheerer, Sebastian (1996) Zwei Thesen zur Zukunft des Gefängnisses – und acht über die Zukunft der sozialen Kontrolle, in Trutz von Trotha (ed.), *Politischer Wandel, Gesellschaft und Kriminalitätsdiskurse: Beiträge zur interdisziplinären wissenschaftlichen Kriminologie – Festschrift für Fritz Sack zum 65. Geburtstag.* Baden Baden: Nomos.

Schumann, Karl F. (1973) Ungleichheit, Stigmatisierung und abweichendes Verhalten: zur theoretischen Orientierung kriminologischer Forschung, *Kriminologisches Journal,* 5: 81–96.

Schumann, Karl F. (1975a) Approaching crime and deviance: a note on contributions by scientists, officials of social control and social activists during the last five years in West Germany, in Bianchi et al. (eds), pp. 59–76.

Schumann, Karl F. (1975b) Was geht die Gewerkschaften der Strafvollzug an? *Kriminologisches Journal,* 7: 227–39.

Schumann, Karl F. (1979) Politische Randgruppenarbeit nach Mathiesen und Foucault – eine Einführung, in Thomas Mathiesen (ed.), *Überwindet die Mauern!: die Skandinavische Gefangenenbewegung als Modell politischer Randgruppenarbeit.* Neuwied: Luchterhand, pp. 1–13.

Schumann, Karl F. (1981) Produktionsverhältnisse und staatliches Strafen: zur aktuellen Diskussion über Rusche und Kirchheimer, *Kritische Justiz,* 14: 64–77.

Schumann, Karl F. (1985) Labeling Approach und Abolitionismus, *Kriminologisches Journal,* 17: 19–28.

Schuyt, Kees J.M. (1991) *Op zoek naar het hart van de verzorgingsstaat.* Leiden: Stenfert Kroese.

Schuyt, Kees J.M. (1993) De omweg van de onverschilligheid, in Nijboer (ed.), pp. 29–34.

Schwendinger, Herman and Schwendinger, Julia (1975) Defenders of order or guardians of human rights?, in Taylor et al. (eds), pp. 113–46.

Scraton, Phil (ed.) (1987) *Law, Order and the Authoritarian State: Readings in Critical Criminology.* Milton Keynes: Open University Press.

Sgubbi, Filippo (1975) *Tutela penale di 'interessi diffusi', La questione criminale, 1 (3): 439–81.*

Sgubbi, Filippo (1990) *Il reato come rischio sociale.* Bologna: Il Mulino.

Shearing, Clifford D. and Stenning, Philip C. (1987) Say 'cheese!': the Disney order that is not so Mickey Mouse, in Clifford Shearing and Philip C. Stenning, (eds), *Private Policing.* Newbury Park, CA: Sage, pp. 317–24.

Sim, Joe (1986) Working for the clampdown: prisons and politics in England and Wales, in Rolston and Tomlinson (eds), pp. 41–63.

Sim, Joe (1994) The abolitionist approach: a British perspective, in Duff et al. (eds), pp. 263–84.

Sim, Joe, Ruggiero, Vincenzo and Ryan, Mick (1995) Punishment in Europe: perceptions and commonalities, in Ruggiero et al. (eds), pp. 1–23.

Simons, David (1911) *Het Wetboek van Strafrecht van 1881 en de bestrijding van de misdadigheid.* The Hague: Belinfante.

Simons, David (1918) Crisisrechtspraak, *Weekblad van het Recht*, no. 10248, 24 May, p. 4.

Simons, David (1929) *Problemen van het strafrecht.* Amsterdam: Wereldbibliotheek.

Smale, Gerard J.A. (1977) *Slachtoffers van ernstige vermogens- en geweldsmisdrijven*, vol. 1: *De materiële problematiek;* vol. 2: *De immateriële problematiek* (1980). Groningen: Kriminologies Instituut.

Smart, Carol (1976) *Women, Crime and Criminology.* London: Routledge and Kegan Paul.

Smart, Carol (1989) *Feminism and the Power of the Law.* London: Routledge.

Smart, Carol (1990) Feminist approaches to criminology or postmodern woman meets atavistic man, reprinted in Carol Smart, *Law, Crime and Sexuality: Essays in Feminism.* London: Sage, 1995, pp. 32–48.

Smaus, Gerlinda (1986a) Gesellschaftsmodelle in der abolitionistischen Bewegung, *Kriminologisches Journal*, 18 (1): 1–18.

Smaus, Gerlinda (1986b) Versuch um eine materialistisch-interaktionistische Kriminologie, *Kriminologisches Journal*, 18 (1): 179–99.

Smaus, Gerlinda (1989) Feministische Beobachtung des Abolitionismus, *Kriminologisches Journal*, 21: 182–94.

Smaus, Gerlinda (1993) Mit Thomas Mathiesen gegen die Ohnmacht der kritischen Kriminologie, in Papendorf and Schumann (eds), pp. 85–102.

Smits, Hans (1994) De harde uitspraken van een procureur-generaal, *Vrij Nederland*, 15 January 1994, pp. 14–16.

Snacken, Sonja, Beyens, Kristel and Tubex, Hilde (1995) Changing prison populations in Western countries: fate or policy?, *European Journal of Crime, Criminal Law and Criminal Justice*, 3 (2): 18–53.

Sola Dueñas, Ángel de (1980) Desarollo democrático y alternativas político-criminales, in UAB, pp. 215–42.

Sorgdrager, Winnie (1994) Strafvordering en criminaliteitsbestrijding; preadvies over het onderwerp 'herbezinning op (de grondslagen van) het Wetboek van Strafvordering', *Handelingen Nederlandse Juristen Vereniging*, 124, no. 1. Zwolle: Tjeenk Willink, pp. 191–242.

Sorgdrager, Winnie (1995) Nederlands gedoogbeleid: pragmatisch en effectief, *Justitiële Verkenningen*, 21 (8): 9–14.

Sparks, Richard (1994) Postmodernism and misgivings about human rights. Paper presented to the American Society of Criminology, Miami, 17 November.

Squires, Peter and Hillyard, Paddy (eds) (1983) *Disputing Deviance: Experiences of Youth in the 80s.* Working papers in European criminology, no. 4. Bristol: EGSDSC.

Stangl, Wolfgang (1984) Kriminologie als Apologie der Macht: über Traditionen der Kriminologie am Beispiel Österreichs, *Kriminologisches Journal*, 16: 287–300.

Stangl, Wolfgang (1985) *Die neue Gerechtigkeit: Strafrechtsreform in Österreich 1954–1975.* Vienna: Verlag für Gesellschaftskritik.

Stangl, Wolfgang (1988) *Wege in eine gefängnislose Gesellschaft: über Verstaatlichung und Entstaatlichung der Strafjustiz.* Vienna: Straatsdruckerei. (Summarised in English as 'Who has the right to prosecute? The reform of criminal procedure in the nineteenth century and the abolitionist trend in contemporary criminology', in Rolston and Tomlinson (1989), pp. 160–72.)

Steenhuis, Dato W. (1986) Coherence and coordination in the administration of criminal justice, in van Dijk et al. (eds), pp. 229–45.

Steenstra, Sietse (1988) Vijfendertig jaar criminologie aan de VU, in van Swaaningen et al. (eds), pp. 77–90.

Steinert, Heinz (1978) Can socialism be advanced by radical rhetoric and sloppy data? Some remarks on Richard Quinney's latest output, *Contemporary Crises,* 2: 303–13.

Steinert, Heinz (1984) Was ist eigentlich aus der Neuen Kriminologie geworden? Einige Thesen um die Suche zu orientieren, *Kriminologisches Journal,* 16 (2): 86–9.

Steinert, Heinz (1985) The amazing new left law and order campaign: some thoughts on anti-utopianism and possible futures, *Contemporary Crises,* 9: 327–33.

Steinert, Heinz (1989) Marxian theory and abolitionism: introduction to a discussion, in Rolston and Tomlinson (eds), pp. 172–91.

Stenson, Kevin and Cowell, David (eds) (1991) *The Politics of Crime Control.* London: Sage.

Sumner, Colin S. (1976) Marxism and deviancy theory, in Wiles (ed.), pp. 159–74.

Sumner, Colin S. (1981) Race, crime and hegemony, *Contemporary Crises,* 5: 277–91.

Sumner, Colin S. (1983) Rethinking deviance: toward a sociology of censures, *Research in Law, Deviance and Social Control,* 5: 187–204.

Sumner, Colin S. (1994) *The Sociology of Deviance: an Obituary.* Milton Keynes: Open University Press.

Swaan, Abram de (1989) *Zorg en staat: welzijn, onderwijs en gezondheidszorg in Europa en de Verenigde Staten in de nieuwe tijd.* Amsterdam: Bert Bakker.

Swaaningen, René van (1988) Ik ben geen zoon van laauwe westerstranden, in van Swaaningen et al. (eds), pp. 3–21.

Swaaningen, René van (1989) Feminism and abolitionism as critiques of criminology, *International Journal for the Sociology of Law,* 17: 287–306.

Swaaningen, René van (1995) Sociale controle met een structureel tekort; pleidooi voor een sociaal rechtvaardig veiligheidsbeleid, *Justitiële Verkenningen,* 21 (3): 63–87.

Swaaningen, René van (1996a) Justitie als verzekeringsmaatschappij: 'actuarial justice' in Nederland, *Justitiële Verkenningen,* 22 (5): 80–97.

Swaaningen, René (1996b) Reclaiming critical criminology. Paper presented to the American Society of Criminology Conference, Chicago, 20–23 November.

Swaaningen, René van (1997) Vingt ans de Déviance et Société sous l'angle de la criminologie critique, *Déviance et Société,* 21 (1): 57–76.

Swaaningen, René van and Jonge, Gerard de (1995) The Dutch prison system and penal policy in the 1990s: from humanitarian paternalism to penal business management, in Ruggiero et al. (eds), pp. 24–45.

Swaaningen, René van, Blad, John R. and Loon, Reinier van (1992) *A Decade of Criminological Research and Penal Policy in The Netherlands: the 1980s – the Era of Business-management Ideology.* Rotterdam: Centre for Integrated Penal Science, EUR working document no. 4.

Swaaningen, René van, Jonge, Gerard de and McMahon, Maeve W. (1989) The laborious conspiracy against the penal system, *Canadian Criminology Forum,* 10: 67–75.

Swaaningen, René van, Snel, Bert, Faber, Sjoerd and Blankenburg, Erhard R. (eds) (1988) *À tort et à travers: liber amicorum Herman Bianchi.* Amsterdam: VU Uitgeverij.

Taverne, B.M. (1941) Boekbespreking no. 31, *Tijdschrift voor Strafrecht,* 51: 38–9.

Taylor, Ian (1981) *Law and Order: Arguments for Socialism.* London: Macmillan.

Taylor, Ian and Taylor, Laurie (1972) *Politics and Deviance.* Harmondsworth: Penguin.

Taylor, Ian, Walton, Paul and Young, Jock (1973) *The New Criminology: for a Social Theory of Deviance.* London: Routledge and Kegan Paul.

Taylor, Ian, Walton, Paul and Young, Jock (eds) (1975) *Critical Criminology.* London: Routledge and Kegan Paul.

Taylor, Laurie (1973) A note on the National Deviancy Conference, in Ian Taylor and Laurie Taylor (eds), pp. 209–14.

Tomlinson, Mike, Varley, Tony and McCullagh, Ciaran (1988) *Whose Law and Order? Aspects of Crime and Social Control in Irish Society.* Belfast: Sociological Association of Ireland.

Tournier, Pierre (1994) The custodial crisis in Europe: inflated prison populations and possible alternatives, *European Journal on Criminal Policy and Research,* 2 (4): 89–100.

Traa, Maarten van (ed.) (1996) *Inzake opsporing* (15-volume report of the parliamentary inquiry committee, including those of the criminological research group of Cyrille Fijnaut, Frank Bovenkerk, Gerben Bruinsma and Henk van de Bunt). The Hague: Sdu.

Tulkens, Françoise (1990) De IKV en de strafrechtswetenschap in België, in Groenhuijsen and van der Landen (eds), pp. 97–113.

Turk, Austin (1969) Introduction, in Willem Bonger, *Crime and Economic Conditions* (abridged). Bloomington, Ind.: Indiana University Press.

Tweedy, John and Hunt, Alan (1994) The future of the welfare state and social rights: reflections on Habermas, *Journal of Law and Society,* 21 (3): 288–316.

UAB (*Universitat Autònoma de Barcelona*) (1980) Sociedad y delito: papers, revista de sociología, no. 13. Barcelona: Península.

Valkhoff, J. (1946) Willem Adriaan Bonger, *de Nieuwe Stem,* 1: 107–13.

Verpalen, Rino J.M. (ed.) (1994) *Druk en tegendruk: constructieve bijdragen aan de discussie over het cellentekort.* Arnhem: Gouda Quint.

Verrijn Stuart, Heikelien (1994) Via onschuld aan de macht: slachtoffers in het strafproces, *Justitiële Verkenningen,* 20 (2): 94–114.

Vervaele, John (1990) *Rechtsstaat en recht tot straffen: van klassiek rechtsindividualisme naar sociaal rechtsdenken – een strafrechtsvergelijkend onderzoek.* Antwerpen/Arnhem: Kluwer/Gouda Quint.

Vijver, Kees D. van der (1993) *De burger en de zin van strafrecht.* Lelystad: Vermande.

Vingtras, Jacques (1972) 'Rote Hilfe' und Politische Justiz in Frankreich, *Kritische Justiz,* 5: 24–42.

Vold, George B. and Bernard, Thomas J. (1986) *Theoretical Criminology,* 3rd edn. New York: Oxford University Press.

Walton, Paul and Young, Jock (eds) *The New Criminology Revisited.* London: Macmillan.

Ward, Tony (1986) Symbols and noble lies: abolitionism, 'just deserts' and crimes of the powerful, in Bianchi and van Swaaningen (eds), pp. 73–82.

Ward, Tony (1991) Rediscovering radical alternatives, in Lasocik et al. (eds), pp. 160–3.

Wentholt, Klaartje (1991) Rekening houden met zorgtaken; een ander perspectief voor het gelijkheidsbeginsel, *Recht en kritiek,* 17: 367–81.

Weringh, Koos van (1981) Van Jesaja tot Bianchi, *Sociologische Gids,* 28: 530–45.

Weringh, Koos van (1986) *De afstand tot de horizon: verwachting en werkelijkheid in de Nederlandse criminologie.* Amsterdam: Arbeiderspers.

Werkentin, Falco, Hofferbert, Michael and Baurmann, Michael (1972) Kriminologie als Polizeiwissenschaft, oder 'wie alt ist die neue Kriminologie?, *Kritische Justiz,* 2: 221–52.

Wichmann, Clara (1912) *Beschouwingen over de historische grondslagen der tegenwoordige omvorming van het strafbegrip.* Leiden: Brill.

Wichmann, Clara (Meijer) (1923) *Mensch en maatschappij.* Arnhem: Van Loghum Slaterus.

Wichmann, Clara (1924) *Bevrijding.* Arnhem: Van Loghum Slaterus.

Wichmann, Clara (Meijer) (1930) *Misdaad, straf en maatschappij.* Utrecht: Bijleveld.

Wijnbergen, A. Baron van (1910) *Hoe staan wij tegenover de moderne strafrechtsleer?* Leiden: Futura.

Wiles, Paul (ed.) (1976) *The Sociology of Crime and Delinquency in Britain,* vol. 2: *The New Criminologies.* London: Martin Robertson.

Willemse, H.M. (1995) Een coup SeC: tien jaar situationele preventie, *Justitiële Verkenningen,* 21 (3): 39–51.

Wilson, James Q. and Herrnstein, Richard J. (1985) *Crime and Human Nature.* New York: Simon and Schuster.

Wit, John de and Outrive, Lode van (1986) *Gevangeniswezen en abolitionisme,* Liga-dossier no. 4, Ghent: Liga voor Mensenrechten.

Witteveen, Willem (1994) Over de grenzen aan het appeleervermogen van de overheid, *Justitiële Verkenningen,* 20 (6): 43–53.

Young, Alison and Rush, Peter (1994) The law of victimage in urbane realism; thinking through inscriptions of violence, in Nelken (ed.), pp. 154–72.

Young, Jock (1970) *The Drugtakers: the Social Meaning of Drug Use.* London: McGibbon and Kee.

Young, Jock (1975) Working-class criminology, in Taylor et al. (ed.), pp. 63–94.

Young, Jock (1979) Left idealism, reformism and beyond; from new criminology to Marxism, in Bob, Fine, Richard Kinsey, John Lea, Sol Picciotto and Jock Young (eds), *Capitalism and the Rule of Law: from Deviancy Theory to Marxism.* London: Hutchinson, pp. 1–29.

Young, Jock (1988) Radical criminology in Britain: the emergence of a competing paradigm, in Rock (ed.), pp. 159–83.

Young, Jock (1992) At the centre and on the periphery: criminal justice research in Canada, in Dawn Currie and Brian MacLean (eds), *Rethinking the Administration of Justice.* Halifax, Nova Scotia: Fernwood. pp. v–vii.

Young, Jock (1994) Incessant chatter: recent paradigms in criminology, in Maguire et al. (eds), pp. 69–124.

Young, Jock (1997) Writing on the cusp of change, in Walton and Young (eds), pp. 259–95.

Young, Jock and Matthews, Roger (eds) (1992) *Rethinking Criminology: the Realist Debate.* London: Sage.

Zaitch, Damián and Sagarduy, Ramiro (1992) La criminología crítica y la construcción del delito: entre la dispersión epistemológica y los compromisos políticos, *Delito y sociedad, revista de ciencias sociales,* 2: 31–52.

Zoomer, Olga (1993) *Zelf doen en overlaten: acties van burgers, politie en lokale overheid tegen overlast en kleine criminaliteit.* Lelystad: Vermande.

Index